# KING AND MESSIAH AS SON OF GOD

# KING AND MESSIAH AS SON OF GOD

*Divine, Human, and Angelic Messianic Figures
in Biblical and Related Literature*

Adela Yarbro Collins *&* John J. Collins

WILLIAM B. EERDMANS PUBLISHING COMPANY
GRAND RAPIDS, MICHIGAN / CAMBRIDGE, U.K.

Published 2008 by

Wm. B. Eerdmans Publishing Co.

2140 Oak Industrial Drive N.E., Grand Rapids, Michigan 49505 /
P.O. Box 163, Cambridge CB3 9PU U.K.

Printed in the United States of America

14  13  12  11  10  09  08      7  6  5  4  3  2  1


**Library of Congress Cataloging-in-Publication Data**

Collins, Adela Yarbro.
 King and Messiah as Son of God : divine, human, and angelic Messianic figures
in biblical and related literature / Adela Yarbro Collins & John J. Collins.
  p.     cm.
 Includes bibliographical references (p.        ) and indexes.
 ISBN 978-0-8028-0772-4 (pbk. : alk. paper)
 1. Messiah — Biblical teaching. 2. Son of God — Biblical teaching. 3. Kings and rulers —
Biblical teaching. 4. Jesus Christ — Messiahship. 5. Messiah — History of doctrines. 6. Son of
God — History and doctrines. 7. Kings and rulers — Religious aspects — History of
doctrines. 8. Middle Eastern literature — History and criticism.
 I. Collins, John Joseph, 1946 –     II. Title.


 BS680.M4C65     2008
 232'.1 — dc22

               2008030616



www.eerdmans.com

# Contents

# *Preface*

This book had its origin in the Speaker's Lectures, delivered at Oxford in May 2006. Originally there were six lectures, three by John J. Collins and three by Adela Yarbro Collins. We have each written an additional chapter; John's new chapter is Chapter 2, and Adela's is Chapter 8.

We would like to thank the Oxford faculty for their extraordinary hospitality on that occasion, especially Chris Rowland, Hugh Williamson, John Day, John Barton, Robert Morgan, Chris Tuckett, Paul Joyce, Christine Joynes, Sue Gillingham, Marilyn Adams, Martin Goodman, Geza Vermes, and Alison Salvesen.

We also benefited from the session with the Oxford biblical faculty after the lectures. Martin Goodman, John Muddiman, and Chris Tuckett each presented a thoughtful and helpfully critical response.

In gratitude for their hospitality and intellectual and social fellowship, we dedicate this book to the Oxford faculty.

# Abbreviations

| | |
|---|---|
| AB | Anchor Bible |
| *ABD* | *Anchor Bible Dictionary* |
| ABRL | Anchor Bible Reference Library |
| *AfO* | *Archiv für Orientforschung* |
| AGSU | Arbeiten zur Geschichte des Spätdjudentums und Urchristentums |
| AnBib | Analecta biblica |
| *ANEP* | *The Ancient Near East in Pictures Relating to the Old Testament* |
| *ANET* | *Ancient Near Eastern Texts Relating to the Old Testament* |
| AOAT | Alter Orient und Altes Testament |
| *ARE* | *Ancient Records of Egypt* |
| *BBR* | *Bulletin for Biblical Research* |
| BETL | Bibliotheca ephemeridum theologicarum lovaniensium |
| *Bib* | *Biblica* |
| *BJRL* | *Bulletin of the John Rylands University Library of Manchester* |
| BJS | Brown Judaic Studies |
| BK | Biblischer Kommentar |
| *BN* | *Biblische Notizen* |
| *BR* | *Biblical Research* |
| BWANT | Beiträge zur Wissenschaft vom Alten und Neuen Testament |

| | |
|---|---|
| BZAW | Beihefte zur Zeitschrift für die alttestamentliche Wissenschaft |
| BZNW | Beihefte zur Zeitschrift für die neutestamentliche Wissenschaft |
| *CAH* | *Cambridge Ancient History* |
| *CBQ* | *Catholic Biblical Quarterly* |
| CBQMS | Catholic Biblical Quarterly Monograph Series |
| CC | Continental Commentaries |
| ConBib OT | Coniectanea biblica: Old Testament Series |
| *DDD* | *Dictionary of Deities and Demons in the Bible* |
| DJD | Discoveries in the Judaean Desert |
| *DSD* | *Dead Sea Discoveries* |
| EA | El-Amarna tablets |
| *EncJud* | *Encyclopaedia Judaica* |
| FAT | Forschungen zum Alten Testament |
| FOTL | Forms of the Old Testament Literature |
| FRLANT | Forschungen zur Religion und Literatur des Alten und Neuen Testaments |
| HSM | Harvard Semitic Monographs |
| HSS | Harvard Semitic Studies |
| *HTR* | *Harvard Theological Review* |
| ICC | International Critical Commentary |
| *JAOS* | *Journal of the American Oriental Society* |
| *JBL* | *Journal of Biblical Literature* |
| *JEA* | *Journal of Egyptian Archaeology* |
| *JNES* | *Journal of Near Eastern Studies* |
| *JSJ* | *Journal for the Study of Judaism* |
| JSJSup | Supplements to Journal for the Study of Judaism |
| *JSNT* | *Journal for the Study of the New Testament* |
| JSOTSup | Journal for the Study of the New Testament: Supplement Series |
| *JSP* | *Journal for the Study of the Pseudepigrapha* |
| *JSS* | *Journal of Semitic Studies* |
| *JTS* | *Journal of Theological Studies* |
| KAT | Kommentar zum Alten Testament |
| *KTU* | *Die Keilalphabetischen Texte aus Ugarit* |
| NovTSup | Novum Testamentum Supplements |
| *NTS* | *New Testament Studies* |

OBO          Orbis biblicus et orientalis
*OGIS*        *Orientis graeci inscriptiones selectae*
SBLDS        Society of Biblical Literature Dissertation Series
SBEJL        Society of Biblical Literature Early Judaism and Its
                Literature
SBLMS        Society of Biblical Literature Monograph Series
*SBLSP*       *Society of Biblical Literature Seminar Papers*
SNTS         Studiorum Novi Testamentum Societas
SNTSMS       Society for New Testament Studies Monograph Series
*STDJ*        *Studies on the Texts of the Desert of Judah*
SUNT         Studien zur Umwelt des Neuen Testaments
SVTP         Studia in Veteris Testamenti pseudepigraphica
*TDNT*        *Theological Dictionary of the New Testament*
*TLZ (ThLZ)*  *Theologische Literaturzeitung*
TSAJ         Texte und Studien zum antiken Judentum
*VT*          *Vetus Testamentum*
VTSup        Supplements to Vetus Testamentum
WBC          Word Biblical Commentary
WMANT        Wissenschaftliche Monographien zum Alten und Neuen
                Testament
WUNT         Wissenschaftliche Untersuchungen zum Neuen Testament
ZAW          Zeitschrift für die alttestamentliche Wissenschaft

# Introduction

Messianism has been a subject of lively discussion in recent scholarship. In 2007 alone at least five books on the subject appeared in English. Joseph Fitzmyer's monograph, *The One Who Is to Come*,[1] is narrowly focused on determining which texts are properly regarded as messianic. *The Messiah in the Old and New Testaments*, edited by Stanley Porter,[2] is an overview. *The Messiah in Early Judaism and Christianity*, edited by Magnus Zetterholm (with contributions by the authors of the present volume),[3] is a different kind of overview, including essays on later Judaism and early Christianity. *Redemption and Resistance: The Messianic Hopes of Jews and Christians in Antiquity*, edited by Markus Bockmuehl and James Carleton Paget, a Festschrift for William Horbury,[4] is a wide-ranging collection of essays, about half of which deal with developments after the New Testament. Andrew Chester's *Messiah and Exaltation*[5] is also a collection of essays, but by a single author, on various themes relating to Jewish messianism and mediator figures and Christology.

The present book differs from all of these insofar as it is focused on the

1. Grand Rapids: Eerdmans, 2007.
2. Grand Rapids: Eerdmans, 2007.
3. Minneapolis: Fortress, 2007.
4. London and New York: T&T Clark, 2007.
5. WUNT 207; Tübingen: Mohr Siebeck, 2007. Five of the eight essays in this book were previously published, but two of these have been substantially expanded.

specific question of the divinity of the messiah.[6] The affirmation of the divinity of the messiah or Christ is often thought to constitute the most fundamental difference between Judaism and Christianity. The recent study by Fitzmyer is typical of much scholarship when it contrasts the Jewish expectation of "a human kingly figure" with "the Christian Messiah (who) is also known to be the Son of God in a transcendent sense."[7] Our study shows that the issue is a good deal more complicated than that. The idea of the divinity of the messiah has its roots in the royal ideology of ancient Judah, which in turn was influenced by the Egyptian mythology of kingship. That ideology was criticized and qualified by the Deuteronomists and prophets, but it remained embedded in texts that attained the status of scripture. The promise to David, recorded in 2 Samuel 7, contained the assurance that the Davidic king would be regarded by God as a son. In the Hellenistic period, when the Davidic line had been broken for centuries, hopes for deliverance often focused on supernatural, heavenly, mediator figures. The rise of the Hasmonean dynasty brought a resurgence of hope for a messiah from the line of David, but messianic expectations were often fused with notions of a heavenly deliverer around the turn of the era. In this context, the old idea of the king as son of God took on new overtones, and it becomes more difficult to maintain a clear distinction between the messiah as a human king and the hope for a transcendent savior figure. The Christian belief in the divinity of Jesus must be seen to have emerged in the context of the fluid and changing Jewish conceptions of the messiah around the turn of the era. To be sure, Christology took its own distinctive forms, culminating a few centuries later in the doctrine of the Trinity. The development of Christology, however, cannot be understood without appreciating the Jewish context in which it had its roots.

The Jewish context of early Christology has been acknowledged increasingly in recent scholarship.[8] Much of this scholarship represents a re-

6. Of the recent books just listed, only Chester's engages this issue, and he does not address the foundational texts in the Hebrew Bible.

7. Fitzmyer, *The One Who Is to Come*, 182-83. Fitzmyer recognizes that at times the Jewish messiah was thought to be preexistent.

8. E.g., C. C. Newman, J. R. Davila, and G. S. Lewis, *The Jewish Roots of Christological Monotheism: Papers from the St. Andrews Conference on the Historical Origins of the Worship of Jesus* (JSJSup 63; Leiden: Brill, 1999); Larry W. Hurtado, *One God, One Lord: Early Christian Devotion and Ancient Jewish Monotheism* (Philadelphia: Fortress, 1988); idem, *Lord Jesus Christ: Devotion to Jesus in Earliest Christianity* (Grand Rapids: Eerdmans, 2003); idem, *How*

action against the influential views of Wilhelm Bousset and the *religions-geschichtliche Schule* of a century ago.[9] Bousset famously argued that the Christ cult, or the worship of Jesus as divine, first emerged in early "Hellenistic Gentile" circles, under the influence of the pagan, polytheistic environment.[10] Larry Hurtado has noted the existence of "principal agents" in monotheistic Jewish texts and notes that they are sometimes given "an amazingly exalted status."[11] He contends that these figures reflect a tendency to binitarianism in Jewish circles that provides a context for the development of Christology, but he insists that the worship of Jesus was a unique "mutation" without any true parallel. Amazingly, Hurtado does not even include "messiah" in his three main types of "principal agents," although he does not deny the importance of messianic expectation.

In a different vein, William Horbury has also written in opposition to "the view that the cult of Christ was essentially a gentilized manifestation of Christianity."[12] Unlike Hurtado, Horbury is not concerned to defend the uniqueness of the cult of Jesus. He argues that "the Christ-cult has so many Jewish elements that it is more likely to originate from the Jewish or the Christian-Jewish community," and specifically that "flourishing messianism" formed "the link between the Judaism of the Hellenistic period and the Christian cult of Christ."[13] Horbury's thesis acquires initial plausibility from the fact that the principal title given to Jesus by his followers, *Christos,* is simply the Greek translation of Hebrew משיח or Ara-

---

*on Earth Did Jesus Become a God? Historical Questions about Earliest Devotion to Jesus* (Grand Rapids: Eerdmans, 2005); J. E. Fossum, "The New religionsgeschichtliche Schule: The Quest for Jewish Christology," in E. Lovering, ed., *SBLSP* 1991, 638-46; Chester, *Messiah and Exaltation,* 13-121, 329-96.

9. Wilhelm Bousset, *Kyrios Christos: A History of the Belief in Christ from the Beginnings of Christianity to Irenaeus* (trans. J. E. Steely; Nashville: Abingdon, 1970; originally published in German in 1913).

10. A similar argument, although quite different in detail, has been put forward more recently by Maurice Casey, *From Jewish Prophet to Gentile God: The Origins and Development of New Testament Christology* (Louisville: Westminster John Knox, 1991).

11. Hurtado, *How on Earth,* 47; compare his earlier books, *One God, One Lord,* and *Lord Jesus Christ,* 29-48. Compare also Chester, *Messiah and Exaltation,* 45-80.

12. William Horbury, *Jewish Messianism and the Cult of Christ* (London: SCM, 1998), 3. See also Horbury's collection of essays, *Messianism among Jews and Christians: Biblical and Historical Studies* (New York and London: T&T Clark, 2003).

13. Horbury, *Jewish Messianism,* 3. Hurtado criticizes Horbury for an unduly broad concept of "cult" (*How on Earth,* 20-22).

maic מְשִׁיחָא. It is undeniable that a figure who is called מָשִׁיחַ is addressed as "my son" by God in Psalm 2.

In the following chapters we address the relations of kingship and messiahship to divinity. John J. Collins has written the first four chapters. Chapter 1, "The King as Son of God," assesses the evidence for the divinity of the Israelite king in the royal psalms. Chapter 2, "The Kingship in Deuteronomistic and Prophetic Literature," shows how the royal ideology was modified in that literature and discusses the relatively modest expectations of early messianism. Chapter 3, "Messiah and Son of God in the Hellenistic Period," discusses the Hellenistic ruler cults, and messianism in the Septuagint and in the Dead Sea Scrolls. A few passages in the Septuagint attribute preexistence to the messiah, or speak of him as an angel. The Scrolls are generally restrained in their references to the messiah(s), but they draw freely on biblical language. The promise of God in Nathan's oracle, that "he [the Davidic king] will be a son to me," is applied to the eschatological "Branch of David" in the *Florilegium*. Psalm 2 probably provides the referential background of two other controversial texts, the *Messianic Rule*, which speaks of God begetting the Messiah, and 4Q246, the *Son of God* text, which refers to an eschatological figure who will be called "Son of God" and "Son of the Most High." Chapter 4, "Messiah and Son of Man," discusses Daniel 7, the *Melchizedek Scroll*, the *Similitudes of Enoch*, and *4 Ezra* 13. It concludes that there is a growing tendency to view the messiah as a preexistent being of heavenly origin. In *4 Ezra*, this heavenly messiah is called "my son" by God, and his activity is described in terms drawn from Psalm 2.

Adela Yarbro Collins has written the last four chapters. Chapter 5, "Jesus as Messiah and Son of God in the Letters of Paul," concludes that Paul's portrayal of Jesus as son of God is closely related to his status as messiah. Chapter 6, "Jesus as Messiah and Son of God in the Synoptic Gospels," concludes that none of the Synoptic Gospels portrays Jesus as preexistent. It also reassesses the evidence for the preexistence of Jesus in the letters of Paul in light of the Synoptic Gospels and the *Similitudes of Enoch*. Chapter 7, "Jesus as Son of Man," discusses the Son of Man sayings in the Synoptic Gospels, the question of their origin, and their relation to traditions about the preexistence and divinity of Jesus. Chapter 8, "Messiah, Son of God, and Son of Man in the Gospel and Revelation of John," concludes that both works present Jesus as preexistent and divine, but do so in quite different ways.

We hope that in this book we have demonstrated that ideas about Jesus as preexistent and divine originated in a Jewish context, in the conviction that he was the messiah, although they were subsequently transformed as Christianity spread in the Gentile world. The Jewish context, even where Semitic languages were spoken, was itself part of the Greco-Roman world, and influenced by Hellenistic culture in various ways. The old antithesis of Judaism and Hellenism cannot be maintained. But it was within the specifically Jewish sector of the Hellenistic world that the idea of the divinity of Christ had its roots. The study of the growth and development of this idea must be interpreted in that context, before its development and transformation in the world of Gentile Christianity can be understood.

# 1. *The King as Son of God*

As is well known, the word מָשִׁיחַ means simply "anointed" and is not used in the Hebrew Bible in an eschatological sense.[1] Several historical kings of Israel and Judah, beginning with Saul, are said to have been anointed.[2] Elijah is told to anoint Hazael king of Syria (1 Kings 19:15-16). The rite was not distinctive to Israelite or Judean kings. Priests as well as kings were anointed, and there is some evidence for the anointing of prophets, although that does not seem to have been commonplace.[3] The word מָשִׁיחַ is used with reference to some specific kings (Saul, David, and Solomon), but it is also used to refer to kings of the Davidic line without further identification (Pss 2:2; 18:51; 20:7; 28:8; 84:10; 89:39, 52; 132:10, 17). In Lam 4:20 it is used with reference to Zedekiah. No special significance can be attached to the fact that it is not used explicitly in connection with every king.[4] It is a generic way of referring to kings, especially those of the Davidic line. When the word מָשִׁיחַ takes on an eschatological connotation in the Second Temple period, the reference is

---

1. Joseph Fitzmyer, *The One Who Is to Come* (Grand Rapids: Eerdmans, 2007), 8-25.

2. Saul, David, Solomon, Jehu, Joash, Jehoahaz. See Fitzmyer, *The One Who Is to Come,* 9. On the anointing of the king, see Tryggve N. D. Mettinger, *King and Messiah: The Civil and Sacral Legitimation of the Israelite Kings* (ConBib OT 8; Lund: Gleerup, 1976), 185-232.

3. In 1 Kings 19:16, Elijah is told to anoint Elisha as his successor. The prophetic speaker in Isa 61:1 says that "God has anointed me."

4. Pace Fitzmyer, *The One Who Is to Come,* 13.

most often to a future king, although it can on occasion refer to a priest or a prophet.[5]

Our concern in this book is with the ideal of kingship, initially with the historical kingship and then with the "messianic" kingship as this would be restored in the eschatological age. Our interest is in the understanding of kingship as a present reality in ancient Judah, and then as a future ideal in the later prophetic texts and in the postexilic period, whether or not the word משיח is used in a particular context.[6] In the words of Tremper Longman, "The field is well beyond the point of thinking that a concept is limited to a single word,"[7] or at least it should be. The king, whether past or future, could be designated by various terms. The word משיח was not *de rigueur*.

## The Royal Ideology

The king is explicitly called "son of God" not only in Psalm 2, but also in Psalm 89 and in the promise to David in 2 Samuel 7. There are also other passages, most notably Psalms 110 and 45, that appear to attribute divinity to the king. There is a long-standing debate, however, about the interpretation of these passages.

On the one hand, beginning with the work of Gunkel, some scholars have viewed the Psalms in the context of ancient Near Eastern mythology, and taken the divinization of the king quite seriously.[8] This line of ap-

---

5. Fitzmyer, *The One Who Is to Come*, 82-102; Andrew Chester, *Messiah and Exaltation* (Tübingen: Mohr Siebeck, 2007), 265-76.

6. Contra Fitzmyer, *The One Who Is to Come*, passim, who maintains a narrow focus on the use of the word משיח. On the terminological issue, see further my comments in *The Scepter and the Star: The Messiahs of the Dead Sea Scrolls and Other Ancient Literature* (ABRL; New York: Doubleday, 1995), 11-12, and a good discussion in Chester, *Messiah and Exaltation*, 193-205. Chester rightly insists that "the use (or lack) of the term משיח should not be allowed to be determinative for the definition of messianism" (204).

7. Tremper Longman III, "The Messiah: Explorations in the Law and Writings," in Stanley Porter, ed., *The Messiah in the Old and New Testaments* (Grand Rapids: Eerdmans, 2007), 14.

8. Hermann Gunkel and Joachim Begrich, *Introduction to the Psalms* (Macon, GA: Mercer University Press, 1998); trans. from the fourth ed. of *Einleitung in die Psalmen* (Göttingen: Vandenhoeck & Ruprecht, 1933), 106-9. See the comments of William Horbury, *Jewish Messianism and the Cult of Christ* (London: SCM, 1998), 15-16.

proach received its classic treatments from Hugo Gressmann[9] and Sigmund Mowinckel.[10] It was carried to extremes by the Myth and Ritual School, exemplified by S. H. Hooke in England[11] and Ivan Engnell in Sweden,[12] which posited a high degree of uniformity throughout the ancient Near East and interpreted elliptic biblical texts in light of supposed "patterns." Partly in reaction to the excesses of the Myth and Ritual School, some scholars insisted that the divine sonship was metaphorical or "a formula of adoption." In the words of Martin Noth, "The use of the formula of adoption shows that the Davidic king in Jerusalem was not god incarnate, was not of divine origin or nature, but is designated 'son' by gracious assent of his God. In this modification, therefore, we have less a proof of a Davidic divine kingship in Jerusalem than indeed an indication of a *rejection* of real divine king ideology."[13] It should be said that even scholars like Gunkel and Mowinckel, who were sympathetic to the mythic context of the kingship, still held an adoptionistic view of the kingship in Israel. While the full ideology of "sacral kingship" promoted by the Myth and Ritual School has fallen out of favor, however, the debate continues between those who take the mythological character of the kingship ideology seriously and those who try to downplay it or explain it away.

## Kingship in Ancient Egypt

The strongest affirmations of the divinity of the king in the ancient Near East are found in ancient Egypt.[14] The titulary of the Pharaoh, from the

9. Hugo Gressmann, *Der Messias* (Göttingen: Vandenhoeck & Ruprecht, 1929).

10. Sigmund Mowinckel, *He That Cometh: The Messiah Concept in the Old Testament and Later Judaism* (Grand Rapids: Eerdmans, 2005). The Norwegian original, *Han Som Kommer,* appeared in 1951. The English translation was originally published by Abingdon in 1955. See John J. Collins, "Mowinckel's *He That Cometh* Revisited," *Studia Theologica* 61 (2007) 3-20.

11. S. H. Hooke, ed., *Myth, Ritual, and Kingship: Essays on the Theory and Practice of Kingship in the Ancient Near East and in Israel* (Oxford: Oxford University Press, 1958).

12. Ivan Engnell, *Studies in Divine Kingship in the Ancient Near East* (Uppsala: Almqvist and Wiksell, 1943). For a broader sampling of the "myth and ritual" school, not only in relation to the ancient Near East but especially in the study of ancient Greece, see Robert A. Segal, ed., *The Myth and Ritual Theory: An Anthology* (Oxford: Blackwell, 1998).

13. Martin Noth, "God, King and Nation," in *The Laws in the Pentateuch and Other Studies* (Philadelphia: Fortress, 1966), 172-73.

14. David O'Connor and David P. Silverman, eds., *Ancient Egyptian Kingship* (Pro-

Middle Kingdom on, included the appellations Horus and "son of Re."[15] In the Hellenistic period, the Ptolemies claimed to be "son of the Sun."[16] After death the king was assimilated to Osiris. The use of these divine titles, to be sure, lent themselves to flattery and propaganda, and can even be used ironically. This is especially evident in the *Tale of Sinuhe*. The death of a pharaoh is described as follows: "The god ascended to his horizon. The King of Upper and Lower Egypt, Sehetepibre, flew to heaven and united with the sun-disk, the divine being merging with its maker."[17] Later, while Sinuhe is seeking refuge outside of Egypt, to escape the turmoil of the succession, one of his hosts asks him, "How then is that land without that excellent god, fear of whom was throughout the lands?" He responds diplomatically, "Of course his son has entered into the palace, having taken his father's heritage. He is a god without peer."[18]

Some Egyptian inscriptions from the New Kingdom period describe the begetting of the king in explicit sexual terms, by telling how the god Amun took the form of the human father, had intercourse with the queen, filling her with his "dew" or "fragrance" and engendering the new ruler.[19]

bleme der Ägyptologie 9; Leiden: Brill, 1994); John Baines, "Ancient Egyptian Kingship: Official Forms, Rhetoric, Context," in John Day, ed., *King and Messiah in Israel and the Ancient Near East* (JSOTSup 270; Sheffield: Sheffield Academic Press, 1998), 16-53. See also the classic study of Henri Frankfort, *Kingship and the Gods: A Study of Ancient Near Eastern Religion as the Integration of Society and Nature* (Chicago: University of Chicago Press, 1948), 15-212.

15. Baines, "Ancient Egyptian Kingship," 19-20.

16. On the Rosetta stone, Ptolemy V is described as "son of the Sun, to whom the Sun has given victory." See *OGIS* 1, p. 43; Edwin R. Bevan, *A History of Egypt under the Ptolemaic Dynasty* (London: Methuen, 1927), 28, 30, 263; Ludwig Koenen, "Die Adaptation ägyptischer Königsideologie am Ptolemäerhof," in W. Peremans, ed., *Egypt and the Hellenistic World* (Studia Hellenistica 27; Leuven: Leuven University Press, 1983), 142-90.

17. Miriam Lichtheim, *Ancient Egyptian Literature,* vol. 1: *The Old and Middle Kingdoms* (Berkeley: University of California Press, 1975), 223.

18. Ibid., 225.

19. Helmut Brunner, *Die Geburt des Gottkönigs. Studien zur Überlieferung eines altägyptischen Mythos* (Ägyptologische Abhandlungen 10; Wiesbaden: Harrassowitz, 1964); Jan Assmann, "Die Zeugung des Sohnes. Bild, Spiel, Erzählung und das Problem des ägyptischen Mythos," in Jan Assmann, Walter Burkert, and Fritz Stolz, *Funktionen und Leistungen des Mythos. Drei altorientalische Beispiele* (OBO 48; Freiburg: Universitätsverlag/ Göttingen: Vandenhoeck & Ruprecht, 1982); Othmar Keel, *The Symbolism of the Biblical World: Ancient Near Eastern Iconography and the Book of Psalms* (Winona Lake, IN: Eisenbrauns, 1997), 247-56.

These texts are admittedly exceptional. The primary examples come from the 18th Dynasty and relate to Queen Hatshepsut (ca. 1479-1458 BCE),[20] who may have felt the need to bolster her claim to the throne, and to the pharaohs Amenhotep III (ca. 1390-1352 BCE) and Haremhab (ca. 1323-1295 BCE). An inscription from the mortuary chapel of Hatshepsut at Der-el-Bahri reads:

> Utterance of Amon-Re, lord of Thebes, presider over Karnak: "He made his form like the majesty of this husband . . . he found her as she slept . . . he imposed his desire on her, he caused that she should see him in his form as a god."

Another inscription gives the response of the queen:

> Utterance by the king's wife and king's mother Ahmose in the presence of the majesty of this august god, Amon, Lord of Thebes: "How great is thy fame! It is splendid to see thy front; thou hast united my majesty with thy favors, thy dew is in all my limbs." After this, the majesty of the god did all he desired with her.[21]

The literalness of the begetting should not be exaggerated, however. The texts variously describe the pharaoh as son of Amun/Re, as Horus, son of Osiris, or fashioned by the potter god Khnum. Haremhab, for example, is said, in the same text, to be son of Horus, god of Hnes, and of Amun.[22] This is mythological language, and it is not easily reduced to modern cate-

---

20. Hatshepsut ruled as regent for Thutmose III from ca. 1479 to 1473, and subsequently ruled jointly with him. See Catharine H. Roehrig, ed., *Hatshepsut: From Queen to Pharaoh* (New Haven: Yale University Press, 2006).

21. James H. Breasted, *Ancient Records of Egypt* (Chicago: University of Chicago Press, 1906), 2:80. Brunner, *Die Geburt des Gottkönigs,* 42-43, and Assmann, "Die Geburt des Königs," 27, translate "dein Duft ist in allen meinen Gliedern," "your fragrance is in all my limbs." I am assured by my colleague Colleen Manassa that "it really is 'dew,' *iAd.t,* that pervades her limbs. Another word, *id.t,* does mean Duft and is often confused with *iAd.t,* and in the Divine Birth scene, they are exploiting both meanings — the scent of the god as well as his 'dew' pervades her limbs. Plus, the term *iAd.t,* 'dew,' is heavily associated in Egyptian religion with the goddesses Hathor/Sakhmet, and by using this term, the queen becomes the goddess of the eye of the sun." On the goddesses see Philippe Germond, *Sekhmet et la Protection du Monde = Aegyptiaca Helvetica* 9 (1981), and John C. Darnell, "Hathor Returns to Medamûd," *Studien zur Altägyptischen Kultur* 22 (1995) 47-94.

22. Alan H. Gardiner, "The Coronation of King Haremhab," *JEA* 39 (1953) 14-15.

gories of literalness.[23] It may be that ancient Egyptians were more conscious of the metaphorical character of such language than modern scholars have often assumed. Recent Egyptologists have pulled back from the tendency to assume that the living pharaoh was regarded as a god incarnate. In the words of David Silverman:

> A pharaoh might be: named a god in a monumental historical text, called the son of a deity in an epithet on a statue in a temple, hailed as the living image of a god in a secular inscription, described as a fallible mortal in a historical or literary text, or referred to simply by his personal name in a letter.[24]

Silverman argues that it was the office of kingship that provided the ruler with the element of the divine, and that "the king lists visibly document this concept of the constant divine office animated by the individual, changeable ruler."[25] He concludes: "It is unlikely, considering the evidence from a variety of sources, that the original mortal nature of the pharaoh was ever totally eclipsed by the divine aspect of the office."[26] Similarly Ronald J. Leprohon writes:

> The evidence shows that the living pharaoh was not, as was once thought, divine in nature or a god incarnate on earth. Rather, we should think of him as a human recipient of a divine office. Any individual king was a transitory figure, while the kingship was eternal.[27]

Even in the royal inscriptions, the dependence of the king on the higher divine power is clear. So we read in one of the hymns of Akhenaten:

> "Thy rays are upon thy beloved son . . . the child who came forth from thy rays. You assign to him your lifetime and your years. . . . He is thy beloved, you make him like Aten. When you rise, eternity is given to him;

---

23. See the comments of J. J. M. Roberts, "Whose Child Is This? Reflections on the Speaking Voice in Isaiah 9:5," *HTR* 90 (1997) 127.

24. David P. Silverman, "The Nature of Egyptian Kingship," in O'Connor and Silverman, ed., *Ancient Egyptian Kingship*, 50.

25. Ibid., 67.

26. Ibid., 68.

27. Ronald J. Leprohon, "Royal Ideology and State Administration in Pharaonic Egypt," in Jack Sasson, ed., *Civilizations of the Ancient Near East* (4 vols.; New York: Scribner's, 1995), 1:275.

when you set, you give him everlastingness. You beget him in the morning like your own forms; you form him as your emanation, like Aten, ruler of truth, who came forth from eternity, son of Re, wearing his beauty."[28]

Pharaohs regularly call on Amun for help in battle. In the words of Henri Frankfort: "Amon, then, was a universal god, while Pharaoh's godhead was of a different order. He was but the son; his power derived from his mighty father."[29]

Nonetheless, there is no doubt that the claims of the pharaoh to divine status were taken seriously in ancient Egypt, in the sense that he was not regarded as an ordinary mortal. While the most explicit claims of divine birth date from the New Kingdom period,[30] the affirmation that the king is "son of Re" persists down to the Ptolemaic period. The title "son of Re" bespoke a special kinship with the divine, both in origin and in ultimate destiny after death.

### Ancient Mesopotamia

In ancient Mesopotamia, a belief in divine kingship is attested for a brief period at the end of the third millennium in ancient Sumer. Naram-Sin was honored as a god in Akkad, and had his own temple, and his son was sometimes, although not always, designated as a god.[31] The divinized Sumerian king claimed superiority to his people and to other city-rulers, but he remained inferior to the gods of the pantheon. He claimed divine parents, and depended on the patronage of the gods.[32] The Sumerian experiment in divine kingship was exceptional in Mesopotamian history, but in the Mid-

28. Breasted, *Ancient Records of Egypt*, 2:409.

29. Frankfort, *Kingship and the Gods*, 161.

30. On the eclipse of the myth of the birth of the pharaoh after the Ramesside era, see Klaus Koch, "Der König als Sohn Gottes in Ägypten und Israel," in Eckart Otto and Erich Zenger, eds., *"Mein Sohn bist du" (Ps 2,7). Studien zu den Königspsalmen* (Stuttgarter Bibelstudien 192; Stuttgart: Verlag Katholisches Bibelwerk, 2002), 10.

31. W. G. Lambert, "Kingship in Ancient Mesopotamia," in Day, ed., *King and Messiah*, 59; Jacob Klein, "Sumerian Kingship and the Gods," in Gary Beckman and Theodore J. Lewis, eds., *Text, Artifact, and Image in the Ancient Near East* (BJS 346; Providence, RI: Brown University Press, 2006), 115-31.

32. Klein, "Sumerian Kingship," 131.

dle and Neo-Assyrian periods the king could still be represented as a son of a god. In the *Epic of Tukulti-Ninurta* (1243-1207 BCE) we are told that

> By the fate determined by Nidimmud [Ea], his mass is reckoned with the flesh of the gods. By the decision of the Lord of all the lands [Enlil], he was successfully engendered through (or cast into) the channel of the womb of the gods. He alone is the eternal image of Enlil. . . . Enlil raised him like a natural father, after his first-born son.[33]

In the words of Peter Machinist, "These lines make clear that one mark of the king as divine child is that he, his body, serves as the image of the god."[34] Thus, there is deliberate ambiguity in referring both to the engendering of the king and to his being cast or poured out like a statue. The sonship is clearly metaphorical. Enlil raises him *like* a father. The text stops short of outright deification. But the theme of divinity also appears in Neo-Assyrian texts, especially in the inscriptions of Asshurbanipal:

> "I knew no [human] father and mother; I grew up on the knees of my goddesses [Ishtar of Nineveh and Ishtar of Arbela]. The great gods brought me up like a baby. The Lady of Nineveh, the mother who bore me, granted me kingship without equal. The Lady of Arbela, who created me, ordered [for me] everlasting life."[35]

As in the Egyptian texts, the language of these inscriptions is mythical, and is imaginatively rhetorical rather than literal. The king seems to regard two goddesses as his mother. Nonetheless, the divine-like character of the Assyrian king is meant to be taken seriously. It entails divine effulgence, which puts his enemies to rout:

> Frightful are his effulgences; they overwhelm all the enemies. . . .
> Like Adad when he thunders, the mountains tremble;

---

33. Trans. Peter Machinist, "Kingship and Divinity in Imperial Assyria," in Beckman and Lewis, ed., *Text, Artifact, and Image*, 152-88, here 161. See also W. G. Lambert, "Three Unpublished Fragments of the Tukulti-Ninurta Epic," *AfO* 18 (1957-58) 48-51 + Taf. IV; Peter Machinist, "The Epic of Tukulti-Ninurta I: A Study in Middle Assyrian Literature" (Ph.D. dissertation, Yale, 1978), 66-71; B. R. Foster, *Before the Muses: An Anthology of Akkadian Literature* (3rd ed.; Bethesda, MD: CDL, 2005), 1:301-2.

34. Machinist, "Kingship and Divinity," 162.

35. Ibid., 167.

And like Ninurta when he raises his weapons, the regions
    [of the world] everywhere are thrown into continual panic.[36]


## Ancient Canaan

It is unfortunate that we do not have comparable texts from ancient Canaan, the sphere that probably had the most direct influence on Israelite conceptions of the monarchy. There is some evidence that kings were associated with divinity. In the Ugaritic king list, each of the names of dead kings are preceded by the word *il*, "god."[37] Just what degree of exaltation this entailed is not clear. Ted Lewis points to the analogy of Samuel in the Hebrew Bible, who is called an *elohim* after his death (1 Sam 28:13). He concludes: "It is safe to say that, upon death, a ruler was not deified in the full sense of becoming one of the god who made up the Ugaritic pantheon," but "entered into the revered company of the Rephaim and continued to exist in the underworld."[38] King Keret was son of El, and was expected to be immortal, but the expectation is disappointed:

> "We rejoiced in your life, our father, we exulted [in] your immortality
> . . . shall you then die, father as men, . . . how can it be said that Keret is a
> son of El . . . or shall gods die?"[39]

It is possible that we have here something analogous to the dual nature of the king in the Egyptian tradition,[40] but Keret is a legendary figure, and

36. *Epic of Tukulti-Ninurta* 12, 14-15. Machinist, "Kingship and Divinity," 161.

37. *KTU*, 2nd ed., 1:113; Manfried Dietrich, Oswald Loretz, and Joaquín Sanmartín, *The Cuneiform Alphabetic Texts from Ugarit, Ras Ibn Hani and Other Places* (Münster: Ugarit-Verlag, 1995), 129. See Theodore J. Lewis, *Cults of the Dead in Ancient Israel and Ugarit* (HSM 39; Atlanta: Scholars Press, 1989), 47-52; John Day, "The Canaanite Inheritance of the Israelite Monarchy," in Day, ed., *King and Messiah*, 82.

38. Lewis, *Cults of the Dead,* 49-59. On the Rephaim see *KTU* 1:20-22, 161, Lewis, *Cults of the Dead,* 5-46; C. E. L'Heureux, "The Ugaritic and Biblical Rephaim," *HTR* 67 (1974) 265-74; B. A. Levine and J. M. Tarragon, "Dead Kings and Rephaim: The Patrons of the Ugaritic Dynasty," *JAOS* 104 (1984) 649-59; Klaas Spronk, *Beatific Afterlife in Ancient Israel and in the Ancient Near East* (AOAT 219; Kevelaer: Butzon & Bercker; Neukirchen-Vluyn: Neukirchener Verlag, 1986), 161-96; H. Rouillard, "Rephaim," *DDD,* 692-700.

39. *KTU* 1:16 i.14-15, 22. J. C. L. Gibson, *Canaanite Myths and Legends* (Edinburgh: Clark, 1977), 95.

40. This was suggested to me by Mark Smith. Nicolas Wyatt, "Degrees of Divinity:

not necessarily representative of Canaanite kingship. Canaanite kings were certainly familiar with Egyptian conceptions of monarchy, as can be seen from the Amarna Letters, where they often greet the Egyptian overlord as "my lord, my Sun, my god,"[41] and from at least one letter found at Ugarit.[42] But much of what is said about Canaanite kingship in modern scholarship depends on inferences from the Hebrew Bible.

It is quite possible in principle that Egyptian conceptions of monarchy were mediated to Israel through ancient Canaan, which had been under Egyptian control for much of the second millennium BCE. It is also entirely possibly that Israelite conceptions were influenced by the Assyrians, during their hegemony in the 8th century. Such influence, of course, is not to be assumed, but the possibility must be given serious consideration.

## Ancient Judah

### Psalm 2

Questions of Egyptian and Assyrian influence have figured prominently in recent discussions of the Psalms, especially Psalm 2.[43] Several German scholars have argued for a postexilic date for this psalm, on the grounds that it contains some Aramaisms and envisions universal kingship.[44] If this

Some Mythical and Ritual Aspects of West Semitic Kingship," in idem, *"There's such Divinity doth Hedge a King"* (Aldershot: Ashgate, 2005), 194-95, suggests that Keret, like Baal, was supposed to die and rise again. He takes the Baal myth as paradigmatic for Ugaritic kingship.

41. *ANET*, 483-90. W. L. Moran, *The Amarna Letters* (Baltimore: Johns Hopkins, 1992). See EA 231, 241, 243, 266, 267, 270, 271, 274, 292-300, 306, 309, 314-16, 319-26, 328, 329, 331, 337.

42. *KTU* (2nd ed.), 2:81; Day, "The Canaanite Inheritance," 87.

43. See especially Eckart Otto, "Psalm 2 in neuassyrischer Zeit. Assyrische Motive in der judäischen Königsideologie," in Klaus Kiesow and Thomas Meurer, eds., *Textarbeit. Studien zu Texten und ihrer Rezeption aus dem Alten Testament und der Umwelt Israels. Festschrift für Peter Weimar* (AOAT 294; Münster: Ugarit-Verlag, 2003), 335-49; idem, "Politische Theologie in den Königspsalmen zwischen Ägypten und Assyrien. Die Herrscherlegitimation in den Psalmen 2 und 18 in ihrem altorientalischen Kontexten," in Otto and Zenger, eds., *"Mein Sohn bist du,"* 33-65; Koch, "Der König als Sohn Gottes," ibid., 11-15.

44. Erhard S. Gerstenberger, *Psalms: Part One, with an Introduction to Cultic Poetry* (FOTL XIV; Grand Rapids: Eerdmans, 1988), 48; Erich Zenger, in Frank-Lothar Hossfeld and Erich Zenger, *Die Psalmen I. Psalm 1–50* (Würzburg: Echter, 1993), 50; Klaus-Peter Adam, *Der königliche Held. Die Entsprechung von kämpfendem Gott und kämpfendem König in Psalm 18* (WMANT 91; Neukirchen-Vluyn: Neukirchener Verlag, 2001), 161-68. The

were so, the Psalm should be considered messianic in the eschatological sense. Erhard Gerstenberger dubs it a "messianic hymn," and informs us that "messianic hopes sometimes rose to feverish heights in exilic and postexilic Israel."[45] In his view, "To oppose all the kings of the world, as visualized in Psalm 2, makes sense only in a political situation of universal dependency."[46] But the dream of universal kingship was an integral part of royal ideology in ancient Egypt and Mesopotamia, in situations far removed from universal dependency. Amun proclaims with reference to Hatshepsut:

> "She is the one who will reign over the two lands while governing all living things . . . as far as every place over which I [as sun god] shine in my circuit."[47]

Egypt's traditional enemies, the Nubians and Asiatics, are depicted beneath the feet of the child pharaoh.[48] Tikulti-Ninurta was described as "he who controls the entire four directions, . . . the assembly of all the kings fear him continually."[49] Assurbanipal claimed to be "king of the universe,"[50] and Nebuchadnezzar II thanked Marduk for granting him kingship over all peoples.[51] To be sure, the Assyrian and Babylonian kings had

---

Aramaisms cited are the verbs רגשׁ (to be in tumult) and רעע (to shatter). Note that Zenger subsequently revised his opinion, and argued that Ps 2:1-9 is preexilic: E. Zenger, "'Es sollen sich niederwerfen vor ihm all Könige'" (Ps 72,11). Redaktionsgeschichtliche Beobachtungen zu Psalm 72 und zum Programm des messianischen Psalters Ps 2-89," in Otto and Zenger, ed., "'Mein Sohn bist du,'" 87. For an overview of the debate about the date of the Psalm see Friedhelm Hartenstein, "'Der im Himmel thront, lacht' (Ps 2,4)," in Dieter Sänger, ed., *Gottessohn und Menschensohn. Exegetische Studien zu zwei Paradigmen biblischer Intertextualität* (Biblisch-Theologische Studien 67; Neukirchen-Vluyn: Neukirchener Verlag, 2004), 158-88, here 160.

45. Gerstenberger, *Psalms: Part One*, 48.
46. Ibid. So also Markus Saur, *Die Königspsalmen* (BZAW 340; Berlin: de Gruyter, 2004), 39-40.
47. Brunner, *Die Geburt des Gottkönigs*, 43; Othmar Keel, *The Symbolism of the Biblical World: Ancient Near Eastern Iconography and the Book of Psalms* (Winona Lake, IN: Eisenbrauns, 1997), 253.
48. Keel, *The Symbolism of the Biblical World*, 254.
49. *Epic of Tikulti-Ninurta*, 13; Machinist, "Kingship and Divinity," 16.1.
50. Benjamin R. Foster, *From Distant Days: Myths, Tales and Poetry from Ancient Mesopotamia* (Bethesda, MD: CDL, 1995), 282.
51. Ibid., 283. On the Assyrian claim of world dominion see further Otto, "Psalm 2 in

some empirical basis for their claims, which the Judahite king did not, but political propaganda is seldom constrained by reality. Neither do Aramaisms require a postexilic date; Aramaic was already the *lingua franca* of the Near East in the Neo-Assyrian period, and Judean leaders could allegedly speak it in the time of Sennacherib (2 Kings 18:26).[52] Psalm 2 has a far more plausible Sitz im Leben in the period of the monarchy, in the context of an enthronement ceremony.[53] Some scholars who regard the psalm in its present form as postexilic recognize that verses 7-9, which tell the decree of the Lord, derive from preexilic tradition.[54]

Eckart Otto has argued persuasively that Psalm 2 combines Egyptian and Assyrian influences.[55] He finds Assyrian influence in the motif of the rebellion of the subject nations, and in the promise that the king will break the nations with a rod of iron and dash them in pieces like a potter's vessel.[56] These motifs suggest a date for the psalm in the Neo-Assyrian period. The declaration that the king is the son of God, however, has closer Egyptian parallels. The idea that the king was the son of a god is not unusual in the ancient Near East. We have noted some Mesopotamian evidence. Kings of Damascus from the 9th century BCE took the name "son of Hadad," and at least one king of the Syrian state of Sam'al was

---

neuassyrischer Zeit," 341-42; J. J. M. Roberts, review of Saur, *Die Königspsalmen*, in *CBQ* 67 (2005) 700.

52. See Edward M. Cook, "Aramaic Language and Literature," in Eric M. Meyers, ed., *The Oxford Encyclopedia of Archaeology in the Ancient Near East* (New York: Oxford, 1997), 182. Mark W. Hamilton, *The Body Royal: The Social Implications of Kingship in Ancient Israel* (Leiden: Brill, 2005), 64, notes the use of the Aramaic word *bar* ("son") in the Phoenician inscription of the Anatolian king Kilamuwa (KAI 24:1, 4, 9) and concludes that scholarly concern with Aramaisms in Psalm 2 are misplaced.

53. Gressmann, *Der Messias*, 9; Gunkel, *Introduction to the Psalms*, 118; Mowinckel, *He That Cometh*, 67; Hans-Joachim Kraus, *Psalms 1–59* (CC; Minneapolis: Fortress, 1993; trans. from the 5th ed. of *Psalmen 1. Teilband, Psalmen 1–59* [BK; Neukirchen-Vluyn: Neukirchener Verlag, 1978]), 126.

54. Hartenstein, "'Der im Himmel thront, lacht,'" 161. He argues that vv. 1-6 are postexilic because of the presence of wisdom motifs, which are characteristic of the editorial phase of the development of the Psalter. Whether such motifs necessarily require a postexilic date, however, is less than certain.

55. Otto, "Psalm 2 in neuassyrischer Zeit"; "Politische Theologie in den Königspsalmen." Not all aspects of the psalm are necessarily explained by these parallels. See Hartenstein, "'Der im Himmel thront, lacht,'" 170-74.

56. Otto, "Psalm 2 in neuassyrischer Zeit," 343-49; cf. Bob Becking, "'Wie Töpfe Sollst Du Sie Zerschmeissen.' Mesopotamische parallelen zu Psalm 2,9b," *ZAW* 102 (1990) 59-79.

called "son of Rakib."[57] Only in the Egyptian evidence, however, do we find the distinctive formulae by which the deity addresses the king as "my son."

The formula, "you are my son, this day I have begotten you," finds a parallel in an inscription in the mortuary temple of Hatshepsut:

> "my daughter, from my body, Maat-Ka-Re, my brilliant image, gone forth from me. You are a king, who take possession of the two lands, on the throne of Horus, like Re."[58]

Reliefs at the temple of Amenophis III at Luxor show Amun touching the royal child and taking it in his arms.[59] Another inscription of Amenophis III has the god declare: "He is my son, on my throne, in accordance with the decree of the gods."[60] At the coronation of Haremhab, Amun declares to him: "You are my son, the heir who came forth from my flesh."[61] Or again, in the blessing of Ptah, from the time of Rameses II: "I am your father, who have begotten you as a god and your members as gods."[62] Such recognition formulae occur frequently in Egyptian inscriptions of the New Kingdom period. Otto suggests that the psalm does not reflect direct Egyptian influence, since the closest Egyptian parallels date from the New Kingdom, before the rise of the Israelite monarchy. Rather, the *Hofstil* of pre-Israelite (Jebusite) Jerusalem may have been influenced by Egyptian models during the late second millennium, and have been taken over by the Judean monarchy in Jerusalem.

The formulation of the psalm, "this day I have begotten you," is widely taken to reflect an enthronement ceremony.[63] The idea that the enthronement ritual in Jerusalem was influenced by Egyptian models was argued by

---

57. For Ben Hadad see 1 Kings 15:18-19 = 2 Chron 16:2; *ANET* 655. For Bar-Rakib, *ANET* 655. P. K. McCarter, *2 Samuel* (AB 9; New York: Anchor, 1984), 207.

58. Brunner, *Die Geburt des Gottkönigs*, 109; cf. 117.

59. Ibid., Plates 10 and 11; Assmann, "Die Zeugung des Sohnes," 16-17, illustrations 10, 14; Keel, *The Symbolism of the Biblical World*, 252 53.

60. Manfred Görg, *Gott-König-Reden in Israel und Ägypten* (Stuttgart: Kohlhammer, 1975), 260.

61. Memphis Stela 3. Alan H. Gardiner, "The Coronation of King Haremhab," *JEA* 39 (1953) 29.

62. Görg, *Gott–König–Reden*, 237; Assmann, "Die Zeugung des Sohnes," 35. For the text, K. A. Kitchen, *Ramesside Inscriptions: Historical and Biographical* (Oxford: Oxford University Press, 1971), II, fasc. 5, 263.

63. Hamilton, *The Body Royal*, 60-61.

Gerhard von Rad, in an article originally published in 1947.[64] He argued that the "decree" (חק) of Ps 2:7 referred to the royal protocol, presented to the king at the time of the coronation. The Egyptian protocol contained the pharaoh's titles, and the acknowledgment that the king was son of Re, and therefore legitimate king. Von Rad noted that a fuller example of a royal protocol can be found in Isa 9:6, where the proclamation of the birth of a son is followed by the titles by which he is to be known, including "mighty god." Von Rad's insights were taken up and developed in a famous essay by Albrecht Alt, who argued that the passage in Isaiah 9 was composed for Hezekiah's enthronement, and celebrated not the birth of a child but the accession of the king.[65] The interpretation of Isaiah 9 in terms of an enthronement ceremony is not certain. The oracle could be celebrating the birth of a royal child.[66] The word ילד is not otherwise used for an adult king.[67] But the accession hypothesis is attractive, nonetheless, in light of Psalm 2. The list of titles is reminiscent in a general way of the titulary of the Egyptian pharaohs.[68] Most importantly, the passage confirms that the king could be addressed as *elohim*, "god." The latter point is further illustrated in Ps 45:6, which is most naturally translated as "Your throne, O God, endures forever."[69] The objection that the king is not

64. Gerhard von Rad, "The Royal Ritual in Judah," in idem, *The Problem of the Hexateuch and Other Essays* (New York: McGraw-Hill, 1966), 222-31, originally published as "Das judäische Königsritual," *ThLZ* 73 (1947) 211-16.

65. Albrecht Alt, "Jesaja 8,23–9,6. Befreiungsmacht und Krönungstag," in Walter Baumgartner, ed., *Festschrift Alfred Bertholet zum 80. Geburtstag gewidmet* (Tübingen: Mohr Siebeck, 1950), 29-49, reprinted in Alt, *Kleine Schriften zur Geschichte des Volkes Israel* (3 vols.; Munich: Beck, 1953), 2:206-25.

66. See the discussion by Hans Wildberger, *Isaiah 1–12* (CC; Minneapolis: Fortress, 1991; trans. from *Jesaja, Kapitel 1–12* [BK; Neukirchen-Vluyn: Neukirchener Verlag, 1980]), 398-89; and by Roberts, "Whose Child Is This?" 115-29. Simon Parker, "The Birth Announcement," in Lyle Eslinger and Glenn Taylor, eds., *Ascribe to the Lord: Biblical and Other Studies in Memory of Peter C. Craigie* (JSOTSup 67; Sheffield: JSOT, 1988), 136-38, argues that the traditional character of the birth announcement shows that it refers to the birth of a child. See the review of the discussion by Paul D. Wegner, *An Examination of Kingship and Messianic Expectation in Isaiah 1–35* (Lewiston, NY: Mellen, 1992), 168-76.

67. Wildberger, *Isaiah 1–12*, 398.

68. The Egyptian protocols had five names. Isaiah 9 has only four, but the odd orthography of the word למרבה in Isa 9:6, with a final *mem* in the middle of the word, is often taken to show that a fifth name has fallen out. See Wildberger, *Isaiah 1–12*, 405; Wegner, *An Examination of Kingship*, 191-92. Wegner rejects this view.

69. See Day, "The Canaanite Inheritance," 83-84; Kraus, *Psalms 1–59*, 451, 455; Zenger, in Hossfeld and Zenger, *Die Psalmen*, 1:282; Hamilton, *The Body Royal*, 51,

otherwise addressed as God loses its force in light of Isaiah 9. The fact that the king is addressed as God in Ps 45:6 is shown by the distinction drawn in the following verse, "therefore God, your God, has anointed you."[70] The king is still subject to the Most High, but he is an *elohim*, not just a man.

In light of this discussion, it seems very likely that the Jerusalemite enthronement ritual was influenced, even if only indirectly, by Egyptian ideas of kingship. At least as a matter of court rhetoric, the king was declared to be the son of God, and could be called an *elohim*, a god. This is not to say that the Judahite and Egyptian conceptions were identical. Most probably, the Israelites took over their conception of kingship from their Canaanite forebears in Jerusalem, and modified it in various ways.

## Psalm 110

The argument that these ideas were mediated through Canaanite traditions finds its strongest evidence in Psalm 110, where the king is told that he is a priest forever after the order of Melchizedek.[71] Melchizedek is known as a venerable priest-king of El Elyon in Jerusalem from Genesis 14.[72] Kingship and priesthood were associated in Assyrian tradition, where the king had the title *shangu*, a term related to the provision and maintenance of sanctuaries. Peter Machinist suggests that the term should be translated as "priest" and that the Assyrian king was honorary chief priest of his realm.[73] A number of Phoenician kings are also said to be priests (Eshmun῾azar, Tabnit).[74] While

---

70. Pace Marc Zvi Brettler, *God Is King: Understanding an Israelite Metaphor* (JSOTSup 76; Sheffield: JSOT, 1989), 39, who argues that *elohim* cannot have more than one referent, or semantic confusion would result.

71. Gerstenberger, *Psalms: Part Two, and Lamentations* (FOTL XV; Grand Rapids: Eerdmans, 2001), 266-67, characteristically dates this psalm to the Second Temple period, because of the supposed "fervent expectations of a restitution of the Davidic empire" in that period. Even he, however, allows that it may contain "pieces of ancient inauguration rituals."

72. Attempts to deny that the reference is to Jerusalem are not convincing. See Day, "The Canaanite Inheritance," 73-74, and especially John A. Emerton, "The Site of Salem," in J. A. Emerton, ed., *Studies in the Pentateuch* (VTSup 41; Leiden: Brill, 1990), 45-71.

73. Machinist, "Kingship and Divinity," 156. See M.-J. Seux, *Épithètes Royales Akkadiennes et Sumériennes* (Paris: Letouzey et Ané, 1967), 287; G. van Driel, *The Cult of Assur* (Assen: van Gorcum, 1969), 170-74.

74. Tabnit, king of Sidon, and his father Eshmun῾azar were "priests of Astarte." KAI 13:1, 2. Day, "The Canaanite Inheritance," 75.

Israelite and Judahite kings do not habitually act as priests, they do offer sacrifice on occasion.[75] Elyon is known apart from the Bible in the Sefire Inscriptions, where he is paired with El,[76] and in the account of Phoenician mythology in Philo of Byblos.[77] There is ample evidence that Yahweh and El Elyon were identified in the Jerusalem cult. Psalm 46:5 refers to Jerusalem as "the holy habitation of Elyon."[78] The association of the king with Melchizedek, then, links him with a cultic tradition that has clear roots in pre-Israelite, Canaanite or Jebusite, Jerusalem.

The invitation to the king to sit at the right hand of the deity, however, has long been recognized as an Egyptian motif, known from the iconography of the New Kingdom.[79] Amenophis III and Haremhab are depicted seated to the right of a deity.[80] The position is not only one of honor, but bespeaks the very close association of the king and the deity. The invitation to the king suggests that at his enthronement he was thought to be seated at the right hand of the deity.[81] Depictions of other pharaohs (Amenophis, Thutmose IV) show them enthroned with their enemies (Nubians and Asiatics) as their footstools.[82]

For our present purposes, the main focus of interest in Psalm 110 is the notoriously corrupt verse 3b:

בהדרי־קדש מרחם משחר לך טל ילדתיך

The corresponding Greek (Ps 109:3) reads:

75. Day, "The Canaanite Inheritance," 75; Hamilton, *The Body Royal*, 71. See further Deborah W. Rooke, "Kingship as Priesthood: The Relationship between the High Priesthood and the Monarchy," in Day, ed., *King and Messiah*, 187-208.

76. KAI 222 A 11.

77. Eusebius, *Preparation for the Gospel* 1.10.15; H. W. Attridge and R. A. Oden, *Philo of Byblos: The Phoenician History* (CBQMS 9; Washington, DC: CBA, 1981), 47.

78. See further Day, "The Canaanite Inheritance," 78-80; E. E. Elnes and P. D. Miller, "Elyon," *DDD*, 293-99.

79. Koch, "Der König as Sohn Gottes," 16; J. de Savignac, "Essai d'interprétation du Psaume CX à l'aide de la littérature égyptienne," *OTS* 9 (1951) 105-35.

80. Keel, *The Symbolism of the Biblical World*, 263.

81. Lorenz Dürr, *Psalm 110 im Lichte der neueren alt-orientalischen Forschung* (Münster: Aschendorff, 1929); Sigmund Mowinckel, *The Psalms in Israel's Worship* (Grand Rapids: Eerdmans, 2004; first English ed., Oxford: Blackwell, 1962), 1:47-48, 63-64.

82. Keel, *The Symbolism of the Biblical World*, 254-55; Scott R. A. Starbuck, *Court Oracles in the Psalms: The So-Called Royal Psalms in Their Ancient Near Eastern Context* (SBLDS 172; Atlanta: Society of Biblical Literature, 1996), 144.

ἐν ταῖς λαμπρότησιν τῶν ἁγίων
ἐκ γαστρὸς πρὸ ἑωσφόρου ἐξεγέννησά σε.

The MT points the last word as *yaldutheka,* "your youth." The NRSV translates accordingly:

> From the womb of the morning
> like dew, your youth will come to you.[83]

Many Masoretic manuscripts, however, read *y<sup>e</sup>lidtika,* the reading presupposed by the Greek, and also supported by the Syriac. In view of the consonantal spelling in the MT, and the parallel in Psalm 2, this reading should be preferred and is accepted by many commentators.[84]

By re-pointing the Masoretic text, but making no changes to the consonants we read:

> In sacred splendor, from the womb, from dawn,
> you have the dew wherewith I have begotten you.[85]

Numerous other emendations have been proposed.

Some commentators read הררי קדש, "holy mountains,"[86] an emendation that seems unnecessary, but has the support of several manuscripts and also of Symmachus and Jerome.

The NRSV's "from the womb of the morning" presupposes either an otherwise unattested noun משחר or dittography, but this reading is widely accepted.[87] William P. Brown retains the *mem,* but translates "towards

---

83. It also emends הדרי, "splendor," to הררי, "mountains."

84. Kraus, *Psalms 60–150,* 344. L. C. Allen, *Psalms 101–150* (WBC 21; Waco, TX: Word, 1983), 81, argues that the LXX reading is a case of harmonization with Psalm 2. See the incisive critique of Allen's position by William P. Brown, "A Royal Performance: Critical Notes on Psalm 110:3aγ-b," *JBL* 117 (1998) 95.

85. So Aubrey R. Johnson, *Sacral Kingship in Ancient Israel* (2nd ed.; Cardiff: University of Wales Press, 1955), 121-22, followed by Day, "The Canaanite Inheritance," 83, except that they read "from the womb of the dawn," which is also possible.

86. Kraus, *Psalms 60–150,* 344.

87. So also Kraus, ibid.; Johnson, *Sacral Kingship,* 121-22; Day, "The Canaanite Inheritance," 83. Gary A. Rendsburg, "Psalm CX 3B," *VT* 49 (1999) 548-53, defends the reading of משחר as "dawn" on the basis of parallel formations. He argues that רחם should be understood as "rain." Rendsburg does not take the Greek translation of the psalm into account at all.

dawn," a reading that has the support of the Greek but makes doubtful sense.[88] It is surely more likely that the king is said to be brought forth from the dawn. The taunt of the king of Babylon in Isa 14:12 refers to him as Helel ben Shachar, usually translated as "Day Star, Son of Dawn."[89] At Ugarit, Shachar is known as a male god, son of El, half-brother of Shalim, evening.[90] Samuel Meier suggests that we should allow for variable gender, in light of the usage in Ps 110:3 (which he reads as "the womb of Dawn").[91] Whether the reference here is to the Canaanite deity is uncertain, however. That which comes forth at, or from, Dawn is the sun, the primary image for the deity in the Egyptian tradition. The imagery of the Psalm associates the king with the rising sun, with all its mythological connotations.[92] Compare the hymn of Akhenaten, cited above at n. 28: "You beget him in the morning like your own forms."

Even more problematic is the reference to dew. The Greek does not reflect the Hebrew words לך טל at all. The Syriac reads talya', "child." Both versions reflect either difficulty of comprehension or theological discomfort. Many commentators ignore the lamed and read, "Like dew I have begotten you."[93] Brown, who acknowledges the problem with that procedure, suggests לך כטל, "go forth/like the dew."[94] He assumes that one kaph

88. Brown, "A Royal Performance," 94. For the construal of the preposition compare the usage in מקדם, "eastward." Brown also cites a Ugaritic parallel from KTU 2:16.6-10, where someone says that he came before the Sun (meaning the king), but this does not seem immediately relevant.

89. See the recent discussion of this passage by R. Mark Shipp, Of Dead Kings and Dirges: Myth and Meaning in Isaiah 14:4b-21 (Academia Biblica 11; Atlanta: Society of Biblical Literature, 2002), 67-79.

90. KTU 1:23. Samuel A. Meier, "Shahar (Deity)," ABD 5:1, 150-51; S. B. Parker, "Shahar," DDD, 754-55.

91. Meier, "Shahar," 1151. Nicolas Wyatt, Myths of Power: A Study of Royal Myth and Ideology in Ugaritic and Biblical Tradition (Ugaritisch-Biblische Literatur 13; Münster: Ugarit-Verlag, 1996), 284, suggests that "womb" and "dawn" are "the geminated mothers of the king" and combares "the geminated pair, Athirat and Rahmay, in KTU 1:23, who represent hypostases of Shapsh, the sun-goddess."

92. Hamilton, The Body Royal, 68-69, suggests that the text refers to a ritual at dawn, in which the king entered the temple from the east. For the association of Yahweh with the Sun, see Mark S. Smith, The Early History of God: Yahweh and Other Deities in Ancient Israel (Grand Rapids: Eerdmans, 2002), 148-59; J. Glenn Taylor, Yahweh and the Sun: Biblical and Archaeological Evidence for Sun Worship in Ancient Israel (JSOTSup 111; Sheffield: JSOT, 1993).

93. Kraus, Psalms 60–150, 344; Starbuck, Court Oracles, 148.

94. So already Joseph Coppens, "Le Psaume CX et l'Idéologie Royale Israélite," in The

was lost by haplography and so requires minimal emendation. (He reads the verb with the preceding words: "towards the dawn, go forth!").[95] Some scholars suggest an allusion to Tallay, daughter of Ba'al ("I have brought you forth like Tallay").[96] Scott Starbuck suggests a more mundane analogy: "Just as Yahweh gives birth to the dew every morning, so too, Yahweh has given birth to the king."[97] If we refrain from any emendation, however, with Johnson and Day, then the dew is the means by which the deity has begotten the king, and it infuses him with divine vitality. We may compare the role of the divine "dew" or "fragrance" in the begetting of Hatshepsut, in the Egyptian inscriptions, where the queen responds to Amun: "Thy dew is in all my limbs."[98] Since the translation of the Egyptian word is disputed,[99] we cannot be sure that the Hebrew "dew" is an allusion to the Egyptian motif. The motifs of seating at the right hand and sun-like emergence from the dawn, however, strongly suggest an Egyptian background. It seems reasonably clear that the psalm refers to the begetting of the king. Like Psalm 2, it should be viewed as reflecting a Jerusalemite enthronement ceremony, which was influenced, if only indirectly, by Egyptian mythology about the divine birth of the king.

### Begotten or Adopted?

But even if we grant that the King of Judah was declared "son of God" and could be addressed as "God," the force of this language remains to be determined. Von Rad and Alt, even while arguing for Egyptian influence, still drew a sharp distinction between Egyptian and Judean conceptions of kingship, and, indeed, most biblical critics have done likewise.[100] Biblical

---

*Sacral Kingship: Contributions to the Central Theme of the VIIIth International Congress for the History of Religions* (Rome, April 1955) (Leiden: Brill, 1959), 333-49, here 341, who credits the suggestion to Geo Widengren.

95. Brown, "A Royal Performance," 96.

96. So, tentatively, John F. Healey, "Dew," *DDD*, 251; cf. Meier, "Shahar," 1,151.

97. Starbuck, "Court Oracles," 150. Cf. Job 38:28-29. So already Gerald Cooke, "The Israelite King as Son of God," *ZAW* 32 (1961) 224

98. *ARE* 2:80. See above, n. 22. Starbuck, *Court Oracles,* 150, notes the parallel but dismisses it.

99. Above, n. 21.

100. See Cooke, "The Israelite King as Son of God," 208-18.

scholars have commonly supposed that in the Egyptian tradition the king was the son of a god in a literal, physical sense. In the Judean context, "You are my son" was taken as a legal formula of adoption. In the words of Sigmund Mowinckel:

> Therefore in spite of all the mythological metaphors about the birth of a king, we never find in Israel any expression of a "metaphysical" conception of the king's divinity and his relation to Yahweh. It is clear that the king is regarded as Yahweh's son by adoption. When, in Ps. ii,7, Yahweh says to the king on the day of his anointing and installation, 'You are My son; I have begotten you today,' He is using the ordinary formula of adoption, indicating that the sonship rests on Yahweh's adoption of the king.[101]

The relevance of the metaphor of adoption has been questioned, however. Herbert Donner pointed to the fact that the legal material in the Hebrew Bible does not provide for adoption.[102] Scholars who argue for understanding the sonship of the Judahite king in terms of adoption usually appeal to the laws of Hammurabi (170-71) where the father recognizes the children of a female slave by declaring "you are my children," but, of course, they may actually have been his children! Even in Babylonian law, positive formulae for adoption (as opposed to formulae for the dissolution of an adoptive relationship) are rare, and there is no actual occurrence of the formula "you are my son."[103] Neither is there any parallel for the use of the verb "to beget" in the context of an adoption.[104]

A number of scholars have argued that the sonship language should be understood in the context of covenants of royal grant.[105] So, for example, the

---

101. Mowinckel, *He That Cometh*, 78.

102. H. Donner, "Adoption oder Legitimation? Erwägungen zur Adoption im Alten Testament auf dem Hintergrund der altorientalischen Rechte," *OrAnt* 8 (1969) 87ff. See also Shalom M. Paul, "Adoption Formulae: A Study of Cuneiform and Biblical Legal Clauses," *Maarav* 2/2 (1979-80) 173-85; J. H. Tigay, "Adoption," *EncJud* (1971), 2:300-301.

103. The classic work is that of Martin David, *Die Adoption im altbabylonischen Recht* (Leipzig: Weicher, 1927). David could find only two examples of positive formulae for adoption. Paul adds one more. See Roberts, "Whose Child Is This?" 119-20.

104. Roberts, "Whose Child Is This?" 121.

105. So especially Moshe Weinfeld, "The Covenant of Grant in the Old Testament and in the Ancient Near East," *JAOS* 90 (1970) 184-203; Roland de Vaux, "The King of Israel, Vassal of Yahweh," in idem, *The Bible and the Ancient Near East* (New York: Doubleday, 1971), 152-80.

Hittite king Shuppululiumash declares to one Mattiwaza: "I shall make you my son, I will stand by (to help in war) and will make you sit on the throne of your father."[106] Adoption could be seen as a way to guarantee an inheritance, and the theme of inheritance is prominent in Psalm 2. According to Kyle McCarter, "Its purpose is to qualify the king for the patrimony Yahweh wishes to bestow on him."[107] But we do not find language of "begetting" in these covenants. The covenantal parallels are more relevant to the formulation of Nathan's oracle, in its Deuteronomistic setting in 2 Samuel 7, than to the Psalms.

The most obvious way in which the "begetting" of the king is qualified in the Psalms is by the assertion in Psalm 2 that the begetting is "today." Most commentators have taken this, quite rightly, as an unequivocal indication of the metaphorical character of the begetting.[108] Similarly, in Ps 89:27 the Lord says of David, "I will make him the firstborn, the highest of the kings of the earth." Even here, the contrast with Egyptian understanding may not be as extreme as is usually assumed. In an account of the Opet festival depicted at Luxor, Lannie Bell writes:

> It should not be forgotten that all reports of oracular nomination to office or divine conception and birth were recorded only after they had manifested themselves undeniably: succession to the throne was normally *de facto* proof of legitimacy.[109]

Again:

> The representation of this *ka* is intended as proof of his divine origins and sufficient evidence that he was predestined to rule. But he actually *becomes* divine only when he becomes one with the royal *ka*, when his human form is overtaken by this immortal element. . . . This happens at the climax of the coronation ceremony when he assumes his rightful place on the "Horus-throne of the living."[110]

This is still different from what we find in the Psalms, as the pharaoh was claimed to be divine from birth, even if this was proclaimed retroac-

---

106. Weinfeld, "Covenant of Grant," 191.

107. McCarter, *2 Samuel*, 207.

108. E.g., Mettinger, *King and Messiah*, 265-66; Keel, *The Symbolism of the Biblical World*, 248.

109. Lannie Bell, "Luxor Temple and the Cult of the Royal Ka," *JNES* 44 (1985) 257.

110. Ibid., 258.

tively when he came to the throne. But the difference between what is met-aphorical and what is mythical is not absolute, and the categories are not incompatible.[111] Both "adoption" and "begetting" are metaphorical when applied to a divinity, but they are different metaphors. Metaphorical "be-getting" suggests a closer kinship between king and god than is conveyed by "adoption." To be sure, the Psalms stop well short of the description of divine begetting, in explicit sexual terms, that we find in some Egyptian texts, but, as we have seen, such language is not universal even in Egypt, and was not necessarily understood literally. The fact that the Israelite king is "chosen" by his God[112] is not at all distinctive. Similar language is used of the pharaoh in the *Blessing of Ptah,* and is also found in Mesopotamian texts. Likewise, the fact that the king is subordinate to a higher deity is a feature shared by all these traditions. The status of the king in Jerusalem was not as exalted as that of the pharaoh, and the testimonies to his divine sonship that have been preserved are relatively few. Nonetheless, the lan-guage of sonship does have mythical overtones, and clearly claims for the king a status greater than human.

### In What Sense Was the King Divine?

Even in ancient Egypt, the king was never thought to be on a par with the gods of the pantheon. Rather, his power derived from his divine father, by whom he was begotten and chosen. Likewise in the Hebrew Bible, to say that the king was son of God was to suggest a special relationship to the Most High, but certainly not parity. Even the one psalm that addresses the king as an *elohim,* or "god," refers to "God, your God" in the next verse, to put the divinity of the king in perspective (Ps 45:7-8).

The main implication of the declaration that the king was son of God is the implication that he is empowered to act as God's surrogate on earth. This entails the promise of divine support, especially in warfare. As God's surrogate, he is sovereign of the whole world by right. He can shatter the nations with an iron rod and execute judgment upon them. The Hebrew

111. Compare the comments of Wyatt, *Myths of Power,* 286, who grants that God's pa-ternity of the king can be understood as a performative utterance but adds: "But that in no way disqualifies it from being mythological at the same time. It is its inherently mythological nature that gives it its significance."

112. Kraus, *Psalms 1–59,* 132.

texts do not emphasize the superhuman wisdom of the king as strongly as do the Egyptian ones (although he is a "wonderful counselor" in Isaiah 9, and a spirit of wisdom rests on the future king in Isa 11:2). They attribute to the king a love for justice and righteousness that is closely associated with kingship in Canaanite tradition.[113] It is an intriguing question whether the king is thought to be immortal. Psalm 72 prays that he may live as long as the sun endures. Psalm 21 declares that "he asked for life and you gave it to him — length of days forever and ever."[114] John Day thinks that there is no good reason to take this as alluding to immortality.[115] But it is at least a possible interpretation. It is true that in the Canaanite legends of Aqhat and Keret, hopes for immortality are regarded as fallacious, even in the case of Keret, who was son of El. But the psalm does not suggest that kings are immortal by nature. Life is something that must be granted by God. Yet the psalm seems to hold out the possibility that a king might be granted life to a fuller and greater extent than an ordinary human being. Here again, the Judahite concept of divine kingship is less explicit and exalted than what we find in Egypt, at least in the New Kingdom period, but it still has a mythical dimension that goes beyond the common human condition.

Ziony Zevit has stressed that there is no evidence that the king in ancient Judah was an object of cult or veneration. Rather, the presence in the Psalter of prayers for the king show that he was "an object of cultic concern."[116] He suggests that "the father-son language [in Ps 2:7 and 89:27] had more to do with expressing the relationship of tutorial deity to the king than anything else. Similar language was also used in prophetic groups to express the relationship between followers and the prophet leader."[117] The lack of evidence for cultic veneration is certainly significant, and it qualifies the sense in which the king may be said to be divine. But the prophetic analogy does not do justice to the mythological language

---

113. Day, "The Canaanite Inheritance," 86-88, citing the legend of King Keret (*KTU* 1:16-17) and a letter from a Ugaritic king to an Egyptian pharaoh.

114. Compare also Ps 61:6: "Prolong the life of the king; may his years endure to all generations." The argument for the immortality of the king has been made by John Healey, "The Immortality of the King: Ugarit and the Psalms," *Or* 53 (1984) 245-54.

115. Day, "The Canaanite Inheritance," 85.

116. Ziony Zevit, "Israel's Royal Cult in the Ancient Near Eastern *Kulturkreis*," in Beckman and Lewis, ed., *Text, Artifact, and Image*, 189-200, here 200.

117. Ibid., 199.

of the Psalms. Granted that the king is not divine in the same sense as the Most High, the claim that he is "begotten" by God is a statement about a nature and status conferred on him, not just about a tutorial relationship. As we shall see in the next chapter, most of the prophets took a dim view of the pretensions of monarchs to divinity, and the claims of the Davidic dynasty were muted in the Deuteronomistic history. Yet they were not entirely suppressed. The fact that the dominant attitude in biblical tradition insists on a sharp distinction between divinity and humanity, and is sharply critical of kingship makes the preservation of the royal psalms all the more remarkable. It requires that we take them seriously as a witness to preexilic religion, before it was chastened by the harsh historical experiences that led to the demise of the monarchy.

# 2. The Kingship in Deuteronomistic and Prophetic Literature

## The Deuteronomistic Literature

### 2 Samuel 7

The fact that divine sonship was an intrinsic part of the royal ideology in Jerusalem is confirmed by the account of Nathan's oracle in 2 Samuel 7.

The literary history of this chapter has been debated endlessly.[1] The chapter as we have it is thoroughly Deuteronomistic.[2] In the words of Kyle McCarter, "It is clear that II Samuel 7 expresses certain important deuteronomistic ideas, for which it stands as a primary point of reference

---

1. T. Veijola, *Die ewige Dynastie. David und die Entstehung seiner Dynastie nach der deuteronomistischen Darstellung* (Helsinki: Suomalainen Akatemia, 1975); P. K. McCarter, *2 Samuel* (AB; New York: Doubleday, 1984), 210-17; W. M. Schniedewind, *Society and the Promise to David: The Reception History of 2 Samuel 7:1-17* (New York: Oxford, 1999), 30-39; M. Pietsch, "*Dieser ist der Spross Davids. . . .*" *Studien zur Rezeptionsgeschichte der Nathanverheissung* (WMANT 100; Neukirchen-Vluyn: Neukirchener Verlag, 2003), 8-53; Tryggve N. D. Mettinger, "Cui Bono? The Prophecy of Nathan (2 Sam. 7) as a Piece of Political Rhetoric," *Svensk Exegetisk Årsbok* 70 (2005) 193-214.

2. On the Deuteronomistic history, see now Thomas Römer, *The So-Called Deuteronomistic History: A Sociological, Historical and Literary Introduction* (London/New York: T&T Clark, 2007). Michael Avioz, *Nathan's Oracle (2 Samuel 7) and Its Interpreters* (Bern: Lang, 2005), 9, is exceptional in dismissing the Deuteronomist as "unknown and indefinable."

in the larger history," and that "the present form of the text is built largely of Deuteronomistic rhetoric."[3] This means that the present form of the chapter is no earlier than the time of Josiah, and possibly postexilic.[4] Timo Veijola drew the radical conclusion that the promise to David had no pre-exilic basis, but was born as an expression of defiant faith in the exile.[5] Many scholars, however, believe that the Deuteronomist was working with an older tradition about the promise to David.[6]

William Schniedewind goes so far as to date all of 2 Sam 7:1-17, except for verse 13a ("he shall build a house for my name"), to the time of David.[7] He makes a good case that this half-verse is both secondary and Deuteronomistic,[8] but he does not allow for the possibility that there was more than one Deuteronomistic edition, as most scholars now assume. The text into which this sentence was inserted was already thoroughly Deuteronomistic, as Cross and others have shown.[9] Tryggve Mettinger recognizes more extensive Deuteronomistic material in the chapter, limiting the original core to verses 1a, 2-4, 5 (except for the messenger formula), 8-9a, 11b-14a, 15a, and 16-17.[10] In verse 13a, however, he limits the Deuter-

---

3. McCarter, *2 Samuel*, 220-21. See the fundamental studies of Dennis McCarthy, "II Samuel 7 and the Structure of the Deuteronomic History," *JBL* 84 (1965) 131-38, and Frank Moore Cross, *Canaanite Myth and Hebrew Epic* (Cambridge, MA: Harvard University Press, 1973), 248-57.

4. On the question whether there were two editions of the Deuteronomistic History, as argued by Cross, *Canaanite Myth*, 274-89, or three, as held by many European scholars, such as Veijola, *Die ewige Dynastie*, and W. Dietrich, *Prophetie und Geschichte* (FRLANT 108; Göttingen: Vandenhoeck & Ruprecht, 1972), see Römer, *The So-Called Deuteronomistic History*, 27-43.

5. Veijola, *Die ewige Dynastie*, 137; idem, *Verheissung in der Krise. Studien zur Literatur und Theologie der Exilszeit anhand des 89. Psalms* (Helsinki: Suomalainen Tiedeakatemia, 1982), 94.

6. See the review of scholarship by McCarter, *2 Samuel*, 211. Influential in this regard was a study by Leonhard Rost, *Die Überlieferung von der Thronnachfolge Davids* (BWANT 3/6; Stuttgart: Kohlhammer, 1926), 47-74.

7. Schniedewind, *Society and the Promise to David*, 35-36. He also grants that the theme of "rest" in 7:1b, 11 is a common Deuteronomistic one, but notes that the Deuteronomistic history elsewhere takes the view that David did not yet have rest from his enemies.

8. It is marked as secondary by the resumptive repetition of the phrase "I will establish his kingdom."

9. See, e.g., the list of Deuteronomistic expressions cited by Cross, *Canaanite Myth*, 252-54.

10. Mettinger, "Cui Bono?" 204.

onomistic insertion to "for my name," and regards the statement that David's son will build the temple as part of Nathan's prophecy. He then dates the core prophecy to the time of Solomon. This seems unlikely. Even apart from the persuasive literary argument advanced by Schniedewind, the divine approval of temple building by the son follows awkwardly on what seemed to be a categorical rejection of the father's proposal.[11] There is a long tradition in German scholarship of identifying redactional layers by verse or half-verse. The classic analysis of Leonhard Rost identified a core consisting of verses 1-4a*, 11b, 16, 18-21, and 25-29, which he dated to the early monarchy.[12] A recent analysis by Michael Pietsch identifies the *Grundbestand* or core of the chapter as consisting of verses 1a, 2-5, 8a-9a, 11b-16, 17, 18-21, and 25-27, but within this core he identifies an older oracle, consisting of verses 11b, 12*, 14a, 15a, and 16, which he also dates to the early monarchy.[13]

It is difficult to have confidence in the minutiae of any such analysis, but there is good reason to believe that the Deuteronomistic writer was working with older traditions. It is difficult to believe that the dynastic promise was formulated only after the dynasty had already been in existence for three hundred years, and still more difficult to imagine that it was a product of the exile, after the Davidic monarchy had been overthrown.[14] The legitimation of kings by oracular decree is well attested in the ancient Near East, and we should expect that the kings of Judah would also avail of this means of establishing their claim to the throne.[15] As we shall see, some

---

11. Scholars who regard the whole composition as Deuteronomistic can point out that what is permitted is a temple "for my name" rather than one "for me to dwell in," as noted by Lyle Eslinger, *House of God or House of David: The Rhetoric of 2 Samuel 7* (JSOTSup 164; Sheffield: Sheffield Academic Press, 1994), 48. But the awkwardness remains. David was not told to refine his understanding of divine presence in the temple, but forbidden to build a temple at all.

12. Rost, *Die Überlieferung,* 47-74.

13. Pietsch, *"Dieser ist der Spross Davids,"* 27, 30-31. Römer, *The So-Called Deuteronomistic History,* 146, thinks that a 7th-century core, containing 2 Sam 7:4, 5a, 8a, b, 9, 11b, 12, and 16, was expanded during the exile. Römer does not allow for a core before the time of Josiah.

14. Compare the comments of Hans Ulrich Steymans, *Psalm 89 und der Davidbund* (Österreichische Studien 27; Berlin: Lang, 2005), 373, in criticism of Veijola.

15. See Antti Laato, "Second Samuel 7 and Ancient Near Eastern Royal Ideology," *CBQ* 59 (1997) 144-69. He argues that "there is no *prima facie* reason to regard the central idea in 2 Samuel 7 — the promise of an eternal dynasty to David — as an anachronistic element in

form of the dynastic promise is presupposed in the Immanuel prophecy of Isaiah, in the 8th century. Frank Moore Cross posits two sources for 2 Samuel 7, which were originally poetic oracles but were reworked by the Deuteronomist. One was an oracle of Nathan prohibiting the building of a temple. The second was the divine decree now found in 7:11b-16.[16] The combination of these two elements is somewhat surprising, since temple building was positively associated with kingship, but it is accomplished elegantly by means of a play on the word "house," which can mean both temple and dynasty. The rejection of David's offer to build a temple becomes the occasion of the dynastic oracle. Whether the two oracles were already combined before the Deuteronomist reworked them is uncertain.[17] For our present purposes, it is sufficient that the promise of an everlasting dynasty was not a late fabrication of the Deuteronomist.

The promise of the dynasty contains a balanced, poetic formula referring to David's son: "I shall be a father to him, and he shall be a son to me."[18] The manner in which the sonship is presented, however, is quite different from what we have found in the Psalms.

To begin with, there is no language of begetting. The Hebrew expression אני אהיה־לו לאב והוא יהיה־לי לבן can be translated "I will become a father to him, and he will become a son to me." This is compatible with the idea in the Psalms that the king becomes son of God on his accession to the throne, but the avoidance of "begetting" language is significant. David himself is not declared to be son of God (although he is so declared in Psalm 89). The very language of the formulation, then, draws back from any suggestion of divine begetting, and might even be described, with Mettinger, as a (limited) demythologization of the royal ide-

---

the account of the reigns of David and Solomon" (263). Also Laato, *A Star Is Rising: The Historical Development of the Old Testament Royal Ideology and the Rise of the Jewish Messianic Expectations* (Atlanta: Scholars Press, 1997), 38-45.

16. Cross, *Canaanite Myth,* 254.

17. McCarter, *2 Samuel,* 222-23, argues that the Deuteronomist would not have introduced the negative oracle about the temple if it had not been part of his source, but compare the questions raised about the temple in Solomon's prayer in 1 Kings 8. McCarter goes on to argue that the dynastic promise was originally made in connection with David's declared intention to build a temple, but that this document was revised by an author with a less favorable view of David and the temple. This seems unduly complicated. The fact that it was not David who built the temple was well known, and had to be accommodated even by authors who had a positive view of David.

18. Cross, *Canaanite Myth,* 256-57.

ology.[19] The demythologization, or accentuation of the human element, is carried further in the following verses:

> When he commits iniquity, I will punish him with a rod such as mortals use, with blows inflicted by human beings. But I will not take my steadfast love from him, as I took it from Saul, whom I put away from before me; your throne shall be established forever.

Amun never spoke to the pharaoh in such terms. The paradigm here is provided by the treaty language of the ancient Near East. Moshe Weinfeld cites a grant by a 13th-century Hittite king to a certain Ulmi-Teshup:

> After you, your sons and grandsons will possess it. Nobody will take it away from them. If one of your descendants sins, . . . the king will prosecute him at his court. . . . But nobody will take away from the descendant of Ulmi-Teshup either his house or his land.[20]

It is unlikely that Israelite or Judean monarchy was influenced by the Hittites at any point: Hittite influence in the region had vanished long before the rise of the monarchy. But analogies with Assyrian treaties are fundamental to the book of Deuteronomy, and the Deuteronomistic project.[21] The model of treaty relations is more likely to have been imposed on the royal ideology by the Deuteronomists than to have been been part of its original conception.

It is widely agreed that the treaty model shaped the understanding of

19. N. D. Mettinger, *King and Messiah* (Lund: Gleerup, 1976), 265. Mettinger, however, also applies this concept to the Psalms.

20. Moshe Weinfeld, "The Covenant of Grant in the Old Testament and in the Ancient Near East," *JAOS* 90 (1970) 184-203, here 189. The analogy has been questioned by Gary Knoppers, "Ancient Near Eastern Royal Grants and the Davidic Covenant: A Parallel?" *JAOS* 116 (1996) 670-97, and Avioz, *Nathan's Oracle*, 26, on the grounds that the grants deal with land ownership rather than kingship, but the significant point is that they guarantee the rights of the descendants in perpetuity.

21. Dennis J. McCarthy, *Treaty and Covenant* (AnBib 21A; Rome: Pontifical Biblical Institute, 1981); Moshe Weinfeld, *Deuteronomy and the Deuteronomic School* (Oxford: Oxford University Press, 1972), 59-157; Eckart Otto, "Das Deuteronomium als Archimedischer Punkt der Pentateuchkritik auf dem Wege zu einer Neubegründung der de Wette'schen Hypothese," in M. Vervenne and J. Lust, eds., *Deuteronomy and Deuteronomic Literature: Festschrift C. H. W. Brekelmans* (BETL 133; Leuven: Peeters, 1997), 321-29; Römer, *The So-Called Deuteronomistic History*, 74-78.

the Mosaic covenant, especially in Deuteronomy. That covenant was conditional, as were the typical vassal treaties of the ancient Near East.[22] The fact that the dynastic promise in 2 Samuel 7 is unconditional, despite the threat of punishment, is a testament to the enduring power of the older royal ideology.[23] In 1 Kings 8, however, the Davidic covenant too is understood as conditional, just like the Mosaic covenant, in accordance with Deuteronomic theology:

> "Therefore, O LORD, God of Israel, keep for your servant my father David that which you promised him, saying, 'There shall never fail you a successor before me to sit on the throne of Israel, if only your children look to their way, to walk before me, as you have walked before me.'" (1 Kings 8:25)[24]

This passage belongs to a later edition of the Deuteronomistic history, in the context of the Babylonian exile. (The exilic situation is evoked explicitly in 8:46: "If they sin against you . . . and you are angry with them and give them to an enemy, so that they are carried away captive to the land of the enemy. . . .")[25] In that context, the view that the covenant with David was conditional was a natural inference from the course of events. Not all Judeans abandoned faith in the promise, but the revision was in line with the critical tendency of the Deuteronomistic tradition. Solomon's paraphrase of the promise makes no mention of the tradition that God regarded the Davidic king as his son.

## The Davidic Covenant in the Psalms

The chastened view of monarchy that we find in 2 Samuel 7 is also reflected in two psalms that allude to the covenant with David, Psalms 89 and 132.

---

22. See, e.g., Jon D. Levenson, *Sinai and Zion* (San Francisco: Harper, 1987), 15-86.

23. Avioz, *Nathan's Oracle*, 27, argues that "the Abrahamic and Davidic covenants are not essentially different from the Sinaitic covenant," but his argument is not persuasive.

24. Avioz, *Nathan's Oracle*, 97-99, notes correctly that Solomon's prayer links the fate of the dynasty to the fate of the people.

25. Römer, *The So-Called Deuteronomistic History*, 119: "But now v. 25 makes the promise of an eternal dynasty conditional, a result of the reflection about the situation after 587 BCE." Schniedewind, *Society and the Promise to David*, 106-10, also regards this passage as exilic.

Psalm 89 is a composite poem, containing three distinct units, skillfully woven together:

1. a hymn in verses 2-3, and 6-19 (Eng. 1-2, 5-18). This is replete with mythological motifs, and may be quite old:
2. a meditation on the covenant with David in verses 4-5 and 20-38 (Eng. 3-4, 19-37); and finally
3. a lament in verses 39-52 (Eng. 38-51).[26]

Our present concern is with the middle part of the psalm. As Nahum Sarna has shown, this passage is an interpretation of Nathan's oracle.[27] The psalm makes no reference to the question of temple building. David himself will call God "father," and will be made "the firstborn, the highest of the kings of the earth." The sonship of the king is understood here in a mythic context that has strong Canaanite overtones. His power is established over the sea and the rivers, the traditional forces of chaos in Canaanite myth.[28] So, while David's own role in 2 Samuel 7 is quite modest, here he is given heroic proportions. The promise is explicitly interpreted as a covenant (v. 2) and is analogous to the covenants of grant in the treaty texts. On the one hand, the promise is guaranteed forever. On the other, there is provision for punishment of his descendants if they "forsake my law and do not walk according to my ordinances, if they violate my statutes and do not keep my commandments" (vv. 30-31). The language is unmistakably Deuteronomistic.[29] Schniedewind argues that the promise that the throne will endure (vv. 29 and 36) implies that there is still a sitting monarch, and that this segment of the psalm "fits nicely into the days of Josiah."[30] At least, the un-

26. Nahum M. Sarna, "Psalm 89: A Study in Inner-Biblical Exegesis," in Alexander Altman, ed., *Biblical and Other Studies* (Cambridge, MA: Harvard University Press, 1963), 30-31. See also E. Gerstenberger, *Psalms: Part Two, and Lamentations* (FOTL XV; Grand Rapids: Eerdmans, 2001), 147-57; Schniedewind, *Society and the Promise to David*, 41; Frank-Lothar Hossfeld, in Frank-Lothar Hossfeld and Erich Zenger, *Psalm 2: A Commentary on Psalms 51-100* (Hermeneia; Minneapolis: Fortress, 2005), 402.

27. Sarna, "Psalm 89," 36-39. For the verbal correspondences between Psalm 89 and 2 Samuel 7 see Veijola, *Verheissung in der Krise*, 48-49.

28. Cross, *Canaanite Myth*, 160-62; John Day, *God's Conflict with the Dragon and the Sea* (Cambridge: Cambridge University Press, 1985), 25-28.

29. The Deuteronomistic affinities of the psalm are argued especially by Veijola, *Verheissung in der Krise*, e.g., 117-18.

30. Schniedewind, *Society and the Promise to David*, 94-95. He dates the last segment of

derstanding of the Davidic covenant corresponds to that of 2 Samuel 7 rather than of 1 Kings 8, insofar as the promise stands in perpetuity, even though individual kings may be punished.

The other psalm that reflects on the Davidic covenant, Psalm 132, is closer to 1 Kings 8. The psalm commemorates the bringing of the ark to Jerusalem as recounted in 2 Samuel 6. In this context it recalls the promise to David:

> The LORD swore to David a sure oath from which he will not
>     turn back:
> "One of the sons of your body I will set on your throne.
> If your sons keep my covenant and my decrees that I shall
>     teach them,
> Their sons also, forevermore, shall sit on your throne."

Frank Moore Cross has argued that this psalm preserves "lore of Davidic date" and is "our earliest witness to the Davidic covenant."[31] We may agree that there is here no hint of the Canaanite ideology of divine sonship,[32] which is found even in 2 Samuel 7 and Psalm 89. Whether it "is in precise agreement with the concept of kingship in the era of Saul and in the later northern kingdom,"[33] however, is another matter.

Scholarship is sharply divided on the date of this psalm.[34] On the one hand are those like Cross, who date the psalm early and see the conditional covenant as a reflection of the ideology of the earliest monarchy. So, for example, Antti Laato argues that the *content* (not necessarily the final form) of Psalm 132 "represents the stage in the development of the Israelite/Jerusalemite royal ideology where the influence of the conditional covenant idea functioning in the tribal society was still very strong."[35] On the

---

the psalm (vv. 39-52) to the exilic period. Veijola, *Verheissung in der Krise*, 117, argues for an exilic date. Steymans, *Psalm 89*, 449, posits both a preexilic "Ur-psalm" stratum and a Persian period redaction throughout the psalm.

31. Cross, *Canaanite Myth*, 232.

32. Ibid., 233. Cross speaks of "divine adoption."

33. Ibid.

34. For a good overview, see Leslie Allen, *Psalms 101–50* (WBC 21; Waco: Word, 1983), 207-9.

35. Antti Laato, "Psalm 132 and the Development of the Jerusalemite/Israelite Royal Ideology," *CBQ* 54 (1992) 49-66. Whether in fact there was a conditional covenant idea in tribal Israel is, however, very much in question.

other hand, many scholars see the conditional nature of the covenant as clear evidence of Deuteronomistic influence.[36] There are several points of affinity with Deuteronomistic language,[37] and with passages in the Deuteronomistic history.[38] Yet it does not speak of finding a place for YHWH's name, but for YHWH himself.[39] The prayer in Ps 132:10, "do not turn away the face of your anointed one," suggests that there was still at least an heir to the Davidic throne.[40] The concluding promise in verse 17 that God will cause a horn to sprout for David, in contrast, would seem to presuppose that the line is no longer flourishing, and suggests genuine messianic expectation.[41] A setting in the time of the restoration is conceivable, when the temple was being rebuilt and there was still hope for the restoration of the Davidic line.[42] The fact that this psalm is cited in 2 Chron 6:41-2, at the end of Solomon's prayer, requires only that it was composed before the end of the 5th century BCE. Whatever the exact date, I am inclined to agree with Mettinger that this psalm too presupposes the Deuteronomistic history, even if it does not share all aspects of Deuteronomistic theology.[43] The view that the covenant with David was conditional, and the eclipse of the motif of divine sonship, reflect the chastened view of the kingship that resulted from the disasters of the Babylonian period.

36. E.g., L. Perlitt, *Bundestheologie im Alten Testament* (WMANT 36; Neukirchen-Vluyn: Neukirchener Verlag, 1969), 51; Veijola, *Verheissung in der Krise*, 161; Mettinger, *King and Messiah*, 256-57.

37. Mettinger, *King and Messiah*, 256, cites such phrases as "for the sake of David your servant" and "the fruit of the womb," and the use of the verb "to choose" with reference to Zion.

38. E.g., 1 Kings 2:4; 6:12-13; 8:25; 9:4-5.

39. Schniedewind, *Society and the Promise to David*, 44.

40. Veijola, *Verheissung in der Krise*, 161, argues, counterintuitively, that "your anointed" refers collectively to the pious.

41. Gerstenberger, *Psalms: Part Two*, 369, takes the psalm as messianic.

42. Corrine L. Patton, "Psalm 132: A Methodological Inquiry," *CBQ* 57 (1995) 643-54. Jean-Marie Auwers, "Le psaume 132 parmi les graduals," *RB* 103-4 (1996) 546-60, also argues for a postexilic date.

43. Mettinger, *King and Messiah*, 276-7. Antti Laato, "Psalm 132: A Case Study in Methodology," *CBQ* 61 (1999) 24-33, here 29, argues less plausibly that the Deuteronomist was influenced by Psalm 132: "The unconditional promise concerning the eternal reign of the Davidic dynasty was reformulated by the Deuteronomist as a conditional promise concerning the Davidides' rule over the whole of Israel, including the northern region." He appears, however, to be harmonizing the different editions of the Deuteronomistic history.

## Kingship in the Prophetic Corpus

One of the standard arguments against the view that the king in Jerusalem was thought to be divine in any sense points to "the absence of criticism of divine pretensions of Israel's kings on the part of the prophets."[44] Contrast the ringing denunciations of the king of Babylon in Isaiah 14 and especially of the king of Tyre in Ezekiel 28:

> Because your heart is proud and you have said, "I am a god;
> I sit in the seat of the gods in the heart of the seas,"
> Yet you are but a mortal, and no god,
> Though you compare your mind with the mind of a god.

These taunts, of course, are directed against foreign kings. Closer to home, Jeremiah upbraided King Shallum, son of Josiah: "Are you a king because you compete in cedar?" (Jer 22:15). One can imagine what he might have said if the hapless king had claimed to be a god. But all these oracles date from the Babylonian era, and there is good reason to think that the monarchy had been downgraded significantly by Josiah's reform and the rise of the Deuteronomic scribes.

## Isaiah

Our only witness to Jerusalemite prophecy before the reign of Josiah is the 8th-century prophet Isaiah. The main passages that touch on the possible divinity of the king are the Immanuel prophecy in chapter 7 and the proclamation "unto us a child is born," in chapter 9. Both of these passages were assigned to the so-called Isaianic "Memoir" *(Denkschrift)* by Karl Budde, in a famous and influential article, and dated to the time of the prophet himself.[45] Budde's theory has repeatedly been challenged in recent years.[46] Unlike chapters 6 and 8, chapter 7 is presented in the third person,

---

44. John Day, "The Canaanite Inheritance," in Day, ed., *King and Messiah* (Sheffield: Sheffield Academic Press, 1998), 82.

45. K. Budde, *Jesaja's Erleben: Eine gemeinverständliche Auslegung der Denkschrift des Propheten (Kap. 6,1–9,6)* (Gotha: Klotz, 1928).

46. See the summary of scholarship in Thomas Wagner, *Gottes Herrschaft. Eine Analyse der Denkschrift (Jes 6,1–9,6)* (VTSup 108; Leiden: Brill, 2006), 18-41.

and several points of contact have been noted between this chapter and the narrative about Hezekiah in chapters 36–39. Nonetheless, a case can be made for at least a modified form of the *Denkschrift,* including some form of 7:1–8:18, although chapter 7 must have subsequently undergone some modification.[47] Isa 8:16-18 would seem to be the end of a unit:

> Bind up the testimony, seal the teaching among my disciples. I will wait for the LORD, who is hiding his face from the house of Jacob, and I will hope in him. See, I and the children whom the LORD has given me are signs and portents in Israel from the LORD of hosts, who dwells in Mount Zion.[48]

But verse 18 presupposes mention of more than one child of Isaiah. If we bracket for the moment the identity of Immanuel, the reference is presumably to Shear-jashub (Isa 7:3) as well as Maher-shalal-hash-baz (8:1-3). Moreover, Isa 8:8, 10 refer back to Immanuel. This reference implies that Immanuel has already been born, and so reflects a later point in time than 7:14. It would seem, then, that Isa 8:1-18 presupposes some form of the narrative in chapter 7. As Ronald Clements has argued,

> It is much easier to understand why the form of such a memoir should have become distorted and partially obliterated in the course of subsequent editing than that, as a construction of later editors, it should have been employed only in a very clumsy and limited fashion.[49]

The present form of these chapters is later than the time of Isaiah, and related to the composition of Isaiah 36–39. Marvin Sweeney dates it to the time of Josiah,[50] but some scholars have argued for redaction in the wake

---

47. Compare Jörg Barthel, *Prophetenwort und Geschichte. Die Jesajaüberlieferung in Jes 6–8 und 28–31* (FAT 19; Tübingen: Mohr Siebeck, 1997), 61. Isaiah 6 may also have been part of this Memoir, but that issue does not concern us here.

48. Barthel, *Prophetenwort,* 60.

49. R. E. Clements, "The Immanuel Prophecy and Its Messianic Interpretation," in idem, *Old Testament Prophecy: From Oracles to Canon* (Louisville: Westminster John Knox, 1996), 67.

50. M. A. Sweeney, *Isaiah 1–39, with an Introduction to Prophetic Literature* (FOTL XVI; Grand Rapids: Eerdmans, 1996), 150. A redaction in the time of Josiah was originally proposed by H. Barth, *Die Jesaja-Worte in der Josia-Zeit. Israel und Assur als Thema einer produktiven Neuinterpretation der Jesajaüberlieferung* (WMANT 48; Neukirchen-Vluyn: Neukirchener Verlag, 1977).

of Sennacherib's invasion in 701 BCE.[51] The story of an encounter between the prophet and Ahaz, and the oracle about the birth of the child, however, surely have a historical basis in the time of Isaiah.[52]

In light of the apparent finality of 8:16-18, Isa 8:23–9:6 (Eng. 9:1-7) should probably be regarded as a separate unit.

### Immanuel

Both the Immanuel prophecy and the proclamation of the birth of the child in Isaiah 9 have been regarded traditionally as messianic prophecies. It is now generally accepted that both passages have their primary frame of reference in the Assyrian period, in the late 8th century BCE. (There are exceptions. Brevard Childs writes with reference to the figure in Isaiah 9 that "the description of his reign makes it absolutely clear that his role is messianic.")[53] The birth of Immanuel was a sign for King Ahaz, and must be an event of his lifetime.[54]

Most probably, Immanuel was the king's own child. The name "Immanuel" brings to mind the promise to David. In 2 Sam 7:9, the Lord tells David that he has been with him wherever he went. In Ps 89:22 he says of David, "my hand shall always remain with him," and three verses later, "my faithfulness and steadfast love shall be with him." The Zion theology expressed in Ps 46:7 professes that "The LORD of hosts is with us; the God of Jacob is our refuge." According to Mic 3:11 the rulers of Judah say, "Surely

51. Barthel, *Prophetenwort*, 55, 64, 153, argues for redaction not too long after 701 BCE. The affinity with Isaiah 36–39 is found primarily in Isa 7:1 (ibid., 63). Some scholars, notably O. Kaiser, *Isaiah 1–12: A Commentary* (2nd ed.; OTL; Philadelphia: Westminster, 1983), 114-17, regard these chapters as postexilic.

52. Jesper Høgenhaven, *Gott und Volk bei Jesaja. Eine Untersuchung zur biblischen Theologie* (Leiden: Brill, 1988), 77-80. See Paul D. Wegner, *An Examination of Kingship and Messianic Expectation in Isaiah 1–35* (Lewiston, NY: Mellen, 1992), 70, n. 14. On the whole question of the Memoir or *Denkschrift*, see further my essay, "The Sign of Immanuel," in *The Proceedings of the Oxford Seminar on Prophecy,* edited by John Day, forthcoming.

53. B. S. Childs, *Isaiah* (OTL; Louisville, KY: Westminster, 2001), 81. He contends that Isaiah 7 was read messianically by the tradents of the Isaianic tradition (ibid., 68-69).

54. This is granted even by relatively conservative scholars, e.g., Daniel Schibler, "Messianism and Messianic Prophecy in Isaiah 1–12 and 28–33," in Philip E. Satterthwaite, Richard S. Hess, and Gordon J. Wenham, *The Lord's Anointed: Interpretation of Old Testament Messianic Texts* (Grand Rapids: Baker, 1995), 87-104, here 99.

the LORD is with us!" In 1 Kings 11:38 the prophet Ahijah tells Jeroboam that if he walks in the way of the Lord, "keeping my statutes and my commandments, as my servant David did, I will be with you, and I will build you an enduring house, as I built for David."[55] The Hebrew translated "an enduring house" is בית־נאמן, which echoes the promise to David in 2 Sam 7:16: נאמן ביתך וממלכתך עד־עולם, "your house and your kingdom is made firm forever." The same root is used in Ps 89:28 ("my covenant is firm for him") and in Ps 132:11 ("the LORD swore to David a sure oath," אמת) The exhortation of Isaiah, אם לא תאמינו כי לא תאמנו, "If you are not firm in faith, you will not be made firm," is playing on the same root.[56] In light of these echoes of the royal ideology, it seems most natural to assume that the child is the king's son.[57] It is sometimes argued on the basis of Ugaritic parallels that the עלמה is the bride of the king.[58] This is not necessarily so in Hebrew usage, but it is nonetheless likely from the context.[59]

There is nothing miraculous about the birth of Immanuel (despite the famous pronouncement of Hugo Gressmann: "Er ist in der Tat ein Wunderkind").[60] The Hebrew word עלמה does not necessarily mean "virgin." In the words of Hans Wildberger, "The main point of the term is not that she is a virgin. The basic meaning of the root is apparently 'strong, marriageable, fully developed for sexual activity."[61] It has sometimes been sug-

---

55. Hans Wildberger, *Isaiah 1–12* (CC; Minneapolis: Fortress, 1991) 311.

56. E. Würthwein, "Jesaja 7,1-9: Ein Beitrag zu dem Thema: Prophetie und Politik," in idem, *Wort und Existenz. Studien zum Alten Testament* (Göttingen: Vandenhoeck & Ruprecht, 1970), 127-43. The positive connotations of the name are also recognized by Barthel, *Prophetenwort*, 141; Wagner, *Gottes Herrschaft*, 165.

57. So also Barthel, *Prophetenwort*, 145, 174-75.

58. Høgenhaven, *Gott und Volk*, 89-90. Cf. Mowinckel, *He That Cometh*, 114.

59. Several scholars have argued that Immanuel was the prophet's own son, by analogy with the other children: J. J. Stamm, "La prophétie d'Emmanuel," *RHPR* 23 (1943) 1-25; idem, "Die Immanuel-Weissagung und die Eschatologie des Jesaja," *ThZ* 16 (1960) 439-55, and in several other publications; Clements, "The Immanuel Prophecy," 71; J. J. M. Roberts, "Isaiah and His Children," in Ann Kort and Scott Morschauser, eds., *Biblical and Related Studies Presented to Samuel Iwry* (Winona Lake, IN: Eisenbrauns, 1985), 193-203. The identification as Isaiah's son was already proposed by Ibn Ezra and Rashi, and even by Jerome (H. G. M. Williamson, *Variations of a Theme: King, Messiah and Servant in the Book of Isaiah* [The Didsbury Lectures, 1997; Carlisle, Cumbria: Paternoster, 1998], 101). The very fact that the prophet begat Maher-shalal-hash-baz at this time, however, argues against the view that he was also the father of Immanuel.

60. Hugo Gressmann, *Der Messias* (Göttingen: Vandenhoeck & Ruprecht, 1929), 238.

61. Wildberger, *Isaiah 1–12*, 308.

gested that "curds and honey" were the food of the gods, and appropriate for the messiah in the end-time.[62] But again, this is not necessarily so. As J. J. Stamm observed, in the Hebrew Bible milk and honey are nothing but the produce of the uncultivated land.[63] According to Isa 7:21-25, everyone left in the land after its desolation will eat curds and honey. What is remarkable about Immanuel is simply that he is born in a time of distress. His birth is a sign that "God is with us," and will not abandon his promise to David. We are not even told that Immanuel will one day become king. His birth is a marker, "For before the child knows how to refuse the evil and choose the good, the land before whose two kings you are in dread will be deserted."[64]

In Jewish tradition, Immanuel is identified as Hezekiah.[65] There are notorious chronological problems with this identification. According to 2 Kings 18:10, the fall of Samaria (722/1 BCE) was in the sixth year of Hezekiah, but according to verse 13 in the same chapter, the campaign of Sennacherib in 701 BCE was in his 14th year. Accordingly, his date of accession is variously given as 728/7 or 715 BCE. In 2 Kings 18:1 we are told that he was 25 years old when he came to the throne, and if this is correct, he would have been born too early to be identified with Immanuel, on either accession date. But the chronology is confused. According to 2 Kings 16:1-2, Ahaz was only 20 when he began to reign, and he reigned for only 16 years. If Hezekiah were 25 when he succeeded to the throne, he would have been born when his father was 11. Blenkinsopp supposes that Hezekiah became king in 715 BCE, in his late teens, rather than at age 25.[66] In that case, the identification with Immanuel might be possible. But it is not clear that Immanuel should be identified with Hezekiah. The reference could be to another son of Ahaz.

In itself Isaiah 7 does not say that the king is son of God, or have any

62. So Gressmann, *Der Messias,* 241. Cf. Wildberger, *Isaiah 1–12,* 314. See Antti Laato, *Who Is Immanuel?* (Åbo: Åbo Akademie, 1988), 151.

63. Stamm, "Die Immanuel-Weissagung," 447.

64. On the question whether Isaiah's oracle is one of judgment or reassurance, or both, see my essay, "The Sign of Immanuel." For a contrasting interpretation see Williamson, "The Messianic Texts in Isaiah 1–39," 253, who finds "radical discontinuity with the present heirs of the Davidic family."

65. See Laato, *A Star Is Rising,* 123-25; idem, *Who Is Immanuel?* 139-44. The identification as Hezekiah is accepted by Schibler, "Messianism and Messianic Prophecy," 99.

66. Joseph Blenkinsopp, *Isaiah 1–39* (AB 19; New York: Doubleday, 2000), 249.

messianic implications. It acquired these implications in later tradition, largely because it was read in conjunction with other passages that were construed as messianic, in Isaiah 9 and 11.

### Isaiah 8:23–9:6 (Eng. 9:1-7)

As we have seen, the oracle in 8:23–9:6 should probably not be regarded as part of the Memoir, or *Denkschrift,* as proposed by Budde, although it is still so regarded by some scholars.[67] Otto Kaiser locates it after the exile, when it could only refer to an ideal future.[68] As Hugh Williamson has observed, however, "The predominant thought of the passage neither demands, nor is even particularly suitable to, a postexilic date."[69] Williamson further remarks that "Its present redactional setting in the aftermath of the Syro-Ephraimite crisis is by no means unreasonable."[70] The proclamation in Isa 9:6-7 may have originated in the royal court, but many critics believe that it was incorporated in an oracle by Isaiah.[71]

The historical setting is suggested by the geographical references in Isa 8:23b-e: "In the former time he brought into contempt the land of Zebulun and the land of Naphtali, but in the latter time he will make glorious the way of the sea, the land beyond the Jordan, Galilee of the nations."[72] There is wide agreement that there is an allusion here to the conquest of Naphtali and Galilee by Tiglath-Pileser III in 732 BCE, when he divided the territory into three provinces, Gilead, Megiddo, and Dor (2 Kings 15:29).[73] It is, then, appropriately associated with the preceding oracles from the time of the Syro-Ephraimite war. The main difficulty presented by 8:23 concerns the ambiguity of the Hebrew word הכביד, which can be taken as either "oppress" or "make glorious." Blenkinsopp takes it as "oppress," and infers

---

67. E.g., Sweeney, *Isaiah 1–39,* 180.

68. Kaiser, *Isaiah 1–12,* 217.

69. H. G. M. Williamson, "The Messianic Texts in Isaiah 1–39," in Day, ed., *King and Messiah,* 257.

70. Ibid., 258.

71. See Wildberger, *Isaiah 1–12,* 389-93.

72. NRSV translation. The connection between Isa 8:23 and 9:1-6 is disputed by Kaiser, *Isaiah 1–12,* 205-6, among others. See the critique of this position by Laato, *Who Is Immanuel?* 174-78.

73. See, e.g., Blenkinsopp, *Isaiah 1–39,* 247; Wildberger, *Isaiah 1–12,* 379.

that the passage refers to two phases of military disaster. He identifies the second of these with the campaign of Tiglath-Pileser, and supposes that the earlier one is a reference to earlier struggles with Syria. But the Syrian wars do not figure at all in the prophecy of Isaiah. Rather, as Albrecht Alt argued, "the land of Zebulun and the land of Naphtali" is equivalent to "the way of the sea, the land beyond the Jordan, Galilee of the nations." These are two ways of referring to the area conquered by the Assyrians.[74] The passage draws a contrast between the "former" and the "latter." Hence הכביד should be read as "make glorious."[75] The contrast is the same as is proclaimed in Isa 9:2: "the people who walked in darkness have seen a great light."[76]

The campaign of Tiglath-Pileser, which brought a significant part of Israel into subjection, brought relief to King Ahaz of Judah. The attempt of Israel and Syria to compel Ahaz to join the anti-Assyrian coalition was the context for the Immanuel prophecy in Isaiah 7. As we have seen, the child in that prophecy is most plausibly identified as a son of the king, but he is not necessarily a future ruler.

In Isaiah 9, it is quite clear that the "son" born to us is a future ruler: authority rests on his shoulders. It is also clear that he is a ruler from the house of David. His reign will entail endless peace for the throne of David and his kingdom. If the oracle is taken literally as an announcement of the birth of a child, then it could possibly refer to Hezekiah, if Blenkinsopp's conjecture about the chronology is correct. Albrecht Alt, however, famously argued, by analogy with Psalms 2 and 110, that the prophecy does not relate to actual birth but to the enthronement of Hezekiah as king in Jerusalem.[77] While the argument is not entirely conclusive, it is persuasive, and it has been widely accepted. If we accept the earlier of the accession dates for Hezekiah (728/7 BCE), the people who had walked in darkness

---

74. A. Alt, "Jesaja 8,23–9,6," in W. Baumgartner, ed., *Festschrift Alfred Bertholet zum 80. Geburtstag gewidmet* (Tübingen: Mohr Siebeck, 1950), 29-49, reprinted in Alt, *Kleine Schriften zur Geschichte des Volkes Israels* (3 vols.; Munich: Beck, 1953), 2:210-11.

75. See Sweeney, *Isaiah 1–39*, 185-86; Wegner, *An Examination*, 153.

76. For further discussion of the problems of this passage, such as the tenses of the verbs, see my essay "Isaiah 8:23–9:6 and Its Greek Translation," in Anssi Voitila and Jutta Jokiranta, eds., *Scripture in Transition: Essays on Septuagint, Hebrew Bible, and Dead Sea Scrolls in Honour of Raija Sollamo* (JSJSup; Leiden: Brill, 2008), and especially J. A. Emerton, "Some Linguistic and Historical Problems in Isaiah VIII.23," *JSS* 14 (1969) 151-75.

77. Alt, "Jesaja 8,23–9,6," 218-19.

could be either the people of the conquered territories or the people of Jerusalem, who had been besieged during the Syro-Ephraimite war, or both. The "great light" that goes forth from Jerusalem (cf. Isaiah 2) has imperialistic implications for the northern kingdom. Alt suggested that Isaiah 9 contained a proclamation by heralds sent from the Judean court to the former Israelite territories, to urge them to accept Hezekiah as their king.[78] Any attempt to incorporate northern Israel into Judah, however, would be far more credible after the fall of Samaria than before it. Moreover, we now know from archeology that Jerusalem expanded greatly in size in the late 8th century,[79] and this accords well with Isaiah's statement that "you have multiplied the nation." It is usually assumed that this expansion came after the fall of Samaria, and was due at least in part to an influx of refugees from the north. It is possible that there was already some migration southward after the earlier Assyrian conquest, but both the increase in the nation and the idea that a Judean king would bring "light" to northern Israel fit better with the later date for the accession of Hezekiah (715 BCE). In that case, however, the failure to mention the fall of Samaria is difficult to explain.

Despite the problems in the chronology, it is highly probable that the child whose "birth" is proclaimed in Isaiah 9 is Hezekiah. The proclamation dates from the king's enthronement, if not his actual birth. It is forward-looking. It is not a retrospective judgment on a reign. Isaiah could be critical of Judahite monarchs, as we can see in his encounter with Ahaz, but he had not abandoned hope for the future of the kingship.

As we have seen already in Chapter 1, the titles given to the king reflect the royal protocol of the Jerusalem kingship, which was probably influenced, if only indirectly, by Egyptian traditions. They are probably quoted from a court proclamation. The most remarkable of these is undoubtedly אל גבור, "mighty god." The divinity of the king, in whatever sense it might be understood, is not otherwise thematized in the book of Isaiah. We would expect the prophet to be skeptical of any claim to divine status, and the people who transmitted and edited his oracles even more so.

---

78. Ibid., 221-22.

79. Israel Finkelstein and Neil Asher Silberman, *The Bible Unearthed: Archaeology's New Vision of Ancient Israel and the Origin of Its Sacred Texts* (New York: The Free Press, 2001), 243-44. They estimate that the city's population may have increased from about one thousand to fifteen thousand inhabitants.

(Compare the taunt of the king of Babylon in Isaiah 14.) Yet the proclamation in Isaiah 9 was allowed to stand, without any hint of criticism. This strongly suggests that Isaiah accepted the ideology of the Davidic house as an ideal, even if historical kings failed to live up to it.

### Messianic Implications

As Blenkinsopp observes, the titles "intimate a certain transcendental aura attaching to royalty in the ancient Near East."[80] Such transcendental language is less objectionable when it is applied to a figure of the future than to an actual historical king. Hence the frequent assumption that this passage is messianic in the eschatological sense. If our reconstruction of the original setting is basically correct, however, the figure called "mighty god" in this passage was a figure of the present, like the kings in the royal psalms, even if the passage describes his potential rather than his accomplishments. Brevard Childs objects that "it is a major misunderstanding of this passage to politicize its message and derive the oracle from an enthusiasm over the accession of one of Judah's kings."[81] But the passage is inherently political, and it is rather a major misunderstanding to disregard its historical specificity. It is an excellent example of Near Eastern royal ideology, as adapted in Jerusalem. It makes claims for the king that no human ruler could fulfill. Neither Hezekiah nor any other ruler could guarantee "endless peace" for the throne of David, or ensure justice and righteousness forevermore. Nonetheless, the passage articulates an ideal of kingship, even though it exceeds the possibilities of history. This ideal was fundamental to later conceptions of the messiah, both in Judaism and in Christianity.[82]

The term "messiah" is usually restricted to a figure who would restore the Davidic line in a definitive way, after it had been disrupted by the Babylonian exile.[83] If the term is restricted in this way, we must agree with

---

80. Blenkinsopp, *Isaiah 1–39*, 250.

81. Childs, *Isaiah*, 80.

82. This point was fundamental to the classic studies of messianic hope by Gressmann (*Der Messias*) and Mowinckel (*He That Cometh*).

83. This was Mowinckel's essential criticism of Gressmann, who had argued that the messianic ideal was implicit in the royal ideology. See my essay, "Mowinckel's *He That Cometh* in Retrospect," *Studia Theologica* 61 (2007) 3-20.

Fitzmyer that Isaiah 9 is not messianic in its original context, quite apart from the fact that it does not use the word משיח.[84] It lent itself readily to a restorationist, "messianic" interpretation in the postexilic period, when there was no longer a king on the throne. It is too simple, then, to say that the passage is not messianic at all. The hope for a reign of everlasting peace and justice is fundamental to messianic expectation. The difference lies only in the continuity or discontinuity between the historical Davidic dynasty and its eschatological fulfillment.

Isaiah 9 affirms the continuity of the promise to David. This affirmation is not necessarily supportive of the Judahite monarchy in the recent past. Isaiah had been severely critical of Ahaz. The new king is set in sharp contrast to the ruler encountered in Isaiah 7, but Isaiah nonetheless reaffirms the promise to David of an everlasting dynasty. This reaffirmation is also implicit in the Immanuel prophecy in chapter 7, where, despite the shortcomings of Ahaz, the name of the child affirms that "God is with us."

## Early Messianism

Messianism proper, in the sense of the hope for restoration of the kingship, may have developed even before the downfall of the Judean monarchy, but the history is obscure because of the difficulties of dating.

The famous oracle in Isaiah 11 can serve as an illustration of the problem. Many scholars think that the reference to the stump of Jesse requires a date after the line had been cut off. So Joseph Blenkinsopp writes: "The anticipation of a new growth from the old stock of Jesse, ancestor of the Davidic dynasty (1 Sam 16:1), aligns with dynastic aspirations that come to expression in other texts from the postdestruction period (Jer 23:5-6; 33:14-22; Ezek 37:24-28; Amos 9:11-15; Mic 5:1-3[2-4])."[85] Against this, Hugh Williamson has pointed out that the later Isaianic tradition, as exemplified in chapters 40–66 of the book, is singularly devoid of messianic expectation.[86] The role of the Davidic figure fits well with the oracle about the

84. Fitzmyer, *The One Who Is to Come,* 37-38.

85. Blenkinsopp, *Isaiah 1–39,* 264. The dates of several of these texts are also debated. For a list of scholars who date Isa 11:1-9 to the postexilic period see Hans Wildberger, *Isaiah 1–12* (CC; Minneapolis: Augsburg Fortress, 1991), 465.

86. Williamson, "The Messianic Texts in Isaiah 1–39," in Day, ed., *King and Messiah,* 239. Williamson suggests that the stump imagery may be derived from the imagery of cutting

birth of the child in Isaiah 9. Williamson is not alone in arguing that the prophecy actually derives from Isaiah. Such weighty names as Duhm,[87] von Rad,[88] and Wildberger[89] have subscribed to this view. Other scholars relate it to the reign of Josiah, whose father was cut down by an assassin and who became king while still a little child.[90] Similar ambiguity attends to the prophecy in Amos 9:11 about the fallen booth of David. Here again some scholars have defended its authenticity as an 8th-century prophecy,[91] while others regard it as transparently postexilic.[92]

It is undeniable that some messianic pronouncements were inserted into prophetic books in the postexilic period. Jer 33:14-16 ("In those days and at that time I will make a righteous shoot to spring up for David") is a clear example, since it is an updating of the prophecy in Jer 23:5-6 and is not found in the LXX.[93] The prominence of the "levitical priests" in Jeremiah 33 is reminiscent of Chronicles, but we really have no information about the historical context in which it was inserted. The date of the original prophecy in Jeremiah 23 is likewise open to dispute. Jeremiah famously declared, in the preceding chapter, that no descendant of King Jehoiachin would ever again sit on the throne of David (Jer 22:30). Nonetheless, the prophecy about the "shoot" is often accepted as authentic because it con-

---

down trees in 10:33-34, but this does not lessen the problem of its application to "the stump of Jesse" (ibid., 269).

87. Bernhard Duhm, *Das Buch Jesaja* (Göttingen: Vandenhoeck & Ruprecht, 1892, 4th ed. 1922), 36, described this passage as the prophet's swan song.

88. Gerhard von Rad, *Old Testament Theology* (New York: Harper & Row, 1965), 2:169-70.

89. Wildberger, *Isaiah 1–12*, 465-69.

90. J. Vermeylen, *Du prophète Isaïe à l'apocalyptique: Isaïe, I–XXXV, miroir d'un demi-millénaire d'expérience religieuse en Israël* (Paris: Gabalda, 1977), 369-75; Sweeney, *Isaiah 1–39*, 204-5; idem, *King Josiah of Judah: The Lost Messiah of Israel* (Oxford: Oxford University Press, 2001), 321. Compare the comment of Schibler, "Messianism and Messianic Prophecy," 102: "A stump requires the cutting of a tree, but its shoot implies that there is still life in it."

91. E.g., von Rad, *Old Testament Theology,* 2:138; Shalom M. Paul, *Amos* (Hermeneia; Minneapolis: Fortress, 1991), 288-89.

92. Wellhausen famously remarked that the passage is "roses and lavender instead of blood and iron." J. Wellhausen, *Die Kleinen Propheten übersetzt und erklärt* (Berlin: Reiner, 1898), 96; H. W. Wolff, *Joel and Amos* (Hermeneia; Philadelphia: Fortress, 1977), 352-53; J. Blenkinsopp, *A History of Prophecy in Israel* (rev. ed.; Louisville: Westminster John Knox, 1996), 77.

93. Michael Fishbane, *Biblical Interpretation in Ancient Israel* (Oxford: Clarendon, 1985), 471-74; Schniedewind, *Society and the Promise to David,* 135-36.

tains an apparent pun on the name of Zedekiah.[94] But here again there is no consensus. The imagery of the "shoot" is used with reference to Zerubbabel in Zechariah, and since Zerubbabel means "shoot from Babylon" Mowinckel claimed that "there can be little doubt that Zechariah's references are earlier."[95] Even Zechariah 9, which is embedded in some of the latest material in the prophetic corpus, has been dated to wildly different periods. Jimmy Roberts dates it to the Assyrian period,[96] Paul Hanson to the early Persian period,[97] Eric and Carol Meyers, in the Anchor Bible commentary, to the mid-5th century,[98] and many scholars associate it with the time of Alexander the Great.[99] Arguments for messianic interests in the editing of the Book of the Twelve, or of sections of the Psalter,[100] are likewise inconclusive for dating, since this editorial work could have taken place at any time from the exile to the second century BCE.

Some scholars infer from this rather scattered evidence that a coherent messianic expectation was prevalent throughout the Second Temple period.[101] I find the inference less than compelling. To be sure, the promise to David was not forgotten, and scribes occasionally inserted pious hopes for its fulfillment into the text. But we only occasionally find an extended messianic oracle, such as Isaiah 11 or Zechariah 9. Several major texts (Chronicles, Ezra Nehemiah, Ben Sira) show little eschatological interest. When we encounter a resurgence of eschatological expectation in the second century BCE, in the books of Daniel and *Enoch*, there is no clear provision for a

---

94. William M. Holladay, *Jeremiah 1* (Hermeneia; Minneapolis: Fortress, 1986), 617; J. J. M. Roberts, "The Old Testament's Contribution to Messianic Expectations," in J. H. Charlesworth, ed., *The Messiah* (Minneapolis: Fortress, 1992), 39-51, here 46.

95. Mowinckel, *He That Cometh*, 19.

96. Roberts, "The Old Testament's Contribution," 44. He bases his argument on the list of places mentioned.

97. Paul D. Hanson, "Zechariah 9 and an Ancient Ritual Pattern," *JBL* 92 (1973) 37-59.

98. Carol L. Meyers and Eric M. Meyers, *Zechariah 9–14* (AB 25C; New York: Doubleday, 1993), 148.

99. Blenkinsopp, *A History of Prophecy*, 231.

100. Christoph Rösel, *Die messianische Redaktion des Psalters. Studien zu Entstehung und Theologie der Sammlung Psalm 2–89\** (Stuttgart: Calwer, 1999). He dates the "messianic redaction" to the Persian period, before the composition of Chronicles.

101. So especially Horbury, *Jewish Messianism and the Cult of Christ* (London: SCM, 1998), 36-108; Joachim Schaper, "The Persian Period," in Markus Bockmuehl and James Carleton Paget, eds., *Redemption and Resistance: The Messianic Hopes of Jews and Christians in Antiquity* (London/New York: T&T Clark, 2007), 3-14.

messianic king. It is only in the Hasmonean period and later that we find substantial evidence for a resurgence of messianic expectation, in the Dead Sea Scrolls and the *Psalms of Solomon.*[102]

Our purpose in this book, however, is not to trace the history of messianic expectation, but only to look for evidence of the view that the messianic king should be regarded as in some way divine. In the prophetic corpus, the only passage that refers to the king, present or future, in language that suggests divinity is Isaiah 9, which, as we have seen, is usually viewed either as an enthronement oracle or as a royal birth announcement. The sweeping put-down of Ezekiel, "you are man, and not god" (Ezek 28:2), is addressed to a foreign, Tyrian king, but would presumably also apply to any Judean king who assumed airs of divinity. Ezekiel's term of choice for the future ruler is נשיא, prince, rather than מלך, king, although he does use the latter on occasion.[103] Most striking, perhaps, is the depiction of the future ruler in Zech 9:9-10:

> Rejoice greatly, O daughter Zion!
> Shout aloud, O daughter Jerusalem!
> Lo, your king comes to you; triumphant and victorious is he,
> humble and riding on a donkey, on a colt, the foal of a donkey.
> He will cut off the chariot from Ephraim
> And the war horse from Jerusalem,
> And the battle bow shall be cut off,
> And he shall command peace to the nations;
> His dominion shall be from sea to sea,
> And from the River to the ends of the earth.

Despite the hope for universal dominion, this prophecy very clearly repudiates the militaristic ambitions of the kings of Israel and Judah, and evokes rather the simpler leadership style of the judges.[104] A similar repudiation of royal pretensions, let alone claims of divinity, is in evidence in the apostrophe to Bethlehem as the birthplace of the future ruler in Mic 5:2.[105]

---

102. I have expounded my views on this issue in *The Scepter and the Star: The Messiahs of the Dead Sea Scrolls and Other Ancient Literature* (New York: Doubleday, 1995), 31-38.

103. See Paul M. Joyce, "King and Messiah in Ezekiel," in Day, ed., *King and Messiah,* 323-37.

104. See the discussion of Meyers and Meyers, *Zechariah 9–14,* 127-33.

105. There is wide agreement that some sections of the book of Micah, and hence the

## Conclusion

I would argue, then, that in the heyday of the monarchy the king in Jerusalem was conceived in mythological terms as the son of God, in a way that was influenced by Egyptian tradition but less emphatic in its presentation. This view of kingship was altered significantly by the Deuteronomistic theologians in the late 7th century BCE. This can be seen already in Deuteronomy 17, where the king is made subject to the law, and this chastened view of the monarchy is reflected first in 2 Samuel 7 and Psalm 89, which provide for punishment of errant monarchs, even though they acknowledge that the king is regarded as God's son. It was carried further in texts from the exilic and early restoration periods (1 Kings 8; Psalm 132), which make the promise conditional. Such messianic predictions as we find in the prophetic books other than Isaiah are relatively modest in their claims for the future king. It is only in the Hellenistic period that we will again find claims that a future king will be in some sense divine.

---

book as a whole, date to the postexilic period. See Ehud Ben Zvi, *Micah* (FOTL XXI B; Grand Rapids: Eerdmans, 2000), 9. There is no consensus on the date of Mic 5:2-5. See Ben Zvi, *Micah*, 129. Many scholars believe that all or part of the prophecy dates to the Assyrian period. See D. R. Hillers, *Micah* (Hermeneia; Philadelphia: Fortress, 1984), 65-69; H. W. Wolff, *Micah* (CC; Minneapolis: Augsburg, 1990), 134-49.

# 3. *Messiah and Son of God in the Hellenistic Period*

The Hellenistic era brought a new culture to the Near East, and while it did not eradicate the native cultures it modified them in various ways. Judea was by no means exempt from its influence.[1] The cult of rulers was widespread in the Hellenistic world. It will be well, then, to begin by reflecting a little on the ways in which monarchs were associated with divinity in the Hellenistic ruler cults.

## Hellenistic Ruler Cults

When Alexander the Great conquered Egypt, he famously interrupted his campaign for six weeks to visit the oracle of the God Ammon in the Libyan desert at Siwah.[2] According to the Greek historian Arrian, one of

1. See the classic discussion by Martin Hengel, *Judaism and Hellenism: Studies in Their Encounter in Palestine during the Early Hellenistic Period* (2 vols.; Philadelphia: Fortress, 1974).

2. Arrian 3.3, extracted in James Romm, *Alexander the Great: Selections from Arrian, Diodorus, Plutarch, and Quintus Curtius* (Indianapolis/Cambridge: Hackett, 2005), 72. Strabo 17.1.13; Callisthenes fragment 14. Peter Green, *Alexander the Great* (New York: Praeger, 1970), 150. See especially Ernst Badian, "The Deification of Alexander the Great," in *Ancient Macedonian Studies in Honor of Charles F. Edson* (Thessaloniki, 1981), 27-71; idem, "Alexander the Great between Two Thrones and Heaven: Variations on an Old Theme," in Alastair Small, ed., *Subject and Ruler: The Cult of the Ruling Power in Classical Antiquity* (Journal of Roman Archaeology Supplementary Series 17; Ann Arbor, MI: Journal of Roman Archaeology, 1996), 11-26.

his motives was to "trace his own birth to Ammon." According to tradition, "The prophet of Ammon gave him salutation from the god as from a father."[3] Presumably, the greeting acknowledged him as pharaoh, son of Ammon-Re, whom the Greeks identified as Zeus.[4] The news spread rapidly, and representatives of two Ionian cities, Miletus and Erythrae, which had not previously detected his divinity, now sent envoys to announce divine communications proclaiming him the son of Zeus.[5] There was, moreover, a story, which some think was spread abroad by his mother Olympias even before the beginning of Alexander's campaign,[6] that Zeus had visited her, either as a thunderbolt or in the form of a snake, before her marriage with Philip was consummated.[7] Scholars dispute whether the status of "son of Zeus" necessarily implied divinity,[8] but later Alexander demanded *proskynesis,* the Persian form of obeisance, which was offensive to many Greeks.[9] In words attributed to Callisthenes:

> But the honors attributed to men have been distinguished from those accorded to the gods in a great many ways. . . . But nowhere is the distinction more plainly marked than in the custom of obeisance. For human beings greet one another with a kiss, but divinity, I suppose because it is seated on high and must not be touched, is honored with

3. Plutarch, *Alexander* 5. Compare the Greek *Alexander Romance,* 30: "Alexander had a vision of Ammon embracing his mother Olympias, and saying to him, 'Child, Alexander, you are born of my seed!'" See Richard Stonemann, *The Greek Alexander Romance* (London: Penguin, 1991), 62.

4. L. Cerfaux and J. Tondriau, *Le culte des souverains dans la civilisation gréco-romaine* (Tournai: Desclée, 1957), 138.

5. Badian, "Alexander the Great between Two Thrones and Heaven," 18. Cerfaux-Tondriau, *Le culte des souverains,* 138.

6. Badian, "Alexander the Great between Two Thrones," 19. In the *Alexander Romance,* 30, Alexander asks Ammon, "If it is true what my mother told me that I am your son, give me a sign!"

7. Plutarch, *Alexander* 3–6; Romm, *Alexander the Great,* 2. According to the *Alexander Romance,* 6, Olympias's dream of being impregnated by Ammon was conjured up by Nectanebo.

8. Cerfaux-Tondriau, *Le culte des souverains,* 138: "La qualité de fils de dieu ne faisait alors de personne une divinité." The offspring of gods and human women were typically regarded as demi-gods or heroes in Greek tradition. See Walter Burkert, *Greek Religion* (Oxford: Blackwell, 1985), 204.

9. Arrian 4.9-12; Romm, *Alexander the Great,* 104-7.

obeisance, and choruses are established for the gods, and paeans are sung to them.[10]

Alexander was the object of cult after his death.[11]

Claims of divinity were commonly associated with rulers in the Hellenistic world.[12] By the end of the fourth century, civic cults had been established for the Diadochi in numerous Greek cities. Here we will comment only on the two dynasties that impinged most directly on the Jews, the Ptolemies and the Seleucids.

The Ptolemies tried to synthesize Greco-Hellenistic and pharaonic traditions.[13] When Ptolemy I delivered Rhodes from a siege in 304 BCE, the inhabitants sent delegates to the oasis of Siwah, to inquire whether Ammon recommended that they honor the king as a god. The answer, as might be expected, was positive, so they established a shrine in his honor and conferred on him the title *Sōtēr*, "savior." Later Delos conferred on Ptolemy I Soter *isotheoi timai*, honors equal to those given to gods. A private inscription records a vow made to the king and his queen Berenice as "savior gods." Several Ptolemies took titles usually given to gods — Soter, Euergetes, Epiphanes. Some included the word *theos* in their Greek titles (Ptolemies IX and X). One, Ptolemy IX Auletes, claimed to be "Neos Dionysos."[14] At the same time, they appropriated the traditional titles of the pharaoh, including "son of Re," or son of the Sun. The victory of Ptolemy IV Philopator over Antiochus III of Syria at Raphia in 217 BCE was celebrated as the victory of Horus over Seth. It was decreed that a statue of the king with the name "Ptolemy Horus who protects his father and whose

---

10. Arrian 4.11; Romm, *Alexander the Great,* 105. See William Horbury, *Jewish Messianism and the Cult of Christ* (London: SCM, 1998), 71.

11. Cerfaux-Tondriau, *Le culte des souverains,* 145-69.

12. Cerfaux-Tondriau, *Le culte des souverains,* 171-267; Martin Nilsson, *Geschichte der griechischen Religion* (3rd ed.; München: Beck, 1974), 132-85; Claire Préaux, *Le monde hellénistique. La Grèce et l'Orient de la mort d'Alexandre à la conquête romain de la Grèce (323-146 av. J.-C.)* (Paris: Presses universitaires de France, 1978), 1:238-71; Christian Habicht, *Gottmenschentum und griechische Städte* (Zetemata 14; München: Beck, 1956); S. R. F. Price, *Rituals and Power: The Roman Imperial Cult in Asia Minor* (Cambridge: Cambridge University Press, 1984), 23-40.

13. Günther Hölbl, *A History of the Ptolemaic Empire* (London: Routledge, 2001), 112. For the following see Cerfaux-Tondriau, *Le culte des souverains,* 189-227; Nilsson, *Geschichte,* 154-65; Préaux, *Le monde hellénistique,* 255-61; Habicht, *Gottmenschentum,* 109-23.

14. Cerfaux-Tondriau, *Le culte des souverains,* 202.

victory is beautiful" would be placed in the large courts of all the temples of Egypt.[15] The Rosetta stone, from 196 BCE, establishes the divine credentials of the young Ptolemy V Epiphanes, who is hailed as "god like the sun," "son of the sun, to whom the sun has given victory,[16] or as "the image of Horus, son of Isis and Osiris." The claim to divine status, then, rested in part on the benefactions attributed to the king, and in part on the traditional association of the pharaoh with the sun god and with Horus.

Ptolemaic influence on Judaism, even in Palestine, was certainly possible. But culturally Judea was closer to Syria, and after 198 BCE it came under Seleucid rule. Here too kings were sometimes hailed as divine in appreciation for their benefactions.[17] The people of Miletus conferred the title "god" on Antiochus II for having delivered their city from a tyrant, and Demetrius I was called "Soter" on the initiative of the Babylonians for similar reasons.[18] Bikerman has emphasized the local character of these honors: the fact that Antiochus II was hailed as a god in Miletus did not necessarily mean that he was so regarded in Antioch or Babylon. Seleucid kings, like the Ptolemies, bore titles such as Soter or Epiphanes, which implied divinity. There was some variation in the honorific titles bestowed by municipal cults from one location to another.[19] From the time of Antiochus III, there was also a state royal cult for the court and army, which was apparently not imposed on municipalities that enjoyed some degree of self-rule, such as Babylon.[20]

Beginning with Antiochus Epiphanes, cultic names were included on coins. In the early part of Epiphanes' reign (175-169) the legend on coins

---

15. Hölbl, *A History,* 164.

16. *OGIS,* no. 90, lines 2-3. Anders Hultgård, *L'eschatologie des Testaments des Douze Patriarches* (Uppsala: Almqvist & Wiksell, 1977), 333.

17. Cerfaux-Tondriau, *Le culte des souverains,* 229-46; E. Bikerman, *Institutions des Seleucides* (Paris: Geuthner, 1938), 236-57; Nilsson, *Geschichte,* 2:165-71; Susan Sherwin-White and Amélie Kuhrt, *From Samarkhand to Sardis: A New Approach to the Seleucid Empire* (Berkeley: University of California Press, 1993), 114-40.

18. Bikerman, *Institutions,* 237; On the nature and motivation of these cults see Price, *Rituals and Power,* 25-40; Habicht, *Gottmenschentum,* 82-108.

19. Bikerman, *Institutions,* 243-45, gives a list of cases where the divinization of a Seleucid king is attested. See also Nilsson, *Geschichte,* 166-67. Price, *Rituals and Power,* 36, observes that cities did not generally adopt dynastic cults that were propagated by the king.

20. Bikerman, *Institutions,* 247-50; Sherwin-White and Kuhrt, *From Samarkhand to Sardis,* 202-10. Three copies of the edict organizing the state royal cult have been found. They are cited in full by Sherwin-White and Kuhrt, pp. 204-5.

minted in Antioch followed the traditional formula: Βασιλέως Αντιόχου, of King Antiochus. After his victory in Egypt in 169 BCE, the words "Theos Epiphanes" were added, and the obverse had a depiction of Zeus Nikephoros enthroned. After the triumphal celebration at Daphne in 166 BCE, the word "Nikephoros" was added. But other mints did not always follow the practice of Antioch. The mint at Tyre retained the simple formula, King Antiochus.[21]

The Seleucids also claimed divine descent. A story was told that when Seleucus was going off on campaign with Alexander, his mother Laodike told him that she had dreamed that she had conceived him by Apollo, and that the god had left her a ring engraved with an anchor. The ring was found in her bed on the morning after the dream. Seleucus allegedly bore the anchor as a birthmark on his thigh, as did his sons and grandsons.[22] This story seems to be modeled on the birth of Alexander (or possibly even on that of Augustus).[23] Seleucus also claimed descent from Heracles, as did the Macedonian royal family.[24] After the death of Seleucus, his son Antiochus I proclaimed him a god and established a cult in his honor. Antiochus III introduced the cult of the living ruler and his queen.[25] Antiochus IV added the words THEOU EPIPHANOUS on his coins, after the traditional ANTIOCHOU BASILEOS. On some of his coins, rays seemed to extend directly from his head, not just from his diadem.[26] Similar imagery is found on coins of Antiochus VI, with the legend BASILEOS ANTIOCHOU EPIPHANOUS DIONYSOU.[27]

Despite the legend of Seleucus's divine birth, however, it remained

---

21. Bikerman, *Institutions*, 220-22, 239-40; Hultgård, *L'eschatologie*, 330-31; Otto Mørkholm, *Antiochus IV of Syria* (Copenhagen: Gyldendal, 1966), 133.

22. Justin 15.4.3. John D. Grainger, *Seleukos Nikator: Constructing a Hellenistic Kingdom* (London: Routledge, 1990), 2-3; Andreas Mehl, *Seleukos Nikator und sein Reich* (Studia Hellenistica 28; Leuven: Leuven University Press, 1986), 5-6. Justin is dated to the 2nd, 3rd, or even 4th century CE. His work was based on the "Philippic Histories" of Pompeius Trogus, a contemporary of Augustus.

23. Suetonius, *Augustus* 94.4. See Mehl, *Seleukos Nikator*, 5-6.

24. Libanius, *Oration* 11 56 and 91. Mehl, *Seleukos Nikator*, 7. Libanius was a Greek rhetorician of the 4th century CE who was born in Antioch. Oration 11 was an encomium on his native city.

25. Cerfaux-Tondriau, *Le culte des souverains*, 233; Nilsson, *Geschichte*, 2:168-69.

26. For the extensive use of astral imagery on Seleucid coins see Hultgård, *L'eschatologie*, 331-32. Also Mørkholm, *Antiochus IV of Syria*, 20.

27. Hultgård, *L'eschatologie*, 331.

true that the divinity of the king was primarily an honor, conferred on him for his benevolence and exploits.[28] Like the Ptolemies, the Seleucids were venerated as "saviors" and benefactors, but the mythology of divine birth was not so firmly rooted as it was in Egypt. Nonetheless, the famous judgment of Arthur Darby Nock, that these honors were "an expression of gratitude which did not involve any theological implications," is too extreme.[29] In Horbury's words, "the ruler-cult was also religion."[30] But it is important to bear in mind that divinity was a status that could be conferred, and that stories about divine birth had only a confirmatory role.

Hellenistic ideas of the divinity of the ruler were inherited by the Roman empire. Octavian was hailed as "divi filius" as early as 40 BCE, and so described on coins beginning in 38.[31] Legends of his divine birth, in the manner of that of Alexander (involving a serpent), were recorded by Suetonius, who claimed to have found the story in a book called *Theologumena* by Asclepias of Mendes.[32] He was hailed as savior of the world and master of the world. A representative decree in his honor begins, "Since Emperor Caesar, son of god, god Sebastos, has by his benefactions to all men outdone even the Olympian gods."[33] The favorable comparison of the emperor with the Olympian gods marks an escalation in rhetoric over against the Hellenistic decrees. After his death, Augustus was "Divus," "inter deos relatus," or "divus factus."[34]

There is no doubt at all that Jews were familiar with Hellenistic ruler cults. Antiochus Epiphanes, for one, brought the phenomenon rather forcefully to their attention. For faithful monotheists, these cults could only be problematic. Accordingly, some scholars have been inclined to rule out the possibility of influence from this quarter on Jewish messianism.[35]

28. Bikerman, *Institutions,* 157. Cf. the comment of Kuhrt and Sherwin-White on Antiochus III's addition of his queen Laodice to the cult of his ancestors and himself: "The cult was an (honour) for the recipient in recognition of religious piety and for devotion as the king's wife" (117-18). Cf. also ibid., 208-10.

29. Nock in *CAH* 10 (1934), 481.

30. Horbury, *Jewish Messianism,* 69. Cf. Price, *Rituals and Power,* 16.

31. Cerfaux-Tondriau, *Le culte des souverains,* 315; cf. Wilhelm Bousset and Hugo Gressmann, *Die Religion des Judentums im Späthellenistischen Zeitalter* (3rd ed.; Tübingen: Mohr Siebeck, 1966), 225-26.

32. Suetonius, *Augustus* 94.

33. Price, *Rituals and Power,* 55.

34. Cerfaux-Tondriau, *Le culte des souverains,* 335-39.

35. Martin Hengel, *The Son of God* (Philadelphia: Fortress, 1976), 30.

William Horbury, however, has astutely remarked that "ruler cult inevitably attracted attention and imitation because it symbolized the focus of power."[36] While faithful Jews stopped short of ruler worship, we need only consider Philo's praise of Augustus to see that conceptions drawn from the ruler cult could be accommodated in a Jewish context:

> He was the first and the greatest and the common benefactor in that he displaced the rule of many and committed the ship of the commonwealth to be steered by a single pilot. . . . But besides all these the whole habitable world voted him no less than celestial honors.[37]

Jewish acclamation of the emperor was of necessity more restrained, but Philo evidently did not regard the divine honors conferred on Augustus by Gentiles as inappropriate. (In contrast, he has nothing but contempt for Caligula's pretensions to divinity.) It should also be noted that even in a Hellenistic or Roman context the divine ruler was often seen as the representative of a heavenly god, and that god in turn as the patron of the human ruler.[38]

## Messianism in the LXX

The argument of William Horbury that Jewish messianism was influenced by Hellenistic ruler cult rests in large part on his interpretation of the LXX, an interpretation that has been further elaborated by his student Joachim Schaper.[39] I have examined elsewhere Horbury's claim that the LXX rendering of three Pentateuchal prophecies, by Jacob, Balaam, and Moses, "form fundamental but often neglected documents of Jewish kingship and messianism."[40] The enigmatic passage in the blessing of Jacob, Gen 49:10,

36. Horbury, *Jewish Messianism*, 68.

37. *Legatio ad Gaium* 143-50.

38. For examples see Horbury, *Jewish Messianism*, 70.

39. Joachim Schaper, *Eschatology in the Greek Psalter* (WUNT 2.76; Tübingen: Mohr Siebeck, 1995); idem, "Der Septuaginta-Psalter als Dokument jüdischer Eschatologie," in Martin Hengel and Anna Maria Schwemer, eds., *Die Septuaginta zwischen Judentum und Christentum* (Tübingen: Mohr Siebeck, 1994), 38-61.

40. Horbury, *Jewish Messianism*, 48; cf. J. J. Collins, "Messianism and Exegetical Tradition: The Evidence of the LXX Pentateuch," in idem, *Jewish Cult and Hellenistic Culture* (JSJSup 100; Leiden: Brill, 2005), 58-81.

עד כי־יבא שילה ולו יקהת עמים ("until שילה comes, and the obedience of the people is his"), was often interpreted as a messianic prophecy in Jewish tradition, but the majority reading of the LXX[41] renders שילה as τὰ ἀποκείμενα αὐτῷ ("the things laid away for him") and so conspicuously fails to associate the future glory of Judah with a monarchic ruler.[42] The blessing of Moses in Deut 33:5 reads in the Hebrew, "there arose a king in Jeshurun." This is rendered in the Greek: "there shall be a ruler in the beloved." This is one of many instances in the Pentateuch where the Hebrew מלך is rendered by the more general term ἄρχων, "ruler." The Greek version of Balaam's oracles (Num 24:7, 17) speaks of an ἄνθρωπος, "man," who will have a kingdom, and this is of some significance for the terminology of messianism in the Hellenistic period.[43] But even this passage refrains from calling the man a king. So there seems to be little influence of Hellenistic kingship ideology on the translation of the Pentateuch. There is no hint that a future king will have more than human status. In the one context where we find reference to a future human king at all, he is explicitly called an ἄνθρωπος. As Ezekiel would say, he is man and not god.

## LXX Psalms

The Hebrew *Vorlage* of the Pentateuch did not provide much basis for the translators to express messianic beliefs. The situation is different in the Psalms and Prophets, especially in the case of Isaiah. While there are great differences of opinion as to the degree to which the translators of the LXX introduced their own beliefs into the translation, even such a stubborn

41. The fact that it deviates from the usual Jewish and Christian understanding of the passage argues for the authenticity of this translation.

42. Pace Schaper, *Eschatology,* 84, who argues that the fact that the Hebrew scepter and staff are interpreted as persons shows "a messianic conception"; Martin Rösel, "Die Interpretation von Genesis 49 in der Septuaginta," *BN* 79 (1995) 54-70, also reads the Greek translation as messianic.

43. On the use of "man" as a messianic term see W. Horbury, "The Messianic Associations of 'The Son of Man,'" in idem, *Messianism among the Jews and Christians* (London and New York: T&T Clark, 2003), 144-51. On the messianic interpretation of the Balaam oracle see Stefan Beyerle, "'A Star Shall Come out of Jacob': A Critical Evaluation of the Balaam Oracle in the Context of Jewish Revolts in Roman Times," in G. H. van Kooten and J. T. A. G. M. van Ruiten, eds., *Balaam: The Prestige of a Pagan Prophet in Judaism, Early Christianity and Islam* (Themes in Biblical Narrative; Leiden: Brill, 2008).

minimalist as Albert Pietersma does not dispute that they did so sometimes and "that messianic interpretation can be found in the Greek Psalter."[44] The scope of our inquiry is narrower, however. Do the translators ever enhance the claims of the king/messiah to divine status, or show influence from the Hellenistic ruler cults?

We have seen that the strongest claims for the status of the king as God or son of God are found in the royal psalms, especially Psalms 2, 45, 72, 89, and 110. Both Psalm 2:7 ("You are my son; today I have begotten you") and Ps 89:27 (= 88:27 LXX: "I will make him firstborn, highest of the kings of the earth") are rendered straightforwardly in the Greek. There is no attempt to evade the implication that the king is son of God, but the literal translations are not necessarily indicative of the translator's own views.

In Psalm 45 (= LXX 44), the translator construes the word אלהים as a vocative: "Your throne, O God, is forever and ever." Schaper is well aware that many scholars, following Gunkel, see this as a quite faithful rendering of the Hebrew text, which preserved a remnant of an early Israelite conception of divine kingship. But, says Schaper, Gunkel "can put forward this theory only on the assumption that Ps 45 is an early text."[45] Schaper, however, follows R. J. Tournay, who argues "that Ps 45 contains a number of Aramaisms and is closely connected with Chronicles."[46] He reads the Hebrew as "your throne, that of God," by analogy with 1 Chron 29:23, where Solomon is said to sit on the throne of the Lord. But Aramaisms do not require a postexilic date, and it is difficult to see why a wedding song for a king should be composed in the postexilic period. In my view, it is much more likely that the LXX preserves here the original meaning of the verse. This in itself is of some significance, as it shows that the translator was not troubled by the "theological problem" that has constrained many modern interpreters, including Schaper.[47] It may be that the appellation "god" addressed to a king seemed unexceptional because of the frequency with which it was used in the titles of kings in the Hellenistic age, and that the thesis of influence from the ruler cults has some basis in that regard.

---

44. Albert Pietersma, "Messianism and the Greek Psalter," in M. A. Knibb, ed., *The Septuagint and Messiah* (BETL CXCV; Leuven: Peeters, 2006), 49-75, here 50.

45. Schaper, *The Eschatology*, 81.

46. R. J. Tournay, *Voir et entendre Dieu avec les Psaumes* (Cahiers de la Revue Biblique 24; Paris: Gabalda, 1988), 175.

47. Schaper, *Eschatology*, 80: "That reading simply avoids the theological problem."

Schaper also finds messianic significance in the superscription of this psalm, which translates ידידת as ὑπὲρ τοῦ ἀγαπητοῦ. Ἀγαπητός is used for יחיד, "only begotten," in Genesis 22 and elsewhere.[48] Whether it had acquired the sense of "only son," as Schaper argues, seems doubtful. "Beloved" appears as a messianic title in the *Ascension of Isaiah,* but the context is Christian,[49] and I am not aware of its use as a messianic title in pre-Christian Jewish texts. It may well be that the translator understood Psalm 45 (and all the royal psalms for that matter) as a psalm about the messiah. If so, he effectively transferred the ideas about the divinity of the king in the Hebrew Bible to the future messiah (and, indeed, that transfer may already have been made in the editing of the Hebrew Bible). It is not the case, however, that he introduced the idea of the divinity of the king into this psalm. Rather, he was faithfully reproducing the original meaning of the text, and the influence of Hellenistic ruler cults is relevant only by way of explanation as to why the idea did not seem problematic.

In the case of Psalm 110 (LXX 109) also, the LXX forthrightly translates the word ילדתיך as "I have begotten you," without theological inhibition. Here again I would argue that it was faithfully reproducing the meaning of the original text, although its willingness to do so may be credited in part to the association of divinity with kingship in the Hellenistic world. As we have already seen, the Hebrew text of Ps 110:3 is difficult, and at least the Masoretic pointing requires emendation. Apart from the rendering of ילדתיך, the Greek differs from the Hebrew at several points. Hebrew נדבת ("willingly"?) is rendered by ἡ ἀρχή ("the rule"), הדרי קדש ("holy splendor") by ἐν ταῖς λαμπρότησιν τῶν ἀγίων ("in the brightness of the holy ones"). The Hebrew "from dawn" is rendered as "πρὸ ἑωσφόρου" ("before the Day Star"), while the words לך טל ("to you the dew") are not translated at all. Schaper argues that "ἑωσφόρος clearly has the very specific meaning of 'Bringer of the morn,' 'the Morning-star.' Interpreting it as 'dawn' misses the point."[50] So, for example, this is the word used to translate Helel ben Shachar in Isa 14:12 (ὁ ἑωσφόρος ὁ πρωὶ ἀνατέλλων). We need not assume that the translator deliberately changed the meaning; he simply took שחר to mean "morning star." The change of the preposition is

48. See Pietersma, "Messianism in the Greek Psalter," 57. Other instances are Judg 11:24; Jer 6:26; Amos 8:19; Zech 12:10.

49. *Ascension of Isaiah* 3:13–4:13. See M. A. Knibb, "The Martyrdom and Ascension of Isaiah," *OTP,* 2:160-61.

50. Schaper, *Eschatology,* 102.

more difficult to justify as a simple translation. As Volz and Bousset already saw, the LXX implies the preexistence of the messianic king.[51] Moreover, the slight change from Hebrew קדש to the plural ἁγίων, "holy ones," can easily be taken to associate the messiah with angelic beings.[52] The association of the messianic king with the heavenly holy ones is interesting in view of the depiction of Melchizedek (who is mentioned in Ps 110:4) as a heavenly being in the *Melchizedek* scroll from Qumran, and more generally in light of the later conflation of traditions about the messiah with those about the Son of Man.

The question of the preexistence of the messiah, or at least of his name, also arises in connection with the Greek translation of Ps 72:17 (= LXX 71:17). The Hebrew is a prayer for the king: "May his name be forever, may his name flourish (or: be propagated) before the sun" (לפני שמש). The Greek reads πρὸ τοῦ ἡλίου. The Targum of Psalm 72 takes the preposition in an explicitly temporal sense: "and before the sun existed, his name had been appointed."[53] Paul Volz argued that the rendering of the LXX should also be taken in a temporal sense, and understood to imply the preexistence of the name of the messiah.[54] In fact, the Greek preposition is ambiguous, and is a perfectly literal translation of the Hebrew לפני. But even a formally literal translation could be interpreted differently. In light of the understanding attested in the Targum and the attestation of the preexistence of the messiah's name in the *Similitudes of Enoch* (1 Enoch 48:2), and especially in light of what we have found in Psalm 110, Volz's interpretation is at least possible.[55]

---

51. Paul Volz, *Jüdische Eschatologie von Daniel bis Akiba* (Tübingen: Mohr Siebeck, 1903), 208; Bousset/Gressmann, *Die Religion*, 265.

52. Pace Gottfried Schimanowski, *Weisheit und Messias* (WUNT 2.17; Tübingen: Mohr Siebeck, 1985), 137-43, who tries to downplay the innovation of the Greek translation. He does not deny that the Greek text was later understood to imply preexistence, and cites the Peshitta and Justin, *Dialogue with Trypho* 45.4, to that effect.

53. Schaper, *Eschatology*, 95. Bousset/Gressmann, *Die Religion*, 263, n. 1.

54. Volz, *Eschatologie*, 208-9.

55. Another possible allusion is found in Mic 5:1-3 LXX, where it is said of the future ruler from Bethlehem, αἱ ἔξοδοι αὐτοῦ ἀπ᾽ ἀρχῆς ἐξ ἡμερῶν αἰῶνος: his goings out (provenance?) are from the beginning, from the days of old. This, however, can be seen as a fairly literal attempt to translate the Hebrew: מוצאתיו מקדם מימי עולם. See Schimanowski, *Weisheit und Messias*, 112-21. Again, the passage was understood to imply preexistence in the Targum, and the LXX could easily be read that way.

## LXX Isaiah

The LXX of the prophetic books also construes a number of passages in an apparently messianic sense, when no such sense is apparent in the Hebrew. Here again I will restrict my focus to passages that have a bearing on the divine or supernatural status of the messiah. The main texts in dispute are found in the book of Isaiah.

The most celebrated of these is undoubtedly Isa 7:14. The Hebrew text reads: הנה העלמה הרה וילדת בן וקראת שמו עמנו אל, "Behold, the young woman is with child and shall bear a son, and shall call his name Immanuel." The עלמה was most probably the wife of the king (or possibly of the prophet) and not necessarily a virgin. The child was not a messiah, and not even necessarily a future king, but his birth was a sign of hope for Ahaz in his embattled circumstances.[56]

The Greek translation reads: ἰδοὺ ἡ παρθένος ἐν γαστρὶ ἕξει καὶ τέξεται υἱὸν καὶ καλέσεις τὸ ὄνομα αὐτοῦ Εμμανουηλ. The Greek word *parthenos* does not necessarily mean *virgo intacta* any more than the Hebrew עלמה,[57] but it is not the usual translation equivalent. In most cases עלמה is rendered in the LXX by the Greek νεᾶνις, "young woman."[58] παρθένος most often corresponds to בתולה, "virgin."[59] The translation choice, then, is remarkable, and the use of this translation in the Gospel of Matthew has heightened the controversy about it.

Martin Rösel has tried to explain the choice of παρθένος by appeal to a much-discussed passage in Epiphanius, which describes a feast of Kore, also called Parthenos, in Alexandria, in celebration of her giving birth to the god

56. See the discussion in Chapter 2 above.

57. G. Delling, "παρθένος," *TDNT*, 5 (1967), 827. R. E. Brown, *The Birth of the Messiah: A Commentary on the Infancy Narratives of Matthew and Luke* (New York: Doubleday, 1993), 148-49, argues that the Greek means that "a woman who is *now* a virgin will (by natural means, once she is united to her husband) conceive the child Emmanuel."

58. Arie Van der Kooij, "Die Septuaginta Jesajas als Dokument jüdischer Exegese. Einige Notizen zu LXX — Jes. 7," in *Übersetzung und Deutung. Studien zu dem Alten Testament und seiner Umwelt Alexander Reinard Hulst gewidmet von Freunden und Kollegen* (Nijkerk: Callenbach, 1977), 97. There is one possible exception in Gen 24:43, where the Greek has *parthenos*.

59. Since the word is most often used in the phrase "virgin daughter of Zion," van der Kooij, "Die Septuaginta Jesajas," 98, suggests that the "virgin" is Zion/Jerusalem. So also Johan Lust, *Messianism and the Septuagint* (BETL 178; Leuven: Peeters, 2004), 222. Nonetheless, the context in Isaiah 7 requires that the reference be to an individual woman.

Aion.[60] The explanation for the festival is that "at this hour on this day ἡ Κόρη τουτέστιν ἡ Παρθένος (Kore, that is, the Virgin) gave birth to Aion."[61] He also cites the testimony of Hippolytus that the birth of Aion was proclaimed at Eleusis by the declaration: ἡ παρθένος ἡ ἐν γάστρι ἔχουσα καὶ συλλαμβάνουσα καὶ τίκτουσα υἱόν[62] (the virgin who was pregnant and conceived and bore a son). He further relates the proclamation to Egyptian tradition. In the Hellenistic period there was a ritual presentation of the birth of Re from Neith and of Horus from Isis, in specially dedicated "birth houses" or Mammisi,[63] and Isis was already identified as a virgin in the New Kingdom period, and could be called *Kore* in Hellenistic times. In light of these parallels, Rösel concludes that Isaiah 7 LXX also refers to a virgin birth, and is evidence for the idea that the messiah should be born from a virgin *before* the New Testament.[64] But whether in fact the use of *parthenos* in the LXX of Isaiah necessarily carries with it these associations is very doubtful. Hippolytus and Epiphanius are unreliable informants for pre-Christian pagan practices,[65] and it is possible that their description of the birth of Aion was itself colored by the language of the LXX. As Seeligmann concluded: "After all, it is not unthinkable that the translator merely conceived the Hebrew word — erroneously of course — to mean 'young virgin' = *parthenos.*"[66] Moreover, the translator had a precedent for rendering עלמה as παρθένος in Gen 24:43, even if that rendering was influenced by harmonization with Gen 24:14, where παρθένος translates נערה.[67]

---

60. Martin Rösel, "Die Jungfrauengeburt des endzeitlichen Immanuel," *Jahrbuch für Biblische Theologie* 6 (1991) 134-51, here 146.

61. Epiphanius, *Refutation of All Heresies* 51.22.5. Rudolf Kittel, *Die hellenistische Mysterien und das Alte Testament* (Stuttgart: Kohlhammer, 1924), 24, 45; R. Pettazzoni, "Aion-(Kronos)Chronos in Egypt," in idem, *Essays on the History of Religions* (Leiden: Brill, 1954), 171-72.

62. Hippolytus, *Refutation of All Heresies* 5.8.40.

63. Helmut Brunner, *Die Geburt des Gottkönigs* (Wiesbaden: Harrassowitz, 1964), 200; F. Daumas, *Les Mammisis des temples égyptiens* (Paris: Les Belles Lettres, 1958).

64. Rösel, "Die Jungfrauengeburt," 151, n. 78.

65. See the comments of P. M. Fraser, *Ptolemaic Alexandria* (Oxford: Clarendon, 1972) 2:336-37, n. 79 on the passage in Epiphanius: "I do not see anything in the passage itself which points to a Ptolemaic origin for this festival of Kore and Aion."

66. Isaac Leo Seeligmann, *The Septuagint Version of Isaiah and Cognate Studies* (Tübingen: Mohr Siebeck, 2004), 292-93. Lust, *Messianism and the Septuagint,* 222, denies that the choice of word is meant to imply virginity *stricto sensu.*

67. Van der Kooij, "Die Septuaginta Jesajas," 97. H. Gese, "Natus ex virgine," in idem,

Nothing in the LXX of Isaiah requires that Immanuel be identified as the messiah. The argument that he should be so identified depends on the assumption that he is the same child to whom reference is made in Isaiah 9. In the latter oracle, the LXX departs strikingly from the Hebrew. The Hebrew titles גבור אל יועץ פלא ("wonderful counselor, mighty god") are rendered by μεγάλης βουλῆς ἄγγελος, which can be translated either "messenger of great counsel" or "angel of great counsel." Moreover, the following titles, שלום שר עד אבי (everlasting father, prince of peace), are translated "for I will bring peace to the princes, peace and health for him." The translator evidently read אבי as a verb and עד as a preposition. Johan Lust suggests that the plus, "peace and health for him," may be either a doublet of the preceding line or a free translation of the missing fifth name of the future king (of which the Hebrew letters לם at the beginning of verse 6 are a remnant).[68] Most significant for our present concerns is the translation of גבור אל as ἄγγελος. Horbury takes this as "angel" and finds support in the "spirit-filled" messiah of Isaiah 11, where the Hebrew והריחו ביראת יהוה ("and his delight shall be in the fear of the LORD") is rendered as ἐμπλήσει αὐτὸν πνεῦμα φόβου θεοῦ, "the spirit of the fear of God will fill him."[69] He points out that David himself was said to be like an angel of God for insight (2 Sam 14:17, 20; 19:28). Moreover, the identification of the "star" of Balaam's prophecy as a "man" could also be taken to imply angelic status, since angels were often represented both as stars and as men. In contrast, Lust points out that in the LXX translation it is God himself who brings peace, not the child/king. He concludes that the passage "emphasizes the role of the Lord over and against that of his human Messiah, who sees his function reduced to that of a messenger."[70]

Lust remarks that the translator "may not have liked the name 'Mighty God' being applied to any human person, king or not."[71] But ἄγγελος may also have been a good faith translation. Heavenly beings other than the Lord are often called אלים in the Dead Sea Scrolls.[72] The

*Vom Sinai zum Zion. Alttestamentliche Beiträge zur biblischen Theologie* (München: Kaiser, 1974), 145, also explains the use of *parthenos* in Isaiah 7 in light of Genesis 24 LXX.

68. Lust, *Messianism and the Septuagint*, 167.

69. Horbury, *Jewish Messianism*, 90-91.

70. Lust, *Messianism and the Septuagint*, 169.

71. Lust, *Messianism and the Septuagint*, 167.

72. אל is translated as ἄγγελος in Job 20:15.

sons of God in Genesis 6 are rendered as "angels" by Philo (*On the Giants* 6), and Josephus (*Jewish Antiquities* 1.73), although the Hebrew was translated literally in the LXX. The role of counselor may have seemed problematic in conjunction with a "god," and the analogy with David, pointed out by Horbury, may apply. I am inclined, then, to think that the title should be translated "angel." This is not so much a demotion as a clarification of his status in relation to the Most High. The fact that it is God who brings peace does not necessarily reduce the role of the messiah, who is conceived as God's agent in any case. Seeligmann comments: "Here we see the Messiah being proclaimed as announcer and bringer of peace,"[73] and this is essentially correct: the reign of the messiah is the occasion on which God will bring peace. Angelic status is also quite compatible with miraculous birth, as can be seen from the *Genesis Apocryphon*, col. 2, where Lamech suspects that Noah was conceived by Watchers or Holy Ones.[74]

## Summary

The evidence of the Septuagint, then, is limited, but includes some items of interest. The translators show no inhibition about reproducing statements that the king is son of God (Psalms 2, 89), begotten by God (Psalm 110), or addressed as God (Psalm 45). Moreover, the idea that the king is preexistent is introduced into Psalm 110 and possibly implied in Psalm 72. The Greek translation of Isaiah 9 does not call the king "mighty god," but instead describes him as an angel, a possible interpretation of the Hebrew word אל, "god," in the Hellenistic period. The willingness of the translators to use divine or transcendent language with reference to the king may have been influenced by the common association of kings with divinity in the Hellenistic world. It is not apparent, however, that the translators introduced language that was associated with the royal cults in passages about the king, past or present. They do not, for example, call the king *sōtēr* or *epiphanēs*. If there is any influence here from the royal cults, it is indirect.

73. Seeligmann, *The Septuagint Version of Isaiah*, 291.
74. See further my essay, "Isaiah 8:23–9:6 and Its Greek Translation," in Voitila and Jokiranta, eds., *Scripture in Transition*.

## The Dead Sea Scrolls

In light of the Dead Sea Scrolls, we can now speak of a revival of messianic expectation in Judaism in the Hasmonean and Herodian periods.[75] Some of the references to the coming messiah or messiahs are quite brief, and say little about him except that he is expected to come. (The famous reference to the coming of the prophet and the messiahs of Aaron and Israel in 1QS 9:11 is a case in point.) Many of the references are in exegetical literature, or at least exegetical contexts, and either interpret or allude to several key texts that were construed as messianic prophecies, Isaiah 11, Genesis 49, Jeremiah 23 (the shoot of David), or Balaam's oracle. Even the extended messianic passages in the contemporary *Psalms of Solomon* are made up of a tissue of biblical allusions.[76] From these passages, there emerges a consistent picture of a righteous figure who is to "save Israel" (4Q174:13) by driving out the Gentiles. The main features of the characterization may be illustrated from the blessing of "the Prince of the Congregation," who is "to establish the kingdom of his people forever":

> With your scepter may you lay waste the earth. With the breath of your lips may you kill the wicked. May he give [you a spirit of coun]sel and of everlasting fortitude, a spirit of knowledge and of fear of God. May justice be the belt of [your loins, and loyalty], the belt of your hips. May he make your horns of iron and your hoofs of bronze. May you gore like a

---

75. J. J. Collins, *The Scepter and the Star: The Messiahs of the Dead Sea Scrolls and Other Ancient Literature* (New York: Doubleday, 1995). See also K. E. Pomykala, *The Davidic Dynasty Tradition in Early Judaism: Its History and Significance for Messianism* (SBLEJ 7; Atlanta: Scholars Press, 1995); Johannes Zimmermann, *Messianische Texte aus Qumran* (WUNT 2.104; Tübingen: Mohr Siebeck, 1998); J. H. Charlesworth, H. Lichtenberger, and G. S. Oegema, *Qumran-Messianism: Studies on the Messianic Expectations in the Dead Sea Scrolls* (Tübingen: Mohr Siebeck, 1998); Stefan Schreiber, *Gesalbter und König. Titel und Konzeptionen der königlichen Gesalbtenerwartung in frühjüdischen und urchristlichen Schriften* (BZNW 105; Berlin: de Gruyter, 2000), 145-403; Géza G. Xeravits, *King, Priest, Prophet: Positive Eschatological Protagonists of the Qumran Library* (Leiden: Brill, 2001); George J. Brooke, "Kingship and Messianism in the Dead Sea Scrolls," in Day, ed., *King and Messiah*, 434-55; Ed Condra, *Salvation for the Righteous Revealed: Jesus amid Covenantal and Messianic Expectations in Second Temple Judaism* (AGJU 51; Leiden: Brill, 2002), 198-271.

76. See now Kenneth Atkinson, *I Cried to the Lord: A Study of the Psalms of Solomon's Historical Background and Social Setting* (JSJSup 84; Leiden: Brill, 2004), 129-79.

bu[ll . . . and may you trample the nation]s like the mud of the streets. For God has raised you to a scepter. . . .[77]

While the ability to kill the wicked with the breath of his lips suggests that the messiah will have supernatural powers, only a few texts suggest that he is son of God. The most securely established of these is the *Florilegium*, 4Q174,[78] where 2 Sam 7:14 is cited and interpreted as follows:

"I shall be a father to him and he will be a son to me": He is the shoot of David who will arise with the Interpreter of the law who [will rise up] in Zion in the last days.

The text makes no comment on how the sonship should be understood. A little later in the same fragment we have a citation and interpretation of Ps 2:1-2:

"[Why ar]e the nations [in turmoil] and the peoples [plot in vain] . . . against the Lord and against [his anointed one." Inter]pretation of the saying: "[the kings of the na]tions [are in turmoil] and pl[ot in vain against] the elect ones of Israel in the last days."

While the latter passage is fragmentary, it is apparent that the word משיחו is read as a plural and understood to refer to "the elect ones of Israel."[79] It should be emphasized that, despite this, the text is in no way an example of "collective messianism." The role assigned to the individual "shoot of David" is unequivocal. Unfortunately the extant text does not interpret the verse "You are my son; today I have begotten you."

The *Florilegium,* as we might expect, shows that the promise to David was understood as grounds for messianic hope, and that the messiah, like the king in 2 Samuel 7, could be regarded as a son of God, in some sense.

A more intriguing text is provided by the *Rule of the Congregation,* which specifies the order of assembly for the occasion "when God begets

77. 1QSb (1Q28b) 5:24-27; trans. F. García Martínez and E. J. Tigchelaar, *The Dead Sea Scrolls Study Edition* (Leiden: Brill, 1997), 109.

78. See Zimmermann, *Messianische Texte,* 99-113.

79. The collective understanding of Ps 2:2 is emphasized especially by Annette Steudel, "Psalm 2 im antiken Judentum," in Dieter Sänger, ed., *Gottessohn und Menschensohn* (Neukirchen-Vluyn: Neukirchener, 2004), 189-97, here 197.

the messiah with them" (1QSa 2:11-12). The reading יוליד (begets) is unclear in the manuscript, and has been endlessly disputed. The scholars who examined the manuscript in the 1950s agreed that the manuscript reads יוליד, although Milik and Cross favored emending it to יוליך (causes to come).[80] Geza Vermes, who has vacillated on the reading, claims that "it seems to be confirmed by computer enhancement."[81] The statement that God begets the messiah "with them" is odd, however, and gives some pause. If the reading is correct, it is simply picking up and endorsing the language of the Psalms.[82] Even if the messiah is divinely begotten, he must still wait for the priest's blessing before stretching out his hand to the bread.

### The "Son of God" Text from Qumran

An even more controversial reference to divine sonship is found in 4Q246, the so-called *Aramaic Apocalypse* or "Son of God" text. This text was first announced by J. T. Milik in a lecture at Harvard in 1972,[83] but remained unpublished for twenty years until it was finally edited by Émile Puech.[84] The extraordinary interest surrounding it arises from the fact that it refers

---

80. P. W. Skehan, "Two Books on Qumran Studies," *CBQ* 21 (1959) 74, cites "the testimony of half a dozen witnesses, including Allegro, Cross, Strugnell, and the writer [Skehan], as of the summer of 1955," that the text reads יוליד. F. M. Cross, *The Ancient Library of Qumran* (3rd ed.; Sheffield: Sheffield Academic Press, 1995), 76, n. 3. The reading יועד, "will be assembled," originally proposed by Theodore Gaster and Jacob Licht, and accepted by L. H. Schiffman, *The Eschatological Community of the Dead Sea Scrolls* (SBLMS 38; Atlanta: Scholars Press, 1989), 54, is emphatically rejected by Cross on palaeographic grounds. Émile Puech, "Préséance sacerdotale et messie-roi dans la Règle de la Congrégation (1QSa ii 11-22)," *RevQ* 16 (1993-1995) 361, proposes to read יתגלה, "will be revealed."

81. G. Vermes, *The Complete Dead Sea Scrolls in English* (rev. ed.; London: Penguin, 2004), 161.

82. J. W. van Henten, "The Hasmonean Period," in M. Bockmuehl and J. Carlton Paget, eds., *Redemption and Resistance* (London and New York: T&T Clark, 2007), 22, declares unequivocally: "This passage alludes to Psalm 2."

83. Milik's interpretation of the text is summarized in his article "Les modèles araméens du livre d'Esther dans la Grotte 4 de Qumrân," *RevQ* 59 (1992) 383.

84. Émile Puech, "Fragment d'une Apocalypse en Araméen (4Q246 = pseudo-Dan^d) et le 'Royaume de Dieu,'" *RB* 99 (1992) 98-131; idem, "246. 4Qapocryphe de Daniel ar," in G. Brooke et al., *Qumran Cave 4, XVII: Parabiblical Texts, Part 3* (DJD XXII; Oxford: Clarendon, 1996), 165-84.

to a figure who is called "son of God" and "son of the Most High," using Aramaic phrases that correspond exactly to the Greek titles given to Jesus in the Gospel of Luke 1:32-35. Milik originally argued that the figure in question was a Syrian king, but this opinion was received so poorly that he never published the text. In recent years, however, several other scholars have rallied to some variant of this view.[85] Vermes, for example, identifies the figure as "the last historico-apocalyptic sovereign of the ultimate world empire, who, like his model Antiochus Epiphanes in Dan xi, 36-37, is expected to proclaim himself and be worshipped as a god."[86] Others, probably the majority, hold that he is a positive, messianic figure.[87] Florentino García Martínez proposed that the "Son of God" be identified with the angelic figure elsewhere called Michael, Melchizedek, or the Prince of Light.[88] The editor, Émile Puech, initially allowed that both interpretations

85. E. M. Cook, "4Q246," *BBR* 5 (1995) 43-66; Klaus Berger, *Jesus and the Dead Sea Scrolls* (Louisville: Westminster, 1995), 77-79; Annette Steudel, "The Eternal Reign of the People of God — Collective Expectations in Qumran Texts (4Q246 and 1QM)," *RevQ* 65-68 (1996) 507-25; Israel Knohl, *The Messiah before Jesus: The Suffering Servant of the Dead Sea Scrolls* (Berkeley: University of California Press, 2000), 87-95.

86. Vermes, *The Complete Dead Sea Scrolls*, 617.

87. To the best of my knowledge, the messianic interpretation was first proposed orally by Frank M. Cross. See his discussion in *The Ancient Library of Qumran* (3rd ed.; Sheffield: Sheffield Academic Press, 1995), 189-91. So also H.-W. Kuhn, "Rom 1,3f und der davidische Messias als Gottessohn in den Qumrantexten," in C. Burchard and G. Theissen eds., *Lesezeichen für Annelies Findeiss* (Heidelberg: Wissenschaftlich-theologisches Seminar, 1984), 103-13; John J. Collins, "The 'Son of God' Text from Qumran," in M. de Boer, ed., *From Jesus to John: Essays on Jesus and New Testament Christology in Honour of Marinus de Jonge* (Sheffield: JSOT, 1993), 65-82; idem, *The Scepter and the Star*, 154-72; Zimmermann, *Messianische Texte*, 162; Xeravits, *King, Priest and Prophet*, 88-89 (Xeravits speaks of a positive eschatological figure with Davidic associations rather than of a messiah); Brooke, "Kingship and Messianism," 447; Chester, *Messiah and Exaltation*, 232; Stefan Beyerle, "'Der mit den Wolken des Himmels kommt,' Untersuchungen zu Traditionsgefüge 'Menschensohn,'" in Sänger, ed., *Gottessohn und Menschensohn*, 48-50. Schreiber, *Gesalbter und König*, 498-508, allows that the messianic interpretation is possible, but finds no interpretation conclusive. J. A. Fitzmyer, "4Q246: The 'Son of God' Document from Qumran," *Bib* 74 (1994) 153-74 (reprinted in idem, the *Dead Sea Scrolls and Christian Origins* [Grand Rapids: Eerdmans, 2000], 41-61), also sees the figure as positive, a Jewish king in an apocalyptic context, but insists that he is not messianic.

88. F. García Martínez, "The Eschatological Figure of 4Q246," in idem, *Qumran and Apocalyptic: Studies on the Aramaic Texts from Qumran* (Leiden: Brill, 1992), 162-79; idem, "Two Messianic Figures in the Qumran Texts," idem, *Qumranica Minora II* (STDJ 64; Leiden: Brill, 2007), 20-24.

are possible,[89] but later decided that the "negative interpretation was preferable."[90]

The text consists of two columns, of which the first is torn down the middle so that only the second half of the lines survives. Someone is said to fall before a throne. There is reference to a vision. The fragmentary text continues:

> affliction will come on earth . . . and great carnage in the provinces. . . . the king of Assyria and [E]gypt . . . shall be great on earth . . . and all will serve. . . . he shall be called, and by his name he shall be named.

The second column is fully preserved:

> Son of God he shall be called, and they will name him "Son of the Most High." Like shooting stars which you saw, so will their kingdom be. For years they will rule on earth, and they will trample all. People will trample on people and city on city, [VACAT] until the people of God arises, and all rest from the sword. His (or its) kingdom is an everlasting kingdom, and all his ways truth. He will judge the earth with truth, and all will make peace. The sword will cease from the earth, and all cities will pay him homage. The great God will be his strength.[91] He will make war on his behalf, give nations into his hand and cast them all down before him. His sovereignty is everlasting sovereignty, and all the depths. . . .

The rulers to whom this passage refers were mentioned in the opening column, and include kings of Assyria and Egypt. The point in dispute is whether the figure who is called "son of God" is one of these pagan kings, and so viewed negatively, or is a positive figure, allied with the people of God. The argument that the figure is negative rests on a construal of the logical progression of the text. The reference to the "son of God" is followed by a situation in which "people will trample on people and city on city, until the people of God arises [or: until he raises up the people of God]." There is a la-

---

89. Puech, "Fragment d'une Apocalypse"; idem, "Notes sur le Fragment d'Apocalypse 4Q246 — 'Le Fils de Dieu,'" *RB* 101-4 (1994) 533-57.

90. É. Puech, "246. Qapocryphe de Daniel ar," in G. Brooke et al., *Qumran Cave 4* (DJD XXII; Oxford: Clarendon, 1996), 178-84.

91. Van Henten, "The Hasmonean Period," 27, reads "He is a great God among the gods" without explanation. This would presuppose reading אלהיא instead of the clear reading of the manuscript, אילה.

cuna before the word "until," which strengthens the impression that this is a point of transition in the text. Those who read the text on the assumption that events are reported in chronological sequence infer that the "son of God" belongs to the time of distress, and so must be a negative, evil figure.

This inference is unsafe for two reasons. First, it is quite typical of apocalyptic literature that the same events are repeated several times in different terms. It is possible to read the text so that the coming of the "son of God" parallels the rise of the people of God rather than precedes it.[92] Moreover, the appearance of a savior figure does not inevitably mean that the time of strife is over. In Dan 12:1 the rise of Michael is followed by "a time of anguish, such as has never occurred since nations first came into existence." In *4 Ezra* 13, the apparition of the man from the sea is followed by the gathering of an innumerable multitude to make war against him. We should note that the statement about the people of God is ambiguous. It can be read either as "the people of God will arise" (יקום) or as "he will raise up the people of God" (יקים). If the latter reading is correct, the nearest antecedent is the one who will be called "son of God," although it is certainly also possible that God is the subject. It is possible, then, that the text envisages an interval of warfare between the appearance of the deliverer and the actual deliverance. So, the fact that the "son of God" appears before the definitive rise of the people of God does not necessarily mean that he belongs to the era of wickedness.

The most detailed argument in favor of the view that the one called "son of God" in this text is a Syrian king has been advanced by E. M. Cook.[93] Cook reads the text against the background of Akkadian predictive texts. These texts are described as follows by A. K. Grayson:

> Akkadian prophecies are actually pseudo-prophecies, for they consist in the main of predictions after the event *(vaticinia ex eventu).* The predictions are divided according to reigns and often begin with some such phrase as "a prince will arise." Although the kings are never named, it is sometimes possible to identify them on the basis of details provided in the "prophetic" descriptions. The reigns are characterized as "good" or "bad." . . .[94]

92. Collins, "The 'Son of God' Text," 70-71; idem, *The Scepter and the Star,* 158.

93. Cook, "4Q246." For a detailed critique of Cook's argument see my response: "The Background of the 'Son of God' Text," *BBR* 7 (1997) 51-62.

94. A. K. Grayson, *Babylonian Historical-Literary Texts* (Toronto: University of Toronto, 1975), 13.

Cook speculates that "the advent of the Seleucids was accompanied by the dissemination of propaganda, including *ex eventu* prophecies of the Akkadian type," and that 4Q246 is a Jewish counterprophecy.[95] But we have no evidence that the Seleucids disseminated such prophecies. All the extant examples are Babylonian. The latest of the series, the Dynastic Prophecy, dates to the Hellenistic age, and may have ended with the capture of Babylon by Seleucus I, and characterized his reign as bad. Grayson suggests that it is "a strong expression of anti-Seleucid sentiment."[96] This interpretation is itself speculative, as the end of the text is not preserved, but it lends no support to the hypothesis that the Seleucids generated *ex eventu* prophecies.

In any case, the generic resemblance of 4Q246 to Babylonian prophecy is not especially close. Most of the parallels cited by Cook are commonplaces of the type "affliction will come on the land." There are far more precise parallels to the book of Daniel ('his kingdom is an everlasting kingdom . . . his sovereignty is an everlasting sovereignty").[97] One important generic clue in 4Q246 is the mention of a vision, in col. 1, and of "shooting stars which you saw" in col. 2. The text is evidently the interpretation of a vision. Most commentators have supposed that the figure who falls before the throne is an interpreter, and that the situation is analogous to that in Daniel 2. In fact, for a long time the text was known as 4QpseudoDaniel[d]. The Akkadian prophecies do not involve visions at all.

Another consideration weighs heavily against the view that the one who is called "son of God" was a Syrian king. While the Seleucids often claimed to be *theos,* or *theos epiphanēs,* the title "son of God," or even "son of a specific god" (Zeus or Apollo), never appears on their coins.[98] The closest analogy Milik could find was Alexander Balas, who used the honorary title Theopator ("of a divine father") on his coins. Balas was trying to bolster his claim that he was son of Antiochus IV Epiphanes, and so

---

95. Cook, "4Q246," 65.

96. Grayson, *Babylonian Literary-Historical Texts,* 17.

97. See further Collins, *The Scepter and the Star,* 157-58.

98. *Elyon* as a divine title also suggests Jewish idiom, but the point is not conclusive. *(El) Elyon* occurs as a divine title in the Aramaic Sefire inscriptions from the 8th century BCE (KAI 222 A). The name is also preserved as *Elioun* in the account of Phoenician theology by Philo of Byblos, in Eusebius, *Preparation for the Gospel* 1.10.15-29. See E. E. Elnes and P. D. Miller, "Elyon," in K. van der Toorn et al., *Dictionary of Deities and Demons in the Bible* (2nd ed.; Leiden: Brill, 1999), 293-99.

Epiphanes, rather than Zeus or Apollo, was the supposed "divine father."[99] This is hardly analogous to being called "son of the Most High." In this respect, Israel Knohl has a better basis for his suggestion that the "son of God" was the Roman emperor Augustus, who was known as "divi filius,"[100] although that suggestion too is outweighed by the evidence that the figure in question is Jewish.

In light of our discussion of the Hellenistic ruler cults, it should be apparent that the formulation "he will be called" and "they will name him" by no means implies that the titles are not appropriate. Divine titles were honors, conferred in appreciation for acts of beneficence. If the author wished to imply that the titles were not appropriate, we should expect that the one so called would be subject to judgment, just as Daniel leaves no doubt that the hybris of Antiochus Epiphanes leads to his downfall.

By far the closest parallel to the titles in question is explicitly messianic. In Luke 1:32 the angel Gabriel tells Mary that her child

> "will be great, and will be called the Son of the Most High, and the Lord God will give to him the throne of his ancestor David. He will reign over the house of Jacob forever, and of his kingdom there will be no end."

In Luke 1:35 he adds: "he will be called the Son of God." The Greek titles "son of the Most High" and "son of God" correspond exactly to the Aramaic fragment from Qumran. Both texts refer to an everlasting kingdom. The fact that these parallels are found in the New Testament does not lessen their relevance to the cultural context of the Qumran text.[101] Despite the claim of Puech that these honorific titles could apply to "n'importe quell autre roi," neither he nor anyone else has been able to adduce a parallel of comparable precision from any other source.[102] Whether Luke is dependent on the Qumran text or the parallel is due to "coincidental use by Luke of Palestinian Jewish titles known to him"[103] makes little difference for the significance of the parallel. Luke would hardly have used

---

99. Norman Davis and Colin M. Kraay, *The Hellenistic Kingdoms: Portrait Coins and History* (London: Thames and Hudson, 1973), Plates 89, 92.

100. Knohl, *The Messiah before Jesus,* 93. The Roman identification is compatible with the paleographic date suggested by Milik and Puech, about 25 BCE (Puech, *DJD* 22, 166).

101. Pace Puech, "Notes," 555.

102. Ibid.

103. Fitzmyer, "4Q246," 174.

the Palestinian Jewish titles with reference to the messiah if they were primarily associated negatively with a Syrian king.

It seems to me, then, that 4Q246 is most plausibly interpreted as referring to a Jewish messiah. The basis for calling him "son of God" is clear, not only in Psalm 2 but also in 2 Samuel 7 and in the *Florilegium* from Qumran. Fitzmyer, who also considers the text to be apocalyptic, and "to be speaking positively of a coming Jewish ruler, who may be a successor to the Davidic throne," nonetheless insists that he is "not envisaged as a Messiah,"[104] apparently because the word משיחא is not used. But this is to fail to distinguish between a word and a concept. A successor to the Davidic throne in an eschatological context is by definition a messiah.[105] Consequently, neither the contention of Wilhelm Bousset, made long before the discovery of the Dead Sea Scrolls, that there is no connection between the title "Son of God" and Jewish messianic expectation,[106] nor that of Fitzmyer that "there is nothing in the Old Testament or Palestinian Jewish tradition that we know of to show that 'Son of God' had a messianic nuance,"[107] can be maintained. "Son of God" was not widespread as a messianic title, insofar as we now know, but it is attested.

In my initial study of this text in 1993, I tentatively suggested that the figure called "son of God" might be understood as an interpretation of Daniel's "one like a son of man."[108] The argument was subsequently made

104. Joseph A. Fitzmyer, "The Aramaic 'Son of God' Text from Qumran Cave 4 (4Q246)," in idem, *The Dead Sea Scrolls and Christian Origins* (Grand Rapids: Eerdmans, 2000), 60.

105. In his most recent publication on the subject Fitzmyer writes: "I agree with Collins that . . . 'a future successor to the Davidic throne in an apocalyptic or eschatological context is by definition a Davidic messiah.' But Collins still has not given any evidence of the use of the title 'Son of God' for a Davidic Messiah either in the Old Testament or in the Qumran literature" (*The One Who Is to Come*, 106-7). But the title "son of God" is applied in this text to a figure whom Fitzmyer himself regards as a future Jewish king "who may be of Davidic lineage" and therefore, by definition, a messiah. Fitzmyer admits that the Hasmonean dynasty does not offer a plausible alternative to Davidic lineage.

106. Wilhelm Bousset, *Kyrios Christos: A History of the Belief in Christ from the Beginnings of Christianity to Irenaeus* (Nashville: Abingdon, 1970; German original, 1913), 207.

107. Joseph A. Fitzmyer, *The Gospel according to Luke I–IX* (AB 28; New York: Doubleday, 1981), 206. Fitzmyer is concerned to argue that the title "Son of God" as applied to Jesus means something more than "messiah" (ibid., 339).

108. Collins, "The Son of God Text," 80-81. Pace J. D. G. Dunn, "'Son of God' as 'Son of Man' in the Dead Sea Scrolls? A Response to John Collins on 4Q246," in S. E. Porter and C. A. Evans, eds., *The Scrolls and the Scriptures: Qumran Fifty Years After* (JSPSup 26; Sheffield:

more forcefully by Johannes Zimmermann.[109] The text is reminiscent of Daniel at many points, including the general situation of an interpreter before a king. The clearest echoes of Daniel are at 2:5, "his kingdom is an everlasting kingdom" (cf. Dan 3:33 [Eng. 4:3]); 7:27), and 2:9, "his sovereignty will be an everlasting sovereignty" (cf. Dan 4:31 [Eng. 4:34]; 7:14). The conflict between nations is reminiscent in a general way of Daniel 11, but such conflict is commonplace in apocalyptic literature, notably also in 4 Ezra 13. Another possible allusion to Daniel lies in the use of the word "to trample" at 2:3. The same word is used with reference to the fourth beast in Daniel 7.

The analogies with Daniel may shed some light on the relation between the one who is called "son of God" and the people of God. In Daniel 7, the eternal kingdom is explicitly given both to the "one like a son of man" and to the people of the holy ones. In the same way, the tensions in 4Q246 can be resolved if the "son of God" is understood as a messianic king, so that the kingdom is given simultaneously both to him and to the people.[110] If the text is read in this way, the figure of the son of God fits well within the spectrum of messianic expectations around the turn of the era. He will exercise judgment and subdue the nations by the power of God.

In light of this situation, it is tempting to suggest that the "son of God" represents an early interpretation of the "one like a son of man" in Daniel 7. If this were so, this would be the earliest instance of the messianic interpretation of the "one like a son of man," which is attested in the *Similitudes of Enoch*, well established in 4 Ezra, and dominant in later Judaism. As we shall find in the next chapter, there are allusions to Psalm 2 in the descriptions of the "Son of Man" figure in both of these texts, and García Martínez may be right that the messiah in 4Q246 is a heavenly "Son of Man" figure too.[111] This would also mitigate the strange absence of inter-

---

Sheffield Academic Press, 1997), 198-210, I have never claimed that this was more than a possibility. Dunn holds to the "negative" view of the "son of God."

109. Zimmermann, *Messianische Texte,* 164-68. See also the comments of Stefan Beyerle, "'Der mit den Wolken des Himmels kommt,'" in Sänger, ed., *Gottessohn und Menschensohn,* 48-50. Beyerle notes the differences between the "Son of God" and "Son of Man," but sees 4Q246 as an early development of the "Son of Man" tradition.

110. This is not "collective messianism," pace Steudel, "The Eternal Reign of the People of God." It is rather analogous to what we find in 4Q174, the *Florilegium,* in which "his anointed" is understood as referring to the elect, but there is still a role for the Shoot of David, of whom God says in 2 Samuel 7, "he will be a son to me."

111. García Martínez, "Two Messianic Figures," 24.

pretations of Daniel 7 in the Dead Sea Scrolls. This interpretation of 4Q246, however, is uncertain. The "Son of God" text is certainly not an exposition of Daniel 7. While some words and phrases are drawn from that source, most elements of the biblical vision are ignored. This is not in itself a decisive objection: there is no mention of beasts from the sea in the *Similitudes of Enoch,* and yet no one doubts that they are dependent on Daniel 7. But unlike the *Similitudes,* the Qumran text does not use specific language associated with the "one like a son of man." The vision that is being interpreted is not preserved, but it seems to be the vision of a king rather than of a visionary like Daniel, and so to be analogous to Daniel 2, or perhaps to the pseudo-Daniel text 4Q243-44 from Qumran, which is also set at the Babylonian court, rather than to Daniel 7.[112] There are no explicit allusions to the interpretation of Daniel here, such as we find in *4 Ezra* 12. Accordingly, the possibility that this text is an interpretation, or adaptation, of Daniel 7 is no more than that. It should be noted that the "Son of God" text is also reminiscent of the *War Scroll,* in its mention of Assyria and Egypt (cf. 1QM 1:2, 4) and the rare word נחשירין, "slaughter" (cf. 1QM 1:9-10).[113] The relation between the son of God and the people might equally well be compared to that between Michael and Israel in the *War Scroll* (1QM 17:7), as suggested by García Martínez.[114]

## Conclusion

The depiction of the 'son of God' in 4Q246 fits nicely with the portrayal of the Davidic/royal messiah in the Scrolls. He functions as a warrior to subdue the Gentiles: God will make war on his behalf and cast peoples down before him. "Son of God" is an honorific title here. Nothing is said about his birth, although, as we have seen, another text from Qumran may speak about God begetting the messiah. Both texts are only applying biblical language to the messiah. If there is any influence from the ruler cults here, it lies in the understanding of "Son of God" as an honorific title and perhaps

---

112. J. J. Collins and P. W. Flint, "243-245. 4Qpseudo-Daniel[a-c] ar," in G. Brooke et al., *Qumran Cave 4, XVII: Parabiblical Texts, Part 3,* 95-164.

113. Zimmermann, *Messianische Texte,* 164-65.

114. García Martínez, "The Eschatological Figure of 4Q246," in idem, *Qumran and Apocalyptic,* 178.

also in the willingness to entertain language of divinity with reference to a future king.

More important than the putative influence of the ruler cults is the tendency that we have noted in a few passages in the LXX to attribute to the messiah preexistence and angelic status. This tendency finds its main expression in another cluster of texts that refer to a heavenly messianic figure who is described as a "man" or "son of man." These texts will be the subject of the next chapter.

## 4. *Messiah and Son of Man*

### The Son of Man Concept

The expression ὁ υἱὸς τοῦ ἀνθρώπου, literally, "the son of the man," occurs more than 70 times in the Gospels with reference to Jesus.[1] The expression is clearly a Semitism, corresponding to Hebrew בן אדם or Aramaic בר אנש, either of which means, normally, "human being" or "someone." The plural, בני אדם, is commonly used to refer to humanity at large. In the book of Ezekiel, the prophet is addressed 93 times as בן אדם. In Aramaic, the expressions בר (א)נש and בר (א)נשא refer to human beings in a generic sense. In the Gospels, however, ὁ υἱὸς τοῦ ἀνθρώπου evidently refers to a specific individual, at least in most cases. Several of these references envision the "Son of Man" coming on the clouds of heaven, a clear allusion to the vision in chapter 7 of the book of Daniel.

For much of the twentieth century, scholars sought to explain this usage of "Son of Man" with reference to an individual, supernatural figure, by appeal to a supposedly widespread myth of a Primal Man, of Iranian origin. Speculation about this Primal Man, or *Urmensch,* is associated especially

---

1. A. Yarbro Collins, "The Origin of the Designation of Jesus as 'Son of Man,'" *HTR* 80 (1987) 391-408, here 396, reprinted in eadem, *Cosmology and Eschatology in Jewish and Christian Apocalypticism* (Leiden: Brill, 2000), 139-58, here 145.

with the "History of Religion School" *(die religionsgeschichtliche Schule)* in the early part of the twentieth century.[2] This approach to scholarship was prompted by the discovery of ancient religious texts, from Egypt to Iran, in the 19th century. Much of the discussion focused on late Hellenistic and even later Mandean and Gnostic materials that date from the 3rd to the 6th centuries of the common era, but it also drew on studies of kingship ideology in the ancient Near East. In the words of Sigmund Mowinckel,

> Conceptions of a more or less divine Primordial Man were widespread in the ancient east. Apparently there is a historical connection between the varying figures of this type, which seem to be derived, directly, or indirectly, from Iranian or Indo-Iranian myths.[3]

The Jewish conception of "the Son of Man" was "a Jewish variant of this oriental, cosmological, eschatological myth of Anthropos."[4] Little attention was paid to the distinctive aspects and historical circumstances of the different bodies of literature. The most recent exponent of this approach to the "Son of Man" problem, F. H. Borsch, summed up his thesis as follows:

> It is our contention that we have good cause for suspecting that there was a mythical conception of relative antiquity concerning a primal hero, conceived of as Man who was once on earth, whose story contains some reference to defeat or death. Yet somehow he was also regarded as one who was or who was very closely allied with a glorious, cosmic Man figure of the heavens. While such legendary beliefs are never found in exactly the same guise and often appear only in fragmentary forms, and while we do not necessarily postulate some one original myth, there is reason to believe that the variant descriptions are related.[5]

Even at the time when Borsch wrote, however, this approach had begun to seem dated. There was a growing realization that composite myths

---

2. Important works in this school include R. Reitzenstein, *Poimandres. Studien zur griechisch-ägyptischen und frühchristlichen Literatur* (Leipzig: Hinrichs, 1904); Reitzenstein and H. H. Schaeder, *Studien zum antiken Synkretismus, aus Iran und Griechenland* (Berlin and Leipzig: Teubner, 1926).

3. S. Mowinckel, *He That Cometh: The Messiah Concept in Israel and Later Judaism* (Nashville: Abingdon, 1956; reprint, Grand Rapids: Eerdmans, 2005), 422.

4. Ibid., 425.

5. F. H. Borsch, *The Son of Man in Myth and History* (London: SCM, 1967), 87.

cannot be constructed from fragmentary sources in different religious traditions, and then retrojected to a time centuries earlier than the extant sources. The problems with the "religionsgeschichtliche" approach were pointed out decisively in a monograph by Carsten Colpe in 1961.[6] Colpe concluded

> not that traditions of a cosmic heavenly macroanthropos, a protoplast put in the end-time, or an archetypal primal man were adopted, but rather that Jewish apocalyptic itself had been fruitful in developing the figure of the Son of Man.[7]

So while Colpe was much more careful than the scholars of the *religionsgeschichtliche Schule* in avoiding anachronism and focusing the discussion within specific historical and cultural limits, he affirmed the existence of a "Son of Man concept" in Judaism around the turn of the era.

Other scholars went further. In 1968, Ragnar Leivestadt had declared the apocalyptic Son of Man to be a phantom.[8] A few years later he reformulated his thesis in English: "Exit the Apocalyptic Son of Man."[9] Geza Vermes argued that "no titular use of the phrase 'the son of man' can be substantiated" from the Jewish sources, and that "the association between ὁ υἱὸς τοῦ ἀνθρώπου and Dan 7:13 constitutes a secondary midrashic stage of development, more understandable in Greek than in Aramaic."[10] Norman Perrin argued that "there is no 'Son of Man' concept, but rather a variety of uses of Son of Man imagery."[11] Barnabas Lindars is typical of much recent scholarship when he declares the "Son of Man" concept to be "a modern myth."[12]

Insofar as the "Son of Man" concept is understood in terms of a syncretistic Anthropos myth, pieced together from late Hellenistic and Gnos-

---

6. C. Colpe, *Die religionsgeschichtliche Schule. Darstellung und Kritik ihres Bildes vom gnostischen Erlösermythus* (Göttingen: Vandenhoeck & Ruprecht, 1961). See also his article "ὁ υἱὸς τοῦ ἀνθρώπου," *TDNT*, 8 (1972), 400-477, especially 408-15.

7. Colpe, "ὁ υἱὸς τοῦ ἀνθρώπου," *TDNT*, 8 (1972), 419-20.

8. R. Leivestadt, "Der apokalyptische Menschensohn ein theologisches Phantom," *Annual of the Swedish Theological Institute* 6 (1967-68) 49-109.

9. Leivestadt, "Exit the Apocalyptic Son of Man," *NTS* 18 (1971-72) 243-67.

10. G. Vermes, *Jesus and the World of Judaism* (Philadelphia: Fortress, 1984), 96-98.

11. N. Perrin, *A Modern Pilgrimage in New Testament Christology* (Philadelphia: Fortress, 1974), 26.

12. B. Lindars, *Jesus, Son of Man* (Grand Rapids: Eerdmans, 1983), 3.

tic sources, the critical reaction is certainly justified. Moreover, it is unwarranted to suppose that all Jewish witnesses to the "Son of Man" draw on a composite myth that encompasses them all. It is now readily granted that "the Son of Man" was not a fixed title in Judaism in the first century CE. The significance of this point should not be exaggerated, however. The text of Daniel's vision was well known, and it inspired further reflections and imaginative elaborations. It is not necessary to posit the existence of any "Son of Man" myth beyond what we find in the texts. Later authors adapt Daniel's vision in ways that are quite creative and are by no means simple reproductions of the original vision. There were, however, some widely held assumptions about the nature of the figure in Daniel's vision, and these go beyond what is explicit in the biblical text. Whether or not these assumptions are thought to amount to a "Son of Man concept," they are important for the development of messianism around the turn of the era.

## The Jewish Texts

### Daniel 7

Since I have written at length on Daniel 7 in the past, on more than one occasion, I trust that it will suffice here to summarize my main conclusions.[13] The "one like a son of man" is not a corporate symbol, but should be identified with the archangel Michael, the "prince of Israel" in chapters 10–12. The "holy ones" are the angelic host, and the "people of the holy ones" are the Jewish people, or at least those who are faithful to the covenant. The imagery of the turbulent sea and the rider on the clouds, and also the white-headed Ancient of Days, is adapted from old mythic traditions that derive from pre-Israelite, Canaanite roots, as can be seen by analogy with the myths from Ugarit.[14] This imagery was always closely associated with

13. J. J. Collins, *The Apocalyptic Vision of the Book of Daniel* (HSM 16; Missoula, MT: Scholars Press, 1977), 123-52; idem, *Daniel: A Commentary on the Book of Daniel* (Hermeneia; Minneapolis: Fortress, 1993), 274-324. For a recent overview of scholarship on the "one like a son of man" in Daniel 7 see S. Beyerle, "'Der mit den Wolken des Himmels kommt,'" in D. Sänger, ed., *Gottessohn und Menschensohn* (Neukirchen-Vluyn: Neukirchener, 2004), 1-52.

14. J. J. Collins, "Stirring Up the Great Sea: The Religio-Historical Background of Daniel 7," in idem, *Seers, Sibyls and Sages in Hellenistic-Roman Judaism* (JSJSup 54; Leiden: Brill, 1997), 139-55.

kingship,[15] and kings and kingdoms figure prominently in Daniel 7. It is not surprising, then, that some scholars see Daniel 7 as "a transformation of Davidic messianism."[16] In antiquity, too, as we shall see, a messianic interpretation prevailed from an early time. Nonetheless, few modern scholars subscribe to the view that the "one like a son of man" was originally meant to be identified with the messiah. The absence of any clear reference to a royal messiah in the remainder of Daniel would appear to be decisive in that regard.

## *11QMelchizedek*

The primary evidence for a "Son of Man" tradition in ancient Judaism is found in the *Similitudes of Enoch* and *4 Ezra*. Before I turn to these texts, however, I want to pause to consider another text that speaks of a heavenly deliverer, although it does not portray him in terms drawn from Daniel 7 and does not call him messiah. This is the document known as the *Melchizedek* scroll, from Qumran Cave 11. It is important for our discussion as a witness to trends in late Second Temple Judaism that provide the context for speculation about the "Son of Man."

11QMelchizedek is a midrashic composition, which explains the law of the jubilee of Leviticus 25 by juxtaposing several other biblical texts, notably Isaiah 61.[17] The editors place the extant fragments in three columns, but only column 2 provides coherent, continuous text. We are told that the jubilee refers to the end of days, and that the Day of Atonement is the end of the tenth jubilee, when expiation will be made for all the sons of light and for the men of the lot of Melchizedek. Melchizedek, then, appears to be equivalent to the Prince of Light in other texts, and the lot of

---

15. See, e.g., Nicolas Wyatt, *Myths of Power: A Study of Royal Myth and Ideology in Ugaritic and Biblical Tradition* (Münster: Ugarit-Verlag, 1996).

16. So H. Gese, *Zur biblischen Theologie* (3rd ed.; Tübingen: Mohr Siebeck, 1989), 140. Compare Paul Mosca, "Daniel 7 and Ugarit: A Missing Link," *Bib* 67 (1986) 496-517, who finds the missing link in the royal psalms, especially Psalm 89.

17. Originally edited by A. S. van der Woude, "Melchisedek als himmlische Erlösergestalt in den neugefundenen eschatologischen Midraschim aus Qumran Höhle XI," *OTS* 14 (1965) 354-73. See now the official edition by F. García Martínez, E. J. C. Tigchelaar, and A. S. van der Woude, *Qumran Cave 11, II* (DJD 23; Oxford: Clarendon, 1998), 22-41. Note also Émile Puech, "Notes sur le manuscrit de XIQMelkisédeq," *RevQ* 12/48 (1987) 483-513.

Melchizedek equivalent to the lot of light. The end of the tenth jubilee is "the time for the year of grace of Melchizedek." The text then applies to Melchizedek the passage from Ps 82:1: "Elohim [God] takes his stand in the assembly of El, in the midst of Elohim [gods] he judges." In interpretation, we are told that "Melchizedek will carry out the vengeance of El's judgments." Several other texts from Isaiah and Daniel are brought into the discussion, including Isa 52:7, where a herald says to Zion, "Your God (*Elohim*) is king." The passage goes on to interpret pesher-style, so that one thing is taken to stand for another. The herald is clearly identified as "the anointed of the spirit" of whom Daniel spoke (presumably in one of the references to an anointed one in Dan 9:25-26, in the interpretation of the 70 weeks of years). Unfortunately, the text is very fragmentary at this point. It has been restored to read, "Your god (אלוהיך) is Melchizedek."[18] This may seem to be a very bold restoration, but in fact Melchizedek had already been identified with the Elohim, or God, of Psalm 82. In the view of this interpreter, the Most High God is El. Elohim is a lesser deity, an angel, if you prefer. But the striking thing about this passage is that the term Elohim, which is usually understood to refer to the Most High in the biblical psalm, is now referred to a lesser heavenly being. There are, at least, two powers in heaven, even if one of them is clearly subordinate to the other.

This interpretation of 11QMelchizedek has not gone unchallenged. The quotation from Psalm 82 is introduced in col. 2, lines 9 and 10, which read:

> It is the time for the year of grace of Melchizedek and of [his] arm[ies, with] the holy ones of God for the rule of judgment (משפט), as was written about him (or it?) (כאשר כתוב עליו) in the songs of David. "Elohim takes his stand. . . ."

18. See García Martínez et al., *DJD* 23, 226, 233. The restoration, proposed by Milik, is very widely accepted: Fred L. Horton, *The Melchizedek Tradition* (SNTSMS 30; Cambridge: Cambridge University Press, 1976), 75; Paul J. Kobelski, *Melchizedek and Melchiresha'* (CBQMS 10; Washington: Catholic Biblical Association, 1981), 23; Claudio Gianotto, *Melchisedek e la sua Tipologia* (Brescia: Paideia, 1984), 70-75; Émile Puech, *La croyance des Esséniens en la vie future: immortalité, résurrection, vie éternelle?* (Paris: Gabalda, 1993), 553 (who restores "the prince Melchizedek"); Johannes Zimmermann, *Messianische Texte aus Qumran* (WUNT 2.14; Tübingen: Mohr Siebeck, 1998), 394; Géza Xeravits, *King, Priest, Prophet* (Leiden: Brill, 2001), 68-75. Van der Woude, "Melchisedek als himmlische Erlösergestalt," *OTS* 14 (1965) 354-73, 366, already suggested that the reference was very probably to Melchizedek.

The standard interpretation of כאשר כתוב עליו is "as it is written about him," taking Melchizedek as the antecedent. The late Jean Carmignac argued that the phrase should be translated "as it is written about it," taking judgment as the antecedent, a theme that is then picked up in the quotation.[19] This is indeed a possible construal of the grammar, but it does not necessarily rule out the identification of Melchizedek with *elohim*. In verse 13 we are told that Melchizedek will carry out the vengeance of El's judgments, and there is a clear antithesis between "the lot of Melchizedek" and "the lot of Belial."

Paul Rainbow, who has revived Carmignac's objection, argues that Melchizedek is "none other than Daniel's anointed one, a prince, whom a later age would call King Messiah."[20] But Daniel's anointed one is clearly identified with the *mebasser,* or herald, in verse 18. This is not the king messiah, but a prophetic figure.[21] The anointing with the spirit is an allusion to Isa 61:1, where the prophet says: "The spirit of the Lord GOD is upon me, because the LORD has anointed me; he has sent me to bring good news (לבשר) to the poor," and prophets are called משיחי רוח קדשו, "those anointed with his holy spirit," in CD 2:12.[22] There is no parallel for making such a prophetic herald the agent of God's vengeance, nor indeed is there any apparent reason why Melchizedek should be cast in the role of a prophet.[23]

---

19. J. Carmignac, "Le document de Qumran sur Melkisédeq," *RevQ* 7 (1970) 343-78.

20. P. Rainbow, "Melchizedek as a Messiah at Qumran," *BBR* 7 (1997) 179-94.

21. J. A. Fitzmyer, "Further Light on Melchizedek from Qumran Cave 11," in idem, *Essays on the Semitic Background of the New Testament* (Missoula, MT: Scholars Press, 1974), reprinted in *The Semitic Background of the New Testament* (Grand Rapids: Eerdmans, 1997), 245-67, here 253-54, also entertained the identification of Melchizedek with the *mebasśer,* but found it "difficult to say." The identification is also endorsed by Anders Hultgård, *L'Eschatologie des Testaments des Douze Patriarches* (Uppsala: Almqvist & Wiksell, 1977), 307-8. Michael O. Wise, *The First Messiah: Investigating the Savior before Christ* (San Francisco: HarperSanFrancisco, 1999), 231, claims that Melchizedek is identical with the messianic herald or prophet, and that both are identical with the Teacher of Righteousness.

22. See further John J. Collins, "A Herald of Good Tidings: Isaiah 61:1-3 and Its Actualization in the Dead Sea Scrolls," in Craig A. Evans and Shemaryahu Talmon, eds., *The Quest for Context and Meaning: Studies in Biblical Intertextuality in Honor of James A. Sanders* (Leiden: Brill, 1997), 225-40. The allusions to Isaiah 61 are set out clearly by Zimmermann, *Messianische Texte,* 402.

23. Gianotto, *Melchisedek,* 70. Fitzmyer, "Further Light," 253, points out that the *mebasśer* of Isa 52:7 was identified as the King Messiah in rabbinic tradition. See Strack-Billerbeck 3:9-10. I would argue, however, that the roles are distinct in the Dead Sea Scrolls. See also

Another recent attempt to avoid the conclusion that Melchizedek is an *elohim,* but distinct from the Most High, has been made by an Italian scholar, Franco Manzi, in a monograph on Melchizedek and angelology in the Scrolls and the New Testament.[24] Manzi accepts that the phrase "as it is written" refers to Melchizedek, but argues that Melchizedek is not the name of a human being or of an angel, but should be translated "king of righteousness" and refers to God. But the variation of names in the text (Melchizedek will exact the vengeance of God's judgment) surely suggests that Melchizedek is distinct from God.[25] The name is not otherwise attested as a divine title.

In support of the angelic interpretation one may cite a couple of other texts from Qumran that are admittedly fragmentary. The name has been reconstructed in two places in the *Songs of the Sabbath Sacrifice.* One, in 4Q401, fragment 22, has only כי צדק[ and must be considered doubtful.[26] The other, 4Q401, fragment 11, is a plausible reconstruction:

:מלכי]צדק הכהן בעד]ת אל

Melchi]sedek, priest in the council of God.[27]

Also plausible is the restoration of Melchizedek in the *Testament of Amram.*[28] This composition is the deathbed speech of the patriarch Amram, son of Qahath, son of Levi, in which he reports a vision in which two angelic figures were quarreling over him. One of them is called a "watcher," like the fallen angels in the book of *Enoch,* and he is said to rule

---

Andrew Chester, *Messiah and Exaltation* (Tübingen: Mohr Siebeck, 2007), 259-61, where he abandons his earlier position that Melchizedek is the herald, and also rejects the messianic interpretation.

24. F. Manzi, *Melchisedek e l'angelologia nell' Epistola agli Ebrei e a Qumran* (AnBib 136; Rome: Pontifical Biblical Institution, 1997), 96-101.

25. Anders Aschim, "Melchizedek and Jesus: 11QMelchizedek and the Epistle to the Hebrews," in C. C. Newman, J. R. Davila, and G. S. Lewis, *The Jewish Roots of Christological Monotheism* (JSJSup 63; Leiden: Brill, 1999), 129-47, here 135.

26. Carol A. Newsom, *Songs of the Sabbath Sacrifice: A Critical Edition* (HSS 27; Atlanta: Scholars Press, 1985), 143-44; idem, "4Q419," in Esther Eshel et al., *Qumran Cave 4, VI: Political and Liturgical Texts, Part 1* (DJD 11; Oxford: Clarendon, 1998), 213; Manzi, *Melchisedek,* 400.

27. Newsom, *Songs,* 134; *DJD* 11.205.

28. J. T. Milik, "4QVisions d'Amram et une citation d'Origène," *RB* 79 (1972) 77-92 (especially 85-86); Kobelski, *Melchizedek and Melchiresha',* 24-36; Gianotto, *Melchisedek,* 75-79; Puech, *La croyance,* 535.

over darkness. He is named Melchiresha', "king of wickedness." The other figure rules over all light and is said to have three names. The obvious counterpart to Melchiresha' is Melchizedek ("king of righteousness"). Other plausible matching pairs are "Prince of Light" and "Prince of Darkness," and Michael and Belial. It is unfortunate that this text is so poorly preserved, especially as it seems to be one of the earliest dualistic texts. The extant fragments, however, are an important witness to the concept of opposing, dualistic angels. Melchiresha' also appears in another fragmentary text (4Q280), where he is cursed, just as Belial is cursed in the second column of the *Community Rule.* The occurrence of Melchiresha' as a demonic name lends at least indirect support to the angelic interpretation of Melchizedek. The only place in the Dead Sea Scrolls where the name Melchizedek is preserved in full in a nonbiblical text (apart from 11QMelchizedek) is the *Genesis Apocryphon,* col. 22, which follows closely the text of Genesis 14, except that it specifies that he provides food and drink to Abram and to all the men who were with him.

The name Melchizedek, of course, was known from two occurrences in the Hebrew Bible, and in at least one of these (and probably in both) it referred to a human Canaanite king in its original context.[29] In Genesis 14, he is king of Salem and priest of El Elyon, and Abraham gives him a tithe of all that he has. In Psalm 110 the king is told: "You are a priest forever according to the order of Melchizedek." The reconstructed reference in 4Q401, fragment 11, identifies Melchizedek as a priest in the council of El. He is not explicitly said to be a priest in 11QMelchizedek, but his activity culminates on the Day of Atonement, which suggests that he has a priestly role after all.[30] His heavenly character, and his role as avenger, are most plausibly derived from the exegesis of Psalm 110. The argument has been summarized nicely by James Kugel.[31] The Hebrew of Psalm 110:4 is ambiguous: אתה כהן לעולם על דברתי מלכי צדק. This is usually translated: "You are a priest forever after the order of Melchizedek," taking the *yod* in דברתי as a connecting vowel *(hireq compaginis).* But the *yod* could have

---

29. Crispin Fletcher-Louis, *All the Glory of Adam: Liturgical Anthropology in the Dead Sea Scrolls* (STDJ 42; Leiden: Brill, 2002), 217, emphasizes this point, to argue that Melchizedek cannot be a purely angelic figure. On the biblical references to Melchizedek see Deborah Rooke, *Zadok's Heirs* (Oxford: Oxford University Press, 2000), 80-103.

30. Fletcher-Louis, ibid., also emphasizes his priestly character.

31. James L. Kugel, *The Traditions of the Bible: A Guide to the Bible as It Was at the Start of the Common Era* (Cambridge, MA: Harvard University Press, 1998), 278-81.

been read as a first-person possessive pronoun, and Melchizedek taken as a vocative, so "you are a priest forever by my order, O Melchizedek." If Melchizedek is the subject addressed here, then he may also be identified with the figure called "my lord" in verse 1, who is invited to sit at God's right hand. "It is from this interpretation of Psalm 110 that there emerged the figure of a heavenly Melchizedek, an angelic being who sits next to the divine throne," concludes Kugel.[32] The violent role of Melchizedek in the Qumran text could then be derived from the Psalm: "The scepter of your might the LORD will send forth from Zion. Rule in the midst of your enemies. . . . he will judge the nations, filling them with corpses." The figure in Genesis 14 would then presumably have been read as "king of peace (shalom)" rather than "king of Salem" since the identity of Salem was uncertain in any case. It is probably significant that the expression "angel of peace," מלאך שלם (which has the same consonants as "angel of Salem"), occurs with some frequency in the *Similitudes of Enoch* and the *Testaments of the Twelve Patriarchs* and is also attested in the Scrolls (4Q228).[33]

Kugel goes on to suggest that Ps 110:3b, which reads in the MT, "From the womb, from dawn, like dew, your youth will come to you," was read as in the LXX: "From the womb, before the morning star, I have begotten you." Melchizedek then would be "son of God," which Kugel takes in the sense of "angel," as in Genesis 6.[34] As we have seen, the LXX translation also implies preexistence. But we do not in fact know that the author of 11QMelchizedek read the text this way. The reading "I have begotten you" reflects the same consonantal text that is found in the MT, and this may be the text presupposed in the midrash.

Much of this exegetical reasoning would also apply if Melchizedek were identified as the "King Messiah," as Rainbow suggested. The name Melchizedek includes the element "king," and the clause "your god is king" is most probably to be interpreted as a reference to Melchizedek. Psalm 110 was interpreted as messianic in early Christianity.[35] The king could be

32. Ibid., 279.

33. Kobelski, *Melchizedek and Melchiresha'*, 52. Cf. 4Q228 1 i 8; *1 Enoch* 40:8; 52:5; *Testament of Dan* 6:5; *Testament of Asher* 6:6; *Testament of Benjamin* 6:1.

34. Kugel, *The Traditions of the Bible*, 280-81.

35. David Hay, *Glory at the Right Hand: Psalm 110 in Early Christianity* (SBLMS 18; Nashville: Abingdon, 1973); Martin Hengel, "Setze dich zu meiner Rechten! Die Inthronisation Christi zur Rechten Gottes und Psalm 110,1," in Marc Philonenko, ed., *Le Trône de Dieu* (Tübingen: Mohr Siebeck, 1993), 108-94.

called an *elohim*, "god," as in Psalm 45. The role of executing judgment is kingly.[36] If Psalm 110 is interpreted as referring to the begetting of the king or Melchizedek by God, this too would lend itself to a messianic interpretation. Rainbow's suggestion that Melchizedek is the King Messiah, then, has some plausibility if it is separated from his assumption that this figure is also to be identified with "the anointed of the spirit" in 11QMelchizedek. Moreover, a messianic interpretation is not necessarily incompatible with an angelic one, as we have seen from the LXX translation of Isaiah 9. Crispin Fletcher-Louis has argued strongly that Melchizedek should not be understood as purely angelic, but rather as an angelomorphic human being.[37] This suggestion draws some support from the legend of the miraculous birth of Melchizedek in 2 *Enoch* 71, where he has no human father and emerges from his mother after her death.[38] He is subsequently preserved from death and taken to the garden of Eden. For Fletcher-Louis, Melchizedek is "a priest with cosmic and divine credentials."[39] He suggests an analogy with the enigmatic figure who claims to be enthroned in heaven in 4Q491, fragment 11 (the "Self-Exaltation Hymn" or "Throne in Heaven" text). While that text is very fragmentary and there is no consensus about its interpretation, it appears to envision an exalted human being rather than an angel.[40] One of the more plausible suggestions about it is that the figure in question may be the eschatological High Priest,[41] and that suggestion is indeed compatible with an association with Melchizedek.

We certainly find a blurring of the lines between human messiah and

---

36. This point is emphasized by Hultgård, *L'Eschatologie*, 307.

37. Fletcher-Louis, *All the Glory of Adam*, 216-21.

38. See F. I. Andersen, "2 Enoch," *OTP*, 1:204-9.

39. Fletcher-Louis, *All the Glory of Adam*, 220.

40. Morton Smith, "Ascent to the Heavens and Deification in 4QMᵃ," in Lawrence H. Schiffman, ed., *Archaeology and History in the Dead Sea Scrolls* (JSPSup 8; Sheffield: JSOT, 1990), 181-88; Philip Alexander, *The Mystical Texts* (Companion to the Dead Sea Scrolls; London/New York: T&T Clark, 2006), 85-92. Note, however, the defense of the angelic interpretation by Florentino García Martínez, "Old Texts and Modern Mirages: The 'I' of Two Qumran Hymns," in idem, *Qumranica Minora I: Qumran Origins and Apocalypticism* (STDJ 63; Leiden: Brill, 2007), 105-25, here 114-18.

41. John J. Collins, *The Scepter and the Star* (New York: Doubleday, 1995), 136-53; Esti Eshel, "The Identification of the 'Speaker' of the Self-Glorification Hymn," in D. W. Parry and E. Ulrich, eds., *The Provo International Conference on the Dead Sea Scrolls* (STDJ 30; Leiden: Brill, 1999), 619-35. For a different interpretation see Michael O. Wise, "מי כמוני באלים: A Study of 4Q491c, 4Q471b, 4Q427 and 1QHᵃ 25:35–26:10," *DSD* 7 (2000) 173-219.

heavenly or angelic deliverer in the Son of Man tradition, as we shall see shortly. García Martínez argues that the three basic functions of Melchizedek are messianic: those of avenging judge, heavenly priest, and ultimate savior of the men of his lot. Consequently, he designates him "a heavenly messiah."[42] It seems to me unlikely, however, that Melchizedek should be identified with a *human* messiah, either royal or priestly. Where do we hear of people belonging to the lot of the messianic king? The antithesis of Melchizedek and Belial also favors an angelic rather than a messianic interpretation, as do the probable references to Melchizedek in the *Songs of the Sabbath Sacrifice* and the *Testament of Amram*. Moreover, in my view the Scrolls were at pains to distinguish the messianic king from his priestly counterpart, in reaction to the combination of the offices by the Hasmoneans[43] (although this is admittedly disputed).[44] Melchizedek, however, is the paradigmatic priest-king.

11QMelchizedek is important for our theme, however, because it shows the growing interest in imagining a savior figure who was divine in some sense, while clearly subordinate to the Most High, and the attempt to ground such a figure in innovative interpretations of traditional texts. This tendency is also in evidence in some of the texts from the LXX that we have examined, which attribute preexistence to the messianic king. The main witnesses to this development, however, are not based on the traditional messianic texts from Isaiah or the Psalms, but on Daniel's vision of "one like a son of man."[45]

## The Similitudes of Enoch

The most important and extensive portrayal of a figure called "Son of Man" in a Jewish text, apart from Daniel 7, is found in the *Similitudes of*

---

42. F. García Martínez, "Two Messianic Figures in the Qumran Texts," in idem, *Qumranica Minora II* (STDJ 64; Leiden: Brill, 2007), 20.

43. See my essay, "What Was Distinctive about Messianic Expectation at Qumran?" in J. H. Charlesworth, ed., *The Bible and the Dead Sea Scrolls* (Waco, TX: Baylor University Press, 2006), 2.

44. Martin G. Abegg, "The Messiah at Qumran: Are We Still Seeing Double?" *DSD* 2 (1995) 125-44.

45. Émile Puech actually regards the "one like a son of man" and Melchizedek as the same: "Le personage 'comme un fils d'homme' dans la tradition daniélique ne serait-il pas déjà Melkîsédeq lui-meme, exalté dans les cieux," *La croyance des Esséniens*, 557.

*Enoch* (*1 Enoch* 37–71).[46] This section of *1 Enoch* is not attested in the Dead Sea Scrolls, and some doubts exist about its date and its Jewish origin.[47] It is hardly conceivable, however, that a Christian author would have written about a figure called "Son of Man" without identifying him explicitly as Jesus. Neither is it likely that a Jewish author would have used this imagery after the Christian identification of Jesus as Son of Man became current. Moreover, the "Son of Man" passages in the Gospel of Matthew (Matt 19:28 and 25:31), which refer to a "glorious throne," are plausibly thought to depend on the *Similitudes*.[48] Michael Knibb concludes justifiably: "The evidence for the view that the Parables are a Jewish rather than a Christian composition is overwhelming."[49] These considerations also suggest a date prior to 70 CE.[50] The allusion to the Parthians in *1 Enoch* 56:5-7 is usually assumed to imply a date after the Parthian invasion in 40 BCE, while the reference to hot springs that serve the kings and the mighty in 67:5-13 may be prompted by Herod's attempt to cure himself in the waters of Callirhoe.[51] So, while the evidence is less than conclusive, a date in the early or middle first century CE seems likely.[52]

The *Similitudes* consist of three "parables" (chapters 38–44; 45–57; and 58–69).[53] Chapter 37 introduces the entire composition as a "vision of wis-

46. A range of opinions on all aspects of the *Similitudes* can be found in Gabriele Boccaccini, ed., *Enoch and the Messiah Son of Man: Revisiting the Book of Parables* (Grand Rapids: Eerdmans, 2007). See also Christfried Böttrich, "Konturen des 'Menschensohnes' in äthHen 37–71," in Sänger, ed., *Gottessohn und Menschensohn*, 53-90.

47. See the reviews of scholarship by D. W. Suter, "Weighed in the Balance: The Similitudes of Enoch in Recent Discussion," *Religious Studies Review* 7 (1981) 217-21; Sabino Chialà, *Libro delle parabole di Enoc* (Studi Biblici 117; Brescia: Paideia, 1997), 39-51; and James R. Davila, *The Provenance of the Pseudepigrapha* (JSJSup 105; Leiden: Brill, 2005), 132-37.

48. Johannes Theisohn, *Der auserwählte Richter* (Göttingen: Vandenhoeck & Ruprecht, 1975), 149-82; Davila, *The Provenance*, 136.

49. M. A. Knibb, "The Date of the Parables of Enoch: A Critical Review," *NTS* 25 (1979) 350.

50. Knibb, ibid., prefers a date after 70 CE, after the destruction of Qumran.

51. Josephus, *Jewish Antiquities* 17.6.5 §§171-73; *Jewish War* 1.33.5 §§657-58.

52. So also D. W. Suter, *Tradition and Composition in the Parables of Enoch* (SBLDS 47; Missoula, MT: Scholars Press, 1979), 32. C. Böttrich, "Konturen des 'Menschensohnes,'" in D. Sänger, ed., *Gottessohn und Menschensohn* (Neukirchen-Vluyn: Neukirchener, 2004), 58, suggests a date at the end of the first century BCE. Note also the several articles on the date in Boccaccini, ed., *Enoch and the Messiah Son of Man*, 415-96.

53. G. W. E. Nickelsburg, "Discerning the Structure(s) of the Enochic Book of Parables," in Boccaccini, ed., *Enoch and the Messiah Son of Man*, 23-47, and M. A. Knibb, "The

dom." Chapter 38 introduces the first parable by asking where the dwelling of sinners will be when "the Righteous One appears in the presence of the righteous." This is followed in chapter 39 by recollection of the ascent of Enoch on a whirlwind (cf. *1 Enoch* 14). The wisdom, then, is based on what he saw when he ascended to heaven: the dwellings of the righteous (39:5-6) and the dwelling of the Chosen One. He also sees the archangels and the judgment that is to come. Finally, he is shown various cosmological secrets, such as the storehouses of the sun and moon, and is told that he has been shown a parable about the holy ones that live on earth and believe in the name of the Lord of Spirits.

The second parable is "about those who deny the name of the dwelling of the holy ones and the Lord of Spirits." These, we are told, will neither ascend to heaven nor come on earth. The main focus of the parable, however, concerns the judgment day when the Chosen One will sit on his throne of glory. This scene is clearly modeled on Daniel's vision, although the older scene is adapted freely. Enoch sees "one who had a head of days, and his head was like white wool. And with him was another, whose face was like the appearance of a man; and his face was full of graciousness like one of the holy angels" (46:1). Enoch proceeds to inquire about "that Son of Man." Again, he is shown the destiny of the righteous and wicked and various cosmological secrets.

The third parable is said in chapter 58 to be about the righteous and the chosen and their destiny. Again, Enoch is shown cosmological secrets, but again a significant segment of the parable is devoted to the "Son of Man" figure and the judgment (chapters 61–64). The work concludes with two epilogues, one in 70:1-4, which begins in the third person but was evidently expanded by two statements in the first person, and the second in 71:1-17.

It is apparent, then, that the "Son of Man" plays a central role in the *Similitudes,* and this is all the more apparent if we recognize that he is the same as the figure referred to as the Righteous, or the Chosen.[54] The clearest allusion to Daniel's vision is in 46:1, cited above. Again in 47:3, the books are opened before the Head of Days, who is surrounded by his court

---

Structure and Composition of the Book of Parables," ibid., 48-64. Citations from the *Similitudes* follow G. W. E. Nickelsburg and J. C. VanderKam, *1 Enoch: A New Translation* (Minneapolis: Fortress, 2004).

54. J. C. VanderKam, "Righteous One, Messiah, Chosen One, and Son of Man in *1 Enoch* 37–71," in J. H. Charlesworth, ed., *The Messiah* (Minneapolis: Fortress, 1992), 169-91.

in the manner of Daniel 7. The Son of Man is initially introduced as one "whose face was like the appearance of a man." This formulation does not suggest that Son of Man was a well-known title. The figure in question is subsequently referred to as "that son of man" — that is, the figure with human appearance who appeared with the "Head of Days." Despite his human appearance, he is not a man, at least in the usual sense of the word. He is "like one of the holy angels" (46:1). While he is distinguished from other angels (Michael in 60:4-5; 69:14; 71:3; the four archangels in 71:8, 9, 13), his rank is higher than theirs.[55]

The exalted nature of the Son of Man is especially in evidence in 48:2-3: "And in that hour that son of man was named in the presence of the Lord of Spirits, and his name before the Head of Days. Even before the sun and the constellations were created, before the stars of heaven were made, his name was named before the Lord of Spirits." The passage continues in 48:6: "For this (reason) he was chosen and hidden in his presence before the world was created and forever." While the context of *1 Enoch* 48:2 is either eschatological or the time of Enoch's ascent, 48:6 seems to state unequivocally that the Son of Man existed before the world was created.[56] Similarly, in *1 Enoch* 62:7 we read:

> For from the beginning the son of man was hidden,
> and the Most High preserved him in the presence of his might,
> and he revealed him to the chosen.

It is sometimes suggested that preexistence here only means "a project in the mind of God,"[57] or that what was hidden was merely his identity.[58] But it is difficult to see why his identity would need to be hidden if he did not yet exist. The clearest parallel for a preexistent figure in pre-Christian Judaism is the portrayal of wisdom in Proverbs 8:22-31.[59] It would seem

---

55. On the transcendent character of the Son of Man see Böttrich, "Konturen des 'Menschensohnes,'" 76-79; H. S. Kvanvig, "The Son of Man in the Parables," in Boccaccini, ed., *Enoch and the Messiah Son of Man*, 179-215, here 189.

56. Gottfried Schimanowski, *Weisheit und Messias. Die jüdischen Voraussetzungen der urchristlichen Präexistenzchristologie* (Tübingen: Mohr/Siebeck, 1985), 153-94.

57. T. W. Manson, "The Son of Man in Daniel, Enoch and the Gospels," *BJRL* 32 (1949-50) 183-85.

58. VanderKam, "Righteous One," 180.

59. Theisohn, *Der auserwählte Richter*, 126-39. On the preexistence of wisdom see Schimanowski, *Weisheit und Messias*, 13-106. The affinity with wisdom is also emphasized by

that the *Similitudes* here have developed the identity of the Son of Man well beyond anything that we found in Daniel by applying to him language that is elsewhere used of wisdom. But, as we have seen in chapter 3, another significant parallel is found in the LXX translation of Psalm 110, where the king/messiah is begotten "before the Day Star."

The *Similitudes* also develop the role of the Son of Man beyond what was found in Daniel in other significant ways. Besides the association with wisdom, he is said to be "the light of the nations" like the servant in Second Isaiah.[60] Of special interest for our present inquiry are passages that associate the Son of Man with the Davidic messiah, although there is no hint of Davidic lineage.[61] The spirit of wisdom and insight that dwells in him (49:1-4) recalls the messianic oracle in Isaiah 11.[62] Moreover, the kings of the earth are condemned in 48:10 for having denied "the Lord of Spirits and his Anointed One," in language reminiscent of Psalm 2. Again in 52:4, Enoch is told that all that he has seen "will serve the authority of his Anointed One." It is not suggested that the Son of Man is a human descendant of David, but he is the Anointed, or Messiah, of the Lord, who takes over the functions of the Davidic king vis-à-vis the nations. He is also installed on a glorious throne, and takes over the function of eschatological judge (51:3; 55:4; 61:8; 62:2; 69:29). The motif of enthronement is reminiscent of Psalm 110. Here again he functions in a manner reminiscent of the traditional messiah: "and the spirit of righteousness was poured out upon him, and the word of his mouth will slay all the sinners" (62:2).

Up to the end of the third parable there is no hint that the "Son of Man" is anything other than a heavenly being, or that he might actually be identical with the visionary Enoch. Not only is there no suggestion that Enoch is seeing himself, but the fact that the Son of Man was hidden before creation would seem to preclude an identification.[63] Nonetheless, the question of an identification is raised in the epilogues to the *Similitudes*. In

---

Kvanvig, "The Son of Man in the Parables," 204. Wisdom is also associated with the Son of Man in *1 Enoch* 49:1-4 and 51:3.

60. For other allusions to the servant passages in 2 Isaiah, see Theisohn, *Der auserwählte Richter*, 114-26; VanderKam, "Righteous One," 189.

61. S. Schreiber, *Gesalbter und König* (Berlin: de Gruyter, 2000), 338.

62. Theisohn, *Der auserwählte Richter*, 138.

63. Chester, *Messiah and Exaltation*, 64, grants that "Enoch and the Son of Man have been clearly separate figures throughout the work." He suggests that the Son of Man is Enoch's heavenly double, with whom he finally becomes one at the end of the work.

71:14, when Enoch ascends to heaven, he is greeted by an angel: "You are that son of man who was born for righteousness, and righteousness dwells on you, and the righteousness of the Head of Days will not forsake you." It is generally held that this passage identifies Enoch with the Son of Man whom he has seen in his visions. There is sharp disagreement, however, as to whether this identification was intended throughout the *Similitudes*.

A major factor in this debate concerns the interpretation of 70:1-2. As noted already, there are two epilogues to the *Similitudes*.[64] 70:1-2 constitutes a brief statement in the third person. 71:1-17 is narrated in the first person. 70:3-4 is also in the first person. *1 Enoch* 70:1-2 is translated as follows by George Nickelsburg:

> And after this, while he was living, his name was raised into the presence of that son of man and into the presence of the Lord of Spirits from among those who dwell on the earth. He was raised on the chariots of the wind, and his name departed from among them.

This translation, based on the majority reading in the manuscripts, makes a clear distinction between Enoch and the Son of Man. In 1976, Maurice Casey proposed a different understanding of the passage based on one important manuscript, Abbadianus 55 (U), and two late MSS, which lack the word *baxaba* (or *baxabehu* in some MSS), "into the presence," before "that son of man."[65] The text could then be rendered: "The name of that son of man was raised into the presence of the Lord of Spirits," thus permitting an identification of Enoch with the Son of Man.[66] (The translation "to the son of man" is also possible.) Since this proposal relied primarily on one manuscript, which was known for capricious omissions, there was little reason to regard it as anything but a scribal mistake. In the meantime, however, four, and possibly five, other manuscripts have come to light that support the minority reading.[67]

---

64. See Nickelsburg, "Discerning the Structure(s)," 42-43; Knibb, "The Structure and Composition," 62-63.

65. P. M. Casey, "The Use of the Term 'Son of Man' in the Similitudes of Enoch," *JSJ* 7 (1976) 11-29.

66. Compare M. Black, *The Book of Enoch or 1 Enoch* (SVTP 7; Leiden: Brill, 1985), 67, who translates: "The name of a son of man (i.e., Enoch) was raised up to the Lord of Spirits."

67. Daniel C. Olson, "Enoch and the Son of Man in the Epilogue of the Parables," *JSP* 18 (1998) 27-38, here 30-31.

Whether this reading is to be preferred, however, remains doubtful. From a literary point of view, one has the impression that 70:3-4 and chapter 71 are appendices, added after 70:1-2 has brought the *Similitudes* to a satisfactory conclusion, by stating in the third person that Enoch, having received his revelations, was finally taken up into the presence of God.[68] The omission of the word *baxaba* in the minority manuscripts is still most easily explained as a scribal mistake.

The apparent identification of Enoch with the Son of Man in 71:14 is not without problems either. The text survives only in Ethiopic. As is well known, three different Ethiopic expressions are translated into English as "son of man," *walda egwala emmaheyaw*, the expression used in 70:1; *walda be'esi*, which is used in 71:14, and *walda sabe'*. The first of these expressions is the one normally used with reference to Christ in Ethiopic tradition, whereas the expression used in 71:14, *walda be'esi*, is never so used. In the Ethiopic tradition, the Son of Man was assumed to be Christ, and Enoch was not identified with him at all.[69] In fact, it is possible to construe the Ethiopic text of *1 Enoch* 71:14 so that it does not require that the two figures be identified.[70] One can translate "you are a son of man," taking the Ethiopic word *we'etu* as a copula rather than as a demonstrative adjective, and it has been read that way in Ethiopic tradition.[71] This is one of only two passages in the *Similitudes* where "son of man" is used in direct address. The other passage is 60:10, where the Ethiopic is *walda sabe'*, and that passage is universally understood as being in the manner of Ezekiel.

There is, then, some reason to entertain the idea that Enoch is not being identified with the Son of Man in 71:14, at least in the Ethiopic version, but only being told that he is a righteous man. The fact that the language here echoes 46:3 ("this is the son of man [*walda sabe'*] who has righteousness") does not exclude this interpretation, as the *Similitudes* emphasize throughout the correspondence between the heavenly and earthly righ-

68. Nickelsburg, "Discerning the Structure(s)," 43; Knibb, "The Structure and Composition," 63; Böttrich, "Konturen des 'Menschensohnes,'" 85.

69. I am dependent here on oral information supplied by Daniel Assefa, who kindly checked two traditional Ethiopic commentaries, but has not checked all that are extant. See also Olson, "Enoch and the Son of Man," 36.

70. See the discussion in John J. Collins, "The Son of Man in First-Century Judaism," *NTS* 38 (1992) 448-66, here 456-57.

71. Olson, "Enoch and the Son of Man," 36.

teous.[72] (Compare 38:2: "and when the Righteous One appears in the presence of the righteous.") A more weighty objection arises from the fact that Enoch was later identified as a heavenly being, Metatron, in *Sefer Hekaloth,* or *3 Enoch.*[73] This lends plausibility to the view that such an identification is made in *1 Enoch* 71. But while it is attractive to posit a trajectory leading from the *Similitudes* to *Sefer Hekalot,* it is remarkable that the titles applied to the Son of Man in the *Similitudes* (Son of Man, messiah, Righteous One, Chosen One) are almost entirely absent from the later text.[74] Nonetheless, in light of the later development, it is probably simplest to accept that the identification was intended in *1 Enoch* 71:14, or at least that the reference would have been understood that way in a Jewish context, especially if the original Aramaic did not use different expressions for the "Son of Man" as the Ethiopic translator did.

This passage, however, is part of a second epilogue, and stands in contradiction to the more probable reading of the first epilogue in *1 Enoch* 70:1-2. This second epilogue is most readily explained as a secondary addition,[75] which may well have been added specifically to identify Enoch as the Son of Man. This identification, in turn, may have been suggested by the Christian appropriation of this title for Jesus.[76] In the body of the *Similitudes,* however, there is no suggestion at all that the Son of Man ever had an earthly career. He is the heavenly representative and vindicator of

72. The flexibility of the various titles in the *Similitudes* is also noted by Böttrich, "Konturen des 'Menschensohnes,'" 86-87.

73. *3 Enoch* 4:1-10. P. Alexander, "3 (Hebrew Apocalypse of) Enoch," *OTP,* 1:258. On the entire tradition see now A. A. Orlov, *The Enoch-Metatron Tradition* (TSAJ 107; Tübingen: Mohr Siebeck, 2005).

74. Only the title "chosen" is applied to Metatron, once. See James R. Davila, "Melchizedek, the 'Youth', and Jesus," in idem, ed., *The Dead Sea Scrolls as Background to Postbiblical Judaism and Early Christianity: Papers from an International Conference at St. Andrews in 2001* (STDJ 46; Leiden: Brill, 2993), 254; Orlov, *The Enoch-Metatron Tradition,* 85.

75. So also Nickelsburg, "Discerning the Structure(s)," 43; Knibb, "The Structure and Composition," 63; Chialà, *Libro delle parabole,* 287. Kvanvig, "The Son of Man in the Parables," 199, argues that ancient readers would not have regarded the passage as a secondary addition, and so would have assumed that Enoch was identified with the Son of Man throughout. See my rejoinder, "Enoch and the Son of Man: A Response to Sabino Chialà and Helge Kvanvig," in Boccaccini, ed. *Enoch and the Messiah Son of Man,* 216-27 (especially 221-27).

76. Schreiber, *Gesalbter und König,* 342; idem, "Henoch als Menschensohn. Zur prolematischen Schlussidentifikation in den Bilderreden des äthiopischen Henochbuches (äthHen 71,14)," *ZNW* 91 (2000) 1-17. Schreiber attributes only the identification in 71:14 to a (Jewish) redactor.

the righteous on earth, but he is a heavenly figure, whose power and glory compensate for the lack of power of the righteous on earth.

Whether the Son of Man is identified with Enoch or not, the *Similitudes* attest to a remarkable development of messianic tradition, insofar as the word "messiah" is used unambiguously with reference to a heavenly judge. The Son of Man is not called "son of God," but his appearance is "like one of the holy angels," and his enthronement indicates a rank higher than that of any angel. He is not said to rule as king on earth, and in that respect he differs from the traditional Davidic messiah, but he functions as king by exercising judgment. In *1 Enoch* 48:5 we are told that "all who dwell on the earth will fall down and worship before him," performing *proskynesis* as had been done before Persian kings and Alexander the Great. Whether this obeisance indicates divinity, or what degree of divinity, might be debated. The same verse continues to say that "they will glorify and bless and sing hymns to the Lord of Spirits," not, at least explicitly, to the Son of Man. But he sits like the Lord on a throne of glory, and this surely bespeaks divine status in some sense, although it does not rule out the possibility that the figure in question is an exalted human being.[77]

### 4 Ezra 13

Another major witness to the interpretation, or adaptation, of the Danielic "Son of Man" in ancient Judaism is found in *4 Ezra,* an apocalypse written at the end of the first century CE. The apocalypse contains three dialogues and four visions.[78] In the third vision (chapter 13) Ezra reports:

> Then after seven days I had a dream in the night. I saw a wind rising from the sea that stirred up all its waves. As I kept looking, that wind

---

77. On traditions of enthronement see J. J. Collins, "A Throne in the Heavens: Apotheosis in pre-Christian Judaism," in J. J. Collins and M. Fishbane, eds. *Death, Ecstasy, and Otherworldly Journeys* (Albany: State University of New York, 1995), 41-58. In addition to the "self-exaltation" hymn from Qumran (4Q491 11) note the enthronement of Moses in Ezekiel the Tragedian. See further D. D. Hannah, "The Divine Throne and Heavenly Mediators in Revelation and the Similitudes of Enoch," *ZNW* 94 (2003) 68-96.

78. For introductory matters see M. E. Stone, *Fourth Ezra: A Commentary on the Book of Fourth Ezra* (Hermeneia; Minneapolis: Fortress, 1990), 1-35; J. J. Collins, *The Apocalyptic Imagination* (2nd ed.; Grand Rapids: Eerdmans, 1998), 195-210.

brought up out of the depths of the sea something resembling a man and that man was flying with the clouds of heaven. . . .

The original language was certainly Semitic, but the composition survives only in translations, of which the Latin and Syriac are most important. The statement "that wind brought up out of the depths of the sea something resembling a man" is missing from the Latin, apparently because of homoioteleuton. Most scholars assume that the missing passage read *homo* for "man" since this is what the Latin uses elsewhere in the chapter. The Syriac, however, reads איך דמותא דברנשא, and this suggests that the original may have read "son of man." It can be argued that the author used the longer phrase initially and the shorter phrase subsequently. Even if *4 Ezra* does not use the expression "Son of Man," however, or use it as a title, it is clearly adapting and reworking Daniel's vision.

There is a further textual problem regarding the relation of the wind and the man. The Ethiopic version reads "this wind came out of the sea in the resemblance of a man." It has been argued that this is the *lectio difficilior,* and should be regarded as a witness to the original text. "Wind" could be understood as a misreading of "spirit" (רוח) in the original Hebrew.[79] This proposal is doubtful, however. Most scholars restore the Latin on the basis of the Syriac, so that the wind is said to bring the man up.

The image of the man flying with the clouds of heaven is a clear allusion to Daniel 7. There is also an explicit reference to Daniel 7 in the preceding chapter, *4 Ezra* 12, where the interpreting angel tells Ezra explicitly: "The eagle you observed coming up out of the sea is the fourth kingdom that appeared in a vision to Daniel your brother. But it was not interpreted to him in the same way that I now interpret it to you" (*4 Ezra* 12:11). Moreover, the interpretation in chapter 13 provides a clear allusion to Daniel 2, when it says that the mountain on which the man takes his stand was "carved out without hands." This detail was not mentioned in the vision.

The allusions to Daniel in *4 Ezra* 13 are woven together with echoes of other sources. Anyone who hears the voice of the man from the sea melts like wax before a fire. (Compare the effect of the theophany in Mic 1:4, for the motif of melting like wax.) Most importantly, a great host comes to make war on the man. He carves out a mountain for himself and takes his

---

79. H. S. Kvanvig, *Roots of Apocalyptic* (Neukirchen-Vluyn: Neukirchener Verlag, 1988), 517-20.

stand upon it. Then he destroys the onrushing multitude with the breath of his lips. The onslaught of the multitude recalls Psalm 2. The mountain is Zion, the holy mountain (Ps 2:6). The breath of his lips is the weapon of the messianic king in Isa 11:4. Taken together, these allusions suggest that the man from the sea has taken on the role traditionally ascribed to the messianic king. This impression is strengthened in the interpretation that follows, where the man is identified, in the Latin and Syriac versions, as "my son" (13:32, 37).[80] The messiah is also called "my son" in *4 Ezra* 7:28.[81] Michael Stone has argued that the Greek original in these passages read παῖς rather than υἱός because of variations in some of the versions, and suggested that the Hebrew original was "servant" rather than "son."[82] But even if the Greek did read παῖς, the word can also mean child or son — compare Wis 2:13, 16, where the righteous man claims to be παῖς of God and boasts that God is his father. In *4 Ezra* 13, in any case, the context strongly suggests an allusion to Psalm 2, so the meaning is "son" rather than "servant."[83]

Stone has also argued that "even if the man in the dream was the traditional 'Son of Man,' the author had to interpret that figure to his readers. Moreover, the author has shorn the Son of Man of all his particular characteristics in the interpretation and treated him as a symbol. This would be inconceivable if the Son of Man concept was readily recognizable to him and his readers."[84] Presumably he is referring to the old composite concept of the Primordial Man of the *religionsgeschichtliche Schule*. It can hardly be doubted, however, that an allusion to Dan 7:13 was intended. The reinterpretation of this figure is apparent already in Ezra's vision, where he carves out a mountain and takes his stand on it. The reinterpretation involves associating motifs traditionally attached to the Davidic messiah with the transcendent figure who comes on the clouds.[85]

---

80. See further J. J. Collins, *The Scepter and the Star*, 184-85.

81. Schreiber, *Gesalbter und König*, 349, raises the possibility of Christian tampering with the text, but there is little other evidence for this in *4 Ezra*.

82. Stone, *Fourth Ezra*, 207-13 ("Excursus on the Redeemer Figure").

83. Cf. M. Knibb and R. J. Coggins, *The First and Second Books of Esdras* (Cambridge Bible Commentary; Cambridge: Cambridge University, 1979), on 7:28.

84. Stone, "The Question of the Messiah in 4 Ezra," in J. Neusner, W. S. Green, and E. Frerichs, eds., *Judaisms and Their Messiahs* (Cambridge: Cambridge University Press, 1987), 209-24, here 213.

85. So also Ulrich B. Müller, *Messias und Menschensohn in jüdischen Apokalypsen und in*

Like the *Similitudes of Enoch, 4 Ezra* 13 is quite free in its adaptation of Daniel's vision. Whereas in Daniel the sea was the source of hostile monsters, here it is the man who rises from the sea. Apparently the sea has become an area of mystery rather than a well of chaos.[86] Nonetheless, the fact that the vision juxtaposes the sea with the man riding on the clouds shows the literary influence of Daniel 7.

The most important departure from Daniel 7, however, is the assimilation of the "Son of Man" to the traditional, Davidic messiah. Unlike the *Similitudes of Enoch, 4 Ezra* has a developed notion of a Davidic messiah. In 7:28-29 he is called "my son the messiah." He is "revealed with those who are with him," a formulation that seems to imply preexistence. After a four-hundred-year reign, however, the messiah dies, and the world reverts to seven days of primeval silence, followed by the resurrection. The messiah, then, is human, despite his preexistence. The heavenly character of the "Son of Man," as we have seen it in Daniel and the *Similitudes,* is significantly qualified here. Nonetheless, the understanding of the messiah is also modified by the correlation with the "Son of Man." While the messiah is said to come from the line of David in 12:32, this is "a traditional element and not at all central to the concepts of the book."[87] Despite his eventual death, the messiah is a preexistent, transcendent figure, whom the Most High has been keeping for many ages.

### Common Assumptions

The relationship between *4 Ezra* 13 and the *Similitudes of Enoch* is complex. The "man from the sea" is very different from the Enochic Son of Man.

---

*der Offenbarung des Johannes* (Gütersloh: Mohn, 1972), 120-22; Schreiber, *Gesalbter und König,* 362.

86. Kvanvig, *Roots of Apocalyptic,* 531, argues that the sea must have the same meaning in both Daniel and *4 Ezra,* and identifies it with Apsu, the subterranean water, in both cases. For a critique of Kvanvig's learned and complex proposal see my essay, "Genre, Ideology and Social Movements in Jewish Apocalypticism," in J. J. Collins and J. H. Charlesworth, eds., *Mysteries and Revelations: Apocalyptic Studies since the Uppsala Colloquium* (JSPSup 9; Sheffield: Sheffield Academic Press, 1991), 25-32 ("Appendix: A New Proposal on Apocalyptic Origins").

87. M. E. Stone, *Features of the Eschatology of Fourth Ezra* (Atlanta: Scholars Press, 1989), 131-32; compare Schreiber, *Gesalbter und König,* 351.

The one is a warrior, concerned with the restoration of Israel. The other is a judge enthroned in heaven, who does not appear on earth at all. Nonetheless, the two texts share some common assumptions about the interpretation of the "one like a son of man" in Daniel 7. Both assume that the figure in Daniel is an individual, not a collective symbol. Both identify him with the messiah, and describe his role in terms usually applied to the Davidic messiah, although they understand his role in different ways. Both the Enochic Son of Man and the man from the sea are preexistent beings of heavenly origin. Both appropriate imagery that was traditionally reserved for God: the Enochic Son of Man sits on the throne of glory and the figure in *4 Ezra* is portrayed in terms of the theophany of the divine warrior. This figure takes a more active role in the destruction of the wicked than was the case in the book of Daniel.

There is no allusion to the *Similitudes* in *4 Ezra,* and no reason to posit literary influence between them. Precisely for that reason, they are independent witnesses to common assumptions about the meaning of Daniel 7 in first-century Judaism. Very similar assumptions underlie the use of Son of Man imagery derived from Daniel in the Gospels.[88]

## Conclusion

In this discussion I have restricted my attention to the major texts that either envision the messiah as son of God or speak of a heavenly deliverer. William Horbury has cast a wider net, including passages where, in his view, "messianic significance attaches to words and expressions for 'man' in interpretation of passages other than Daniel 7."[89] Not all of these passages are relevant to my theme. The LXX translation of Balaam's oracle speaks of a man who will rule many nations (Num 24:7), and Philo also uses *anthrōpos* in a messianic context.[90] But while "man" may be a messi-

88. See further my essay, "The Son of Man in First-Century Judaism," *NTS* 38 (1992) 448-66. Compare T. B. Slater, "One like a Son of Man in First-Century-CE Judaism," *NTS* 41 (1995) 183-98.

89. William Horbury, "The Messianic Associations of 'The Son of Man,'" in idem, *Messianism among Jews and Christians* (London and New York: T&T Clark, 2003), 125-55, here 144.

90. Philo, *On the Life of Moses* 1.290; *On Rewards and Punishments* 95. Horbury, "The Messianic Associations," 145.

anic term in these cases, it does not clearly indicate divinity or heavenly origin. In contrast, the mysterious "man from heaven" in *Sibylline Oracles* 5:414, who wields a scepter and restores Jerusalem, would seem to be a heavenly deliverer analogous to the Son of Man, whether the terminology is chosen to make that association or not. The Sibyl also refers to "a king sent from God" (108), and "an exceptional man from the sky" (256).[91] If these references are all to the same figure, he might reasonably be called a heavenly messiah. Whether he should be related to traditions about the Son of Man is more difficult to say. If the Sibyl is influenced by the Daniel tradition, she has thoroughly recast the idiom, so the allusion is uncertain. We also read of "a great king" sent from heaven in the *Oracle of Hystaspes,* and some scholars have defended the authenticity of that oracle as a pagan composition of Iranian background in the Hellenistic age.[92] There is no consensus, however, on the provenance of the *Oracle of Hystaspes,* and the suspicion remains that Lactantius, who cites it, may have imported Christian beliefs into it. The texts we have reviewed, however, enable us to draw some conclusions about the association of messiah and divinity around the turn of the era. On the one hand, there is some evidence, not very extensive but certainly not negligible, for the use of "son of God" as a messianic title, not only in the "Son of God" text, but also in the *Florilegium* from Qumran and in *4 Ezra.* This title can be viewed as honorific, in the manner of the divine titles of Hellenistic kings. There are no Jewish stories about the miraculous birth of the messiah that might be compared with those about Alexander and Augustus (unless we make dubious assumptions about the implications of the word *parthenos* in the LXX of Isa 7:14). Even if God is said to "beget" the messiah in 1QSa, it is not at all clear how this was supposed to take place. On the other hand, we find a growing tendency in this period to conceive of the messiah as a preexistent being of heavenly origin (or, conversely, to speak of a heavenly, angelic deliverer as messiah). Pre-existence seems to be attributed to the Davidic messiah in the LXX (at least in Psalm 110) and again in *4 Ezra.* In 11QMelchizedek an *elohim* exercises some of the traditional functions of the messiah, and in

---

91. J. J. Collins, "Sibylline Oracles," *OTP,* 1:390-405. *The Sibylline Oracles* 5 dates to the early 2nd century CE.

92. Lactantius, *Epitome of the Divine Institutes* 7.17. The pagan origin of the oracle is defended by John R. Hinnells, "The Zoroastrian Doctrine of Salvation in the Roman World," in E. J. Sharpe and J. R. Hinnells, eds., *Man and His Salvation: Studies in Memory of S. G. F. Brandon* (Manchester: Manchester University Press, 1973), 125-48.

the *Similitudes of Enoch* a heavenly figure who resembles one of the holy angels is called "messiah." In light of this fluidity, it is plausible that the LXX of Isa 9:6 should be understood to refer to the future king as an "angel" rather than simply as a messenger.

There was evidently no orthodoxy, and only limited consistency, in the ways in which the messiah might be imagined. Many of the references to the shoot of David or prince of the congregation in the Dead Sea Scrolls say nothing to indicate supernatural status. But there were clear biblical precedents for speaking of the messiah as God or son of God, and there was plenty of speculation about heavenly deliverers. There was also a tendency to conflate different conceptions of future rulers, as we see especially in the development of the Son of Man tradition.[93] In the context of first-century-CE Judaism, it is not surprising or anomalous that divine status should be attributed to someone who was believed by his followers to be the messiah. At the same time, it should be noted that neither the king in ancient Judah nor the messiah in most instances was the object of worship. There is, however, an important exception in the case of the Son of Man in the *Similitudes of Enoch,* before whom all who dwell on earth are said to perform *proskynesis* by falling down and "worshipping" before him (*1 Enoch* 48:5), but this is distinguished from the honors paid to the Lord of Spirits. Whether *proskynesis* should be deemed to constitute "worship" is a matter of definition, on which there were different opinions already in antiquity. At the least, it acknowledges the superior status and power of the figure who is honored, in this case the Messiah, Son of Man.

93. See further Müller, *Messias und Menschensohn;* Klaus Koch, "Messias und Menschensohn," in idem, *Vor der Wende der Zeiten. Beiträge zur apokalyptischen Literatur* (Neukirchen-Vluyn: Neukirchener Verlag, 1996), 235-66.

# 5. Jesus as Messiah and Son of God in the Letters of Paul

In 1901 William Wrede famously argued that the tradition about the earthly activities of Jesus was unmessianic. It was only after his resurrection that his followers conceived the idea that he was the messiah.[1] In any case, it is clear that the identification of Jesus as the messiah was established very soon after his death, if not before.

## 1 Thessalonians

In Paul's earliest letter, which we know as his first letter to the Thessalonians, he uses the term "Christ" (Χριστός) with reference to Jesus ten times.[2] In none of these instances does he explain to his audience what the expression signifies. It is likely that Paul explained it to the Thessalonians when he proclaimed the gospel to them during his stay in their city.[3] The fact that the term "Christ" appears to be more of a personal name in this letter than a title is probably due to the Gentile character of his audience

---

1. William Wrede, *The Messianic Secret* (Cambridge, UK: J. Clarke, 1971; reprinted, Greenwood, SC: Attic Press; 1st German ed. 1901), 209-43.

2. 1 Thess 1:1, 3; 2:7, 14; 3:2; 4:16; 5:9, 18, 23, 28. Gerd Lüdemann dates this letter to ca. 41 CE; *Paul, Apostle to the Gentiles: Studies in Chronology* (Philadelphia: Fortress, 1984; German 1980), 262. Abraham J. Malherbe dates it to 50 CE; *The Letters to the Thessalonians* (AB 32B; New York: Doubleday, 2000), 73.

3. Paul describes his visit and his proclamation of the gospel in 1:4; 2:1-13.

and to the fact that the Greek term χριστός was "never related to persons outside the Septuagint, the New Testament and writings dependent on them."[4] No doubt Paul received the practice of calling Jesus "Christ" from Greek-speaking, probably Jewish, followers of Jesus, who were active members of the movement before him. They apparently used the term to signify that Jesus was God's anointed, in other words, the messiah of Israel. Paul's continuing use of the term as an epithet for Jesus thus reflects very early tradition, which he passed on to the Thessalonians. Even though the term "Christ" appears to be used as a personal name, it can be and probably was also understood as an epithet or title signifying authority.[5] It also served to make the point that there is only one anointed person of the last days, only one messiah.[6]

As was pointed out in chapters 1 and 2 above, the king of Israel was explicitly presented as the "son of God" in Psalm 2, Psalm 89, and in 2 Samuel 7.[7] Although Paul does not cite these scriptures in 1 Thessalonians, it is likely that his portrayal of Jesus as the son of God is informed, at least in part, by the use of this epithet for the king of Israel.[8] We have also seen that the designation of the messiah of Israel as son of God is attested in the Dead Sea Scrolls. This usage suggests that Psalm 2 and other biblical texts were being read messianically in Paul's time.

4. Walter Grundmann, "χρίω κτλ., A. General Usage," *TDNT,* 9 (1974), 495. Günther Zuntz claimed that Gentiles finding the phrase "Jesus Christ" in the opening titular sentence of Mark would take it to mean "Jesus-ointment" or perhaps "Jesus the painted/made up one." Or they might infer that χριστοῦ was a mistake and that χρηστοῦ was meant. The phrase would then mean "Jesus (presumably a slave of Semitic origin who was given a new name, as was customary) Chrestos (i.e., good or serviceable). See Günther Zuntz, "Ein Heide las das Markusevangelium," in Hubert Cancik, ed., *Markus-Philologie. Historische, literargeschichtliche und stilistische Untersuchungen zum zweiten Evangelium* (WUNT 33; Tübingen: Mohr Siebeck, 1984), 205-22, especially 205. Andrew Chester suggests that Gentiles in the cities of the Roman empire would have understood χριστός to mean "smeared with oil" (*Messiah and Exaltation: Jewish Messianic and Visionary Traditions and New Testament Christology* [WUNT 207; Tübingen: Mohr Siebeck, 2007], 383).

5. Chester concluded that the use of the term signifies that Paul took Jesus' messianic status for granted; "The Christ of Paul," in Markus Bockmuehl and James Carleton Paget, eds., *Redemption and Resistance: The Messianic Hopes of Jews and Christians in Antiquity* (London/New York: T&T Clark, 2007), 109-21, especially 111.

6. Cf. Grundmann, "χρίω κτλ., III. Χριστός in Paul's Epistles," 540-43.

7. Pss 2:7; 89:26-27; 2 Sam 7:14.

8. There may be an allusion to 2 Sam 7:14 in 2 Cor 6:18. That text, however, speaks about the faithful as potential sons and daughters of God, inspired (also) by Isa 43:6.

Paul speaks of Jesus as the son of God in only one place in 1 Thessalonians, in the emphatically placed ending of the thanksgiving following the opening address. In that context he compliments his audience by remarking that they, collectively, have become an example (τύπος) to all the believers in Macedonia and Achaia. Their exemplary behavior includes turning to God from idols "and awaiting his son from the heavens, whom he raised from the dead, Jesus who delivers us from the wrath that is coming" (1 Thess 1:10). That Jesus will come from heaven reflects the view that he was exalted to heaven when God raised him from the dead.[9]

## The Synoptic Sayings Source (Q) and Paul

The expectation of Jesus from heaven is also reflected in other early Christian traditions. Although the coming of Jesus from heaven is not explicitly mentioned in the critical reconstruction of the Synoptic Sayings Source (Q), it is implied in several sayings:

> "But know this: If the householder had known in which watch the robber was coming, he would not have allowed his house to be dug through. You also must be ready, for the Son of Man is coming at an hour you do not expect."[10]

> "If they say to you: 'Look, he is in the wilderness,' do not go out; 'look, he is indoors,' do not follow. For as the lightning streaks from the East and flashes as far as the West, so will the Son of Man be on his day."[11]

> "For as in those days they were eating and drinking, marrying and giving in marriage, until the day Noah entered the ark and the flood came and took them all, so will it be also on the day the Son of Man is revealed."[12]

---

9. Cf. Malherbe, *The Letters to the Thessalonians,* 121; Ernest Best, *A Commentary on the First and Second Epistles to the Thessalonians* (Black's New Testament Commentaries; London: Adam & Charles Black, 1972), 83.

10. Q 12:39-40; translation (modified) from James M. Robinson, Paul Hoffmann, and John S. Kloppenborg, eds., *The Critical Edition of Q* (Hermeneia; Minneapolis: Fortress; Leuven: Peeters, 2000), 360, 364.

11. Q 17:23-24; translation (modified) from ibid., 502, 506.

12. Q 17:27, 30; translation (modified) from ibid., 514, 518.

It is likely that Paul knew about the identification of Jesus with the one like a son of man in Daniel 7. This identification was probably made quite early and was one of several ways in which the conviction was expressed that God had vindicated Jesus after his death. If Paul had not already heard about this interpretation, he could well have learned about it in his fifteen-day visit with Peter three years after he had been called to be apostle to the Gentiles (Gal 1:18).

But instead of using the epithet "Son of Man" for the exalted Jesus with reference to his coming from heaven, Paul employed the idea of Jesus as the son of God. Again, the reason is probably that "the Son of Man" is translation-Greek, based on a Semitic idiom, and would not have been immediately intelligible to his Gentile audience.

In the sayings from Q cited above, it is highly likely that Jesus is identified with the one like a son of man in Dan 7:13. In the context of Daniel 7, the apparently human figure is presented to the Ancient of Days, who is seated on a throne in a heavenly scene. Furthermore, the one like a son of man is given "dominion, and glory and kingship, that all peoples, nations, and languages should serve him."[13] In the application of this scene to Jesus, the presentation of the human-like figure to God in heaven is interpreted as Jesus' resurrection and exaltation. Since he was not granted universal kingship in a generally observable way during his earthly lifetime, his installation as king of the whole earth is envisaged as becoming manifestly effective in the future, upon his "coming" or at his "revelation" to all humanity. This web of interrelationships suggests that "son of God" and "Son of Man" in early Christian tradition are both equivalent to "messiah of Israel" or "Christ."[14]

As noted earlier, Paul characterizes Jesus, the son of God, as the one "who delivers us from the wrath that is coming." The wrath in question here is the manifestation of the anger and judgment of God upon the Gentiles in some formulations and upon all unrepentant sinners in others. The expectation of this wrath in the last days is widespread in Second Temple Jewish texts.[15]

Paul does not explain in this context *how* Jesus would rescue his fol-

13. Dan 7:14; NRSV translation.
14. Adela Yarbro Collins, "The Influence of Daniel on the New Testament," in John J. Collins, *Daniel* (Hermeneia; Minneapolis: Fortress, 1993), 90-105.
15. Erik Sjöberg and Gustav Stählin, "ὀργὴ κτλ., D. The Wrath of God in Later Judaism," *TDNT*, 5 (1967), 414-15.

lowers from the wrath that is coming. One way in which the claim could be understood is that the exalted Jesus will serve as a witness at the last judgment.[16] This idea is reflected in another saying from the Synoptic Sayings Source:

> "Everyone who acknowledges me before human beings, the Son of Man will also acknowledge him before the angels of God. But whoever denies me before human beings will be denied before the angels of God."[17]

### Deliverance from Wrath in 1 Thessalonians

Paul does, however, give some clues later in this letter about the deliverance in question. In the prayer that concludes the account of his interaction with the Thessalonians, Paul asks that God strengthen their hearts in holiness so that they may be blameless before the Father "at the coming of our Lord Jesus with all his holy ones."[18] Immediately thereafter, he gives them ethical instruction so that they may fulfill God's will for their sanctification (1 Thess 4:3-12). So compliance with ethical standards is a factor in maintaining hope for deliverance through Christ.

In chapter 5, Paul refers to "the day of the Lord" as a time when sudden destruction will come upon those "who are of night or of darkness," that is, upon the wicked (1 Thess 5:3-5). In contrast, God has not destined those who are of the day or of light for wrath but for obtaining salvation "through our Lord Jesus Christ, who died for us in order that, whether we wake or sleep, we might live together with him" (1 Thess 5:9-10). Chapters 4 and 5 thus imply that it is the death of Jesus that has enabled the Gentiles to serve the living and true God and to live ethically. It is God's faithfulness to them, Christ's faithfulness, and their faithfulness to God and Christ that will then enable Christ to deliver them from the imminent wrath at the time of his coming. He will do so by raising the faithful dead and transforming the faithful living so that they can be with the Lord forever (1 Thess 4:15-17).

---

16. Paul speaks sometimes of God as judge (Rom 14:10) and sometimes of Christ as judge (2 Cor 5:10); Victor Paul Furnish, *II Corinthians* (AB 32A; Garden City, NY: Doubleday, 1984), 275.

17. Q 12:8-9; cf. Robinson et al., *The Critical Edition of Q*, 302, 304.

18. 1 Thess 3:13. The "holy ones" here are probably angels; see Malherbe, *The Letters to the Thessalonians*, 214.

## Galatians

Galatians is another early letter of Paul; at least it is earlier than Romans.[19] In this letter Paul uses the term "Christ" (Χριστός) to refer to Jesus 38 times. In all these cases, the expression is unexplained and could be taken as a proper name.[20] It is likely, however, that in Galatia, as in Thessalonica, Paul had proclaimed and explained Jesus' messiahship.

Paul refers to Jesus as the son of God in four passages in Galatians. The first occurs in Paul's account of how and why he changed from being a persecutor of the eschatological community founded by God to being God's apostle to the Gentiles. In that context, he says that God was pleased "to reveal his son to me."[21] Paul gives no details. It is likely, however, that the event referred to here is identical with the one that he describes as the last appearance of the resurrected Christ in 1 Corinthians 15, the one to Paul himself (1 Cor 15:8). If that inference is correct, the experience probably involved seeing Jesus in glory and exalted to heaven. If so, the event implies, as does 1 Thessalonians, that Jesus, as "son of God," is one who has been exalted to heaven. Given the frequent designation of Jesus as "Christ" in both letters, it is likely that here, too, "son of God" is equivalent to "messiah."

The second application of the phrase "son of God" to Jesus in Galatians occurs in a passage in which Paul articulates his own position in relation to the conflict at Antioch:[22]

For I died through the law to the law, in order that I might live to God.[23] I have been crucified with Christ; so I live, no longer I, but Christ lives in me; the life I now live in the flesh, I live by faith, that is, by the faith of the son of God, who loved me and gave himself for me. (Gal 2:19-20)[24]

19. Hans Dieter Betz, *Galatians* (Hermeneia; Philadelphia: Fortress, 1979), 11.

20. In three cases, the article is used with Χριστός. In all three instances, the term is in the genitive case; it has the article because the related noun has an article. See Grundmann, "χρίω κτλ., III. Χριστός in Paul's Epistles," 540.

21. Gal 1:16; ἐν ἐμοί is parallel to ἐν τοῖς ἔθνεσιν. Since the latter phrase should be translated "to the Gentiles," the former should be translated "to me" rather than "in me." See John Bligh, *Galatians in Greek: A Structural Analysis of St. Paul's Epistle to the Galatians with Notes on the Greek* (Detroit: University of Detroit, 1966), 94.

22. Betz, *Galatians*, 113-14, 121.

23. Although neither occurrence of νόμος in this verse has the article, it is surely the Mosaic law that is meant; W. Gutbrod, "νόμος κτλ., D. The Law in the New Testament," *TDNT*, 4 (1967), 1070.

24. On the translation of τῇ τοῦ υἱοῦ τοῦ θεοῦ with "by the faith of the son of God," see

Here the expression "son of God" is associated with the effective and vicarious death of Jesus. As we have noted, the same association is made in 1 Thessalonians. Jesus, the son of God, "who delivers us from the wrath that is coming," is also the one "who died for us in order that, whether we wake or sleep, we might live together with him."[25] Both letters imply that Jesus' death on behalf of others is an important aspect of his messiahship.

The third instance occurs in the argument based on the legal point that an heir is no better than a slave until he comes of age:[26]

> So also is the case with us; when we were minors, we were enslaved under the elements of the world; but when the fullness of time came, God sent his son, born of woman, born under the law, in order that he might redeem those under the law, so that we might receive adoption. (Gal 4:3-5)

The parallel between "enslaved under the elements of the world" and "born under the law" suggests an equivalence between the states of Jews and Gentiles prior to the sending of the son of God. The law was ordered (by God) through angels (Gal 3:19). The gods of the Gentiles are analogous intermediary beings from Paul's point of view, perhaps demons.[27] The statement that "God sent his son" in this context does not necessarily imply that Jesus existed as some kind of heavenly or divine being before his birth as a human being. The Jewish scriptures often refer to God "sending" a prophet.[28]

A new element here in comparison with 1 Thessalonians is that the son of God is sent in order to make others sons (and daughters) of God as well. In an earlier passage of Galatians, Paul had argued as follows:

---

Richard B. Hays, *The Faith of Jesus Christ: The Narrative Substructure of Galatians 3:1–4:11* (2nd ed.; Grand Rapids: Eerdmans; Dearborn, MI: Dove Booksellers, 2002; 1st ed. 1983), 153-55.

25. 1 Thess 1:10; 5:10. See also 2 Cor 5:14-15.

26. Gal 4:1-7; Betz, *Galatians*, 202.

27. Cf. 1 Cor 10:20.

28. Judg 6:8; Jer 7:25; Ezek 3:5-6; the verb in the LXX of all three passages is the same as in Gal 4:4, ἐξαποστέλλω. See also Christopher M. Tuckett, *Christology and the New Testament: Jesus and His Earliest Followers* (Louisville: Westminster John Knox, 2001), 51, 67, n. 21. For the view that the sending is of the preexistent son of God into the world, see Martin Hengel, *The Son of God: The Origin of Christology and the History of Jewish-Hellenistic Religion* (Philadelphia: Fortress, 1976; German ed. 1975), 10-11; Chester, *Messiah and Exaltation*, 389-90.

Now that faith has come, we are no longer under a guardian. For in Christ Jesus you are all sons of God, through faith. (Gal 3:25-26)[29]

In Gal 4:5 that point is elaborated by specifying that God's son "redeems (ἐξαγοράζειν)" people so that they may become sons of God.[30] This affirmation is analogous to the teaching of 1 Thessalonians that Christ died for others in order that through him God might transform the living and raise the dead for eternal life. The argument of Galatians focuses more on the present: the Galatians do not need to be circumcised because they are already sons of Abraham and sons of God. 1 Thessalonians focuses on the future: those who are alive when Christ comes will not have an advantage over those who have died in Christ. Being "sons (and daughters) of God" has implications both for the present and the future. But the depiction of the future in 1 Thessalonians implies that, ultimately, being a son or daughter of God means being granted eternal life. As Jesus was raised from the dead and made immortal, so also will his followers be raised as or transformed into heavenly beings who will live forever.

## The Corinthian Correspondence

### 1 Corinthians

A letter perhaps written around the same time as Galatians, but to a very different set of circumstances, is the one we know as the First Letter to the Corinthians. As in 1 Thessalonians and Galatians, the term "Christ" is used without explanation.[31] A few passages, however, indicate that the term means "messiah" and that the audience of this letter had been instructed about the messianic tradition. Near the end of the thanksgiving, Paul expresses confidence that the Corinthians are:

not lacking in any spiritual gift as you wait for the revealing of our Lord Jesus Christ. (1 Cor 1:7)

---

29. On the translation, see Hays, *The Faith of Jesus Christ,* 155-56.

30. The theme of sonship is elaborated in Gal 4:6-7.

31. The term "Christ" (χριστός) is used at least 63 times in 1 Corinthians and perhaps 65 times, depending on the resolution of the textual problems in 10:9 and 16:23.

As we have seen, the Synoptic Sayings Source (Q) spoke about the "coming" or the "revealing" of the Son of Man. That the "revealing of our Lord Jesus Christ" here also refers to the coming of the risen Jesus at the end is made clear by the following verse:

> [God] will also strengthen you until the end [so that you will be] blameless on the day of our Lord Jesus Christ. (1 Cor 1:8)[32]

Recall that a similar expectation was expressed in 1 Thessalonians, that God would strengthen the hearts of Paul's audience in holiness so that they might be blameless before the Father "at the coming of our Lord Jesus with all his holy ones."[33] The "day of our Lord Jesus Christ" brings the judgment,[34] but it is also the day on which the risen Jesus, as messiah, is manifested to all.

Christ is portrayed as God's son only twice in 1 Corinthians, once in chapter 1 and once in chapter 15, the two chapters in which the term "Christ" appears most frequently. The first instance follows immediately upon the two verses that speak about Christ being revealed and "the day of our Lord Jesus Christ":

> God is faithful, by whom you were called into fellowship with his son, Jesus Christ our Lord. (1 Cor 1:9)

The context suggests that this fellowship with God's son, if it continues, will protect those who have it so that they will be acquitted in the judgment that is coming. As Paul put it in 1 Thessalonians, God's son delivers us from the wrath that is coming (1 Thess 1:10).

The fifteenth chapter of 1 Corinthians argues for the reality of the (general) resurrection of the dead in part by emphasizing the reality of the resurrection of Jesus. If Christ has not been raised:

> we are even found to be misrepresenting God, because we testified in contradiction to God that he raised Christ, whom he did not raise if indeed the dead are not raised. (1 Cor 15:15)

32. On God as the strengthener here, see Hans Conzelmann, *1 Corinthians* (Hermeneia; Philadelphia: Fortress, 1975; 1st German ed. 1969), 28.

33. 1 Thess 3:13; the vocabulary is synonymous but varied. "Strengthen" in 1 Cor 1:8 is βεβαιόω; in 1 Thess 3:13 στηρίζω. "Blameless" is ἀνέγκλητος in the Corinthians passage and ἄμεμπτος in the Thessalonians passage.

34. Conzelmann, *1 Corinthians*, 28.

Later in the chapter, Paul puts the general resurrection in the context of the events of the end:

> But each in [his] own order: Christ as first fruits, then those who belong to Christ at his coming, then the end, when he hands over the kingdom to God and Father, when he brings to an end every rule and every authority and power. For he must reign until "he puts all the enemies under his feet." As the last enemy, death will be abolished. For "he has put all things in subjection under his feet." But when it says that all things have been subjected, it is clear that he who subjected all things to him is excepted. So when all things are subjected to him, then the son himself will also be subjected to the one who subjected all things to him, in order that God may be all in all. (1 Cor 15:23-28)

The first thing to be noted about this passage is its messianic interpretation and application of two psalms.[35] The two psalms alluded to here are Psalm 110 and Psalm 8.[36] As was shown in chapter 1 above, Psalm 110 is a royal psalm that attributes divinity to the king. In 1 Corinthians 15, Paul conflates the first verse of Psalm 110 with Ps 8:6.[37] Psalm 8 is a hymn praising God for exalting humanity. Its references to "man" and "the son of man" are open to being interpreted as a king for two reasons. First, the passage in the first chapter of Genesis that says that God created "man" in his "image and likeness" draws upon royal ideology.[38] Second, once the human-like figure of Daniel 7 was identified with Jesus as messiah, the phrase "son of man" could take on royal connotations in relation to Jesus.

Another thing to notice about this passage is that the depiction of "ev-

---

35. On this procedure as characteristic of early reflection on the person and work of Jesus, see Donald Juel, *Messianic Exegesis: Christological Interpretation of the Old Testament in Early Christianity* (Philadelphia: Fortress, 1988).

36. Ps 109:1 and Ps 8:7 LXX.

37. The same portions of these psalms are also conflated in Mark 12:36; Matt 22:44; Eph 1:20-22; Heb 1:13–2:8; David M. Hay, *Glory at the Right Hand: Psalm 110 in Early Christianity* (Nashville: Abingdon, 1973), 35; Joel Marcus, *The Way of the Lord: Christological Exegesis of the Old Testament in the Gospel of Mark* (Louisville: Westminster/John Knox, 1992), 130; Martin C. Albl, *"And Scripture Cannot Be Broken": The Form and Function of the Early Christian Testimonia Collections* (NovTSup 96; Leiden: Brill, 1999), 227.

38. Phyllis A. Bird, "'Male and Female He Created Them': Gen 1:27b in the Context of the Priestly Account of Creation," *HTR* 74 (1981) 129-59. See Albl's discussion of the use of Ps 8:4-6 in constructing an Adam-Christ typology (*"And Scripture Cannot Be Broken,"* 228).

ery rule and every authority and power" as "enemies" of Christ is similar to a passage in chapter 2 of this letter:

> Yet in the presence of the mature we do speak wisdom, but a wisdom that does not belong to this age or to the rulers of this age who are being brought to an end. Rather, we speak, in the form of a secret, God's hidden wisdom which God decided upon before the ages for our glory, which none of the rulers of this age knew. If they had known [it], they would not have crucified the Lord of glory. (1 Cor 2:6-8)

The expression "Lord of glory" is common in *1 Enoch* as an epithet of God.[39] It "alludes to the effulgent splendor that envelops the enthroned deity."[40] Here that epithet is transferred to Jesus. One need not infer from this usage that Jesus was preexistent and descended from heaven through the cosmos.[41] Rather, in light of the connection between the phrases "for our glory" and "the Lord of glory," one may infer that Jesus is the "Lord of glory" because God raised and glorified him and through him will raise and glorify those who have fellowship with him. This inference is supported by the following verse, which speaks about the wonderful things that God has prepared for those who love him.

Analogously, the affirmation that "to those who are called, both Jews and Greeks, [we proclaim] Christ the power of God and the wisdom of God" (1 Cor 1:24) does not necessarily imply that Paul identifies Christ here with preexistent, personified wisdom. In the context, the force of the statement is that those who are called do not need human power and wisdom because they share in God's power and wisdom manifested in Christ.[42] This interpretation is supported by 1:30, which states that Christ *became* wisdom for us from God, that is, by his death and resurrection.[43]

Nevertheless, Paul may sometimes speak of Christ as preexistent in the Corinthian correspondence. In the discussion about meat sacrificed to idols in 1 Corinthians, Paul makes the following statement:

---

39. *1 Enoch* 22:14; 25:3, 7; 27:3, 5; 36:4; 63:2; 83:8. Cf. 81:3.

40. George W. E. Nickelsburg, *1 Enoch* 1 (Hermeneia; Minneapolis: Fortress, 2001), 316.

41. As Conzelmann argued (*1 Corinthians*, 63).

42. Similarly, Conzelmann, ibid., 47-48. For a different view, see Chester, *Messiah and Exaltation*, 388-89.

43. Conzelmann describes the statement as "exposition of the cross" (*1 Corinthians*, 52).

> For even if there are so-called gods, whether in heaven or on earth, just as indeed there are many gods and many lords, yet for us there is one God, the Father, from whom are all things and for whom we exist, and one Lord, Jesus Christ, through whom are all things and through whom we exist. (1 Cor 8:5-6)

This confession attributes the activity of creation to God and identifies Jesus Christ as the means through which God created all things. One way to interpret this passage is to affirm that Paul has identified the preexistent Christ with the wisdom of God, God's agent in creation.[44] Another possibility is that Paul is taking the idea of a new creation seriously here and implying that the resurrection and exaltation of Christ made him equivalent to God's wisdom.[45]


## 2 Corinthians 4

A similar statement occurs in the discussion of the ministry of the new covenant in 2 Corinthians:

> And even if our gospel is veiled, it is veiled among those who are perishing; in their case the god of this age has blinded the minds of the unbelievers so they will not see the light of the gospel of the glory of Christ, who is the image of God. (2 Cor 4:3-4)

Here again, Paul seems to identify Christ with wisdom. In a text roughly contemporary with Paul's letters, the Wisdom of Solomon, wisdom is described as follows:

> For she is a breath of the power of God, and a pure emanation of the glory of the Almighty; therefore nothing defiled gains entrance into her. For she is a reflection of eternal light, a spotless mirror of the working of God, and an image of his goodness. (Wis 7:25-26)[46]

44. The role of wisdom in creation is hinted at in Prov 8:22-31 and more fully developed in Wis 7:22–8:1; 9:2. Cf. Conzelmann, *1 Corinthians*, 144-45. Hengel interprets 1 Cor 8:6 in terms of Christ as the preexistent mediator of creation (*The Son of God*, 13). Chester seems to take this position as well (*Messiah and Exaltation*, 389).

45. On Paul's notion of a new creation in Christ, see 2 Cor 5:16-17.

46. NRSV translation. In both Wis 7:26 and 2 Cor 4:4, the word translated "image" is εἰκών. See also Furnish, *II Corinthians*, 222.

The passage about the new covenant in 2 Corinthians may imply that Christ, as God's wisdom, existed before the birth of Jesus. Alternatively, it may signify that Christ *became* the image of God when he was raised and exalted to heaven. The latter interpretation is perhaps supported by the context. A little later Paul says:

> For it is the God who said, "Light shall shine out from darkness," who has shone in our hearts to bring to light the knowledge of the glory of God in the face of Jesus Christ. (2 Cor 4:6)

This passage seems to make an analogy between God's creation of light, on the one hand, and God's self-revelation through Christ in the last days, on the other.

## Philippians

Paul's letter to the Philippians is probably later than 1 Thessalonians, Galatians, and 1 Corinthians. It was apparently written in prison, probably in Ephesus, before the writing of 2 Corinthians and Romans. The latter two were written after he was released from prison.

As in the earlier letters, Paul associates the epithet "Christ" (Χριστός) with Jesus many times in Philippians without explaining its significance.[47] Its messianic connotations, however, come through in the opening thanksgiving. Paul says that he gives thanks to God:

> being sure of this very thing, that the one who began a good work in you will bring [it] to an end by the day of Christ Jesus. (Phil 1:6)

And he prays:

> that your love may abound yet more and more in knowledge and all discernment so that you may approve the things that matter, in order that you may be pure and blameless until the day of Christ. (Phil 1:9-10)

The similarities between these statements and passages in 1 Thessalonians and 1 Corinthians make clear that "the day of Christ" is the day of the com-

---

47. The term occurs at least 36 times in this relatively short letter (perhaps 37 times, depending on the resolution of the text-critical problem in 2:30).

ing of Jesus from heaven or the day of the revealing of Jesus Christ.[48] The contexts in all three letters make clear that judgment is associated with that day.[49] 1 Corinthians also associates the kingship of Jesus with his coming (1 Cor 15:23-28). There are good grounds, therefore, for reading "Christ Jesus" in Philippians as "the messiah, Jesus."

It is noteworthy that the prose hymn[50] in chapter 2 of Philippians is introduced with reference to "Christ Jesus" and that it ends with the acclamation of "Jesus Christ" as Lord. If "Christ" here has a messianic significance, one would expect the hymn to have political connotations. That is exactly what we do find.

The hymn begins as follows:

> Think in this way among yourselves, a way that was also in Christ Jesus, who, although he was in the form of God, did not consider equality with God something to be seized, but emptied himself, taking the form of a slave, being in the likeness of men. (Phil 2:5-7)

Commentators have debated whether one should translate "did not consider equality with God something to be seized" or "something to be held onto tenaciously." Those who choose the latter translation seem to affirm that "being in the form of God" is equivalent to "being equal to God." This reading is undercut by the last part of the hymn in which God highly exalts Jesus. If he had been equal to God at the beginning, then he would simply return to that state. The hymn implies that the exaltation is something new and climactic.

The word translated "something to be seized" here is ἁρπαγμός. This exact word does not occur in the Jewish scriptures that were written in or translated into Greek. But members of its word-family occur frequently in these works, and they always have the negative connotation of robbery or taking plunder. Except for the usage of being snatched up to heaven, the word-group usually has a negative connotation in the Greek Pseudepigrapha, Philo, Josephus, and the New Testament.[51] In some cases, plundering

---

48. Cf. Phil 1:6, 10 with 1 Thess 1:10; 4:16-17; 5:2; 1 Cor 1:7-9. Compare also Phil 3:20 with 1 Thess 1:10; 4:15-17; 5:9-10.

49. The association of "the day of Christ" with judgment in Phil 2:14-16 is also clear.

50. For an argument that the so-called christological hymn of Philippians 2 is better defined as "rhythmic prose," a "prose hymn," or a brief encomium, see Adela Yarbro Collins, "Psalms, Phil. 2:6-11, and the Origins of Christology," *Biblical Interpretation* 11 (2003) 361-72.

51. Samuel Vollenweider, "Der 'Raub' der Gottgleichheit: Ein religionsgeschichtlicher Vorschlag zu Phil 2.6(-11)," *NTS* 45 (1999) 413-33, especially 417-18.

is portrayed as the typical activity of rulers.[52] Furthermore, the notion of equality with God on the part of entities that are not aspects of God has a strongly negative connotation in biblical, Jewish, and early Christian literature.[53] Finally, an important cultural context for such imagery is traditions about the typical ruler who is violent and who presumes to take a divine role.[54] Verse 6, therefore, means that, although Christ had a divine form, he did not attempt to make himself equal to God, unlike the typical arrogant ruler.[55]

The implicit contrast in Philippians 2 between Jesus and arrogant rulers is similar to Philo's contrast of Moses with those "who thrust themselves into positions of power by means of arms."[56] Philo goes on to say that God bestowed kingship upon Moses as a gift of honor that he deserved. Although he was a ruler of Egypt, as the son of the daughter of the reigning king, he renounced his expected inheritance. Since he rejected material wealth and power, God granted him the greatest and most perfect wealth by making him a partner in the divine rule of the universe. This partnership was magnified by the honor of being accounted worthy to bear the same name as the deity. For Moses was called god and king of the whole nation.[57]

Since Philippi was a Roman colony and the imperial cult was practiced there,[58] the hymn would evoke a comparison of Jesus with the emperor on the part of its audience.[59] If Philippians was written after 54 and before 68

---

52. Nah 2:13 LXX of the Assyrians; *Testament of Judah* 21:7; *Lives of the Prophets* 4:7; Josephus, *Jewish War* 6.3 §353 of the Romans; Ernest Moore points out that Josephus often uses this word group in connection with the Jewish rebels; "ΒΙΑΖΩ, ΑΡΠΑΖΩ and Cognates in Josephus," *NTS* 21 (1975) 519-43, especially 526.

53. Vollenweider, "Raub," 418; see, e.g., John 5:18.

54. Vollenweider, "Raub," section 2, beginning on p. 419.

55. Ibid., 429.

56. Philo, *On the Life of Moses* 1.27 (§148); trans. Loeb Classical Library.

57. Ibid., 1.28 (§§155-58).

58. Yarbro Collins, "Phil. 2:6-11," 371.

59. Cf. Paul's depiction of himself and other apostles as "serving as ambassadors for Christ" in 2 Cor 5:20. The verb used there (πρεσβεύειν) and its related noun (πρεσβευτής) were "used in the Greek-speaking part of the Roman empire for an official representative of Caesar (Latin: *legatus*)"; Furnish, *II Corinthians,* 339. Cf. also Paul's attribution of kingly virtues to Christ in 2 Cor 10:1 (πραΰτης καὶ ἐπιείκεια); see Donald Dale Walker, *Paul's Offer of Leniency (2 Cor 10:1): Populist Ideology and Rhetoric in a Pauline Letter Fragment* (WUNT 2.152; Tübingen: Mohr Siebeck, 2002).

CE, as seems likely, Nero would have been the reigning emperor. He was one of the emperors who actively encouraged worship of himself as a divine being. Jesus, on the contrary, as Paul implies, humbled himself and, as a result, was highly exalted by God. This exaltation may be interpreted as the installation of Jesus as messiah or universal king. The name given him, the name that is above every other name, is Lord (κύριος). It is noteworthy that this name or epithet was used absolutely, as here, "of gods and human rulers in the ancient world of the eastern Mediterranean. . . . Indeed, it occurs once in the NT itself for Nero (Acts 25:26)."[60]

Jesus is clearly depicted as preexistent in this hymn. This depiction lends some support to the idea that Jesus is presented as preexistent in the Corinthian correspondence, in at least one or two of the occasions when he is identified with the wisdom of God. This issue will be taken up again in the next chapter.

## Romans

Romans is recognized by many commentators as Paul's latest letter, written in Corinth[61] in the mid- or late fifties.[62] It is striking that Paul gives more information about Jesus as son of God and messiah in the address and greeting of Romans than he gives anywhere in his other letters. The reason is probably that he did not found and had not visited the community in Rome and thus had to introduce himself, as well as his understanding of the gospel, to his audience.[63]

---

60. Joseph A. Fitzmyer, S.J., "The Semitic Background of the New Testament *Kyrios*-Title," in idem, *A Wandering Aramean: Collected Aramaic Essays* (SBLMS 25; Missoula, MT: Scholars Press, 1979); reprinted with the same page-numbering in idem, *The Semitic Background of the New Testament* (Biblical Resource Series; Grand Rapids: Eerdmans; Livonia, MI: Dove Booksellers, 1997), 117 and n. 26. Fitzmyer notes that "the *kyrios*-title has regal connotations" in Mark 12:36 and parallels; he also points out that "the entire tradition of the royal character of Yahweh in the OT would seem to be associated with the *kyrios*-title" (ibid., 131-32).

61. Joseph A. Fitzmyer, S.J., *Romans* (AB 33; New York: Doubleday, 1993), 85.

62. Ibid., 87.

63. Ibid., 227.

*Romans 1:1-15*

Paul refers to "the gospel of God,"[64] which is "about his son, who was born from the seed of David according to the flesh" (Rom 1:3). The reference to Jesus as God's son here and the phrase "according to the flesh" are open to two quite different readings. One is that "son of God" means that Jesus was preexistent as God's son before he was born "according to the flesh." "Son of God" could then be interpreted as equivalent to "being in the form of God" in Philippians. The implication is not necessarily that the pre-existent Jesus was God or an aspect of God. The force of the expression may be that his similarity to God consisted in his existence as a heavenly being and in his being immortal.

The other reading is to take "son of God" as a biblical epithet of the king transferred to Jesus as the messiah.[65] In this reading, it is taken as equivalent to being descended from David.[66] The phrase "according to the flesh" could then be taken as a contrasting parallel to the appointment of Jesus as son of God "in accordance with a spirit of holiness" in the following verse.

That verse supports the reading of the hymn in Philippians expressed earlier, since it makes clear that Paul considers the epithet "son of God" to apply to Jesus in a stronger sense from the moment of his resurrection: "who was appointed son of God in power in accordance with a spirit of holiness by[67] his resurrection from the dead, Jesus Christ our Lord" (Rom 1:4). The two verses, taken together, may be read as implying that Jesus was indeed the messiah of Israel during his lifetime, but only as messiah designate. In other words, he actually became the messiah only at the time of his resurrection and exaltation to heaven. This interpretation is supported by

64. As he does also in Rom 15:16; 2 Cor 11:7; 1 Thess 2:2, 8, 9.

65. Pss 2:7; 89:26-27; 2 Samuel 7:14.

66. For the messiah of Israel as a descendant of David, see, e.g., 4QpIsa[a] (4Q161), fragments 8-10 (col. III); for text and translation see Florentino García Martínez and Eibert J. C. Tigchelaar, eds., *The Dead Sea Scrolls Study Edition* (2 vols.; Leiden: Brill, 1997-1998), 1: 314-17. For further examples and discussion, see John J. Collins, *The Scepter and the Star: The Messiahs of the Dead Sea Scrolls and Other Ancient Literature* (New York: Doubleday, 1995), 49-73.

67. This translation understands the preposition ἐκ here as expressing the effective cause; see Walter Bauer, *A Greek-English Lexicon of the New Testament and Other Early Christian Literature,* ed. William F. Arndt, F. Wilbur Gingrich; 3rd ed. rev. by Frederick W. Danker (Chicago: University of Chicago Press, 2000), *s.v.* 3.d.

the hypotheses already mentioned, namely, that Daniel 7 and Psalm 110 were interpreted by Paul's predecessors as prefiguring or prophesying Jesus' resurrection from the dead. Paul seems to presuppose the latter interpretation of Psalm 110 in 1 Corinthians 15. It is also supported by the end of the hymn in Philippians: after his death, Jesus was exalted to heaven and given the name "Lord" so that all creatures should venerate him and submit to him with obedience. This submission appears to be both cultic and political.[68]

In the thanksgiving of Romans, Paul continues the language of the address by saying that he serves God "in the gospel of his son" (Rom 1:9). This is the only time that the phrase "the gospel of [God's] son" occurs in the undisputed letters of Paul. When the term "gospel" is not used absolutely, the most common phrase with the genitive case following it is "the gospel of Christ."[69] Assuming that "Christ" in these cases carries the connotation of "messiah," this is further evidence that "son of God" in the opening of Romans is equivalent to "messiah."

## Romans 5

In chapter 5 of Romans, Paul discusses the results of justification:

> Having been justified, therefore, on the basis of [Jesus'] faith,[70] we have peace in relation to God through our Lord Jesus Christ. (Rom 5:1)

Paul goes on to say that we boast about our hope for (sharing in) the glory of God. We even boast about our sufferings because they produce hope:

> and hope will not disappoint, because the love of God has been poured out into our hearts through (the) holy spirit which has been given to us. (Rom 5:5)

68. Cf. Adela Yarbro Collins, "The Worship of Jesus and the Imperial Cult," in Carey C. Newman, James R. Davila, and Gladys S. Lewis, eds., *The Jewish Roots of Christological Monotheism: Papers from the St. Andrews Conference on the Historical Origins of the Worship of Jesus* (JSJSup 63; Leiden: Brill, 1999), 234-57, especially 247.

69. Rom 15:19; 1 Cor 9:12; 2 Cor 2:12; 4:4 (the gospel of the glory of Christ); 2 Cor 9:13; 10:14; Gal 1:7; Phil 1:27; 1 Thess 3:2.

70. Cf. Rom 5:19; Hays, *The Faith of Jesus Christ*, 151-52.

Then he goes on to elaborate the initial statement about having peace in relation to God through Jesus Christ:

> For while we were still weak, yet at the right time, Christ died for the ungodly. . . . God demonstrates his own love for us, for, while we were still sinners, Christ died for us. Being justified now by his blood, how much more, therefore, will we be saved through him from the wrath. For if, while we were enemies, we were reconciled to God through the death of his son, how much more, being reconciled, will we be saved by his life. (Rom 5:6, 8-10)

Paul uses a political metaphor about hostility between two parties to illustrate the way in which the death of Jesus has affected the relations between God and humanity. The language suggests that Paul is reflecting on and interpreting the entirely unexpected and shocking event of the crucifixion of the messiah. The terms "Christ" and "son of God" recall the royal ideology in the Bible and the expectation of the messiah of Israel in Second Temple Jewish texts. Paul interprets the apparently shameful death of Jesus as an expression of God's love for humanity, especially the Gentiles. He also links that death closely to the resurrection. This link provides a basis for hoping to be acquitted at the judgment of the end-time and to share in the glorious, eternal existence of God.

### Romans 7–8

The final text that speaks about Jesus as the son of God in some detail is the eighth chapter of Romans. In chapter 7, Paul had made a vivid argument, using speech in character, that the Gentiles were so weakened by sin and their own passions that any attempt on their part to relate rightly to God by observing the law of Moses was doomed to failure.[71] In chapter 8 he shows how the Gentiles are now able to please God through "the law of the spirit of life in Christ Jesus" that has "freed you from the law of sin and death" (Rom 8:2). Summarizing the argument of chapter 7 and elaborating on the possibility of new life in Christ, he goes on to say:

---

71. Cf. Rom 7:7-25 with 1:18-32. For discussion see Emma Wasserman, "The Death of the Soul in Romans 7: Sin, Death, and the Law in Light of Hellenistic Moral Psychology" (Ph.D. diss., Yale University, 2005).

> For what was impossible for the law, because it was weakened by the flesh, [God has done, namely,] by sending his own son in the likeness of sinful flesh and [to atone] for sin, he has passed sentence on sin in the flesh, in order that the requirement of the law might be fulfilled in us, who walk, not according to the flesh, but according to the spirit. (Rom 8:3-4)

The reference to God "sending his own son" can be interpreted in two rather different ways. The first is to read it without any implication of Jesus' preexistence. Like the passage in Galatians discussed earlier, this one can be interpreted by analogy with the biblical expression regarding God sending prophets. From this point of view, the genitive ἑαυτοῦ may be taken simply as a marker of possession: "his son" rather than "his own son." Or if one opts to translate "his own son," the intensification of the relationship could be explained in terms of election, as God chose Israel, for example. In this case the phrase "in the likeness of sinful flesh" would not imply that he had been in a heavenly or divine form before his birth. Rather, he shared fleshly existence with other human beings, but he did not share their sinfulness.

The second reading involves taking "his own son" to indicate a significant degree of similarity between God and Jesus.[72] This similarity can be interpreted in light of the hymn in Philippians and thus as implying preexistence. Jesus, as God's "own" son, was "in the form of God" before he was born as a human being. We will come back to this question after discussing the rest of Paul's argument in this passage.

His next main point is:

> If then the spirit of the one who raised Jesus from the dead dwells in you, the one who raised Christ from the dead will make alive also your mortal bodies through his spirit that dwells in you. (Rom 8:11)

Walking according to the spirit, rather than according to the flesh, has ethical implications. Those who live up to them are like Christ:

> For those who are led by the spirit of God, these are sons of God. For you did not receive a spirit of slavery again so that you should fear, but

---

72. Chester interprets the reference to mean that God sends his son into the world (*Messiah and Exaltation*, 389-90).

you have received a spirit of adoption in which we cry, "Abba, Father." The same spirit testifies with our spirits that we are children of God. If then children, also heirs. And as heirs of God, [we are] also fellow heirs with Christ, provided that we suffer with him in order that we may be glorified with him. (Rom 8:14-17)

Being glorified with Christ means "adoption, the redemption of our bodies" (Rom 8:23), which ultimately means resurrection to or transformation into a heavenly body and eternal life, events described by Paul in 1 Thessalonians and 1 Corinthians.

This whole ethical and bodily process of transformation is then summed up by Paul as follows:

For those whom he knew beforehand, he also predetermined to be conformed to the appearance[73] of his son, in order that he might be the firstborn among many brothers (and sisters). (Rom 8:29)

The goal in the plan of God is that human beings become like the resurrected and glorified Christ, that is, that they attain a heavenly, eternal existence.

So in the eighth chapter of Romans, the epithet "son of God" is used in the sense of being like God in having a glorious appearance and eternal life. We can now return to the question raised earlier, whether the statement that God "sent his own son" implies preexistence in this context. The argument as a whole is certainly compatible with the idea that Jesus was preexistent in the sense expressed in the hymn of Philippians. But explicit references to Christ's resurrection (8:11) and his glorification (8:17) in connection with that event indicate that a reading involving preexistence is not necessary. The equation of "adoption" and "the redemption of our bodies" (8:23) suggests that "being conformed to the appearance of Christ" means sharing in his death and subsequent glorification, rather than in his "being in the form of God" before his birth.[74]

---

73. Although the Greek term used here is εἰκών, translated "image" in Gen 1:26-27 LXX and 2 Cor 4:4, its usage and sense here are different; see Bauer et al., *A Greek-English Lexicon,* *s.v.* 3.

74. It may be surprising to some that there is no passage in Romans in which Paul clearly affirms the preexistence of Christ, even though he affirms it in Philippians, which was written earlier. This state of affairs may be explained by inferring that Paul's interpreta-

## Conclusion

In conclusion, the use of the epithet "Christ" in the letters of Paul is evidence that the messiahship of Jesus was a well-established tradition before Paul joined the movement. Further, his use of it without explanation or debate indicates that the proclamation of Jesus as the messiah of Israel was a fundamental part of his announcement of the good news to those who formed the core membership of the communities that he founded. It also appears that the portrayal of Jesus as the son of God is closely related to his status as messiah. It is a biblical expression that is taken over in the characterization of the messiah. The passages in which Jesus' status as son of God is linked with his death on behalf of others reflect the result of the reinterpretation of the messianic tradition in light of the crucifixion of Jesus. What appeared to be a refutation of Jesus' status as messiah was interpreted by Paul, and probably others before him, as an expression of faithfulness and love for humanity on the part of both Jesus and God.[75]

---

tion of Christ differed from letter to letter depending on the circumstances he was addressing and on the variety among his audiences.

75. Chester argues that Paul deliberately avoided messianic traditions about an earthly or material kingdom because such a proclamation of the kingdom of God would be misunderstood and the proclaimers could not in any case bring about the changes implied in such a message. He also sees Paul's shift from the original thrust of the movement to a more cosmic and future kind of expectation in terms of accommodation of the message to the new setting in the cities of the Roman empire (*Messiah and Exaltation,* 382-88, 394-96). Once Jesus was crucified, however, and his vindication was understood in terms of resurrection, exaltation, and glorification, and in terms of the universal kingship of Dan 7:14, the transformation of the idea of Jesus' messiahship from earthly king into a cosmic, heavenly messiah was virtually inevitable.

# 6. Jesus as Messiah and Son of God in the Synoptic Gospels

The previous chapter showed how Paul adapted and elaborated the tradition that Jesus was the messiah and son of God. This chapter focuses on the same two epithets in the Synoptic Gospels. It begins, however, with the question whether these Gospels present Jesus as preexistent and concludes with a reassessment of the question of the preexistence of the messiah in Paul's letters in light of certain Synoptic traditions.

## Jesus as Preexistent in the Synoptic Gospels?

Recently Simon J. Gathercole has revived the traditional view that Jesus is presented as preexistent in the Synoptic Gospels.[1] In making his case, he focused on the sayings about Jesus' "coming" for a specific purpose.[2] In spite of the fact that both the verb meaning "come" varies and the syntax of the expression of purpose varies as well, he claims that there is a pattern or formula common to these sayings and labels it the "'I have come' + purpose" formula.[3] The first part of his argument is that there is a *prima facie*

---

1. Simon J. Gathercole, *The Preexistent Son: Recovering the Christologies of Matthew, Mark, and Luke* (Grand Rapids/Cambridge, UK: Eerdmans, 2006).

2. Ibid., 84. The sayings are Mark 1:24//Luke 4:34//Matt 8:29; Mark 1:38//Luke 4:43; Mark 2:17//Matt 9:13//Luke 5:32; Matt 5:17; Luke 12:49; Matt 10:34//Luke 12:51; Matt 10:35; Mark 10:45//Matt 20:28; Luke 19:10.

3. Ibid., 85.

123

(logical) case for concluding that preexistence is implied in these sayings. His warrants are: (1) the sayings speak about coming *with a purpose,* and therefore the coming is portrayed as a deliberate act; (2) a "deliberate act requires a before-and-after, and, in the case of a 'coming,' an origin from which the speaker has come"; (3) "if the person is referring to his whole earthly activity as the goal of the coming, the place of origin is logically somewhere outside of the human sphere."[4] Next he argues that none of the previous interpretations of these sayings is acceptable.[5] Then he proposes that the best parallel to the relevant Synoptic sayings is the use of the "formula" by angels in Jewish and Christian texts.[6] He also provides an exegesis of the Synoptic sayings in support of his thesis.[7]

Gathercole's case for preexistence has some serious flaws. He admits that his argument that "coming with a purpose" logically implies a movement from one place to another is refuted if there is "some kind of idiom in operation." The latter seems indeed to be the case. The probability of an idiomatic usage is illustrated by a saying that Gathercole excludes from the discussion as a "red herring," namely, Matt 11:18-19//Luke 7:33-34.[8] He excludes it because there is no expression of purpose. The saying is relevant, however, because it uses a verb meaning "come" (ἔρχομαι) without any mention or implication of coming from one specific earthly place to another. It is also relevant because it characterizes the whole of both John's and Jesus' public ministries. The problem that this saying raises for Gathercole's thesis is of course the necessity of attributing preexistence to John the Baptist, if such is inferred for Jesus.

The idiom that this saying seems to presuppose is that the "coming" in question is not spatial, but concerns the idea that certain individuals are "sent" by God to the people to fulfill a certain divine purpose. Luke recognized this idiomatic way of speaking when he rewrote Mark 1:38. Mark wrote, "for this [purpose] I have come [or, I have come forth]" (εἰς τοῦτο γὰρ ἐξῆλθον). Luke wrote, "for this [purpose] I was sent" (ἐπὶ τοῦτο ἀπεστάλην).[9] The catalyst for Mark's usage of the idiom may be Mal 3:1,

---

4. Ibid., 86-87; emphasis his.

5. Ibid., 92-112.

6. Ibid., 113-47.

7. Ibid., 148-76.

8. Ibid., 88-89. Gathercole defines the saying as Matt 11:19a//Luke 7:34, ignoring the part of the double saying referring to John the Baptist.

9. The "I have come" sayings are formally different from "being sent" sayings, as Gather-

which reads, "Behold, I am sending [or, I shall send] my messenger, and he will look upon [or, prepare] the way before my face" (ἰδοῦ ἐγῶ ἐξαποστέλλω τὸν ἄγγελόν μου, καὶ ἐπιβλέψεται ὁδὸν πρὸ προσώπου μου). This is most likely one of the passages alluded to in Mark 1:2-3. For Luke, Isa 61:1b, "he has sent me to bring good news to the oppressed," may provide the context, since it is cited in Luke 4:18.

In the parable of the two sons, the Matthean Jesus says, "For John came to you in the way of righteousness, and you did not believe him, but the tax collectors and the prostitutes believed him" (Matt 21:32). The context suggests a purpose for John's coming: to turn the people from sin to righteousness. Similarly, by identifying the return of Elijah with the activity of John the Baptist, Mark implies that John "came" with the purpose of restoring all things.[10]

Another flaw was touched on above in characterizing the subject of Matt 11:18-19//Luke 7:33-34 as "the public ministries of John and Jesus." Gathercole's argument that the "I have come" sayings concern the person's "whole earthly activity" is tendentious.[11] It obviously prepares for the "logical" inference that "the place of origin" is "somewhere outside of the human sphere."[12] The sayings, however, do not refer to "the whole earthly life" of Jesus, but rather to his public activity of destroying demons, preaching the good news or gospel of God, calling sinners, fulfilling the law, and so forth.

Gathercole points out, apparently without seeing their significance, that the Qumran literature contains sayings about messiahs and other figures with an eschatological role as "coming" without any local specification.[13] The word "come" is not technical, as Gathercole rightly notes.[14] Nevertheless, its usage in the Dead Sea Scrolls shows that it could be used

---

cole points out (ibid., 105). Even so, the latter are substantively relevant as synonymous with the former.

10. Compare Mark 9:9-13, especially vv. 12a and 13, with Mal 3:22-23 LXX (Eng. 4:5-6). See also the parallel in Matt 17:10-13.

11. Gathercole, *Preexistent Son*, 87.

12. Ibid.

13. Ibid., 111-12. See 4Q252 5:3 for the coming of the messiah of righteousness; CD-B 19:10-11 for the messiah(s) of Aaron and Israel; 1QS 9:11 for "the prophet" and the messiahs of Aaron and Israel; and CD 7:18-19 for the interpreter of the law. The latter is expected to come "to Damascus." That city, however, is symbolic here and is probably equivalent to "to you" or "to the people." Cf. Matt 21:32.

14. Ibid., 112.

to express an eschatological role (being "sent" by God) without implying preexistence.

With regard to Gathercole's argument that the "I have come" sayings in the Synoptics have their closest parallels in texts about angels making a visit to earth, it should be noted that there is an important difference between the summing up of Jesus' public ministry as a whole and the summing up by angels of their earthly activity *in a particular visit* to earth.[15] In any case, the vast majority of the texts involving angels cited in support of this thesis are considerably later than the Synoptic Gospels.

This assessment of Gathercole's book leads to the conclusion that the "I have come" sayings cannot be used to argue that any of the Synoptic Gospels portrays Jesus as preexistent. Other passages that seem to do so will be discussed below. Since Mark is probably the earliest of the Synoptic Gospels, let us turn to it first.

## Mark

### Opening and the Baptism of Jesus

The opening sentence of Mark is variously represented in the manuscripts. The majority read, "[The] beginning of the good news of Jesus Christ, son of God." A significant number of manuscripts from various text-groups lack the phrase "son of God." The shorter reading is likely to be original for a number of reasons. It seems unlikely that an accidental omission would occur at the very beginning of a work. Further, it is far easier to explain the deliberate addition of the phrase "son of God" than its omission. It may have been added out of piety or to combat too human an understanding of Jesus.[16]

So the good news in question is about "Jesus Christ." In that phrase, the term "Christ" (Χριστός) may be taken either as a proper name or in a titular sense. We saw the same ambiguity in the letters of Paul. The narrative of Mark as a whole evokes the titular sense, "messiah." This is most

---

15. Ibid., 113; emphasis his.

16. Adela Yarbro Collins, "Establishing the Text: Mark 1:1," in Tord Fornberg and David Hellholm, eds., *Texts and Contexts: Biblical Texts in Their Textual and Situational Contexts: Essays in Honor of Lars Hartman* (Oslo: Scandinavian University Press, 1995), 111-27.

clear in Peter's statement in 8:29, "You are the Messiah" (Σὺ εἶ ὁ χριστός). It is also implied by the portrayal of the baptism of Jesus:

> And in those days, Jesus came from Nazareth in Galilee and was baptized in the Jordan by John. And immediately, while he was coming up out of the water, he saw the heavens split and the spirit coming down to him like a dove. And a voice came from the heavens, "You are my beloved son; I take delight in you."

In the Hebrew Bible, the gift of the divine spirit signifies the endowment of the charisma of leadership as judge or king.[17] The spirit of God is also associated with the gift of prophecy[18] and with the qualities of the ideal king.[19] The narrative context of Mark suggests an intertextual relationship with Isaiah 61:

> "The Spirit of the Lord is upon me, because he has anointed me;
> He has sent me to proclaim good news to the poor,
> To heal those whose hearts are broken,
> To proclaim release to the captives,
> The recovery of sight to the blind,
> To announce the year of the Lord's favor,
> And the day of recompense of our God,
> To comfort all who mourn. . . ."[20]

From the perspective of Mark, the speaker of this passage may be understood to be the prophet or the messiah. The conflation of the two offices is also possible, since David was remembered as both king and prophet.[21]

In addition, the voice from heaven indicates the significance of the descent of the spirit. The first part of the saying is an actualization of Ps 2:7, a royal psalm in which the Lord says to the king of Israel, his anointed, "You are my son." The descent of the spirit makes it likely that God establishes Jesus as his "son" with these words. The allusion to Psalm 2 implies that God thus appoints Jesus as messiah at the time of his baptism by John.

Mark adds the word "beloved" to the clause from Psalm 2, "you are my

---

17. Judg 3:10; 1 Sam 16:13.
18. Mic 3:8; Neh 9:30.
19. Isa 11:1-9, especially v. 2.
20. Isa 61:1-2 LXX.
21. E.g., Mark 12:35-37; Acts 1:16, 20-21.

son." Some have argued that the word "beloved" evokes the story of Abraham's near-sacrifice of Isaac.[22] Another, more likely, explanation is that the addition was inspired by the other passage that is actualized in the speech of the divine voice, Isa 42:1, which reads, "Behold my servant, whom I uphold, my chosen, in whom my soul delights." The authors of Mark and Matthew may have known a text of Isa 42:1 in which the word "beloved" occurred.[23] Or the term may have been inspired by the use of the related verb in "the parallel and related passages Isa 41:8-9 and 44:2 in the Greek version."[24] These passages suggest that "chosen" and "beloved" are synonyms.

By combining Psalm 2 and Isaiah 42, the text of Mark interprets Jesus both as the messiah and as the servant of the Lord. The close association of the two epithets has several implications. One is that the author of Mark, and perhaps his predecessors as well, read the poems about the servant of the Lord in Isaiah messianically, at least some of them. The striking similarities between the fate of the servant as described in Isaiah 53, on the one hand, and the fate of Jesus as interpreted by his followers, on the other, may have been the impetus for the messianic interpretation of these poems. Another implication is that the messiahship of Jesus is not presented in royal and military terms; instead the idea of the messiah of Israel is reinterpreted in prophetic terms.[25]

### A Markan Summary and the Appointment of the Twelve

As we have seen, in the baptismal scene the divine voice declares to Jesus, "You are my son." The next passage that presents Jesus as the son of God is the summary of Jesus' activites in Mark 3:7-12. A great multitude is follow-

---

22. Jon D. Levenson, *The Death and Resurrection of the Beloved Son: The Transformation of Child Sacrifice in Judaism and Christianity* (New Haven, CT: Yale University Press, 1993), 30-31, 200-202, 228-29. See also Jeffrey B. Gibson, "Jesus' Wilderness Temptation according to Mark," *JSNT* 53 (1994) 3-34, especially 25-26.

23. Cf. Mark 1:11 with Matt 12:17-21, especially v. 18.

24. Joel Marcus, *The Way of the Lord: Christological Exegesis of the Old Testament in the Gospel of Mark* (Louisville: Westminster/John Knox, 1992), 51.

25. See "Jesus as Prophet" and "Jesus as Messiah," in "5. Interpretation of Jesus," in the "Introduction" of Adela Yarbro Collins, *Mark: A Commentary* (Hermeneia; Minneapolis: Fortress, 2007).

ing Jesus because he had healed many, and all who had diseases pressed upon him to touch him. "And the unclean spirits, whenever they saw him, would fall down before him and cry out, saying, 'You are the son of God!'" Jesus rebukes them "in order that they not make him known." The words of the spirits and the rebuke of Jesus suggest that they have special knowledge, concealed from the human beings who surround Jesus.

The allusion to the special knowledge of the unclean spirits, the acclamation of Jesus as "the son of God," and his rebuke of the spirits are all related to an important theme in the Gospel of Mark, the question of the identity of Jesus, often described as the "messianic secret."[26] The first time that Jesus is described as son of God in Mark, at his baptism, Jesus is the only character within the narrative who hears the divine voice. In chapter 3, it is only the unclean spirits who know Jesus' identity. These features of the narrative call the attention of the audience to Jesus' identity as son of God and lead them to ponder its meaning. Those who link the expression "son of God" with the Davidic messiah, inspired by Psalm 2 and related passages, may assume that Jesus is keeping his identity secret until the appropriate time, to be revealed perhaps by some divine signal. Those who hold that all religious Jews are children of God are led by this passage to recognize that Jesus is God's son in some special sense.

In the passage that follows this summary (Mark 3:13-19), Jesus chooses twelve disciples to be with him, to be sent out to proclaim, and to cast out demons. The number "twelve" probably reflects the twelve tribes of Israel. The stated purposes for sending out the Twelve reflect the intention of preparing the people of Israel for the dawning kingdom of God.[27] The act of choosing a special group of twelve for such a purpose reinforces the inference that Jesus is presented as the Davidic messiah in the baptismal scene. According to the *War Scroll* from Qumran, the prince of the congregation was to have the names of the twelve tribes of Israel written upon his shield (1QM 5:1-2). The epithet "prince of the congregation" probably refers to the messiah of Israel since the oracle of Balaam (Num 24:15-19) is cited later in the work (1QM 11). Although the "scepter" that shall arise out of Israel is not interpreted in the latter passage, it is explained as "the prince of the whole congregation" in the *Damascus Document* 7:20, a work also found at Qumran (4Q266 3 iii 21).

---

26. See the excursus on the messianic secret in the commentary on Mark 1:21-28 in ibid.
27. Cf. Mark 1:14-15 and 6:7-13.

## The Declaration of Peter and the Transfiguration

As indicated earlier, a very important passage for the development of the theme of "Jesus as messiah" in Mark is the scene in which Peter declares, "You are the messiah" (Mark 8:27-30). It is clear from the context that ὁ χριστός, literally "the anointed," means the Davidic messiah or royal messiah here, because the acclamation is offered as an alternative to the opinion of some of the people that Jesus is "one of the prophets." The response of Jesus makes clear that the acclamation is accepted; the immediate response is not to reject or reinterpret, but to command the disciples to keep the identity of Jesus secret.

The reinterpretation comes in the next, closely related scene. Evidently, Jesus and the disciples, as characters in the narrative, on the one hand, and the author of Mark and his audience, on the other, have a shared understanding of the notion of the Davidic messiah and a shared assumption that "the messiah" and "the Son of Man" are equivalent. That such information is commonly understood is clear from the fact that the use of the epithet "Son of Man" as equivalent to "messiah" needs no comment, explanation, or defense.[28]

The epithet "Son of Man" will be treated in the next chapter below. For now the important point is that the speech of Jesus following the command to secrecy does introduce new and controversial information: that the messiah must suffer, be rejected, be killed, and rise again. Suffering, rejection, and death were not part of the traditional picture of the role of the messiah of Israel. But suffering and rejection, even death, were typically associated with the prophetic role.[29] The combination of the rebuking, indicting, sentencing, and teaching activities of the prophet with the royal messianic role was not unusual in Jewish circles at the time of Mark, as the *Psalms of Solomon*, the *Similitudes of Enoch*, and *4 Ezra* (= 2 Esdras 3–14) make clear.[30]

---

28. On the equivalence of "messiah" and "Son of Man" in the first century CE, see Adela Yarbro Collins, "The Influence of Daniel on the New Testament," in John J. Collins, *Daniel* (Hermeneia; Minneapolis: Fortress, 1993), 90-112, especially 90-105.

29. See, e.g., Reinhold Liebers, *"Wie geschrieben steht"; Studien zu einer besonderen Art frühchristlichen Schriftbezuges* (Berlin/New York: de Gruyter, 1993), 369-76.

30. *Psalms of Solomon* 17:21-43; *1 Enoch* 37–71; *4 Ezra* 11–13; on the messiah in the *Similitudes* or *Parables of Enoch*, see James C. VanderKam, "Righteous One, Messiah, Chosen One, and Son of Man in 1 Enoch 37–71," in James H. Charlesworth, ed., *The Messiah: Developments in Earliest Judaism and Christianity* (Minneapolis: Fortress, 1992), 169-91.

The combination of the prophetic motifs of suffering, rejection, and even death with the royal messianic role, however, was very unusual. That this was so is indicated by the reaction of Peter and Jesus' strong correction of his attitude (Mark 8:32-33).

After the teaching on discipleship that follows Peter's acclamation and the first passion prediction, Jesus takes Peter, James, and John to a high mountain where they can be alone. In their presence he is transformed and his clothes become very white and shining (Mark 9:2-3). Then the three disciples see Elijah and Moses conversing with Jesus. After Peter suggests that the disciples make three tents, a cloud covers "them," presumably Jesus, Moses, and Elijah, and a voice speaks from the cloud, "This is my beloved son; listen to him" (Mark 9:7).

The presence of Moses together with the divine command, "listen to him," evokes the statement of Moses to the people in Deut 18:15, "The LORD your God will raise up for you a prophet like me from among you, from your brethren; listen to him."[31] A similar statement in the same chapter of Deuteronomy inspired the expectation of an eschatological prophet reflected in the Dead Sea Scrolls.[32] This line of interpretation suggests that Elijah is present in the vision because of the expectation that he would return in the last days.[33] The rhetoric of the scene seems to make the point that all the expectations related to the prophet like Moses and Elijah's return are to be fulfilled in Jesus.

The motif of secrecy is implicit here, as in 3:7-12, because Jesus has allowed only three disciples to share in this experience. Once again the idea that Jesus is the son of God is shrouded in secrecy. The context suggests a reason for that. The messiahship of Jesus has just been affirmed, again secretly, to the disciples only. This affirmation has been followed by a prediction of the suffering, death, and resurrection of Jesus. The whole complex from the discussion of Jesus' identity to the end of the transfiguration suggests that the heart of Jesus' teaching, the message to which the disciples should listen, is that the messiah, the son of God, must suffer.

At the same time, the account of the transfiguration suggests that Jesus is a divine being walking the earth. Although the portrayal of the baptism

31. Marcus, *The Way of the Lord*, 81.

32. Deut 18:18-19 is cited in the *Testimonia* or *Messianic Anthology* (4Q175), lines 5-8; cf. CD 6:11. For discussion see John J. Collins, *The Scepter and the Star: The Messiahs of the Dead Sea Scrolls and Other Ancient Literature* (New York: Doubleday, 1995), 112-14, 116-17.

33. See Mal 3:23-24 (4:5-6 Eng.).

seems to indicate that Jesus was chosen as messiah on that occasion, certain features of the transfiguration suggest that it is the self-manifestation of a deity.[34] Similarly, the motif of secrecy in Mark has an affinity with the notion of a deity disguising him- or herself as a human being. From the point of view of traditional Greek religion, the identification of Jesus in this scene as God's son is equivalent to identifying him as a divine being.[35]

The account of the transfiguration, read in the traditional Greek way, is in tension with the description of the baptism. This tension has been resolved for later Christian readers by the assumption that Mark presupposed the preexistence of Jesus, even though he does not mention it.[36] For the author and earliest audiences of Mark, the tension may have been resolved by the assumption that the transfiguration is a preview of the resurrection of Jesus. In the first century of the common era, not only Elijah, but also Moses, was believed to have been taken up in bodily form to heaven.[37] Similarly, after his death, Jesus would be raised from the dead and exalted to heaven.

### The Entry into Jerusalem and the Passion Narrative

In Mark 11:1-10, Jesus enters the city of Jerusalem in a way that suggests the fulfillment of Zech 9:9-10, understood as a messianic prophecy. The people acclaim Jesus as "the coming one" and associate him with the kingdom of their father David. He is not said explicitly to be the messiah, but such seems to be implied.

The passion narrative of Mark is full of ironic affirmations of the kingship of Jesus. The anonymous woman of 14:3-9 is a culturally unlikely

---

34. Adela Yarbro Collins, "Mark and His Readers: The Son of God among Greeks and Romans," *HTR* 93 (2000) 85-100; Candida R. Moss, "The Transfiguration: An Exercise in Markan Accommodation," *Biblical Interpretation* 12 (2004) 69-89.

35. Yarbro Collins, "The Son of God among Greeks and Romans," 86-87.

36. This is the traditional reading of Mark that Gathercole has attempted to revive; see the discussion above.

37. On Elijah, see Josephus, *Jewish Antiquities* 9.2.2 §28. On Moses, see Josephus, *Jewish Antiquities* 4.8.48 §§325-26. In spite of the statement in Deut 34:5 that Moses died, Josephus did not believe that he did; see Christopher Begg, "Josephus' Portrayal of the Disappearances of Enoch, Elijah and Moses: Some Observations," *JBL* 109 (1990) 691-93, especially 692; see also Adela Yarbro Collins, *The Beginning of the Gospel: Probings of Mark in Context* (Minneapolis: Fortress, 1992), 142-43.

choice for the role of choosing and anointing Jesus as king, but her action suggests that such is what she is doing: she pours a bottle of aromatic oil upon his head.[38] Yet the gesture is reinterpreted by Jesus as anointing for burial; this reinterpretation contributes to the author's redefinition of messiahship to include suffering and death.

In one scene of the passion narrative, the kingship of Jesus is directly affirmed, in a non-ironic way (14:53-65). When the high priest asks him, "Are you the messiah, the son of the Blessed?" Jesus responds, "I am; and you will see the Son of Man sitting on the right of the Power and coming with the clouds of heaven" (14:62). The relation between the question and the answer, especially the opening statement "I am," shows clearly the equivalence of "messiah" and "Son of Man" for the author of Mark and the assumption that the audience would understand and accept it. This passage also makes clear that the rejection and suffering of Jesus belong to the period in which he is the hidden Son of Man[39] and that his exercise of the messianic office will commence after his resurrection and exaltation.

The interrogation of Jesus by Pilate forms a transition from Jesus' direct affirmation of his messiahship to the renewed irony that characterizes the final stage of the hiddenness of the Son of Man. Pilate asks him, "Are you the king of the Jews?" Jesus' response, "You say [so]," is not a denial, but it is evasive and noninformative. The irony appears in full strength in the scene in which the crowd rejects the nonviolent Jesus for the rebel Barabbas (Mark 15:6-15). It is present in powerful and poignant form in the mocking of Jesus as king by the Roman soldiers (15:16-20), in the inscription of the charge against him, "the king of the Jews" (15:26), and in the mockery of the passersby (15:32).[40] The irony is shattered by the splitting of the temple veil and by the acclamation of the centurion, "This man really was God's son!" (15:38-39).[41] Just as it is not entirely clear how Peter came to the insight that Jesus is the messiah, so the reason for the centurion's affirmation in the narrative logic of the scene is somewhat obscure. Never-

---

38. Cf. 1 Sam 10:1; 1 Kings 19:15-16.

39. Cf. Mark 8:30-31.

40. Graham Stanton, "Messianism and Christology: Mark, Matthew, Luke and Acts," in Bockmuehl and Paget, eds., *Redemption and Resistance* (London and New York: T&T Clark, 2007), 78-96, especially 83.

41. On the ambiguity of the centurion's statement, see Yarbro Collins, "The Son of God among Greeks and Romans," 93-97. See also Whitney T. Shiner, "The Ambiguous Pronouncement of the Centurion and the Shrouding of Meaning in Mark," *JSNT* 78 (2000) 3-22.

theless, the link between the affirmation and the death of Jesus is unmistakable. This scene is, therefore, the climax of the reinterpretation of the traditional understanding of the royal messiah by the author of Mark.

The splitting of the temple veil recalls the baptism, when the heavens were split. At the baptism God is present and speaks. At the cross God seems to be absent and is silent. But the splitting of the temple veil may be interpreted as a mysterious theophany, indicating that, in the death of Jesus, the will of the hidden God is manifested.

The denouement comes in the last chapter of Mark (16:1-8). The author, building upon the tradition formulated by his predecessors, innovates in his portrayal of Jesus as messiah by including a narrative concerning the resurrection of the messiah from the dead. The authors of the *Similitudes of Enoch* and *4 Ezra* (2 Esdras 3–14) innovated in a different way, with the similar result of a heavenly messiah. They achieved this innovation in large part through their appropriation of Daniel 7, transforming the expectation of a royal messiah, who would be primarily a warrior and a king, into belief in an exalted, heavenly messiah whose role would be to execute judgment and to inaugurate a new age of peace and rejoicing.[42]

## Matthew

Let us now turn to the Gospel according to Matthew, which follows Mark closely in many ways.

### Opening and Genealogy

Matthew begins with a titular sentence similar to Mark's:

> [The] account of [the] descent of Jesus Christ, son of David, son of Abraham. (Matt 1:1)

The primary purpose of this sentence is to introduce the genealogy that follows. The use of the term βίβλος (usually translated "book"), however,

---

42. The transformation of the earthly Jesus as messiah designate into the exalted, heavenly messiah explains why the Markan Jesus questions the idea of the messiah as the son of David (Mark 12:35-37; cf. Matt 22:41-46).

may suggest that the opening sentence introduces the whole Gospel as well.

It is interesting that Matthew elaborates Mark's reference to "Jesus Christ," not with "son of God," but with "son of David, son of Abraham." The mention of Abraham prepares for the genealogy and could make the point that Jesus is Jewish, since he is descended from the ancestor of the Jewish people. Alternatively or in addition, the mention of Abraham could prepare for the command of Jesus to preach the good news to all nations at the end of the Gospel, since Abraham was by birth and upbringing a Gentile. In the first century of the common era he was described as the first proselyte.[43] The mention of Abraham at the beginning and of the mission to the Gentiles at the end together evoke God's promise that the nations would bless themselves by Abraham.[44] This promise was read by Paul in terms of the justification of the Gentiles by faith.[45]

In any case, the phrase "son of David" makes clear that Matthew understood the epithet "Christ" to mean "messiah of Israel." Apart from the genealogy, Matthew uses the epithet "son of David" in contexts of healing and elsewhere.[46] The association of the title "son of David" with healing may be explained in two ways. One way is to argue that the model for this association is the prophecies of healing associated with the restoration in the Greek version of Isaiah 40–55: opening the eyes of the blind (42:7) and freeing captives from their bonds (42:7; 49:8-9).[47] These have been read in the context of messianic expectation and thus associated with the royal messiah, the son of David. The other possibility is that the association derives from the connection of Solomon, the son of David, with healing and especially with exorcism.[48]

---

43. Philo, *On the Virtues* 212, 219.

44. Gen 18:18; cf. 12:3.

45. Gal 3:8; cf. Acts 3:25.

46. Matt 9:27; 12:23; 15:22; 20:30-31.

47. Under this interpretation, the prophecy about the liberation of captives is understood as fulfilled in the exorcisms of Jesus.

48. Dennis C. Duling, "Solomon, Exorcism, and the Son of David," *HTR* 68 (1975) 235-52; Bruce Chilton, "Jesus *ben David*: Reflections on the *Davidssohnfrage*," *JSNT* 14 (1982) 88-112; J. H. Charlesworth, "The Son of David: Solomon and Jesus (Mark 10.47)," in Peder Borgen and Søren Giversen, eds., *The New Testament and Hellenistic Judaism* (Peabody, MA: Hendrickson, 1995), 72-87; Stephen H. Smith, "The Function of the Son of David Tradition in Mark's Gospel," *NTS* 42 (1996) 523-39. For criticism of this interpretation, see Marcus, *Way of the Lord*, 151-52.

## The Birth of Jesus

In the passage immediately following the genealogy (Matt 1:18-25), Matthew reprises the opening titular sentence:

"Now the birth [or descent] of Jesus Christ was like this" (1:18). The notion of Jesus as the son of God is indirectly expressed in this passage, as we will see presently.

The plot of this short narrative and the formula quotation near its end make clear that Mary is still a virgin at the time the story is set. Yet she had become pregnant before she began to live with Joseph, to whom she was engaged to be married. The narrator informs the audience that the pregnancy is ἐκ πνεύματος ἁγίου. This phrase may be translated "from or of *a* holy spirit" or "from or of *[the]* holy spirit," that is, the spirit of God.[49] In either case, the idea would seem to be that the spirit in question is the efficient cause employed by God, the actual agent, in bringing about the pregnancy of a virgin.[50] Mark uses the definite article in speaking about "the spirit" that descended to Jesus at his baptism, implying that it was God's spirit, a divine force or power. The phrase in Matthew, even though it lacks the article, probably has the same sense.[51]

A bit further on, the same phrase is used by an angel of the Lord who appears to Joseph in a dream and informs him that "what has been begotten in her is ἐκ πνεύματος . . . ἁγίου," that is, from or of (the) holy spirit (1:20). The angel says that Mary will bear a son and that Joseph is to call his name "Jesus" because "he will save his people from their sins" (1:21). This explanation of the name is based on a popular etymology of the Hebrew name, Joshua, expressed in Greek with Ἰησοῦς.[52]

Then the narrator comments, in the first of a number of formula quotations in Matthew:

49. The preposition ἐκ here is apparently used as a marker denoting origin or cause; see Walter Bauer, *A Greek-English Lexicon of the New Testament and Other Early Christian Literature,* ed. William F. Arndt and F. Wilbur Gingrich; 3rd ed. rev. by Frederick W. Danker (Chicago: University of Chicago Press, 2000), *s.v.* 3.

50. Cf. Ulrich Luz, *Matthew 1–7: A Commentary* (Minneapolis: Fortress, 2007), 93.

51. Cf. Raymond E. Brown, S.S., *The Birth of the Messiah: A Commentary on the Infancy Narratives in the Gospels of Matthew and Luke* (new updated ed.; ABRL; New York: Doubleday, 1993; 1st ed. 1977), 124-25; W. D. Davies and Dale C. Allison, *The Gospel according to St. Matthew* (3 vols.; ICC; Edinburgh: T&T Clark, 1988-97), 1:200.

52. Brown, *Birth of the Messiah,* 130-31.

All this happened in order that what was said by the Lord through the prophet might be fulfilled, saying, "Behold, the virgin will conceive and will bear a son, and they will call his name Emmanuel." (Matt 1:22-23)

The text cited is Isa 7:14. In the Hebrew, the identity of the child is ambiguous. The context may be read as implying that the child is the second child of Isaiah himself; alternatively, he is the son of King Ahaz.[53] It is a young woman who is with child, not a virgin. The Greek manuscripts vary with regard to who will call the child Emmanuel.[54] Three manuscripts read "you will call" and imply that King Ahaz is the father of the child.[55] Matthew apparently changed "she will call" or "you will call" to "they will call" to adapt the text to its new context: all the followers of Jesus will call him Emmanuel.[56] All the known manuscripts representing the Old Greek translate the Hebrew's "young woman" with παρθένος, which also means young woman. It sometimes has the connotation of virginity, but not necessarily. In Matthew, the context makes clear that "virgin" is meant.[57]

It has been pointed out that the Old Greek translation "probably means only that she who is now a virgin will later conceive and give birth; no miracle is involved."[58] Therefore, "the Isaian prophecy did not give rise either to the idea of the virginal conception or to Matthew's narrative. . . ."[59] What then was the catalyst that evoked a miraculous reading of Isa 7:14?[60]

The best explanation is that the author of Matthew and his predecessors were aware of Greek and Roman stories about great men being fa-

---

53. Joseph Blenkinsopp, *Isaiah 1–39* (AB 19; New York/London: Doubleday, 2000), 232-34. See also chapter 2 above.

54. On the Greek version of Isaiah 7, see chapter 3 above.

55. B (Vaticanus), A (Alexandrinus), and C (Catena of prophets) read κάλεις ("you [sing.] will call"). S (Sinaiticus) reads καλέσει ("she will call") in conformity with the MT. Q (Codex Marchalianus) and L (Lucian) read καλέσετε ("you [pl.] will call"). About a quarter to a half of the known minuscules read καλέσουσι(ν) ("they will call"). These MSS may have been influenced by the text of Matthew. See the critical apparatus in Alfred Rahlfs, *Septuaginta* (2 vols.; Stuttgart: Württembergische Bibelanstalt, 1935), vol. 2, *ad loc.*

56. Cf. Davies and Allison, *Matthew*, 1:213-14.

57. See the discussion in Brown, *Birth of the Messiah*, 145-49; Luz, *Matthew 1–7*, 96.

58. Davies and Allison, *Matthew*, 1:214. So also Brown, *Birth of the Messiah*, 149.

59. Brown, *Birth of the Messiah*, 149. So also Davies and Allison, *Matthew*, 1:214.

60. Davies and Allison discuss proposals regarding "a historical catalyst," but find these theories problematic (*Matthew*, 1:216).

thered by deities with human women.⁶¹ The Isaian prophecy enabled followers of Jesus to interpret the origin of Jesus as equally or even more miraculous, since his Father is not just one among many so-called gods, but the Creator of all things himself.

There is no exact or even very close parallel to Matthew's story in Greek and Latin literature for two reasons. First, the story is analogous to and probably inspired by Greek and Roman stories, but the typical form of the story is adapted to a Jewish context. Second, like some Greeks and others roughly contemporary with Matthew, the evangelist rejected the mythological expression of the idea. An analogy to this rejection is found in Plutarch's *Life of Numa:*

> And yet the Egyptians make a distinction here which is thought plausible, namely, that while a woman can be approached by a divine spirit and made pregnant, there is no such thing as carnal intercourse and communion between a man and a divinity. (Καίτοι δοκοῦσιν οὐκ ἀπιθάνως Αἰγύπτιοι διαιρεῖν ὡς γυναικὶ μὲν οὐκ ἀδύνατον πνεῦμα πλησιάσαι θεοῦ καί τινας ἐντεκεῖν ἀρχὰς γενέσεως, ἀνδρὶ δὲ οὐκ ἔστι σύμμιξις πρὸς θεὸν οὐδὲ ὁμιλία σώματος.)⁶²

Aeschylus wrote in similar language about the impregnation of Io by Zeus:

> Whence [Argos] we boast ourselves sprung, from the breath of Zeus' nostrils, And the touch of his procreant finger laid, For a dynasty's founding, on a king's daughter, Even the gnat-tormented heifer-maid.⁶³

---

61. See the list given in ibid., 1:214. See also David R. Cartlidge and David L. Dungan, *Documents for the Study of the Gospels* (Philadelphia: Fortress, 1980), 129-36.

62. Plutarch *Life of Numa* 4.4; text and translation (slightly modified) from Bernadotte Perrin, *Plutarch's Lives* (11 vols; Loeb Classical Library; Cambridge, MA: Harvard University Press; London: Heinemann, 1914), 1:318-19. For discussion see Hans Dieter Betz, "Plutarch's Life of Numa: Some Observations on Graeco-Roman 'Messianism,'" in Bockmuehl and Paget, eds., *Redemption and Resistance*, 44-61, especially 49. Davies and Allison refer to this passage (*Matthew*, 1:201). See also the discussion in François Bovon, *Luke 1* (Hermeneia; Minneapolis: Fortress, 2002), 43-47, especially 46 and n. 27.

63. Aeschylus, *The Suppliant Maidens* 17-19; trans. by G. M. Cookson in Robert Maynard Hutchins, ed., *Great Books of the Western World* (Chicago: William Benton/Encyclopedia Britannica, 1952), 1. On Io, see Ken Dowden, "Io," in Simon Hornblower and Anthony Spawforth, eds., *Oxford Classical Dictionary* (3rd ed.; Oxford: Oxford University Press, 1996), 762-63.

The term "breath" here translates the Greek word πνεῦμα, the same word used by Plutarch, Matthew, and Mark.

The conclusion that Jesus is portrayed as God's son in this passage suggests how the name "Emmanuel" in the formula quotation should be understood.[64] Matthew explains it as meaning "God with us" (1:23). If Jesus is portrayed as son of God, it is too much to say that "Emmanuel" implies that Jesus is "God."[65] But it is too little to infer, as Davies and Allison do, that Jesus is a human being "in whom God's active presence, that is, the divine favor and blessing and aid, have manifested themselves."[66] As son of God, Jesus is divine, yet subordinated to God.[67] God's active presence is manifest in him not only because he is divine, but also because he is God's appointed agent, the messiah of Israel.

### The Flight into Egypt

In the passage about the flight into Egypt, Jesus is again portrayed as son of God in relation to another formula quotation:

> And he was there until the death of Herod in order that what was said by the Lord through the prophet might be fulfilled, saying, "Out of Egypt I have called my son." (2:15)

The quotation is from Hos 11:1, and the wording of Matthew is closer to the Hebrew text than to the Old Greek. This state of affairs can be explained in one of three ways: the author of Matthew could read the Hebrew text; he used a Greek translation closer to the Hebrew than Old Greek; or he was using a collection of scriptural testimonies.[68]

---

64. Brown concluded that Matt 1:18-25 portrays Jesus as God's son (*Messiah*, 161); so also Luz, *Matthew 1–7*, 95-96. Davies and Allison, however, argued that others had "exaggerated the importance in 1.18-25 of Matthew's Son of God Christology" (*Matthew*, 1:201, n. 9). This perspective leads them to disregard the notion of Jesus as son of God in their interpretation of the name "Emmanuel" (ibid., 1:217).

65. See the criticisms of this view in Davies and Allison, *Matthew*, 1:217.

66. By ignoring the implication that Jesus is son of God here, Davies and Allison seem to imply this kind of interpretation (ibid.).

67. The subordination of the son to the Father seems to be implied in Mark 13:32 and its parallel in Matt 24:36; cf. 1 Cor 15:27-28.

68. On the use of such collections, see Martin C. Albl, *"And Scripture Cannot Be Bro-*

Assuming that the context of the passage in Hosea is significant, Jesus' stay in Egypt is compared to the sojourn of the people of Israel in Egypt and especially to their deliverance from the oppression they were suffering there.[69] The depiction of Jesus as son of God in this context is significant on two levels. On one level, Jesus recapitulates the experience of the people of Israel as a whole. The same recapitulation occurs in the testing of Jesus by Satan, which recalls the behavior of the Israelites during the wilderness wandering. In that passage, Satan introduces the first two of the three tests with the phrase, "If you are the son of God."[70] On another level, the exodus from Egypt provided language for speaking about new acts of deliverance.[71] The evocation of this tradition through the citation of Hosea 11 suggests that Jesus, as messiah, will play a major role in the definitive deliverance of the last days.

### The Baptism of Jesus and His Authority

Matthew follows Mark in the portrayal of the divine voice at the baptism of Jesus, except that the the statement is addressed to all present, rather than to Jesus alone (3:17). An important contextual difference is that the audience of Matthew will connect the statement "This is my son" with the story about Jesus' conception in chapter 1.

In a later passage of the Gospel (11:25-30), Matthew portrays Jesus as praising God for revealing "these things" to babes rather than to the wise and understanding. Then Jesus announces:

> "All things have been handed over to me by my father, and no one knows the son except the father, and no one knows the father except the son and anyone to whom the son may choose to reveal [the father]."

The first statement, that the father has handed all things over to Jesus, implies that Jesus has full authority as the primary agent of God. It recalls the

---

ken": *The Form and Function of the Early Christian* Testimonia Collections (NovTSup 96; Leiden: Brill, 1999).

69. Cf. Hos 11:1 with Exodus 1–3.

70. Matt 4:3, 6. On the relation of the testing of Jesus to the experience of Israel in the desert, see Davies and Allison, *Matthew*, 1:263, 352.

71. Hos 2:14-15; Isa 40:1-3; 51:9-11; Ezek 20:33-44; for further references, see Davies and Allison, *Matthew*, 1:263.

statement of the risen Jesus to the Eleven at the end of the Gospel, where such authority is explicitly mentioned. The second statement, that no one knows the son except the father, qualifies the first statement. Although God has handed over all things to him, his role as agent of God remains hidden to all but God. The implication is that Jesus will exercise his role as divine agent, son of God and messiah, only after the resurrection.[72]

The third and last statement of this initial saying portrays Jesus in the role of revealer, one who makes the Father known to those whom he chooses.

In the next short speech, Jesus is portrayed speaking as personified wisdom might speak:

> "Come to me, all who labor and are burdened, and I will give you rest. Take my yoke upon you and learn from me, for I am gentle and humble of heart, and you will find rest for your souls. For my yoke is easy and my burden is light."[73]

The content of what Jesus says here is similar to the concluding autobiographical poem of Sirach:

> Draw near to me, unlearned ones, and live in the house of learning. Why do you say that you are lacking in these things, and your souls thirst greatly? I opened my mouth and said, "Acquire for yourselves without money." Put your necks under the yoke and let your souls receive learning. For it is near to be found. See with your eyes that I have labored little and have found for myself great rest. (Sir 51:23-27 LXX)

Jesus speaks in the Matthean passage as a teacher, as Sirach does, but the text hints that Jesus is wisdom embodied.[74] This hint does not necessarily imply that Jesus is preexistent. The Wisdom of Solomon states that wisdom passes into holy souls in every generation and makes them friends of God, and prophets (Wis 7:27). The Matthean text may signify something

---

72. In the account of the stilling of the storm, the disciples do obeisance to him and say, "Truly you are God's son" (Matt 14:33). In light of the sayings in 11:25-27, the miracle account may be interpreted as an instance of God revealing the son to the disciples by enabling Jesus to make the wind cease.

73. Cf. Matt 11:28-30 with Prov 9:5-6 LXX.

74. The same idea may be expressed in Matt 11:19; see Davies and Allison, *Matthew*, 2:264-65, 272.

similar. As the son of God, he is a holy soul and prophet, even divine, though neither preexistent nor equal to God.

### The Acclamation of Peter, the Transfiguration, and the Entry into Jerusalem

In the discussion of the identity of Jesus, Matthew rewrites Mark so that Peter acclaims Jesus, not only as the messiah, but also as "the son of the living God" (16:16). The close association of the two epithets here makes clear that they are equivalent for Matthew.

Matthew follows Mark in the account of the transfiguration with minor changes. One of these is that he makes the divine statement more similar to its counterpart in the baptismal scene.

In the entry of Jesus into Jerusalem, Matthew quotes the passage from Zechariah 9 to which Mark only alludes. The result is that Jesus is explicitly presented as a king (Matt 21:5). Matthew also portrays the crowd as crying out, "Hosanna to the son of David."[75] In association with the citation of Zechariah 9, this epithet has a clearly messianic and political sense.

### The Passion Narrative

Whereas Mark portrayed Jesus as speakly openly to the high priest and evasively to Pilate, Matthew presents Jesus as speaking evasively to the high priest. To the question, "Are you the messiah, the son of God?" Jesus answers, "You have said so." Perhaps here Matthew is maintaining the view that the son is hidden from the world at present and is known only by God.[76] The rest of Matthew's answer implies that Jesus will exercise his messiahship after his resurrection as Son of Man:

> "But I say to you, from now on you will see the Son of Man sitting on the right of the Power and coming with the clouds of heaven." (26:64)

The expression "from now on" may express imminent expectation of the revelation of the Son of Man.

---

75. Matt 21:9; cf. 21:15. The crowd in Mark refers to Jesus as "the one coming in the name of the Lord," and acclaims "the coming kingdom of our father David" (11:9-10).

76. Cf. Matt 11:27.

# Luke

Luke begins much differently from Mark and Matthew, with a formal preface that does not even mention Jesus explicitly. Jesus is introduced for the first time in the scene traditionally referred to as the annunciation (1:26-38).

## *The Annunciation*

In contrast to Matthew, the angel is named, rather than unnamed, and sent to Mary, rather than Joseph. As in Matthew, Mary is identified as a virgin (παρθένος) engaged to be married to Joseph. That she is a virgin and not just a young woman is made clear in her statement to the angel, "How will this be, since I do not know a man?" (1:34).[77] But first the angel announces to Mary:

> "And behold, you will conceive in your womb and will bear a son, and you shall call his name 'Jesus.' He will be great, and will be called 'son of the Most High,' and the Lord God will give him the throne of David, his father, and he will rule over the house of Jacob forever, and of his kingdom there will be no end." (Luke 1:31-33)

As in Matthew, his name is to be "Jesus," although here Mary names him, rather than Joseph. Then Gabriel reveals that Jesus will be both son of God and messiah. The notion of his being son of God is formulated in terms of his being called "son of the Most High."

In Mark, the Gerasene demoniac addresses Jesus as "son of the most high God."[78] In the Old Greek translation of the Hebrew Bible, "the Most High" is the usual translation of Elyon.[79] Mark's "most high God" is probably a translation of the Hebrew or Aramaic El Elyon.[80] A striking parallel to Luke's usage occurs in the so-called "son of God text" from Qumran,

---

77. The verb "to know" (γινώσκω) is used here for sexual relations; Brown, *Birth of the Messiah*, 289; Joseph A. Fitzmyer, *The Gospel according to Luke (I–IX)* (AB 28; Garden City, NY: Doubleday, 1981), 348; François Bovon, *Luke 1* (Hermeneia; Minneapolis: Fortress, 2002), 51.

78. υἱὸς τοῦ θεοῦ τοῦ ὑψίστου; Mark 5:7.

79. ὁ ὕψιστος; Deut 32:8; for further examples, see Edwin Hatch and Henry A. Redpath, eds., *A Concordance to the Septuagint and Other Greek Versions of the Old Testament* (Oxford: Clarendon, 1897), *s.v.*

80. In 1QapGen 21:2 Abram says that he offered sacrifices to God Most High (אל עליון); see Florentino García Martínez and Eibert J. C. Tigchelaar, eds., *The Dead Sea Scrolls Study Edition* (2 vols.; Leiden: Brill, 1997-1998), 1:42-43.

which reads, "He will be called son of God, and they will call him son of the Most High."[81] The latter text probably refers to the messiah of Israel.

Gabriel goes on to say that God will give Jesus "the throne of David, his father." Thus Luke closely links his being "son of the Most High" with his messiahship, that is, his role as king in the restoration of the house of David and the kingdom of Israel in the last days.

The definitive and eternal character of his rule and kingdom are expressed in synonymous parallel statements: "He will rule over the house of Jacob forever, and of his kingdom there will be no end." This affirmation is probably inspired by the promise in 2 Samuel 7 that God will "establish *the throne of his kingdom forever*" and that "your *house* and your *kingdom* will be made sure *forever*."[82]

It also evokes the book of Daniel. In his interpretation of the dream of Nebuchadnezzar, Daniel says:

> "And in the days of those kings, the God of heaven will set up a kingdom that will never be destroyed, and the kingdom will never be left to another people. It will shatter and bring to an end all these kingdoms, and it will stand forever. . . ."[83]

Even more pertinently, when kingship is given to the one like a son of man, Daniel says:

> His dominion is everlasting dominion, which will not pass away, and his kingdom is indestructible.[84]

Then Mary asks her question, "How will this be," and Gabriel replies:

> "[The] holy spirit will come upon you, and [the] power of [the] Most High will overshadow you; therefore, the child to be born will be called holy, son of God." (Luke 1:35)[85]

---

81. *Aramaic Apocalypse* (4Q246) 2:1. See the discussion in chapter 3 above.

82. 2 Sam 7:13, 16; Brown, *Birth of the Messiah*, 310; emphasis his. So also Bovon, *Luke 1*, 51.

83. Dan 2:44; translation from Collins, *Daniel*, 152.

84. Dan 7:14; translation from Collins, *Daniel*, 275. Fitzmyer concludes that Luke may allude here to Isa 9:6 LXX or to Dan 7:14; *Luke (I–IX)*, 348.

85. On the translation of the last clause, see Brown, *Birth of the Messiah*, 286; Fitzmyer, *Luke (I–IX)*, 334, 351; Bovon, *Luke 1*, 43, 52.

The language about the "power of the Most High" overshadowing Mary is theophanic language. For example, near the end of Exodus, it is said:

> And the cloud covered the tent of testimony, and the tent was filled with [the] glory of [the] LORD; and Moses was not able to enter the tent of testimony, because the cloud overshadowed it, and the tent was filled with [the] glory of [the] LORD. (Exod 40:34-35)[86]

The conception is brought about by the holy spirit coming upon Mary and by the power of the Most High overshadowing her. The parallel expressions may be read as implying that the holy spirit is equivalent to "the power of God" and thus the efficient cause of the conception. The answer to Mary's question is therefore similar to the account in Matthew: God is the ultimate agent of the conception, so that God may be called the Father of the child.

As we have noted, the name "Most High" applied to God is biblical and continued to be employed in the period of the Second Temple. The use of this name, however, has the effect of opening the text to a traditionally Greek reading. In non-Jewish, non-Christian Greek texts, "Most High" occurs as a name for Zeus. Zeus Hypsistos was revered from Athens, through Asia Minor and Syria, and on into Egypt.[87] Thus for members of Luke's audience familiar with the cult of "Zeus Most High," the designation of Jesus as "son of the Most High" could call to mind stories about Zeus fathering sons by human women.

Luke's narrative does not speak of God in an anthropomorphic or mythological way. The event is described in an elevated and subtle manner. Nevertheless, the scene evokes the myths and legends of the births of famous Greek and Roman men.[88] As in Matthew, the narrative about the virginal conception of Jesus in Luke implies that he is divine. In both Gospels, Jesus is "son of God" in a stronger sense than in Mark. The narratives in Matthew and Luke do not imply preexistence, but the notion of virginal conception was easily combined with ideas about preexistence later on.

---

86. The verb translated "overshadowed" is the same one used by Luke (ἐπισκιάζω). Cf. Luke 9:34; Bovon, *Luke 1*, 52.

87. Cilliers Breytenbach, "Hypsistos," *DDD*, 439-43.

88. In his discussion of the context of this narrative in the history of religion, Bovon emphasizes Egyptian religion and pharaonic ideology (*Luke 1*, 43-47, especially 46). See, however, his references to Plutarch and Philo.

## The Birth of Jesus

In the narrative of the birth of Jesus (2:1-20), Jesus' Davidic descent is emphasized (2:4). This emphasis prepares for the announcement to the shepherds that a child has been born in the city of David who is χριστὸς κύριος (literally, "messiah lord" or "lord messiah"). The juxtaposition of the two epithets seems to have as its purpose the explanation of the Jewish term "messiah" for a Gentile audience.[89] The epithet "lord" had royal connotations.[90]

Although Luke does not emphasize Davidic messianic themes in the account of the baptism of Jesus (3:21-22), the prayer in Acts 4 seems to interpret his baptism as God's anointing of Jesus "to do whatever your hand and your plan had predetermined to take place" (4:28).[91]

## Jesus' Public Activity

Luke's portrayal of the inauguration of Jesus' public activity, with its citation of Isa 61:1-2, seems to present him as a prophetic messiah rather than a Davidic.[92] If so, this would mean that Luke, like Mark, combined prophetic and royal traits in his portrait of Jesus as the messiah.[93]

In chapters 1–2 Luke sets up the expectation of a Davidic messiah who will redeem Israel in a political sense. This expectation is alluded to in 24:21 and Acts 1:6. It had already been reinterpreted in Jesus' inaugural speech

89. Stanton, "Messianism and Christology," 89-90. Stanton also discusses the possibility that the passage is intended as a counterpoint to the imperial cult (ibid., 89). See also his discussion of the portrayal of Jesus as the Davidic messiah in the account of the presentation of Jesus in the temple (2:25-38) (ibid., 90).

90. See the discussion of the poem in Philippians 2 in the previous chapter.

91. See also Acts 13:32-34; Stanton, "Messianism and Christology," 90-91.

92. Isa 61:1-3 is also cited in 4Q521 in a messianic interpretation, and that interpretation also seems to be a kind of prophetic messianism; see John J. Collins, "A Herald of Good Tidings: Isaiah 61:1-3 and Its Actualization in the Dead Sea Scrolls," in Craig Evans and Shemaryahu Talmon, eds., *The Quest for Context and Meaning: Studies in Biblical Intertextuality in Honor of James A. Sanders* (Biblical Interpretation Series 28; Leiden: Brill, 1997), 225-40; see also idem, *The Scepter and the Star*, 117-22. 11Q13 (11QMelchizedek) also speaks about an anointed herald who goes before Melchizedek (ibid., 229-30).

93. Cf. Luke 4:41 and Acts 9:20-22, where Jesus' Davidic messianic status is emphasized with the epithet "son of God"; Stanton, "Messianism and Christology," 91.

with its hints that Jesus would be accepted more fully outside Israel than within it (4:24-30). It is more clearly reinterpreted in the commands of the risen Jesus to proclaim repentance and forgiveness of sins to all the nations (24:47) and to be his witnesses to the ends of the earth (Acts 1:8).[94]

## Conclusion: A Reassessment of the Preexistence of the Messiah in Paul's Letters

Let us now turn to a reassessment of the notion of the preexistence of the messiah in the letters of Paul. As concluded in the previous chapter, there is one passage in Paul's letters that clearly speaks about the preexistence of Jesus, the prose hymn in Philippians. That passage does not imply that Jesus was God or equal to God before his birth as a human being. It does, however, state that he was "in the form of God."[95]

As noted in the same chapter, there are two other passages in Paul's undisputed letters that may refer to the preexistence of Jesus. One is the passage about there being one God and one Lord, Jesus Christ, "through whom are all things and through whom we exist" (1 Cor 8:5-6). The other is the one about "our gospel" being "veiled among those who are perishing," which describes Christ as "the image of God" (2 Cor 4:3-4). If these two passages imply the preexistence of Jesus, he appears to be identified with wisdom as a personified aspect of God.

The previous chapter also included a discussion of Paul's reference at the beginning of Romans to "the gospel of God" as being "about his son, who was born from the seed of David according to the flesh." This passage may be read as implying that Jesus existed as God's son before he was born "according to the flesh." In that case, Paul would assume a preexistent messiah. Such a messiah is attested in the Greek version of Psalm 110 (Psalm

---

94. Cf. ibid., 92.

95. ἐν μορφῇ θεοῦ (Phil 2:6). It is unlikely that this phrase is an allusion to Gen 1:26-27. The phrase used in the Greek version refers to the "image" (εἰκών) of God, not to God's "form" (μορφή). Thus Christ is not presented here as the second Adam, pace James D. G. Dunn, *Christology in the Making* (London: SCM, 1980), 114-25. It is doubtful that the hymn "is integrally connected with Adam speculation," as Andrew Chester concludes (*Messiah and Exaltation* [WUNT 207; Tübingen: Mohr Siebeck], 392). For criticism of Dunn's position, see Otfried Hofius, *Der Christushymnus Philipper 2,6-11* (2nd ed.; WUNT 17; Tübingen: Mohr Siebeck, 1976), 113-16.

109 LXX), the *Similitudes of Enoch,* and in *4 Ezra* (2 Esdras 3–14).[96] But Paul shares with the Synoptics an emphasis on the exaltation of Jesus to his messianic office at the time of his resurrection.

So what does "in the form of God" in Philippians mean? As argued in the previous chapter above, the hymn alludes to the violent, plundering activities of rulers and to their arrogant claims to be godlike. Since references to Jesus as "Christ" frame the poem and since its rhetoric is political, it is likely that the phrase "in the form of God" portrays Jesus as the preexistent messiah. The evidence indicating that Paul may portray the preexistent Jesus elsewhere as personified wisdom does not tell against this interpretation. On the contrary, there is evidence that the two portrayals were combined in the cultural context of Paul's letters.

In the *Similitudes of Enoch,* the preexistent Son of Man is presented as the messiah. He is also, however, described in terms of divine wisdom:

> And in that hour that son of man was named in the presence of the Lord of Spirits, and his name, before the Head of Days. Even before the sun and the constellations were created, before the stars of heaven were made, his name was named before the Lord of Spirits. . . . And for this [reason] he was chosen and hidden in his presence before the world was created and forever. (*1 Enoch* 48:2-3, 6)[97]

Here language from Prov 8:22-31 is applied to the Son of Man as preexistent messiah. So, like the author of the *Similitudes of Enoch,* Paul may also have conceived of Jesus, as the preexistent messiah, in terms of preexistent and personified divine wisdom.[98]

Although there is less evidence that Mark presented Jesus as preexistent, if the hypothesis about Paul just discussed is correct, it would be analogous to Mark's presentation of Jesus as the hidden Son of Man. It is to the origin and character of the Synoptic Son of Man tradition that we turn in the next chapter.

---

96. *1 Enoch* 62:7; *4 Ezra* 7:28; 12:32; 13:25-26. On the Greek version of Psalm 110, see chapter 3 above.

97. Translation from George W. E. Nickelsburg and James C. VanderKam, *1 Enoch: A New Translation Based on the Hermeneia Commentary* (Minneapolis: Fortress, 2004), 62.

98. See pp. 89-90 above; cf. Martin Hengel, *The Son of God: The Origin of Christology and the History of Jewish-Hellenistic Religion* (Philadelphia: Fortress, 1976; German ed. 1975), 71-76.

# 7. Jesus as Son of Man

It is virtually impossible to come to an understanding of Christian origins without having a theory about the teaching and life of Jesus. In particular, it is difficult to discuss early christologies without being clear about what basis they have in the life of Jesus. This is especially true of the portrayal of Jesus as Son of Man.

In the Synoptic Gospels, "Son of Man" is a title used to characterize Jesus, even though it most often occurs in his own speech. This chapter begins with a discussion of the use and significance of that title in the Synoptic Gospels. Following that is a treatment of the question of the origin of these sayings in the life of Jesus.

## Son of Man in the Synoptic Gospels

Since the work of Rudolf Bultmann, commentators generally divide the Son of Man sayings in the Synoptic Gospels into three groups: sayings "which speak of the Son of Man (1) as coming, (2) as suffering death and rising again, and (3) as now at work."[1] I will use these categories for their practical value.

---

1. Rudolf Bultmann, *Theology of the New Testament* (2 vols.; New York: Scribner, 1951), 1:30.

## *Mark*

In the Gospel according to Mark, the Son of Man sayings are closely bound up with the theme of the identity of Jesus and the secrecy about it. The author of Mark takes Dan 7:13-14 as prophecy and seems to see its fulfillment in Jesus in two stages. During his public activity, he is the Son of Man who has authority to forgive sins and to interpret the commands of God concerning the sabbath (2:10, 28). As argued in the previous chapter, "Son of Man" and "messiah" are equivalent in Mark. So Mark implies that Jesus has such authority as the messiah, since he was appointed to this office by God at the time of his baptism.

Yet the messiahship of Jesus is hidden from the human characters in the narrative until the acclamation of Peter. In the depiction of Jesus as the authoritative Son of Man in chapter 2, there is no obvious allusion to Daniel. The audience of the narrative, having been instructed, can appreciate "the Son of Man" as a title for Jesus. But the characters are not enlightened about its significance. Although they do not object or question Jesus, there is no indication that they understand what the phrase means. The scribes, for example, are silenced by the miraculous healing of the paralyzed man.

In the middle section of Mark, the title "Son of Man" is used in the three passion predictions. The disciples are the only characters within the narrative to hear these predictions. Both the disciples and the audience seem to accept the equivalence of "messiah" and "Son of Man." The messianic use of the title "Son of Man" seems to presuppose a messianic interpretation of Dan 7:13-14. When Dan 7:13-14 is evoked in association with the passion predictions, a shocking paradox emerges. The interpretation of Daniel's dream-vision refers to a battle between the fourth beast and the holy ones, that is, between the mythic symbol of the Greco-Syrian king and the angels of heaven.[2] This cosmic battle has its counterpart in the king's persecution of the people of Judea. The one like a son of man is a glorious, heavenly figure who is given eternal kingship. Yet Mark portrays this Son of Man, identified with the earthly Jesus, as undergoing great suffering, rejection, and death. The tension of this paradox was too great to maintain for long. Ignatius of Antioch, early in the second century, already resolves the tension. He was the first among many to take

---

2. Dan 7:21-22, 25.

"Son of Man" as representing the humanity of Jesus[3] and "Son of God" as expressing his divinity.

The second stage of the fulfillment of Dan 7:13 according to Mark will take place in the future. The sayings about the Son of Man "coming," or, more broadly, the apocalyptic Son of Man sayings, express the expectation of this second fulfillment. The first such saying in Mark also occurs in the middle section:

> "For whoever is ashamed of me and of my words in this adulterous and sinful generation, the Son of Man will also be ashamed of him when he comes in the glory of his Father with the holy angels." (8:38)

In contrast to the version of this saying in Q,[4] the Markan one is not forensic. There is no indication that Jesus is acting as a witness or judge in the final judgment. Instead, the reference to the coming of the Son of Man here is closely related to the depiction of the coming of the Son of Man in the apocalyptic discourse of chapter 13. The significance of the saying about the Son of Man being ashamed when he comes is that he will not gather those who were ashamed of him. They will lose their place among the elect who are gathered by the angels to be with the Son of Man.

The final Son of Man saying in Mark occurs in the trial before the Sanhedrin, or, more accurately, the Judean council. When the high priest asks Jesus, "Are you the messiah, the son of the Blessed?" he responds, "I am, and you will see the Son of Man sitting on the right hand of the Power and coming with the clouds of heaven" (14:62). In one way, this saying is a turning point in the theme of Jesus' identity in Mark. He reveals openly that he is the messiah and will be the heavenly, coming Son of Man. In another way, this trial and the rest of the account of Jesus' rejection, suffering, and death still portray him as the hidden Son of Man. This is so because the high priest and all the others in authority do not recognize him as messiah and Son of Man. Further, no revelation of the glory and power of Jesus takes place to convince them otherwise. For the audience, however, the saying makes clear that Jesus will exercise his messianic office when he comes as Son of Man.

3. Delbert Burkett, *The Son of Man Debate: A History and Evaluation* (SNTSMS 107; Cambridge, UK: Cambridge University Press, 1999), 3, 7-8, 13-21.

4. Matt 10:32-33//Luke 12:8-9; James M. Robinson et al., *The Critical Edition of Q* (Hermeneia Supplements; Minneapolis: Fortress; Leuven: Peeters, 2000), 304-7.

The saying of Jesus before the high priest conflates allusions to Ps 110:1 and to Dan 7:13. Psalm 110 is used to depict the exaltation of Jesus after death, and Daniel 7 to portray his coming in glory. The introduction to the saying, "you will see," makes clear that the emphasis in relation to the narrative context is on the public vindication of Jesus as Son of Man.

## Matthew

Two distinctive features of the Son of Man sayings in Matthew are the emphasis on the Son of Man as eschatological judge and the notion that the Son of Man has a kingdom. The portrayal of the Son of Man as judge is clearest in the response of Jesus to Peter's question, "Look, we have left all things and have followed you. What then will be for us [in return]?" Jesus replies:

> "Truly I say to you, that you who have followed me, in the renewal of the world, when the Son of Man sits on the throne of his glory, will also sit on twelve thrones judging the twelve tribes of Israel." (Matt 19:27-28)

The phrase "the throne of his glory" also occurs in the *Similitudes of Enoch* with reference to the throne of "the Son of Man," that is, the figure of Daniel 7 whom the *Similitudes* portray as a preexistent, heavenly messiah.[5]

In the parable of the weeds, which is unique to Matthew, the man who sowed good seed in his field is interpreted as the Son of Man (13:24, 37). The enemy who sowed weeds among the grain is interpreted as the devil (13:25, 39). The harvest is the end of the age (13:30, 39). The interpretation of the parable is notable for its explicit teaching that the Son of Man has a kingdom (13:38, 41). Since the field is interpreted as "the world" (13:38), the kingdom of the Son of Man is also the whole world. This portrayal is similar to that of 1 Corinthians 15, in which the risen "Christ" also has a kingdom (1 Cor 15:24).

---

5. Johannes Theisohn, *Der auserwählte Richter* (Göttingen: Vandenhoeck & Ruprecht, 1975), 153-61. Leslie W. Walck has argued that Matthew is dependent on the *Similitudes of Enoch* in the use of this phrase; "The Son of Man in the *Similitudes of Enoch* and the Gospels," in Gabriele Boccaccini, ed., *Enoch and the Messiah Son of Man: Revisiting the Book of Parables* (Grand Rapids: Eerdmans, 2007), 299-337.

The Son of Man of Matthew's parable

> "will send his angels, and they will gather all causes of stumbling and all who practice lawlessness from his kingdom and will cast them into the furnace of fire; in that place there will be weeping and gnashing of teeth. Then the just will shine like the sun in the kingdom of their Father." (13:41-43a)

This passage depicts the Son of Man as judge, as well as king. The reference to "the kingdom of his Father" shows that he is God's agent in exercising judgment. Similarly, Paul argued that, after he had conquered all the enemies, Christ would hand the kingdom over to his Father. The portrayal of the Son of Man as judge is also found in the *Similitudes of Enoch*.[6]

As noted earlier, Mark has a saying about the Son of Man being ashamed of those who are ashamed of him. Matthew rewrites that saying to introduce once again the notion of the Son of Man as judge:

> "For the Son of Man is about to come in the glory of his Father with his angels, and then he will repay each in accordance with his activity." (Matt 16:27)

Immediately following the saying about the Son of Man being ashamed of those who are ashamed of him, the Markan Jesus states:

> "Truly I say to you, some of those who are standing here will surely not experience death until they see that the kingdom of God has come with power." (Mark 9:1)

Matthew rewrites this saying to introduce the idea that the Son of Man has a kingdom:

> "Truly I say to you, some of those who are standing here will surely not experience death until they see the Son of Man coming in his kingdom." (Matt 16:28)

This change is related to the theme of the Son of Man having a kingdom in the parable of the weeds. Both passages are probably dependent on Dan 7:13-14.

6. *1 Enoch* 46:4-8; 69:29.

The Son of Man also appears in the description of the final judgment that closes the apocalyptic discourse of Jesus in Matthew. The scene is introduced with the statement:

> "When the Son of Man comes in his glory, and all the angels with him, then he will sit on the throne of his glory." (Matt 25:31)

The narrative that follows combines an explicit forensic setting with the dispensation of rewards and punishments. As in the *Similitudes of Enoch,* the Son of Man here acts as God's agent in judging the just and the wicked.

Another important feature of the Son of Man theme in Matthew is that the title "Son of Man" is so strongly associated with Jesus that it is equivalent to the first-person pronoun and is interchangeable with it. This feature is clear in the opening of the scene in which Peter acclaims Jesus as messiah and son of God:

> "When Jesus had come to the region of Caesarea Philippi, he asked his disciples, 'Who do people say that the Son of Man is?' They then said, 'Some say John the Baptist, others Elijah, and others Jeremiah or one of the prophets.' He said to them, 'But as for you, who do you say that I am?'" (Matt 16:13-15).[7]

## Luke

The Gospel of Luke seems to present Jesus, the Son of Man, as both the advocate of his faithful followers in the heavenly court and as the eschatological judge. He appears as advocate in the following saying:

> "Truly I say to you, everyone who acknowledges me before human beings, the Son of Man will also acknowledge him before the angels of God. But the one who denies me before human beings, I will deny before the angels of God." (Luke 12:8-9)[8]

---

7. For further discussion of this point, see Adela Yarbro Collins, "The Influence of Daniel on the New Testament," in John J. Collins, *Daniel* (Hermeneia; Minneapolis: Fortress, 1993), 99.

8. In the form of this saying in Matthew, Jesus speaks in the first person and does not use the phrase "Son of Man" (Matt 10:32-33).

This saying envisages a scene in the heavenly court in which Jesus as Son of Man plays the role of advocate of those who have acknowledged him in public on earth. The second half of the saying may imply that he will act as the accuser of those who have denied him. This passage shares with Daniel 7 the characteristics of the heavenly scene, the forensic setting, and the presence of the Son of Man. It is likely that Daniel 7 had an influence in the creation of this saying.[9]

The role of the Son of Man as eschatological judge is not as clear in Luke as in Matthew. It seems to be implied, however, in several sayings. At the end of the Lukan version of the apocalyptic discourse, the audience is exhorted to watch and pray so that they may "stand before the Son of Man" (Luke 21:36). The language seems to portray defendants standing before a seated judge and thus evokes the tradition of the final judgment. In this case, as in Matthew's, the judge is Jesus, the Son of Man.

In another context, the Lukan Jesus says that, as Jonah became a sign to the Ninevites, so the Son of Man will be "to this generation":

"The queen of the South will rise up at the judgment with the men of this generation and will condemn them, because she came from the ends of the earth to hear the wisdom of Solomon, and look, something greater than Solomon is here." (Luke 11:31)

The point is that the general resurrection and final judgment will reveal that Jesus is the Son of Man and thus confound those of "this generation" who rejected him. Not only will the wicked see that Jesus has been vindicated by God, but they will also discover that he has an exalted role as the agent of God in the process of the eschatological judgment. Although it is not explicit, it is likely that the implied role is that of judge. The queen of the South and the Ninevites will play the role of witnesses at the judgment.[10]

---

9. On this saying as a creation of followers of Jesus after his death, see Adela Yarbro Collins, "The Origin of the Designation of Jesus as 'Son of Man,'" *HTR* 80 (1987) 391-407, especially 401-2; reprinted in eadem, *Cosmology and Eschatology in Jewish and Christian Apocalypticism* (Leiden: Brill, 1996), 139-58, especially 151-52.

10. For a discussion of the role of the Son of Man in Luke 6:22 and 18:1-8, see Yarbro Collins, "The Influence of Daniel on the New Testament," 100.

## The Origin of the Synoptic Son of Man Sayings

There are two main theories about the origin of all these sayings.[11] One is that the oldest Son of Man sayings are the ones that allude to Daniel 7 and that the other types derive from these.[12] The second is that all the Son of Man sayings derive from the use by Jesus of a Semitic idiom in which "son of man" means "a man" or "man" in general.[13]

### Derivation from a Semitic Idiom

The second theory was proposed by Arnold Meyer in 1896.[14] He argued that some Gospel sayings use the phrase "the son of man" to refer to "man" in general, as the Aramaic phrase בר נש is sometimes used. He identified the sayings "the son of man has authority on earth to forgive sins," "the son of man is lord of the sabbath," and "whoever speaks a word against the son of man will be forgiven" as exemplifying the usage.[15] He argued that other Gospel sayings use the phrase "son of man" to mean "I," especially when the "I," a human being, is contrasted with God, other beings, or animals. He identified the sayings about "the son of man" having "nowhere to lay his head" and "the son of man" coming "eating and drinking" as belonging to this group.[16] He based his argument for the second group on an alleged parallel usage in Galilean Aramaic of הָהוּא גַבְרָא (that man = I) and הָהוּא בַר נשא (that son of man).[17]

---

11. Cf. Burkett, *The Son of Man Debate*, 5.

12. Cf. ibid., 4-5, 22-31.

13. The second theory has been adopted by John Dominic Crossan, *The Historical Jesus: The Life of a Mediterranean Jewish Peasant* (San Francisco: HarperSanFrancisco, 1991), 258; Larry W. Hurtado adopts a variant of it in *One God, One Lord: Early Christian Devotion and Ancient Jewish Monotheism* (Grand Rapids: Eerdmans, 2003), 290-306.

14. Arnold Meyer, *Jesu Muttersprache: Das galiläische Aramäisch in seiner Bedeutung für die Erklärung der Reden Jesu und der Evangelien überhaupt* (Freiburg im Breisgau/Leipzig: Mohr Siebeck, 1896). He profited from the work of Emil Kautzsch and Gustaf Dalman (ibid., 27-28) and of Adolf Neubauer (ibid., 31-32), among others. See also the discussion of Meyer by Geza Vermes, "The Use of בר נש/בר נשא in Jewish Aramaic," Appendix E in Matthew Black, *An Aramaic Approach to the Gospels and Acts* (3rd ed.; Oxford: Clarendon, 1967), 311; reprinted with an introduction by Craig A. Evans (Peabody, MA: Hendrickson, 1998).

15. Mark 2:10, 28; Matt 12:32 (Meyer, *Jesu Muttersprache*, 93-95).

16. Matt 8:20//Luke 9:58; Matt 11:19//Luke 7:34 (ibid., 95-97).

17. Ibid., 95-96.

In the same year, Hans Lietzmann argued, on the basis of five tractates from the Palestinian Talmud, that the phrase בר נש (son of man) is a common expression and that it is a kind of indefinite pronoun meaning "someone."[18] He denied that בר נש (son of man) and הַהוּא גַבְרָא (that man = I) were interchangeable.[19] Since, in his view, the Aramaic phrase "son of man" could not be used as a title, he concluded that the formula ὁ υἱὸς τοῦ ἀνθρώπου (the son of man) in the Gospels must be a technical term of "Hellenistic theology." It could have arisen already in Jewish circles.[20]

So there was disagreement and controversy about the issue from the beginning. That state of affairs continues to this day.

In 1898, Gustaf Dalman put forward a quite different interpretation.[21] He argued first of all that the singular construction in Hebrew, בֶּן אָדָם, is rare, apart from its frequent use in Ezekiel, and found only in poetic language.[22] It does not mean "'the son of a certain man,' but the member of the genus man." He concluded that the biblical Aramaic usage is the same as the Hebrew.[23] This means that the ordinary word for "man" in biblical Aramaic is אֲנָשׁ, whereas the expression found in Dan 7:13, בַּר אֱנָשׁ, is uncommon and poetic.

The same situation holds for early Palestinian Aramaic, by which he meant the Targum Onkelos and the Targum to the Prophets, also known as

18. Hans Lietzmann, *Der Menschensohn: Ein Beitrag zur neutestamentlichen Theologie* (Freiburg im Breisgau/Leipzig: Mohr Siebeck, 1896), 38. See also the discussion of Lietzmann by Vermes, "The Use of בר נש/בר נשא in Jewish Aramaic," 311-12.

19. Lietzmann, *Menschensohn,* 84.

20. Ibid., 95.

21. Gustaf Dalman, *Die Worte Jesu mit Berücksichtigung des nachkanonischen jüdischen Schrifttums,* vol. 1: *Einleitung und wichtige Begriffe, nebst Anhang. Messianische Texte* (Leipzig: Hinrichs, 1898); ET *The Words of Jesus Considered in the Light of Post-Biblical Jewish Writings and the Aramaic Language* (Edinburgh: T&T Clark, 1909); the ET is cited here. See also the discussion of Dalman by Vermes, "The Use of בר נש/בר נשא in Jewish Aramaic," 312.

22. Num 23:19; Isa 56:2; Jer 49:18, 33; 50:40; 51:43; Job 16:21; 25:6; Pss 8:5 (8:4 Eng.); 80:18 (80:17 Eng.); 146:3.

23. Dalman, *The Words of Jesus,* 235. Erik Sjöberg attested in 1953 that most subsequent scholars agreed with Dalman on this point; "בר אנש und בן אדם im Hebräischen und Aramäischen," *Acta Orientalia* 21 (1953) 57-65, 91-107, especially 91-92. Sjöberg's claim that the definite form of the former phrase, that is, בן האדם, is unattested (ibid., 91) must be corrected now in light of 1QS 11:20. In that passage, the article is written above the line before the noun אדם.

the Targum Jonathan. The expression בַּר אֱנָשׁ is not found in Onkelos at all, and only rarely, in poetry, in Jonathan.[24] It is only in later Jewish-Galilean and Christian-Palestinian Aramaic that בַּר אֱנָשׁ is commonly used to signify "'a human being,' although in both these types of language the simple אֱנָשׁ remains current for 'any one.'"[25] He emphasizes that, in Jewish Palestinian Aramaic of the earlier period, the singular בַּר אֱנָשׁ was not in ordinary oral use.[26]

Dalman also argued that the definite form בַּר אֱנָשָׁא, like the Hebrew בֶּן הָאָדָם, is unheard of in the older Jewish Aramaic literature, that is, in the time of Jesus. In that literature "the human being" is expressed by the simple word אֱנָשָׁא.[27] Contradicting Lietzmann, Dalman concluded that the definite form was entirely suitable for use as a special designation of a particular individual.[28] But he noted that in idiomatic Greek, the phrase ὁ υἱὸς τοῦ ἀνθρώπου, which is common in the Synoptic Gospels, would have to be translated "the man's son," whereas the definite form of the Aramaic should be translated "the son of man."[29]

In 1901 Paul Fiebig disagreed with Dalman's conclusion that the phrase בַּר אֱנָשָׁא in the time of Jesus would still have the meaning "son of man," rather than simply "man."[30] But he also disagreed with Lietzmann's argument that, in the Palestinian Talmud, בר נש is simply an indefinite pronoun, meaning "someone." It could also mean "a man" or "man" in general.[31] Further, Fiebig argued that, in the Palestinian Talmud and in the

24. Dalman, *The Words of Jesus,* 236-37. Similarly Sjöberg, "בר אנש und בן אדם im Hebräischen und Aramäischen," 62, 91-92.

25. Dalman, *The Words of Jesus,* 237. Similarly Sjöberg, "בר אנש und בן אדם," 92-93, 98-99. Sjöberg also discusses Samaritan Aramaic (ibid., 95-96, 102) and Syriac (ibid., 99-100).

26. Dalman, *The Words of Jesus,* 236-37. Similarly Sjöberg, "בר אנש und בן אדם," 101.

27. Dalman, *The Words of Jesus,* 238.

28. Ibid., 238-41.

29. Ibid., 241. The translator reproduces Dalman's German translation of the two phrases: "des Menschen Sohn" ("the man's son") and "der Menschensohn" ("the son of man").

30. Paul Fiebig, *Der Menschensohn: Jesu Selbstbezeichnung mit besonderer Berücksichtigung des aramäischen Sprachgebrauches für "Mensch"* (Tübingen/Leipzig: Mohr Siebeck, 1901), 25. See also the discussion of Fiebig by Vermes, "The Use of בר נש/בר נשא in Jewish Aramaic," 312-13. Sjöberg agreed with Fiebig's conclusion, even though he rejected his argumentation ("בר אנש und בן אדם," 102).

31. Fiebig, *Der Menschensohn,* 28.

Midrashim, both the definite and indefinite forms can be used to mean either "the man" or "a man," but not "the son of man" or "a son of man."[32]

Against Meyer, Fiebig argued that the relevant Aramaic expressions never do and in fact cannot directly signify the first-person singular pronoun "I."[33] Against Meyer and others he argued that the sayings "the son of man has authority on earth to forgive sins," "the son of man is lord of the sabbath," and "whoever speaks a word against the son of man will be forgiven" are not due to the mistranslation of the Aramaic idiom. Rather, they represent sayings of Jesus in which "the man" is a self-reference.[34]

The Greek translators of Jesus' sayings did not use ὁ ἄνθρωπος to render the Aramaic idiom because by using the definite, unidiomatic Greek expression ὁ υἱὸς τοῦ ἀνθρώπου they pointed to the humanlike figure of Dan 7:13.[35]

Finally, Fiebig argued, on the basis of *1 Enoch* and *4 Ezra* (= 2 Esdras 3–14), that "the man" in Aramaic was a messianic title in oral circulation.[36] Jesus adopted that title to speak of himself as the messiah because it concealed as well as revealed his messianic identity. Fiebig assumed that the portrayal of the messianic secret goes back to the historical Jesus himself.[37]

Matthew Black published an article in the 1940s in which he, like Fiebig, rejected the idea that *bar-nāsh* was used to refer directly to the speaker, as the idiom "that man" was used. When it means "one" or "a man," however, it can refer to the speaker in his view.[38]

Also like Fiebig, Black argued that Jesus used the ambiguous phrase *bar-nāsh* as a "veiled allusion to His own identity as Son of Man."[39]

Then Geza Vermes stimulated a lot of discussion by publishing a study in 1967 entitled "The Use of בר נש/בר נשא in Jewish Aramaic," as an appendix to the third edition of Matthew Black's *An Aramaic Approach to the Gospels and Acts*.[40] He argued that the Son of Man sayings originated in Je-

---

32. Ibid., 44.

33. Ibid., 74-75.

34. Ibid., 61-66.

35. Ibid., 67.

36. Ibid., 80-100.

37. Ibid., 100.

38. Matthew Black, "Unsolved New Testament Problems: The 'Son of Man' in the Teaching of Jesus," *Expository Times* 60 (1948-1949) 32-36, especially 34-35.

39. Ibid., 35. This is the case, in his view, in Matt 11:19//Luke 7:34 (ibid., 34-35); Mark 2:10, 28; Luke 22:69 (ibid., 35).

40. Geza Vermes, "The Use of בר נש/בר נשא in Jewish Aramaic," Appendix E in Black,

sus' use of the Semitic idiom mentioned in his title in a generic or indefinite sense and, more importantly, as a circumlocution for "I." In other
words, he argued, with Meyer and against Lietzmann, Fiebig, and Black,
that בר נש (son of man) and הָהוּא גָּבְרָא (that man = I) are interchangeable and equivalent. He doubted that "son of man" was originally a
christological formula. If it had been, it would have occurred in Paul's letters or in the other epistles. He, like others, was struck by the fact that the
phrase occurs almost exclusively on the lips of Jesus. He reminded his
readers that the phrase ὁ υἱὸς τοῦ ἀνθρώπου (the son of man) is not idiomatic in Greek; it would normally mean the son of the man or the man's
son.

The Aramaic form of the idiom occurs in Dan 7:13. By the time Vermes
wrote, it was generally accepted that the idiom was used in virtually all periods in a generic sense to mean "man" as such (the human being in general). It was also generally recognized that the idiom was used widely in an
indefinite sense to mean "one" or "someone." But Vermes did not use any
of these established uses to explain the origin and meaning of any saying in
the New Testament. Rather, the crucial underpinning of his thesis is the
premise that there existed in Aramaic literature what he calls a circumlocutional use of the idiom. In other words, an Aramaic speaker would use
the phrase "son of man" to refer to himself when a direct statement about
himself would have seemed immodest or have been uncomfortable for the
speaker. For example, Vermes takes the saying of Mark 2:10 as probably an
actual saying of Jesus:

> "But that you may know that the son of man has authority on earth to
> forgive sins . . . 'I say to you, get up, lift up your pallet, and go home.'"

According to Vermes, the phrase "son of man" was used by Jesus because
the direct claim, "I have the authority to forgive sins on earth," would have
sounded immodest.[41] He argued further that the Son of Man sayings that
contain the prediction of Jesus' suffering, death, and resurrection were

---

*An Aramaic Approach to the Gospels and Acts,* 310-30; reprinted with an introduction by
Craig A. Evans. See also Geza Vermes, *Jesus the Jew: A Historian's Reading of the Gospels*
(Philadelphia: Fortress, 1973), 160-91. For brief discussions of Vermes' work, see Burkett, *The
Son of Man Debate,* 70, 75, 86-87. Vermes has revisited the topic and restated his views in
idem, *The Authentic Gospel of Jesus* (London: Allen Lane/Penguin Books, 2003), 234-63.

41. Vermes, *Jesus the Jew,* 180.

originally only predictions of his imminent martyrdom. In these cases, the Aramaic idiom was used to avoid direct reference by the speaker to his own violent death.[42] Finally, Vermes argued that the apocalyptic Son of Man sayings were created by the apocalyptically minded Galilean followers of Jesus. These followers gave an eschatological interpretation of Jesus' neutral manner of speech by connecting it with Dan 7:13.[43]

A major problem with Vermes' approach is that none of the texts he cited supports his claim that the Aramaic idiom is used to refer to the speaker exclusively.[44] For example, one of the texts cited by Vermes is the following story:

> "If a son of man is despised by his mother, but honoured by another of his father's wives, where should he go?" Yohanan replied: "He should go where he is honoured." Thereupon Kahana left. Then Rabbi Yohanan was told: "Kahana has gone to Babylon." He exclaimed: "What! Has he gone without asking leave?" They said to him: "The story he told you was his request for leave."[45]

It should be clear that, in this story, "son of man" is used in an indefinite sense, meaning "a man," any man. The saying is applied to the speaker, but only as a particular example of a general rule.

Furthermore, this text, and it is typical of Vermes' data, does not help us understand the Son of Man sayings as we have them in the Gospels. For example, in Mark 2:10, such a reference by Jesus to himself would merely mean that a man, any man, has the authority to forgive sins on earth. In the context, the saying surely means that Jesus has this power by virtue of

---

42. Ibid., 181-82.

43. Ibid., 186.

44. See also Yarbro Collins, "The Origin of the Designation of Jesus as 'Son of Man,'" 397-98; eadem, *Cosmology and Eschatology*, 146-47. Joseph A. Fitzmyer, S.J., noted that "Many of the examples which are cited by Vermes from the Palestinian Talmud and *Genesis Rabbah* and said to mean 'I' or 'me' can just as easily be translated 'a man' or 'man' in the indefinite or generic sense"; Joseph A. Fitzmyer, "The New Testament Title 'Son of Man' Philologically Considered," in idem, *A Wandering Aramean: Collected Aramaic Essays* (SBLMS 25; Missoula, MT: Scholars Press, 1979); reprinted with the same page-numbering in idem, *The Semitic Background of the New Testament* (Biblical Resource Series; Grand Rapids: Eerdmans; Livonia, MI: Dove Booksellers, 1997), 153; see also 159, n. 58.

45. Vermes, *Jesus the Jew*, 164. In his translation of the text, Vermes left *bar nash* untranslated. I have translated it, but otherwise quote from his version.

his special nature or role. Even Matthew, who comments that the crowds glorified God, who had given such authority to men, probably implies the extension of Jesus' authority to his disciples, not to some general ability any person might exercise.[46]

Although Vermes' thesis regarding a circumlocutional use of the phrase "son of man" in Aramaic has been severely criticized, it has continued to be used in a modified form, even by some of his critics.[47] For example, Maurice Casey claimed that the idiom in question has two levels of meaning. The first is a general statement. The second level is that at which the speaker says something about himself. Casey assumed that the saying about the son of man having authority to forgive sins in Mark 2:10 was spoken originally by Jesus in Aramaic. He took it as a general statement used by Jesus deliberately to say something about himself. So far so good, but then Casey claimed that the general statement was that healers could forgive sins. Thus the "general statement" is not general at all, but allegedly applies to a particular group.[48] The Aramaic evidence outside the New Testament does not support such a restricted use of the idiom.

Barnabas Lindars, like Casey, rejected the circumlocutional theory. He also rejected Casey's solution. But his own is equally vulnerable. He proposed that there was an "idiomatic use of the generic article," that is, the emphatic state, *bar (e)nasha*. In this usage, "The speaker refers to a class of persons, with whom he identifies himself."[49] He thought this usage was the key to the Synoptic Son of Man sayings. The phrase "son of man" in this idiomatic usage should be translated "a man in my position." His only example is one of the texts cited by Vermes. Lindars cited it as follows:

> At the end of those thirteen years, he said: "I will go forward and see what is happening in the world. . . ." He sat down at the entrance to the

46. Matt 9:8; cf. 16:18-19 and 18:18.

47. See also Yarbro Collins, "The Origin of the Designation of Jesus as 'Son of Man,'" 397-98, nn. 31, 33; eadem, *Cosmology and Eschatology,* 146-47, nn. 31, 33; John R. Donahue, S.J., "Recent Studies on the Origin of 'Son of Man' in the Gospels," in Raymond E. Brown, S.S., and Alexander A. DiLella, O.F.M., eds., *A Wise and Discerning Heart: Studies Presented to Joseph A. Fitzmyer in Celebration of His Sixty-Fifth Birthday, CBQ* 48 (1986) 484-98, especially 489, 490-94.

48. Maurice Casey, *Son of Man: The Interpretation and Influence of Daniel 7* (London: SPCK, 1979), 228-29. See also Burkett, *The Son of Man Debate,* 90, 92-96.

49. Barnabas Lindars, *Jesus, Son of Man* (London: SPCK, 1983), 24. See also Burkett, *The Son of Man Debate,* 90-96.

cave. There he saw a fowler trying to catch birds by spreading his net. He heard a heavenly voice saying [in Latin!], *Dimissio!* [release], and the bird escaped. He then said: "Not even a bird perishes without the will of heaven. How much less *bar nasha*."[50]

It should be clear that *"bar nasha"* here may perfectly well and more simply be understood in the indefinite sense, "a man," any man. In the situation envisaged, the indefinite sense includes the speaker.

In a way similar to Casey's approach, Lindars took the saying about the son of man forgiving sins in Mark 2:10 as a generic use of the idiom. But he denied that the reference is to any man.[51]

In the 1970s Joseph A. Fitzmyer criticized Vermes for using Aramaic texts of a later provenance to interpret sayings of the New Testament.[52] In his own survey of the relevant Aramaic evidence, Fitzmyer discussed the earliest occurrence of בַּר אֱנָשׁ.[53] It occurs in an Old Aramaic inscription and means "'a man,' a member of the human race" (the indefinite usage).[54] Fitzmyer points out that the context is "scarcely poetic," although, as part of the stipulations of a treaty, it could "be regarded as solemn." This

---

50. Lindars, *Jesus, Son of Man,* 22.

51. Ibid., 44-45. Carsten Colpe occasionally made a similar argument; "ὁ υἱὸς τοῦ ἀνθρώπου," *TDNT,* 8 (1972), 430-31. Douglas R. A. Hare argued that the historical Jesus employed the phrase *bar enasha* as a modest self-reference in six Synoptic sayings and probably also in a saying that underlies the passion predictions; *The Son of Man Tradition* (Minneapolis: Fortress, 1990), 257-82. See the criticism of this position by Burkett, *The Son of Man Debate,* 87.

52. Fitzmyer, "The Study of the Aramaic Background of the New Testament," in idem, *The Semitic Background of the New Testament: A Wandering Aramean,* 13-14. This essay was originally published in 1975 (ibid., 21, n.*).

53. Fitzmyer, "The New Testament Title 'Son of Man' Philologically Considered," in idem, *The Semitic Background of the New Testament: A Wandering Aramean,* 147. This essay was originally one of the Speaker's Lectures at Oxford University, May 1974; it was published for the first time in 1979 (ibid., 155, n.*). For a discussion of other Old Aramaic inscriptions, see Sjöberg, "בן אדם und בר אנש im Hebräischen und Aramäischen," 62-64; of later Aramaic inscriptions, ibid., 64-65. At the time Sjöberg wrote, as Fitzmyer points out ("The New Testament Title 'Son of Man,'" 147), Dan 7:13 was the oldest occurrence of the Aramaic phrase בר אנש.

54. Ibid., 147. See also the discussion by Paul Owen and David Shepherd, "Speaking Up for Qumran, Dalman and the Son of Man: Was *Bar Enasha* a Common Term for 'Man' in the Time of Jesus?" *JSNT* 81 (2001) 81-122, especially 116-18. In their view, the context implies that, here, "The term בר אנש does not simply mean 'a man', but rather a 'descendant' of the royal line" (ibid., 118).

remark is an indirect criticism of Dalman. Since the phrase is not poetic or literary, he concludes that it reflects the ordinary usage of the time.[55]

In the next oldest historical phase of the Aramaic language, which Fitzmyer calls "Official Aramaic," the only occurrence of the idiom is in Dan 7:13. This usage is generic, that is, a reference to the human being as such. He translates the passage: "'and lo, with the clouds of heaven one like a human being was coming' [or, more literally, 'one like a son of man']."[56]

The literature from Qumran falls into the next phase of the history of the Aramaic language. In the texts already published at the time Fitzmyer was writing, both "the indefinite sense of 'someone' and the generic sense of 'a human being'" are attested.[57]

Fitzmyer agreed with Lietzmann and Fiebig, quoting Joachim Jeremias to the effect that there is an essential difference between the two idioms that Meyer and Vermes had equated:

> *Hāhū gabrā,* referring to the person who speaks, means "I (and no other)," and thus is strictly limited to the speaker; *bar 'enāšā,* on the other hand, keeps its generic or indefinite significance, "the [or a] man, and therefore also I," "the [or a] man like myself," even where the speaker does include himself.[58]

Fitzmyer also argued that the literature used by Vermes to make his case belongs to the Late Phase of Aramaic, that is, "Palestinian Jewish Aramaic of the classic, rabbinic period (between the Mishnah and the closing of the Talmud)."[59] Only Aramaic evidence from the first century of the common era, that is, belonging to the phase he calls "Middle Aramaic,"[60] is relevant for the

---

55. Fitzmyer, "The New Testament Title 'Son of Man' Philologically Considered," 147.

56. Ibid., 147-48. Owen and Shepherd argue ("Speaking Up for Qumran," 119-20) that the phrase "son of man" here contrasts with the expected "son of God," that is, an angel. But it is more likely that "son of man" here contrasts with the mythic animals used to portray the four kingdoms.

57. 1QapGen 21:13; 11QtgJob 9:9; 26:2-3 (Fitzmyer, "The New Testament Title 'Son of Man' Philologically Considered," 148).

58. Joachim Jeremias, *New Testament Theology: The Proclamation of Jesus* (New York: Charles Scribner's Sons, 1971), 261, n. 1; cited by Fitzmyer, "The New Testament Title 'Son of Man' Philologically Considered," 152.

59. Fitzmyer, "The New Testament Title 'Son of Man' Philologically Considered," 151.

60. Ibid., 153.

Son of Man tradition in the Gospels.[61] Finally, he concludes "that the NT usage is special." As the phrase now occurs in the Gospels, ὁ υἱὸς τοῦ ἀνθρώπου, it "must be understood as a title for Jesus." It could be "an attempt to translate the emphatic state of the Aramaic; but it may be something more. I suspect that it was deliberately fashioned to carry the nuance of a title."[62]

When Fitzmyer wrote, many, but not all, of the texts from Qumran had been published. The rest appeared in the 1990s. In 2001, Paul Owen and David Shepherd published a new review of the Aramaic evidence relevant to the Son of Man sayings in the Gospels, taking into account the previously unpublished materials from Qumran.[63] As Fitzmyer had done, but in more detail, they pointed out a major philological flaw in the work of Vermes, Lindars, and Casey. These scholars claimed that the distinction between absolute or indefinite states of nouns and their emphatic or definite states had been lost in the Aramaic dialect of Jesus and his contemporaries. This means that the emphatic state could be translated either "a son of man"/"man" or "the son of man"/"the man."

The problem is that Vermes, Lindars, and Casey relied on Eastern Aramaic texts to make their case. The printed editions of some Western Aramaic texts seemed to support their view. But there is evidence that the earliest recoverable text of those works had been modified under the influence of the Eastern Aramaic dialect. Owen and Shepherd also discussed evidence that the distinction was maintained in the common speech of Palestine in both Middle and Late Aramaic.[64] They also made a case for the conclusion that the emphatic state had not lost its determinative state in the Aramaic texts from Qumran.[65]

Casey and Lindars argued that the origin of the Son of Man sayings may be explained by the use by Jesus of the phrase "son of man" in the emphatic state. Since, in their view, the emphatic and the absolute states were interchangeable, Jesus used this definite form "to make generic statements about himself in the third person." But this hypothesis is based on "Eastern Aramaic materials that derive from a period several centuries removed from the historical Jesus."[66]

61. Ibid., 151, 153-54.
62. All these quotations are from ibid., 154.
63. Owen and Shepherd, "Speaking Up for Qumran."
64. Ibid., 88-96.
65. Ibid., 96-104.
66. Ibid., 105.

Finally, they showed that the singular emphatic form בר אנשא would have meant "*the* son of man" in the idiom of Qumran Aramaic.[67] Even the absolute form, בר אנש, does not seem to be a common expression for "man" in the generic sense in the time of Jesus.[68]

## Derivation from Daniel 7

The other approach, as mentioned at the beginning of this chapter, is to argue that the apocalyptic Son of Man sayings are the oldest and that all the others derive from these. In 1921 Bultmann concluded that a few Son of Man sayings were spoken by Jesus, namely, those that distinguished Jesus from a Son of Man figure who was to have a role in the eschatological judgment.[69] In the 1950s and 1960s, this conclusion was disputed by Philipp Vielhauer[70] and Norman Perrin.[71] Both of these men argued that none of the Son of Man sayings goes back to Jesus. The tradition rather originated

---

67. Ibid., 112.

68. Ibid., 121-22.

69. Mark 8:38//Luke 9:26 and the Q form of the saying adapted in Matt 10:32-33//Luke 12:8-9; Luke 17:24//Matt 24:27; and possibly Matt 24:37-39//Luke 17:26-27, 30; Matt 24:43-44//Luke 12:39-40; Rudolf Bultmann, *The History of the Synoptic Tradition* (rev. ed.; New York: Harper & Row, 1968), 112, 122, 128, 151-52. On Bultmann's view and those of his predecessors in this line of argumentation, see Burkett, *The Son of Man Debate*, 37-39.

70. Philipp Vielhauer, "Gottesreich und Menschensohn in der Verkündigung Jesu," in Wilhelm Schneemelcher, ed., *Festschrift für Günther Dehn* (Neukirchen: Buchhandlung des Erziehungsvereins, 1957), 51-79; idem, "Jesus und der Menschensohn: Zur Diskussion mit Heinz Eduard Tödt und Eduard Schweizer," *Zeitschrift für Theologie und Kirche* 60 (1963) 133-77; these two essays were reprinted in Philipp Vielhauer, *Aufsätze zum Neuen Testament* (Theologische Bücherei 31; München: Kaiser Verlag, 1965); subsequent references are to this volume. See also Burkett, *The Son of Man Debate*, 53-54.

71. Norman Perrin, "Mark XIV. 62: The End Product of a Christian Pesher Tradition?" *NTS* 12 (1965-66) 150-55; idem, "The Son of Man in Ancient Judaism and Primitive Christianity: A Suggestion," *BR* 11 (1966) 17-28; idem, "The Creative Use of the Son of Man Traditions by Mark," *Union Seminary Quarterly Review* 23 (1967) 357-65; idem, "The Son of Man in the Synoptic Tradition," *BR* 13 (1968) 3-25. These four articles were reprinted in idem, *A Modern Pilgrimage in New Testament Christology* (Philadelphia: Fortress, 1974). See also idem, *Rediscovering the Teaching of Jesus* (New York: Harper & Row, 1967), 154-206. See also the discussion of Perrin's work in Donahue, "Recent Studies on the Origin of 'Son of Man' in the Gospels," 485-86, 494-96, and Burkett, *The Son of Man Debate*, 54-56, 73-74. Hans Conzelmann also concluded that none of the Son of Man sayings goes back to Jesus; *An Outline of the Theology of the New Testament* (New York: Harper & Row, 1969), 135-36.

as one attempt to make sense of the death and vindication of Jesus. According to Vielhauer, the designation of Jesus as Son of Man was the earliest Christology, which arose in connection with the experience of Easter.[72]

Perrin argued that all the apocalyptic Son of Man sayings originated in early Christian interpretation of scripture in light of the experience of Jesus as risen. This conclusion was based in large part on another of his arguments, namely, that there was no defined concept of the apocalyptic Son of Man in ancient Judaism.[73] Since, in his view, the apocalyptic Son of Man sayings in the Synoptic tradition presuppose a well-defined concept of the Son of Man and his eschatological role, that concept must have developed during the time between the resurrection of Jesus and the writing of the oldest texts we possess. Using especially the work of Barnabas Lindars[74] and Heinz Eduard Tödt[75] as models, Perrin attempted to reconstruct the development of a very early Christology, that is, the understanding of the risen Jesus as the apocalyptic Son of Man.[76]

I agree that the rediscovery of the importance of the interpretation of scripture among the followers of Jesus is an advance. Likewise, it is crucial to keep in mind the diversity of eschatological ideas in Jewish texts of the late Second Temple period. There is, however, a weak link in Perrin's impressive chain of argument. It is the failure to consider seriously the likelihood that there were certain features in the understanding of Daniel 7 common to many Jews around the turn of the era.[77]

Perrin argued that the "one like a son of man" in Daniel 7 represents:

"the people of the saints of the Most High," almost certainly the Maccabean martyrs, and his coming to dominion, glory and greatness is

72. Vielhauer, "Gottesreich und Menschensohn," 90-91.

73. Ragnar Leivestad took the same position; for a discussion of his views, see Chapter 3. See also Hare, *The Son of Man Tradition*, x, 4-5.

74. Barnabas Lindars, *New Testament Apologetic: The Doctrinal Significance of the Old Testament Quotations* (London: SCM, 1961).

75. Heinz Eduard Tödt, *The Son of Man in the Synoptic Tradition* (Philadelphia: Westminster, 1965).

76. Perrin, *Rediscovering the Teaching of Jesus*, 197-98; idem, *A Modern Pilgrimage in New Testament Christology*, 23-40.

77. John J. Collins has made a case for this view in "The Son of Man in First Century Judaism," *NTS* 38 (1992) 448-66. See also Adela Yarbro Collins, "The Apocalyptic Son of Man Sayings," in Birger A. Pearson, ed., *The Future of Early Christianity: Essays in Honor of Helmut Koester* (Minneapolis: Fortress, 1991), 220-28.

their coming to their reward for the sufferings they have endured. In other words, the use of Son of man in Daniel is a cryptic way of assuring the [Maccabean] readers of the book that their suffering will not go un-rewarded.[78]

An interpretation that fits the evidence better by far is that the one like a son of man is an angelic being.[79]

Perrin was quite correct in pointing out the considerable differences between the use of Daniel 7 in the *Similitudes of Enoch* and in *4 Ezra* (2 Esdras) 13. He was wrong, however, in saying that the only thing the two have in common, apart from the attribution of a kind of preexistence to the two redeemer-figures, is their dependence on Dan 7:13.[80] Perrin over-looked the fact that there is another similarity between the two: both works assume that the manlike figure of Daniel 7 is the messiah.[81]

Since the *Similitudes of Enoch* and *4 Ezra* are literarily independent of one another, it appears that a tradition had developed prior to the compo-sition of both works that the "one like a son of man" in Daniel 7 should be understood as the messiah. Although *4 Ezra* was written after the first Jew-ish war with Rome,[82] the *Similitudes* were written between 40 BCE and 70 CE.[83] Thus the reading of Daniel that they presuppose was probably cur-rent before 70.

### The Historical Jesus

A further point that needs to be made is that the history of scholarship on the Son of Man sayings must be placed in the context of scholarly attitudes

---

78. Perrin, *Rediscovering the Teaching of Jesus,* 166-67.

79. Collins, *Daniel,* 304-10. See also Yarbro Collins, "The Apocalyptic Son of Man Say-ings," 221-23.

80. Perrin, *Rediscovering the Teaching of Jesus,* 167-72; idem, *A Modern Pilgrimage in New Testament Christology,* 24-26, 28-32.

81. Perrin recognized the messianic character of the man from the sea in *4 Ezra* 13, but not that of the Son of Man in the *Similitudes* (*Rediscovering the Teaching of Jesus,* 167-70; *A Modern Pilgrimage in New Testament Christology,* 25-26, 31-32). For further discussion, see Yarbro Collins, "The Apocalyptic Son of Man Sayings," 223-24.

82. John J. Collins, *The Apocalyptic Imagination* (2nd ed.; Grand Rapids: Eerdmans, 1998), 194-95.

83. Ibid., 178.

to the apocalyptic tradition. Bultmann was quite willing to speak of Jesus as an apocalyptic prophet, building as he did upon the work of Johannes Weiss and Albert Schweitzer.[84] Perrin and Vielhauer, in contrast, wanted to distinguish between Jesus as an eschatological teacher and prophet, on the one hand, and the oldest Christian community in Jerusalem as an apocalyptic movement, on the other.[85] This allegedly historical distinction is based on a theological bias in favor of eschatology and against apocalypticism. The tendency is evident in the title of Vielhauer's major article on the subject — "Gottesreich und Menschensohn" ("Kingdom of God and Son of Man"). In this article he argued that kingdom of God and Son of Man are two totally distinct and separate elements in the history of the Synoptic tradition. Vielhauer is correct that these two elements are not closely intertwined in the Synoptic tradition. But since the two belong to the same complex of ideas in roughly contemporary Jewish texts, the claim that they are totally separate in the tradition related to Jesus seems tendentious. For example, in Daniel 7 the dominion of the one like a son of man is closely associated with the kingdom of the people of the holy ones of the Most High.[86] The context suggests that both the dominion of the one like a son of man and the kingdom of the people result from the decree of the Most High. In other words, they are manifestations of the kingdom of God.

In the 1980s, Burton Mack and other members of the Jesus Seminar argued that Jesus was not even eschatological, let alone apocalyptic.[87] During the same decade, however, E. P. Sanders made a well-conceived attempt to reconstruct the historical Jesus as an eschatological prophet.[88]

---

84. Bultmann, *Theology of the New Testament*, 1:4; Johannes Weiss, *Die Predigt Jesu vom Reiche Gottes* (Göttingen: Vandenhoeck & Ruprecht, 1892); ET *Jesus' Proclamation of the Kingdom of God* (Lives of Jesus; Philadelphia: Fortress, 1971); Albert Schweitzer, *Von Reimarus zu Wrede: Eine Geschichte der Leben-Jesu-Forschung* (Tübingen: Mohr Siebeck, 1906); ET *The Quest of the Historical Jesus* (New York: Macmillan, 1968; first complete ed., London: SCM, 2000).

85. Vielhauer, "Gottesreich und Menschensohn," 87-91. Perrin, *Rediscovering the Teaching of Jesus*, 154-206. See also Norman Perrin and Dennis Duling, *The New Testament: An Introduction* (2nd ed.; New York: Harcourt Brace Jovanovich, 1982), 71-79, 411-12.

86. Dan 7:13-14, 27.

87. Burton L. Mack, *A Myth of Innocence: Mark and Christian Origins* (Philadelphia: Fortress, 1988). On the work of the Jesus Seminar in the 1980s and of other scholars who denied that Jesus' teaching and work were eschatological, see Yarbro Collins, "The Origin of the Designation of Jesus as 'Son of Man,'" 393-94 and nn. 9-11.

88. E. P. Sanders, *Jesus and Judaism* (Philadelphia: Fortress, 1985). M. Eugene Boring ar-

Sanders' book, *Jesus and Judaism,* provides a good answer to one of Perrin's arguments that none of the Son of Man sayings goes back to Jesus. Perrin did not argue that Jesus could not have alluded to scripture in his teaching. His argument was that the use of Dan 7:13 in the New Testament presupposes the resurrection of Jesus. Such an argument is difficult to refute, given that all the books of the New Testament presuppose the resurrection, exaltation, or at least vindication of Jesus. The surviving uses and contexts of most, if not all, of the sayings are colored by this presupposition. Further, many, if not all, of Jesus' sayings are ambiguous if read without a context.

Because of the difficulty of reconstructing a setting for the sayings, I agree with Sanders' judgment that it is methodologically more sound to begin with the events of Jesus' life that are generally accepted as historical in attempting to reconstruct his teaching.[89] The events of Jesus' life that are generally accepted as historical, or for which one could make a sound case for historicity, imply that Jesus understood himself and was understood in an apocalyptic or restoration-eschatological context. He accepted the apocalyptic message of John the Baptist by going to him to be baptized.[90] He chose twelve disciples to play a special role, apparently in relation to the expected restoration of the twelve tribes of Israel.[91] He performed actions in the temple that implied the need to reform or restore the practices in the temple related to its sanctity.[92] He was executed by the Romans as a threat to public order, possibly for claiming to be or allowing himself to be treated as the king of the Jews (the messiah of Israel).[93] Shortly after Jesus was crucified, his death and subsequent vindication were interpreted by a

---

gued that the point of origin of the Synoptic Son of Man tradition was Jesus himself; *Sayings of the Risen Jesus: Christian Prophecy in the Synoptic Tradition* (SNTSMS 46; Cambridge: Cambridge University Press, 1982). See also A. J. B. Higgins, *The Son of Man in the Teaching of Jesus* (SNTSMS 39; Cambridge: Cambridge University Press, 1980).

89. Sanders, *Jesus and Judaism,* 3-13. See the list on p. 11.

90. Ibid., 91-93. Compare the Synoptic presentation of the activity and teaching of John the Baptist with the apocalyptic eschatology of *Sibylline Orcles* 4.152-92.

91. Ibid., 95-106.

92. Adela Yarbro Collins, "Jesus' Action in Herod's Temple," in eadem and Margaret M. Mitchell, eds., *Antiquity and Humanity: Essays on Ancient Religion and Philosophy Presented to Hans Dieter Betz* (Tübingen: Mohr Siebeck, 2001), 45-61. Sanders argued that Jesus performed a prophetic symbolic action in the temple that alluded to its destruction and possibly to its replacement by the eschatological temple (*Jesus and Judaism,* 61-90).

93. Sanders, *Jesus and Judaism,* 294-318.

significant and influential number of his disciples in an apocalyptic context.[94] The origin of Jesus' activity in the apocalyptic movement of John the Baptist, the known events of his life, and the apocalyptic movement initiated by his followers after his death suggest that Jesus understood himself and his mission in apocalyptic terms.

The most likely charge against Jesus, from a Roman point of view, was sedition.[95] As noted in the chapter on Paul above, Jesus was identified as the royal messiah well before Paul wrote his letters. These two types of historical evidence suggest that Jesus drew large crowds and was probably identified as the messiah of Israel by some who saw and heard him, already in his lifetime.[96] It could be that Jesus considered himself to be the royal messiah, but it seems somewhat more likely that he understood himself to be a prophet sent by God in the last days, analogous to John the Baptist. A Hebrew text, found among the Dead Sea Scrolls and known as 4Q521, speaks about "[God's] anointed one" or "[God's] messiah." The works to be performed by this messianic figure as God's agent[97] have more in common with prophetic texts than with the usual expectations of the messiah of Israel.[98] They also have much in common with the activities of Jesus as described in the Gospels, especially in the scene in which Jesus replies to a question from John the Baptist.[99]

In any case, if Jesus understood himself in an apocalyptic or restoration-eschatological context, it is illegitimate to exclude all the apocalyptic sayings from the material attributed to Jesus. Consider the saying in the apocalyptic discourse attributed to Jesus in Mark:

94. Ibid., 93-95.

95. See Adela Yarbro Collins, *Mark: A Commentary* (Hermeneia; Minneapolis: Fortress, 2007), especially "History of the Tradition and Historical Reliability" in the commentary on 14:53-72 and the commentary on 15:1-15.

96. Nils Alstrup Dahl argued that Jesus began to be called "messiah" or "Christ" by his followers because he was executed as a messianic pretender and did not deny that he was the messiah; *The Crucified Messiah and Other Essays* (Minneapolis: Augsburg, 1974), 24-28.

97. Grammatically, "the Lord" is the subject of the relevant verbs, but since the actions include the role of herald, it is likely that the Lord performs them through an agent; see John J. Collins, *The Scepter and the Star* (ABRL; New York: Doubleday, 1995), 117-18.

98. See the discussion of 4Q521 in ibid., 117-22. See also idem, "A Herald of Good Tidings: Isaiah 61:1-3 and Its Actualization in the Dead Sea Scrolls," in Craig Evans and Shemaryahu Talmon, eds., *The Quest for Context and Meaning: Studies in Biblical Intertextuality in Honor of James A. Sanders* (Biblical Interpretation Series 28; Leiden: Brill, 1997), 225-40.

99. Matt 11:2-6//Luke 7:18-23.

"And then the Son of Man will be seen coming in clouds with great power and glory. And then he will send the angels, and he will gather the elect from the four winds, from [one] end of the earth to the other." (Mark 13:26-27)

This saying is remarkably similar in substance to a saying that Paul refers to as "a saying of the Lord":

For the Lord himself, when the command is given, at the utterance of an archangel and at the sounding of the trumpet of God, will descend from heaven, and the dead in Christ will rise first. Then we who are alive, who are left, will be taken up together with them on clouds to meet the Lord in the air. (1 Thess 4:16-17a)

As I have argued elsewhere, these passages look very much like oral variants of a tradition that may well go back to Jesus.[100]

Bultmann excluded the saying in Mark 13:26-27 because he believed that it reflected Jewish tradition, rather than the teaching of Jesus. But this and other sayings that do not explicitly identify Jesus with the figure of Dan 7:13, yet allude to that passage, are plausible as expressing Jesus' view that after his work of proclaiming the kingdom, a heavenly messiah would be revealed.

The hypothesis that Jesus alluded to the fulfillment of Dan 7:13-14 in his teaching makes it easier to understand how and why his disciples identified him, in his exalted state, with the one like a son of man depicted in that passage. Vielhauer's thesis that it was the experience of Jesus as risen, and this experience alone, that led the disciples to identify him with that figure puts too much hermeneutical weight on such an experience. After the death of Jesus, the exalted Jesus and the heavenly manlike figure whose coming Jesus had announced were easily collapsed into one.[101]

The Dead Sea Scrolls and the Jewish historian Josephus provide evidence for widespread eschatological expectation in some Jewish circles in the first century of the common era. In such a context, if Jesus viewed

---

100. Adela Yarbro Collins, "Composition and Performance in Mark 13," in the Festschrift for Seán Freyne, ed. Anne Fitzpatrick McKinley, Margaret Daly-Denton, Brian McGing, and Zuleika Rodgers (Leiden: Brill, forthcoming); eadem, *Mark*, section on "History of the Tradition" in the commentary on chapter 13.

101. Compare the secondary identification of the exalted and transformed Enoch with the preexistent Son of Man in *1 Enoch* 71:14; see Chapter 4 above.

himself as an eschatological prophet, it is likely that he understood the book of Daniel to refer to his own time and to the near future. He need not have been a scribe or a professional interpreter of scripture to have known the major characters and basic contents of Daniel. He could have acquired this knowledge from the reading of scripture in synagogues or from the teaching of professional scribes that became part of oral tradition in Palestine.

## Conclusion: Early Worship of Jesus?

So how then did Jesus become a god, as Larry Hurtado asks in a recent book?[102] Although Jesus may have considered or presented himself more as a prophet than as a king, he proclaimed the kingdom of God, and in Daniel 7 the one like a son of man was closely associated with the kingdom. It is plausible, then, that Jesus spoke about the one like a son of man in Daniel as a heavenly messiah who was coming soon or who would be revealed soon. The text of Daniel already presents this figure as God's agent in exercising eternal kingship. The *Similitudes of Enoch* present the same figure as God's agent in the final judgment. *4 Ezra* presents him as God's agent in defeating the nations, gathering the people of Israel, and defending them.[103]

After his crucifixion, some of his followers had visions of Jesus as raised from the dead and exalted to heaven. These visions were interpreted in terms of Dan 7:13-14 and Psalm 110, both read messianically. In other words, Jesus himself was identified with the one like a son of man whom he had proclaimed. He was also identified with the figure seated at the right hand of God in Ps 110:1, a kingly warrior who appears to be more than human.

If his followers had hoped that Jesus would take the role of messiah of Israel during his earthly lifetime, this hope was transformed by his death and resurrection into an expectation of his coming or being revealed as a heavenly messiah, the Son of Man. At that time he would act as God's agent in ruling, judging, and defending God's people.

102. Larry W. Hurtado, *How on Earth Did Jesus Become a God? Historical Questions about Earliest Devotion to Jesus* (Grand Rapids: Eerdmans, 2005).
103. *4 Ezra* 13:33-50.

## The Issue of Worship

One of the key questions in the debate about the divinity of Jesus has been whether he is worshipped in a way that "principal agents" of God are not.[104] It is difficult to distinguish ancient texts and practices expressing political submission and respect, on the one hand, from practices that we would call religious, which express worship and devotion, on the other.[105] If Jesus was seen as taking over God's functions as king, warrior, and judge at the End, as God's agent, his divinity may have been perceived primarily in functional terms at first.

But the idea of a heavenly messiah opens the door to speculation and rhetoric about preexistence.[106] The notion of preexistence intensifies the divine status of the heavenly messiah. Similarly, the honorific recognition as God's son is intensified in language about a virginal conception.

The cultural environment must also be taken into account. In the Hellenistic ruler cults and especially in the imperial cults, men who were once human beings were honored and worshipped as gods. Some were even worshipped as gods during their earthly lifetimes. The messiah of Israel was conceived at first primarily as a king, of his own nation first of all and then of the whole world.

The understanding of Jesus that emerged after his resurrection involved his kingship over Israel and over the entire world. Given the practices of the imperial cults, it is not surprising that Jesus was viewed as a god and that worship of him became an alternative to the worship of the emperor.[107]

---

104. Hurtado, *How on Earth Did Jesus Become a God?* 46-53.

105. The use of the verb προσκυνέω in the book of Revelation with God and the Lamb as objects, as well as with the community in Philadelphia as object (3:9), is a case in point. The honor given to the highly exalted Jesus in Phil 2:10-11 is also ambiguous in this way.

106. Cf. the Greek version of Psalm 110, especially v. 3.

107. See Adela Yarbro Collins, "Psalms, Phil. 2:6-11, and the Origins of Christology," *Biblical Interpretation* 11 (2003) 361-72.

# 8. *Messiah, Son of God, and Son of Man in the Gospel and Revelation of John*

## The Gospel of John

### *The Prologue*

In the published form of his Cadbury lectures, Maurice Casey put foward his conviction that "The Gospel attributed to St. John is the only New Testament document in which the deity and incarnation of Jesus are unequivocally proclaimed."[1] This statement is somewhat misleading. If the proclamation of the Gospel were really unequivocal, it would be hard to explain the extended christological controversies in the early church.[2] For example, the third clause of John 1:1 may be translated either "the word was God" or "the word was a god."[3] Justin Martyr apparently understood the

1. P. Maurice Casey, *From Jewish Prophet to Gentile God: The Origins and Development of New Testament Christology* (Cambridge, UK: James Clarke; Louisville: Westminster John Knox, 1991), 23.

2. On these controversies, see Henry Chadwick, *The Early Church* (Pelican History of the Church 1; Harmondsworth, UK/Baltimore: Penguin Books, 1967; reprinted 1969), 85-90, 133-51, 192-212.

3. B. A. Mastin considers it "overwhelmingly probable" that John 1:1 "describes the pre-existent Logos as God" ("A Neglected Feature of the Christology of the Fourth Gospel," *NTS* 22 [1976] 32-51; quotation from 37). This conclusion, however, is based on his

passage in the latter way. According to Henry Chadwick, "Justin had boldly spoken of the divine logos as 'another God' beside the Father, qualified by the gloss 'other, I mean, in number, not in will.'"[4] Casey describes John 1:14 as involving "incarnation in the strong sense in which I use that term, that is, of the process by means of which a fully divine being is born as a person."[5] It is not precisely clear what Casey means by "a fully divine being" here. If he means something like the second person of the trinity, it is doubtful that John 1 supports this interpretation.[6]

Casey refers to John 1:18 as "a brief summary of Jesus' nature and mission on earth" and translates "No-one has seen God. Only-begotten God, who is in the bosom of the Father, he has revealed him."[7] He is right to take μονογενὴς θεός ("only-begotten god") as the earliest recoverable reading, rather than ὁ μονογενὴς υἱός ("only-begotten son").[8] The translation of the earliest reading is problematic, however, because earlier and contemporary Greek texts attest only the usages *"the only member of a kin or kind:* hence, generally, *only, single"* and *"unique"* (apart from specialized idiomatic usages).[9] If applied to John 1:18, however, the first usage does not make good sense. It would imply that the one who is in the bosom of the father is the only God and that the father is not God. The force of the second usage would be unclear, unless one includes the contrast between one unbegotten God and one begotten god. With reference to Jesus Christ, the usage of μονογενής to signify "only-begotten" is well attested in later

view that Thomas's acclamation in 20:28 "is the one verse in the New Testament which does unquestionably describe Christ as God" (ibid., 42). This view fails to recognize, however, that the phrase *dominus et deus,* and presumably its Greek equivalent, is an honorific acclamation, used, e.g., by those who wished to flatter Domitian; see Leonard L. Thompson, *The Book of Revelation: Apocalypse and Empire* (New York: Oxford University Press, 1990), 105-7.

4. Justin, *Dialogue with Trypho* 56; 127; 129; Chadwick, *Early Church,* 85-86.

5. Casey, *New Testament Christology,* 23.

6. See the discussion below of Hellenistic Jewish speculation on wisdom and the logos.

7. Casey, *New Testament Christology,* 23.

8. See Bruce M. Metzger, *A Textual Commentary on the Greek New Testament* (2nd ed.; Stuttgart: German Bible Society/United Bible Societies, 1994), 169-70.

9. Henry George Liddell and Robert Scott, eds., *A Greek-English Lexicon* (9th ed. Henry Stuart Jones; Oxford: Clarendon, 1940), *s.v.* (hereafter LSJ). These are also the only usages listed in Walter Bauer, William F. Arndt, and F. Wilbur Gingrich, eds., *A Greek-English Lexicon of the New Testament and Other Early Christian Literature* (3rd ed. Frederick William Danker; Chicago/London: University of Chicago Press, 2000), *s.v.* (hereafter BAGD).

Christian texts.[10] It may well be that this new usage is already present in John 1:18.[11]

The "word" (λόγος) in John 1:1 plays a major role in creation. All things are said to have come into being through it (or him, in light of vv. 10-17), and nothing at all has come into being apart from him (1:3). This role in creation is analogous to the role assigned to the logos by Philo and Justin Martyr.[12] Both writers adapted this aspect of Middle Platonic philosophy in order to explain how the transcendent God could also be the creator of the material world.[13] This philosophical notion of the "logos," with which the author of the prologue seems to have been familiar, is linked to scripture by the fact that the "word" of God in the Hebrew Bible is translated with λόγος in the Septuagint.[14]

It is also linked to the biblical and postbiblical wisdom tradition by the claims in John 1:4 that in the "word" or "logos" was life, and the life was the light of human beings.[15] Personified wisdom was linked with life already in Proverbs.[16] Most strikingly, she declares, "Whoever finds me finds life."[17] Similarly, Sir 4:12 says, "The one who loves her, loves life." In Wis 7:10, "Solomon" says that he chose wisdom rather than light (φῶς) because her radiance (φέγγος) never ceases. She is also said to be a reflection

10. Geoffrey W. H. Lampe, *A Patristic Greek Lexicon* (Oxford: Clarendon, 1961), *s.v.*, B.

11. This tentative conclusion is supported by John 1:14, since otherwise one would have to conclude that this verse signifies that Jesus was the only one ever sent by God, a sense that seems unlikely. It is also supported by the language concerning "being begotten by God" in 1:13. Verses 13 and 18 could be reconciled by arguing that the word was begotten by God in a different sense from the human beings who can be said to have been "begotten" of or from God. Some NT scholars have argued for a heightening of the usage of μονογενής signifying "unique" to the sense "uniquely begotten" in 1:18; see Bauer et al., *s.v.* 2.

12. See also Wis 7:22.

13. On Philo, see Thomas H. Tobin, "Logos," *ABD*, 4:348-56, especially 350-51; David Winston, *Logos and Mystical Theology in Philo of Alexandria* (Cincinnati: Hebrew Union College Press, 1985), 9-25, especially 15-16; Daniel Boyarin, *Borderlines: The Partition of Judaeo-Christianity* (Philadelphia: University of Pennsylvania Press, 2004), 113-19. Boyarin rightly emphasizes that Philo was "as much a producer as a consumer of Middle Platonism" (ibid., 115). On Justin Martyr, see Chadwick, *Early Church*, 77; Boyarin, *Borderlines*, 37-73.

14. Winston, *Logos*, 15.

15. Or "that which came to be in him was life," depending on how one punctuates John 1:3-4.

16. Prov 3:16, 18.

17. Prov 8:35 MT; the LXX reads "for my doors (ἔξοδοι) are doors of life (ζωή, the same word used in John 1:4)."

(ἀπαύγασμα)[18] of eternal light (φῶς) in Wis 7:26, and compared with light (φῶς), she is superior (7:29). According to Tobin, "The closest conceptual parallels to the use of *logos* in the hymn from the Prologue of John are to be found in Jewish wisdom literature."[19] Yet the hymn was not modeled directly on the wisdom literature; rather, it has its roots in Hellenistic Jewish speculation about logos/wisdom.[20]

Wisdom was portrayed as God's first creature in Prov 8:22-23 and Sir 24:9. In the Wisdom of Solomon, however, wisdom "glorifies her noble birth by living with God" (Wis 8:3).[21] Analogously, Philo takes "the house of Bethuel" in Gen 28:2 to be the house of wisdom. He then interprets the name to mean "daughter of God" and speaks of God begetting her (*On Flight and Finding* 9 §§48-50).[22] Wisdom 7:26, however, implies that she is eternal.[23] Whether Jesus was viewed as wisdom or as logos, whether as created or eternal, the prologue of John (1:1-18) implies that he was a preexistent figure who became incarnate.

## Jesus as the Messiah and Son of God

Immediately following the prologue is a scene in which "the Jews" send priests and Levites from Jerusalem to Bethany beyond the Jordan to ask John the Baptist who he is (1:19-28). John replies that he is not the messiah (ὁ χριστός) (1:20). His reference to "the one who is coming after me" (1:27)

18. David Winston translates "effulgence" (*The Wisdom of Solomon: A New Translation with Introduction and Commentary* [AB 43; Garden City, NY: Doubleday, 1979], 184, 186-87).

19. Tobin, "Logos," 353. See the chart in which the parallels are laid out (ibid., 353-54).

20. Ibid., 354-55. Boyarin argues that "the Logos of the Prologue — like the theological Logos in general, in accord with the view of Burrus cited above — is the product of a scriptural reading of Genesis 1 and Proverbs 8 together." He defines the type of scriptural reading involved as "an intertextual interpretive practice" akin to midrash (*Borderlines*, 95).

21. Prov 8:30, if "little child" is read, supports the idea of wisdom living with God as a daughter. Winston, however, translated Wis 8:3 with "magnifies her noble birth by enjoying intimacy with God" (*Wisdom of Solomon*, 191). He remarks that "The multiplication of images which we find [in the Wisdom of Solomon] (Wisdom as Bride of Solomon, Daughter of God, Bride of God) is also characteristic of Philo." He also argues, with regard to Wis 8:4, that the text implies that "Wisdom is essentially synonymous with the Divine Mind, and thus represents the creative agent of the Deity" (ibid., 194).

22. Winston, ibid., 193-94.

23. Ibid., 186-87.

suggests that Jesus is the messiah.[24] In the next scene (1:29-34), John identifies Jesus as the lamb of God (v. 29) and as the man who is coming after him (v. 30). The scene ends with John's testimony that Jesus is the son of God (ὁ υἰὸς τοῦ θεοῦ) (v. 34). The juxtaposition of these two scenes strongly implies that on at least one important level of meaning, "son of God" in the Gospel of John is equivalent to "messiah."

This impression is reinforced by the next scene, in which John's declaration that Jesus is the lamb of God leads two of his disciples to follow Jesus. One of these is Andrew, who then goes to his brother Simon Peter and tells him, "We have found the messiah" (ὁ μεσσίας). The narrator then explains, "which is, translated, 'anointed' (χριστός)" (1:41).[25]

The question of Jesus' messiahship is also raised by the people of Jerusalem (7:26). They seem to reject the idea because they think they know where Jesus comes from, whereas when the messiah (ὁ χριστός) comes, no one will know where he is from (7:27). Irony lies in the presentation of the people as expecting a preexistent or heavenly messiah, yet not recognizing that Jesus is just that kind of messiah. They assume that they know where he is from. The irony of their assumed knowledge is developed further when Jesus proclaims that he has been sent by one whom they do not know (vv. 28-29). They try to arrest him, but many in the crowd believe in him, asking whether the messiah (ὁ χριστός), when he comes, would do more signs than Jesus (vv. 30-31). In the scene after next, when Jesus makes his proclamation about living water (7:37-39), some of the people conclude that Jesus is the messiah (ὁ χριστός), but others doubt it because they define Jesus as from Galilee and the messiah is not supposed to come from there (7:41), but from Bethlehem (v. 42).

The portrayal of Jesus as messiah occurs also in John 9. Jesus heals a blind man (9:1-12). The Pharisees criticize the healing because it was done on the sabbath, and the healed man identifies Jesus as a prophet (9:13-17). The Pharisees interrogate the healed man's parents, and they affirm that their son was born blind but profess ignorance about the healing. The narrator then comments, "His parents said this because they feared the Jews; for [they] had already decided that whoever acknowledged him as messiah

---

24. John's testimony and its implication of the messiahship of Jesus are repeated in 3:28.

25. Similarly, in 4:25 the Samaritan woman says, "I know that messiah (μεσσίας) is coming, the one called 'anointed' (χριστός)." In 4:29 she asks, expecting a negative answer, whether Jesus might be the messiah (ὁ χριστός).

(χριστός) should be put out of the synagogue" (9:22). It is likely that this statement reflects controversy in the synagogues of the author's time over the messiahship of Jesus.[26] In any case, it makes clear that Jesus' identity as messiah was important to the author(s) of the Gospel of John.

In 10:24, "the Jews" ask Jesus to tell them plainly whether he is the messiah (ὁ χριστός). Jesus' response in v. 25 makes clear that this identity is affirmed, "I have told you, and you do not believe." In the rest of the dialogue, Jesus' messiahship is elaborated in terms of his oneness with the father (10:30)[27] and his identity as God's son (υἱὸς τοῦ θεοῦ) (v. 36). This sonship is defined in terms of the father's sanctifying and sending Jesus into the world (v. 36). Although the preexistence of the son is presupposed, the emphasis is on his relationship to the father as his agent who does the father's works (vv. 37-38). The fact that Jesus does the works of the father signifies that "the father is in me, and I am in the father" (v. 38).[28]

Finally, the importance of the messiahship of Jesus is also clear in two key passages. In response to Jesus' declaration that he is the resurrection and the life, Martha affirms, "Yes, lord, I believe that you are the messiah (ὁ χριστός), the son of God who is coming into the world" (11:27). In the original conclusion to the Gospel, the narrator states, "These [signs] are written in order that you [plural] may believe that Jesus is the messiah (ὁ χριστός), the son of God, and that believing you may have life in his name" (20:31).

The juxtaposition of "messiah" and "son of God" in both of these passages, like the inclusion of both epithets in 1:19-34, suggests that the term

26. Fear of speaking openly about Jesus because of "the Jews" is mentioned already in 7:13; on being put out of the synagogue, see also 12:42; 16:2; the latter passage makes clear that this type of event belongs to the author(s)' time; Rudolf Schnackenburg, *The Gospel according to St. John* (3 vols.; London: Burns & Oates, 1968-1982; 1st German ed. 1965-1975), 2:250; James Louis Martyn, *History and Theology in the Fourth Gospel* (rev. ed.; Nashville: Abingdon, 1979; 1st ed. 1968), especially 24-62.

27. This oneness signifies Jesus' "working together with the Father (5:17, 19), his agreement with the Father (cf. 5:30; 8:16, 18), his acting in accordance with the Father's will and direction (6:38; 8:26, 28; 10:18). All this is included; but in the leading and protection of the sheep the unity becomes oneness, since the sheep belong commonly to the Father and the Son (17:10) and are admitted into the fellowship of the Father and the Son (cf. 10:14; 17:21-23, 26)" (Schnackenburg, *John,* 2:308). The "oneness" does not yet signify a trinitarian (or binitarian) theology (ibid., 511, n. 121).

28. This "reciprocal Johannine formula" expresses the oneness of the father and the son mentioned in 10:30 (Schnackenburg, *John,* 2:313).

"son of God" is used for the messiah in an adaptation of the traditional royal epithet.[29] It would seem, then, that "son of God" for the Gospel of John means first and foremost "the (royal, Davidic) messiah." That traditional epithet, however, and the notion of a royal, Davidic messiah (a messiah of Israel) are reinterpreted in a variety of ways in John, not least by the incorporation of a hymn or poem in the prologue. As we have seen, the prologue explicitly identifies Jesus Christ, that is, Jesus as the messiah, with "the word," the "logos," in a way that shows some knowledge of the philosophical use of that term in Hellenistic Jewish speculation. This identification implies that Jesus is preexistent and divine in the sense of being an emanation of God or being "a god."

This reinterpretation of messiahship is analogous to Paul's portrayal of Jesus as preexistent "in the form of God" in Phil 2:6 and as God's agent in creation in 1 Cor 8:6. What Paul mentions in passing, the editor or author who composed the prologue elaborates a bit more, yet in a brief, ambiguous, and poetic way.

### Other Instances of Jesus as Son of God

One of the most famous sayings from the Gospel of John is 3:16, "For God so loved the world that he gave his only son, so that everyone who believes in him may not perish but may have eternal life." One important thing to notice about this saying is that Jesus' death is effective for those who believe in him.[30] Another is that the phrase "[his] only son" (ὁ υἱὸς ὁ μονογενής) distinguishes between Jesus and those who believe in him as "begotten" in different ways and therefore as sons (and daughters) in different senses.[31] Finally, one should note that this verse, like 3:14-15, interprets the death of Jesus in light of scripture. Here the reference to an *only* son who is *loved* recalls the willingness of Abraham to sacrifice Isaac when God commanded him to do so (Gen 22:2, 12).[32]

---

29. Ps 2:7; 2 Sam 7:12-16.

30. See the discussion of 1 Thessalonians, Galatians, 1 Corinthians, and Romans in the chapter on Paul above. See also Schnackenburg, *John*, 1:398-99.

31. See the subsection on the prologue above, especially the discussion of John 1:18.

32. Raymond E. Brown, *The Gospel according to John* (2 vols.; AB 29; Garden City, NY: Doubleday, 1966-1970), 1:147. In Second Temple and rabbinic literature, the role of Isaac gradually received more emphasis, e.g., the idea that his choice to give up his life benefited

As noted above, the saying about God giving his only son follows the comparison of the effectiveness of the death of Jesus with that of the bronze serpent lifted up by Moses on a pole. Both intertextual interpretations occur in the monologue of Jesus that follows his dialogue with Nicodemus. The last section of the monologue, 3:17-21, elaborates on how those who believe in the son will receive eternal life. The world is saved through him insofar as he is the light that has come into the world, and those who believe in him come to the light. This link between v. 16 and what follows suggests that the phrase "the only son of God" (ὁ μονογενὴς υἱὸς τοῦ θεοῦ) in 3:18 continues the allusion to Abraham and Isaac, begun in v. 16.

The discourse in 3:31-36 is loosely attached to the speech of John the Baptist, arguing that he must decrease and Jesus must increase (3:27-30), yet in terms of content it seems to continue the dialogue with Nicodemus. The last saying in the discourse picks up the theme of judgment from 3:17-21 and the topic of eternal life from 3:16: "The one who believes in the son has eternal life, but the one who disobeys the son will not see life because the wrath of God remains on him" (3:36).[33] The second last saying takes up the topic of the father's love for the son in 3:16 and adds a new element: "The father loves the son and has put all things in his hand" (v. 35).[34] This saying seems to be a variant of the one that appears in Matt 11:27, "All things have been handed over to me by my father, and no one knows the son except the father, and no one knows the father except the son and anyone to whom the son may choose to reveal the father."[35] Both sayings express the idea that Jesus is the fully authorized agent of the father.[36]

The simple statement of 3:35 is elaborated in 5:19-23, part of Jesus' discourse directed to those who were trying to kill him.[37] The son can do nothing of his own accord. Whatever he sees the father doing, he does like-

---

many; Jon D. Levenson, *The Death and Resurrection of the Beloved Son: The Transformation of Child Sacrifice in Judaism and Christianity* (New Haven, CT/London: Yale University Press, 1993), 173-99.

33. Cf. the theme of the wrath of God in 1 Thessalonians; see the chapter on Paul's letters above.

34. Cf. 13:3 (Jesus knew that the father had put all things in his hands).

35. See the discussion of this saying in the chapter on the Synoptic Gospels above.

36. For an interpretation of John 3:35 in the context of the Gospel as a whole, see Schnackenburg, *John*, 1:388.

37. See the discussion of chapter 5 in the subsection, "Son of Man," below.

wise (v. 19). In particular, the son gives life to those whom he wishes, just as the father raises the dead and gives them life (v. 21). Similarly, the father has given the son the authority to judge (v. 22).

As noted above, John 1:18 and 3:16 imply that Jesus is son of God in a unique way. The opponents of Jesus are presented as recognizing that this is his claim, so they accuse him of a capital offense: blasphemy (5:18; 10:33; 19:7).[38]

## Son of Man

As is the case in Mark, the identity of Jesus as "messiah" appears to be equivalent to his identity as "Son of Man" in the Gospel of John, although each epithet of course has its own particular connotations. This equivalence is shown in the scene in which Jesus calls Philip and Nathanael (1:43-51). When Jesus reveals his suprahuman knowledge, Nathanael says, "Rabbi, you are the son of God! You are king of Israel!" (v. 49). This speech clearly indicates the equivalence of "messiah" (king of Israel) and "son of God" in John. Jesus replies that Nathanael will see greater things than these, for example, he will see "heaven opened and the angels of God ascending and descending upon the Son of Man" (v. 51). The first part of Jesus' reply implies that Nathanael's characterization of Jesus as son of God and king of Israel is correct. The second part suggests that "Son of Man" is also equivalent to the first two epithets. The saying about the Son of Man is opaque, however, at this point. It becomes clear only much later in the narrative.[39]

The next Son of Man saying occurs in the dialogue of Jesus with Nicodemus. In the second part of the dialogue, when it is becoming a monologue, Jesus says, "No one has ascended into heaven except the one who has descended from heaven, the Son of Man" (3:13). This is a clear reference to the preexistence of Jesus[40] and a restatement of 1:14 in different

---

38. Schnackenburg (*John*, 3:258) connects the charge of blasphemy with Lev 24:16, which was one of the key texts for the notion of blasphemy in Second Temple Jewish texts (Adela Yarbro Collins, "The Charge of Blasphemy in Mark 14:64," *JSNT* 26 [2004] 379-401; reprinted in Geert van Oyen and Tom Shepherd, eds., *The Trial and Death of Jesus: Essays on the Passion Narrative in Mark* [Leuven: Peeters, 2006], 149-70).

39. See the discussion of John 12 below.

40. See also 3:31-34.

terms.[41] Then Jesus goes on to say, "And just as Moses lifted up the serpent in the wilderness, so must the Son of Man be lifted up, in order that everyone who believes in him may have eternal life" (3:14-15). This saying refers to the statement in Num 21:9 that each person bitten by a poisonous serpent who looked at the bronze serpent Moses had put on a pole would "live." In the Johannine saying, the earlier one is taken as a prefiguration of Jesus being lifted up on the cross.[42] His crucifixion, which is also a "being lifted up," gives eternal life,[43] a greater benefit than the physical life mediated by Moses.[44] This saying is the first hint in John that the crucifixion of Jesus is also his exaltation.

The next Son of Man saying occurs in the dialogue between Jesus and "the Jews" after the healing of a man near the pool called Beth-zatha in chapter 5. When his interlocutors pursue or persecute Jesus for healing the man on the sabbath, he defends himself by saying that his father is still working, and he himself is also working (5:17). They then wish to kill him for "making himself equal to God" (v. 18). Jesus then discourses on the authority that God has delegated to him because he is God's son. A little later he reveals that the father "has given [the son] authority to execute judgment because he is the Son of Man" (v. 27). The Son of Man also has the role of judge in the *Similitudes of Enoch,* the Synoptic Sayings Source (Q), Matthew, and Luke.[45] In those texts, the judgment is eschatological in the sense that it occurs at the end of this age and the dawning of the next. In John the judgment is eschatological in a partially realized sense because it begins already in the public activity of Jesus: "Truly, truly, I say to you, the one who hears my word and believes the one who sent me has eternal life, and does not come to judgment, but has already passed from death to life" (5:24).[46]

41. Cf. the preexistence of the messianic Son of Man in the *Similitudes* or *Parables of Enoch* (1 Enoch 37–71) and of the "man from the sea" in 4 Ezra 13:25-26.

42. That the death of Jesus is involved is implied by the following saying about God giving his only son (3:16); Brown argued that the "giving" involves both the incarnation and the crucifixion (*John,* 1:134). See the subsection "Other Instances of Jesus as Son of God" above.

43. Cf. John 6:39-40.

44. Cf. John 1:17.

45. See the discussion above in the chapter on the Synoptic Gospels.

46. See also John 3:17-21, where the eschatological theme of judgment is also expressed in at least partially realized terms. There it is associated with Jesus as son of God rather than as Son of Man.

The idea of the Son of Man as judge also occurs in Jesus' final dialogue with the blind man whom he had healed. Jesus asks, "Do you believe in the Son of Man?" (9:35). After Jesus explains that he himself is the Son of Man and the man declares that he does believe, Jesus says, "I have come into this world for judgment so that those who do not see may see, and those who see may become blind" (v. 39). This saying once again implies Jesus' pre-existence. Also, as is the case with 5:27, the context suggests that this judgment has already begun.

In 6:26-27, Jesus criticizes the crowd for seeking food that perishes and exhorts them to work for the food "that remains unto eternal life, which the Son of Man will give you." Like the saying of 3:14-15, this saying (in context) connects the Son of Man with the crucifixion of Jesus, which grants eternal life to those who believe. The context makes this clear when the food that does not perish is defined as "the flesh of the Son of Man" and his blood (6:53). In the first part of the scene that follows the discourse on the bread of life, many of the disciples find the idea of eating the flesh of the Son of Man and drinking his blood "difficult" (σκληρός). Jesus then asks, if this idea offends them, what will happen "if you see the Son of Man ascending where he was before" (6:62)? Like the other sayings mentioned in this paragraph, this one alludes to Jesus' death by crucifixion. His being lifted up on the cross is described as an ascent, and his death as a return to the heavenly world whence he came. On the one hand, the question recognizes that it will be difficult for many to interpret the crucifixion as exaltation. On the other, it suggests that Jesus' death, properly understood, is actually an ascent to heaven.

The claim that Jesus' "being lifted up" is actually his glorification is clearest in chapter 12.[47] After he has entered Jerusalem, he says, "The hour has come for the Son of Man to be glorified" (v. 23). Here "glorification" refers to the death of Jesus. This is clear from 7:30: when the opponents of Jesus try to take him into custody, they are unable to do so because "his hour had not yet come." It is also clear from the following statement about the seed having to die in order to bear fruit (12:24) and the next saying (v. 25), which recalls the teaching on discipleship following the first passion prediction in Mark (8:35). This reading is supported by 12:32, "And

---

47. See also 13:31, where the glorification of the Son of Man is linked to his death by 13:1 and the immediately preceding departure of Judas, whose betrayal Jesus has foretold (vv. 18-30).

when I am lifted up from the earth, I will draw all people to myself." The narrator comments, "Now he said this to signify by what kind of death he was about to die" (v. 33). The image of drawing all people to himself is clarified by 12:26, "If anyone serves me, let him follow me, and where I am, there will be my servant; if anyone serves me, the father will honor him." This saying, like v. 25, recalls the Markan teaching on discipleship in 8:34-38. It also suggests what Jesus means by saying that when he is lifted up, he will draw all people to himself. Through the crucifixion Jesus will ascend to the father and draw his followers to the heavenly realm as well.

It is at this point in the narrative that the first Son of Man saying, the one addressed to Nathanael in 1:51, becomes more intelligible. The specific image of the angels ascending and descending upon the Son of Man comes from Jacob's dream at Bethel (Gen 28:10-17). When Jacob awakes after his dream of a ladder on which angels are ascending and descending, he concludes that the place is the house of God (Bethel) and the gate of heaven (v. 17). The saying of Jesus in John 1:51 suggests that the story of Jacob at Bethel is a prefiguration of Jesus' mission, which is completed on the cross (cf. 19:30). Jesus has become the house of God (cf. 2:19-21) and the gateway to heaven. Those who believe in him will follow him into the heavenly realm (cf. 14:1-3).[48]

The lifting up of the Son of Man is also a revelatory event. Jesus says to his opponents that when they have lifted him up, "then you will know that I am, and that I do nothing by myself, but as the father has taught me, these things I speak" (8:28). To know that "I am" means to recognize that in Jesus "God is present to reveal his eschatological salvation" and offer it to all humanity.[49] Whether this event issues in salvation or not depends on the response of human individuals.[50]

The Gospel of John uses the traditional phrase "son of God" to identify Jesus as the messiah. The term "son of God," however, is elaborated so that Jesus is portrayed as a preexistent, heavenly messiah. He is son of God in a unique way as "the only-begotten god." He is also identified with the philosophical notion of the logos in Hellenistic Jewish speculation, based on Middle Platonic philosophy, Genesis 1–2, and the wisdom tradition.

---

48. See also Adela Yarbro Collins, "The Influence of Daniel on the New Testament," in John J. Collins, *Daniel* (Hermeneia; Minneapolis: Fortress, 1993), 90-112, especially 100-102.

49. Schnackenburg, *John*, 2:200.

50. Ibid., 2:202-3.

The author of John was heir to the Synoptic Son of Man tradition or to similar traditions. Yet the presentation of Jesus as Son of Man is distinctly Johannine.

## The Book of Revelation

### *Jesus as the Messiah*

Like Paul, the author of the book of Revelation (John the prophet) appears to use the epithet χριστός ("Christ" or "messiah") as a proper name for Jesus.[51] This usage may be found in 1:1, 2, and 5.[52] Several other passages in the work, however, make clear that the epithet still had the connotation "messiah" (11:15; 12:10; 20:4, 6).[53]

When the seventh angel blew his trumpet, John heard loud voices in heaven saying, "The kingdom of the world has become the kingdom of our lord and of his messiah."[54] The past tense is used because the action is presented as having taken place before John's eyes and ears. The content of 11:15-19, however, makes clear that the audition concerns the future. Only then will the final judgment take place, which includes the reward of the the servants of God and the punishment of those who destroy the earth (v. 18).[55] Even though John hears the voice of many angels declaring Jesus, as the lamb, worthy to receive power, wealth, wisdom, strength, honor, glory, and praise (5:12) and every creature in heaven, on earth, under the earth, and in the sea blessing and glorifying God and the lamb (5:13), the

51. See the chapter on the letters of Paul above.

52. David E. Aune translates Ἰησοῦ χριστοῦ in these three instances with "Jesus Christ" (*Revelation* [3 vols.; Word Biblical Commentary 52; Dallas: Word; Nashville: Thomas Nelson, 1997-1998), 1:12, 19, 37.

53. Aune translates χριστός in all these cases with "Messiah" (*Revelation*, 2:669, 699; 2:1,089, 1,093).

54. The link between the lord (κύριος) and kingship (ἡ βασιλεία) is also found in Ps 22:29 (21:29 LXX; 22:28 Eng.) and Obad. 21. The phrase "of our lord and of his messiah" (τοῦ κυρίου καὶ τοῦ χριστοῦ αὐτοῦ) seems to be an allusion to Ps 2:2 LXX. In the original social and historical context of Psalm 2, the phrase χριστὸς αὐτοῦ referred to the king of Israel and should be translated "his anointed."

55. See Adela Yarbro Collins, *The Combat Myth in the Book of Revelation* (Harvard Dissertations in Religion 9; Missoula, MT: Scholars Press for the Harvard Theological Review; reprinted Eugene, OR: Wipf & Stock, 2001), 34-36.

rule of God and the lamb at the time John wrote was fully effective, in his view, only in heaven. He portrayed the devil, as dragon or serpent, having power over the earth (12:7–13:1; 13:4-10).[56]

Chapters 12–13 make clear that, at the time John was writing, the devil ruled the earth through the Roman emperor and empire. In the future God and Christ, the messiah, would conquer the devil and his servants (chapters 18–19). This depiction of the last days corresponds to the apocalyptic distinction between the present evil age or world and the coming new age or world.[57] The ruler or god of this age or world is the devil or Satan.[58]

According to Rev 12:10, John heard a loud voice in heaven, saying, "Now the salvation and the power and the kingdom of our God and the authority of his messiah have come because the accuser of our brothers [and sisters] has been thrown down, the one who accuses them before our God day and night." This declaration takes place after a battle in heaven, in which Michael and his angels defeat the devil and his angels, casting them down to earth. This victory signifies that God and Jesus, as messiah, have unchallenged power in heaven. It also means salvation for those who have conquered Satan by means of the blood of the lamb and their own testimony, which has led to their deaths (v. 11). Thus God rules and Jesus has authority over those who accept the testimony of Jesus and who refuse to worship the beast, Satan's agent. In its typical recapitulatory way, the book of Revelation portrays in chapter 12 events that take place before those associated with the seventh trumpet in 11:15-19.[59]

After the beast from the sea and the beast from the land (chapter 13) are defeated by Jesus (19:11-21) and the devil is confined in the bottomless pit for a thousand years, the messianic rule of Jesus on earth begins (20:4-6).[60] At the end of v. 4, it is said that those who had been beheaded for refusing to worship the beast "came to life and reigned with the messiah for a

---

56. Yarbro Collins, *Combat Myth*, 142-45, 158-90, 207-11, 219-34.

57. Cf. Matt 12:32; Mark 10:30; Luke 16:8; 20:34-36; Rom 12:2; 1 Cor 1:20; 2:6-8; 3:18-19; Gal 1:4.

58. 2 Cor 4:4.

59. Yarbro Collins, *Combat Myth*, 8-9, 32-44.

60. On the question whether the messianic reign is located on earth or in heaven, see Adela Yarbro Collins, "The Apocalypse of John and Its Millennial Themes," in Martin McNamara, ed., *Apocalyptic and Eschatological Heritage: The Middle East and Celtic Realms* (Dublin: Four Courts Press, 2003), 50-60.

thousand years." The double function of χριστοῦ as a virtual second name of Jesus and as an indication of his messiahship makes clear that he is the anointed one who is meant. Similarly, in v. 6 those who take part in this first resurrection are declared blessed and holy because they will not experience the second death; rather, "they will be priests of God and of the messiah and will reign with him for a thousand years." This vision anticipates the fulfillment of the prophecy or promise in 5:10 that the saints will reign on earth.[61]

John also portrays Jesus indirectly as the messiah by alluding to biblical passages that were read messianically in his time, for example, as the "lion from the tribe of Judah" (Gen 49:9)[62] and "the root [or sprout] of David"[63] in Rev 5:5.[64] In 12:5 the woman clothed with the sun is said to give birth to a son (ἔτεκεν υἱόν); this phrase may allude to Isa 7:14 LXX, "and she will give birth to a son" (καὶ τέξεται υἱόν). According to Rev 12:5, the woman's son (Jesus) "is about to rule all the nations with a rod of iron," a clear allusion to Ps 2:8-9 LXX.

### Christ as an Angel, as Angelomorphic, or Angelic

The letter to the Hebrews strongly and clearly rejects the idea that Christ is an angel (Hebrews 1).[65] Revelation, however, seems to portray the risen Jesus as an angel or at least in angelomorphic terms.[66] The first passage that

---

61. Cf. Rev 1:6; 22:5.

62. There may be a messianic allusion to Gen 49:9 in 1QSb 5:29; see John J. Collins, *The Scepter and the Star* (New York: Doubleday, 1995), 60-61.

63. Cf. Isa 11:1, 10 LXX, which refer to "the root of Jesse"; Rev 22:16; Rom 15:12. The "sprout [or branch] of David" (צמח דויד) occurs in 4Q285, frg. 5, line 3, in synonymous parallelism with "the stump [or root] of Jesse." It also occurs in several other texts from Qumran; on these passages, see Collins, *The Scepter and the Star*, 56-63; Johannes Zimmermann, *Messianische Texte aus Qumran* (WUNT 2.104; Tübingen: Mohr Siebeck, 1998), 49-127.

64. The risen Jesus affirms his role as the root or sprout of David in 22:16. In the latter passage, he also affirms himself as "the offspring of David" (τὸ γένος Δαυίδ); Aune, *Revelation*, 3:1226.

65. For discussion see Harold W. Attridge, *Hebrews* (Hermeneia: Philadelphia: Fortress, 1989), 35-62.

66. Peter R. Carrell, *Jesus and the Angels: Angelology and the Christology of the Apocalypse of John* (SNTSMS 95; Cambridge: Cambridge University Press, 1997); Charles A.

may present Jesus as an angel is the opening of the book. The prologue or preface (1:1-3) speaks of John the prophet in the third person: "[The] revelation of Jesus Christ, which God gave him to show his servants what must happen soon, and he made it known by sending [it] through his angel [or messenger] to his servant John" (1:1). In the phrase "which God gave him," the pronoun "him" is clearly Jesus. Jesus possesses the revelation because God gave it to him. In the phrase "he made it known," it is not so clear whether God or Jesus is meant. In favor of taking the unexpressed subject of the verb as God is the fact that the only nominative noun expressed so far is θεός (God). In that case, it would be God who sent his angel to John. Since God gave the revelation to Jesus, that angel could be Jesus. Further, the risen Jesus is the first heavenly being to appear to John in his account (1:13-20).[67] In addition, in 22:6 someone, probably the angel who showed John the new Jerusalem (21:9-10), states that God sent his angel to show his servants what must happen soon. Against taking the angel of 1:1 as Jesus, however, is the fact that Jesus is quoted in 22:16 as saying that he has sent his angel to declare these things to you (plural) about the (seven) congregations. The "you" here could refer to the servants mentioned in 1:1. It seems, then, that whatever angel is referred to in 1:1 is sent both by God and Jesus.[68] The ambiguity in the use of pronouns in 1:1 may be deliberate. In any case, it is not a problem if "God" is understood instead of "Jesus" or vice versa.

In the description of the appearance of the risen Christ to John in 1:12-16, it is not said that he is an angel or messenger (ἄγγελος).[69] Yet a number

---

Gieschen, *Angelomorphic Christology* (AGJU 42; Leiden: Brill, 1998), 245-69; Darrell D. Hannah, *Michael and Christ: Michael Traditions and Angel Christology in Early Christianity* (WUNT 2.109; Tübingen: Mohr Siebeck, 1999), 144-45, 151-55.

67. Carrell takes it for granted that Jesus and the angel of 1:1 are distinct beings, but notes a functional equivalence between them (*Jesus and the Angels,* 15, 119-27). Gieschen argues that the first figure mentioned in the opening Christophany is the Spirit, citing 1:10-11 (*Angelomorphic Christology,* 266). This argument is problematic, however, because "being in [the] spirit" (1:10) is more likely to mean being possessed by the spirit, as a power of God effecting an altered state of consciousness, than experiencing a vision of the Spirit as a heavenly being. He goes on, however, to argue that the voice of 1:12 and 4:1 belongs to or is the Spirit (ibid., 265-66).

68. Gieschen (*Angelomorphic Christology,* 261) points out that this joint sending would explain why John refers to what he received from this angel as both the word of God and the testimony of Jesus (1:2).

69. Hannah argues that Christ is neither identified with nor described as an angel in this passage (*Michael and Christ,* 151-55).

of features of that description are attributed elsewhere to angels. The first thing to notice is that the author of Revelation does not use "the Son of Man" as a title for Jesus. Rather, in 1:12-13 he wrote that he saw [one] like a son of man" (εἶδον . . . ὅμοιον υἱόν ἀνθρώπου). The accusative υἱόν here is a violation of the rules of Greek grammar; it should be dative or genitive.[70] The phrase ὅμοιον υἱὸν ἀνθρώπου ("one like a son of man") is probably a translation of the Aramaic כבר אנשׁ (*kĕbar 'ĕnāš*) in Dan 7:13 or of the Hebrew כדמות בני אדם (*kidĕmût bĕnê 'ādām*) in Dan 10:16.[71] In Dan 7:13 the phrase, in its original historical context, referred to an angel, probably Michael.[72] Later, the phrase came to be understood as the messiah.[73]

Since the figure of 1:12-20 is identified with the risen Jesus (v. 18) and he is called messiah elsewhere in the book,[74] it is likely that John shared the view of his contemporaries that the "one like a son of man" in Dan 7:13 is the messiah. Yet a number of scholars have pointed out that the imagery of Rev 1:13-16 is adapted from Dan 10:5-9.[75] The figure in Daniel is best understood as an angel.[76] Some of the imagery comes from Ezekiel 9–10 (an angel with priestly and scribal characteristics), some from Ezek 28:13 (the

---

70. LSJ, *s.v.*, B.2; note that the accusative may be used to express that in which a person or a thing resembles another (ibid., 3); such is not the case here. See also BAGD, *s.v.*, a., b., and c.; Friedrich Blass and Albert Debrunner, *A Greek Grammar of the New Testament and Other Early Christian Literature* (trans. from the 9th-10th Germ. ed.; ed. Robert W. Funk; Chicago/London: University of Chicago Press, 1961), §182 (4).

71. Both the Old Greek and Theodotion read ὡς υἱὸς ἀνθρώπου. Gieschen argues that the allusion is to Ezek 1:26 LXX (ὁμοίωμα ὡς εἶδος ἀνθρώπου); *Angelomorphic Christology*, 249.

72. Collins, *Daniel*, 304-10.

73. See the chapters on the Son of Man above.

74. See the subsection "Jesus as the Messiah" immediately above.

75. Christopher Rowland, "The Vision of the Risen Christ in Rev. I.13ff.: The Debt of an Early Christology to an Aspect of Jewish Angelology," *JTS* 31 (1980) 1-11; idem, *The Open Heaven* (London: SPCK; New York: Crossroad, 1982), 94-113; idem, "A Man Clothed in Linen: Daniel 10.6ff and Jewish Angelology," *JSNT* 24 (1985) 99-110; Adela Yarbro Collins, "The 'Son of Man' Tradition and the Book of Revelation," in James H. Charlesworth, ed., *The Messiah: Developments in Earliest Judaism and Christianity* (Minneapolis: Fortress, 1992), 536-68, especially 548-51; reprinted in eadem, *Cosmology and Eschatology in Jewish and Christian Apocalypticism* (JSJSup 50; Leiden: Brill, 1996), 159-97, especially 173-77; Carrell, *Jesus and the Angels*, 150-54; Gieschen, *Angelomorphic Christology*, 246-47; Hannah, *Michael and Christ*, 151-52. See also the chart in Aune, *Revelation*, 1:72, comparing Rev 1:13-16 with Dan 10:5-9 and the *Apocalypse of Zephaniah*.

76. Collins, *Daniel*, 373; Carrell, *Jesus and the Angels*, 40-41.

primal man), and some from Ezekiel 1 (of the four living creatures, the chariot, and the one seated on the throne).[77]

Carrell concludes that Jesus is divine in the book of Revelation and not an angel. He infers the divinity of Christ from his position in the midst of God's throne (5:6) and his relation with God as father and son (3:21). Christ's close association with the throne of God makes him similar to the four living creatures, whom Carrell calls "the most exalted of all heavenly beings apart from God"; nevertheless they worship him.[78] A problem with this conclusion is that sonship of God is highly ambiguous. It may, but need not, imply divinity. The risen Jesus being seated on the throne certainly implies his exaltation and his sharing in important activities of God, such as ruling and judgment. Yet divinity admits of different degrees. Carrell also concludes that the "christology of Apocalypse 1.13-16 is appropriately described as an 'angelomorphic christology,'" that is, Jesus has the form of an angel, but is not an angel.

Gieschen argues that "the *theophany* in Ezekiel 1" has influenced the *angelophany* of Daniel 10; the connection between the two texts leads him to conclude, "The Christ in Revelation 1 was not only understood as Gabriel (from Daniel), but as the Glory (from Ezekiel 1 and 8), the very manlike form of God."[79] He also concludes "that 'the angel' of Rev 20.1 is Christ."[80] The elements adapted in Rev 1:13-16 from Ezekiel 1, however, are not all taken from the description of the one seated on the throne-chariot. For this reason it seems unwarranted to conclude that the risen Christ in Revelation 1 is identified with the manlike form of God in Ezekiel 1. The argument that the angel of 20:1 is Christ is based on texts from the Gospels and non-Pauline epistles; the relevance of these texts for the interpretation of Revelation is dubious. Ultimately, the hypothesis seems to be dependent, directly or indirectly, on Augustine's interpretation of Rev 20:1, namely, that it was Jesus who bound Satan.[81]

77. Rowland, *Open Heaven*, 98-99; Collins, *Daniel*, 373-74.

78. Carrell, *Jesus and the Angels*, 143-44.

79. Gieschen, *Angelomorphic Christology*, 248; emphasis his. He accepts the view that the angel of Daniel 10 is Gabriel and my suggestion that the author of Revelation considered Gabriel to be the principal angel and the risen Christ to be identified with Gabriel (ibid.); Yarbro Collins, "The 'Son of Man' Tradition," 558; *Cosmology and Eschatology*, 185.

80. Gieschen, *Angelomorphic Christology*, 250.

81. Augustine, *City of God* 20; for discussion see Judith Kovacs and Christopher Rowland, *Revelation* (Blackwell Bible Commentaries; Oxford: Blackwell, 2004), 207-8.

Hannah concludes that, with the exception of Jude 5-6,[82] Christ is never called or portrayed as an angel in the New Testament. Motifs related to principal angels, however, "are used to elucidate Christ or his work," so "angelology did have some effect on NT Christology" and "we are justified in speaking of NT angelic Christology."[83] It is noteworthy in this context that the Greek version of Isaiah 9 refers to the ideal king as an angel.[84]

Hannah's conclusions, on the whole, are more judicious than those of Carrell and Gieschen. As argued above, the risen Jesus is clearly identified as the messiah in Revelation. The author of the work used some traditions about angels in order to portray Christ as a messiah of the heavenly type. The idea of a heavenly messiah, however, is compatible with the notion that he is also the principal angel. The strongest evidence for the conclusion that the author considered the risen Jesus to be an angel are the ways he uses the phrase "one like a son of man" in 1:13 and 14:14. These ways will be discussed in the next subsection.

As we have seen, the notion of a heavenly messiah was combined with the portrayal of preexistent, personified wisdom in *1 Enoch* 48:2-3, 6 and probably in the letters of Paul.[85] The same two ideas appear in Revelation, so it seems that the author considered them compatible. Christ is portrayed in terms of personified wisdom in the message to Laodicea: "Thus says the amen, the faithful and true witness, the beginning of the creation of God" (Rev 3:14).[86]

The tradition about personified wisdom is probably also the best context in which to understand the sayings of Rev 1:17 and 22:13. In the former, Christ affirms that he is "the first and the last" (ὁ πρῶτος καὶ ὁ ἔσχατος); in the latter that he is "the alpha and the omega, the first and the last, the beginning and the end" (τὸ ἄλφα καὶ τὸ ὦ, ὁ πρῶτος καὶ τὸ ἔσχατος, ἡ ἀρχὴ καὶ τὸ τέλος). God also affirms "I am the alpha and the omega" in 1:8, and the same in 21:6 along with being "the beginning and the end."

---

82. Hannah argues that it was the preexistent Christ, "as the Exodus angel" who saved a people out of the land of Egypt according to Jude 5 (*Michael and Christ*, 139-40); cf. Metzger, *Textual Commentary*, 657.

83. Hannah, *Michael and Christ*, 161-62; see also 151-61.

84. See Chapter 3 above.

85. See the last part of the chapter on the Synoptic Gospels above.

86. On the connections between the phrase "the beginning of the creation of God" (ἡ ἀρχὴ τῆς κτίσεως τοῦ θεοῦ) and the Jewish (and Christian) wisdom tradition, see Aune, *Revelation*, 1:256-57.

It is not necessarily the case that the same attributes have exactly the same significance for Christ as they have for God. For example, in light of 3:14, the affirmation that Christ is the beginning and the end in 22:13 may be understood as signifying that he is both the beginning and the fulfillment of the creation of God. Thus his being "the first and the last" (an affirmation not made about God in Revelation) could also mean the first creature of God and the agent of God at the end. All of the affirmations are more like poetry than like philosophy, so it is difficult to determine whether the author considered Jesus to be an aspect or emanation of God or the first creature of God, or whether he thought about this issue at all. The notion that Christ was the first creature of God is compatible with his being the principal angel.

### One like a Son of Man

The previous subsection focused on the angelic motifs in the vision of the risen Christ as "one like a son of man" in Rev 1:12-16. As noted above, the author of Revelation does not use the phrase as a title for Jesus, "the Son of Man," as the Synoptic Gospels (and Acts 7:56) do. In 1:13, the author seems to be alluding to Dan 7:13. This conclusion is supported by 1:14, which reads "and his head and his hair were white as white wool, as snow" (ἡ δὲ κεφαλὴ αὐτοῦ καὶ αἱ τρίχες λευκαὶ ὡς ἔριον λευκὸν ὡς χιών). This statement seems to reflect a Jewish apocalyptic tradition, based on Dan 7:9 ultimately, but varying in wording. The Aramaic original of that text says that an ancient of days took his throne, that his garment was white as snow, and that the hair of his head was like pure wool.[87] It is striking that in Rev 1:13-14 the risen Christ is associated with both the manlike figure of Dan 7:13 and the ancient of days, usually understood as God, in 7:9.

In his edition of the Old Greek version of Daniel, Rahlfs followed the cursive manuscript 88 and the literal Syriac translation of the fifth column[88] of Origen's Hexapla made by the monophysite bishop Paul of Tella in the early seventh century (Syh, the Syro-Hexapla)[89] in reading ὡς

---

87. Yarbro Collins, "The 'Son of Man' Tradition," 551-52; *Cosmology and Eschatology*, 177.

88. The fifth column of Origen's Hexapla was the Septuagint; see Melvin K. H. Peters, "Septuagint," *ABD*, 5:1,093-1,104, especially 1,098-99.

89. These witnesses are cited at the beginning of the text of the Old Greek version of

παλαιὸς ἡμερῶν in Dan 7:13. This reading has the one like a son of man coming *as* the ancient of days, rather than *to* the ancient of days.[90] If the author of Revelation was familiar with the reading *as* the ancient of days, this could explain why he combined attributes of the two figures in his portrayal of the risen Christ.

James A. Montgomery, however, had already suggested that this reading was an ancient error for ἕως παλαιοῦ ἡμερῶν, but an error that was made before the time that Revelation was written. He rejected Wilhelm Bousset's suggestion that the change was made deliberately in order to express the idea of a preexistent messiah, suggesting that the change was accidental.[91] He reasoned that ἕως was misread as ὡς and that this error resulted in the "correction" of παλαιοῦ to παλαιός.[92] Since Rev 1:14 seems to identify the two figures, Montgomery inferred that the author of Revelation read ὡς παλαιός in his text of Daniel. Sharon Pace Jeansonne followed Montgomery and Joseph Ziegler in arguing that the reading ὡς παλαιὸς ἡμερῶν ("as an ancient of days") is a corruption of the original reading.[93]

The arguments of Montgomery and Pace Jeansonne are convincing. It is better to explain variants as mechanical errors when such an explanation is credible. As Montgomery suggested, this error may be very ancient. Papyrus 967 provides evidence that the error was made in the second century or earlier.[94] As an inadvertent error, it could have been made as easily by a Jewish scribe as by a Christian one.

---

Daniel in Alfred Rahlfs, *Septuaginta* (2 vols.; 7th ed.; Stuttgart: Württembergische Bibelanstalt, 1935), 2:870. On the Old Greek version, see Collins, *Daniel*, 4-7. See also Peters, "Septuagint," 1,094, 1,098-99.

90. The Greek version attributed to Theodotion follows the sense of the Aramaic version in having the latter reading. In his edition Rahlfs printed the Old Greek version on the upper half of the page and Theodotion's version on the lower half.

91. James A. Montgomery, *A Critical and Exegetical Commentary on the Book of Daniel* (ICC; Edinburgh: T&T Clark, 1927; reprinted 1979), 304. See also Yarbro Collins, "The 'Son of Man' Tradition," 553 and nn. 89 and 90; *Cosmology and Eschatology*, 179 and nn. 89 and 90.

92. James A. Montgomery, "Anent Dr. Rendel Harris's 'Testimonies,'" *Expositor* 22 (1921) 214-17, especially 214.

93. See the discussion in Yarbro Collins, "The 'Son of Man' Tradition," 554-55; *Cosmology and Eschatology*, 180-81.

94. Angelo Geissen, *Der Septuaginta-Text des Buches Daniel Kap. 5-12, zusammen mit Susanna, Bel et Draco sowie Esther Kap. 1,1a-2, 15* (Papyrologische Texte und Abhandlungen 5; Bonn: Habelt, 1968), 18; Yarbro Collins, "The 'Son of Man' Tradition," 539-40, 553-55; *Cosmology and Eschatology*, 162-64, 179-81.

The prototypes of the Masoretic text of the Hebrew Bible (in this case Aramaic) and of Theodotion and the earliest recoverable reading of the Old Greek as reconstructed by Ziegler[95] may be read as revealing that alongside God (the ancient of days) there is a primary angel or there will be an exalted messiah (the one like a son of man). This point of view was apparently opposed by certain rabbis in the second century CE, who argued exegetically that the ancient of days and the one like a son of man were two different manifestations of the one and only God. Greek-speaking Jews of this persuasion would have welcomed the reading of Pap. 967 and MS 88-Syh as support for their point of view. They could have argued that Dan 7:9-12 and 7:13-14 are two parallel accounts of the same event. Supporters of the notion of two powers in heaven could have replied that neither the ancient of days nor the one like a son of man was the one and only transcendent God; the two figures are variant manifestations of the principal angel.[96]

If the form of Dan 7:13 known to the author of Revelation was ὡς παλαιὸς ἡμερῶν ("as an ancient of days"), he apparently interpreted *both* the ancient of days *and* the one like a son of man as manifestations of the principal angel whom he identified with the exalted messiah.[97]

The other important passage related to John's depiction of the risen Jesus as son of man is Rev 14:14-20. This vision is the sixth in a series that begins with the vision of the woman clothed with the sun.[98] It depicts a symbolic harvest and vintage inspired by Joel 4:13 (3:13 Eng.), which uses the images of harvest and vintage for divine judgment on the nations on the day of the lord. This application is made clear by 4:12 and 14. That the symbolic vision in Revelation concerns judgment is made clear by the way in which the description of vintage shifts into battle imagery in 14:20.[99]

The vision opens with a white cloud, and upon the cloud "one like a

---

95. Joseph Ziegler, *Susanna, Daniel, Bel et Draco* (Septuaginta: Vetus Testamentum Graecum 16.2; Göttingen: Vandenhoeck & Ruprecht, 1954), 169-70; cited by Yarbro Collins, "The 'Son of Man' Tradition," 540; *Cosmology and Eschatology,* 163.

96. See the more detailed discussion in Yarbro Collins, "The 'Son of Man' Tradition," 555-57; *Cosmology and Eschatology,* 182-84.

97. Cf. Yarbro Collins, "The 'Son of Man' Tradition," 557-58; *Cosmology and Eschatology,* 184.

98. For the enumeration of the visions, see Yarbro Collins, *Combat Myth,* 13-19. The seventh vision in this series is 15:2-4.

99. Cf. *1 Enoch* 100:3.

son of man" (ὅμοιος υἱὸς ἀνθρώπου)[100] was seated. Louis Vos has argued that the motif of the seated son of man comes from Mark 14:62 or its parallel in Matt 26:64, since the one like a son of man is not portrayed as seated in Daniel 7.[101] Although the son of man is not seated in Daniel 7 or *4 Ezra* 13, he *is* so described in the *Similitudes of Enoch* (*1 Enoch* 37–71). In 69:27 "that son of man" is depicted as sitting on the throne of his glory for the purpose of judgment. Although the *Similitudes* were probably composed prior to the writing of Revelation,[102] it could be that the respective authors either independently adapted Daniel 7 or were familiar with a common tradition based ultimately on Daniel.

Another difference between this vision and Daniel 7 is that Dan 7:13 says that the one like a son of man was coming with the clouds of heaven, whereas Rev 14:14 portrays him as seated on a single cloud. The fact that Luke 21:27 also speaks of one cloud does not prove a connection between the two texts. The author of Revelation may have chosen to refer to a single cloud to create a more vivid image.[103]

The crown on the head of the one like a son of man in Rev 14:14 can be explained as a visual representation of the remark in Dan 7:14 that he was given dominion and glory and kingship. The sickle derives from Joel 4:13 (3:13 Eng.). George B. Caird and Louis Vos interpreted the image of the harvest in Rev 14:14-16 as the ingathering of the elect. It is better understood, however, as an image for judgment, since the ripeness of the harvest in Joel is in synonymous parallelism with the fullness of the winepress, which is associated with the wickedness of the nations in Joel 4:13. Furthermore, the motif of salvation in this series comes at its end in Rev 15:2-4.[104]

Vos also argued that the depiction of an angel coming out of the temple to inform the one like a son of man that it is time to reap is dependent

---

100. This is the same phrase used in Rev 1:13; see the discussion of it above in the subsection "Christ as an Angel, as Angelomorphic, or Angelic."

101. Louis A. Vos, *The Synoptic Traditions in the Apocalypse* (Kampen, the Netherlands: Kok, 1965), 146-52; for a more detailed discussion of Vos's arguments, see Yarbro Collins, "The 'Son of Man' Tradition," 562-64; *Cosmology and Eschatology*, 189-92.

102. The *Similitudes of Enoch* were composed between 40 BCE and 70 CE (John J. Collins, *The Apocalyptic Imagination* [2nd ed.; Grand Rapids: Eerdmans, 1998], 178), and Revelation around 95-96 CE (Adela Yarbro Collins, *Crisis and Catharsis: The Power of the Apocalypse* [Philadelphia: Westminster, 1984], 54-83).

103. Yarbro Collins, "The 'Son of Man' Tradition," 564; *Cosmology and Eschatology*, 192.

104. Cf. Yarbro Collins, "The 'Son of Man' Tradition," 562-66; *Cosmology and Eschatology*, 190-94.

on Mark 13:32 or its parallel in Matt 24:36, the saying in which Jesus declares that only the father knows the day and the hour of the end. He is right that the angel of Rev 14:15 should be taken as an agent of God announcing the arrival of the time for judging the nations. There is no need, however, to connect this verse with the saying of Mark 13:32 and parallels. The alleged "subordination" of the one like a son of man to God through his angelic agents is perfectly compatible with an early christology in which the conception of the risen Christ is that he is the principal angel and a messianic figure like the Son of Man in the *Similitudes of Enoch*.[105]

It is striking that the risen Jesus performs a task, the harvest of grain (14:16), parallel to that of an angel, the harvest of grapes (14:17-19). Hannah seeks to overcome this difficulty by inferring from 19:11 that Christ is the unexpressed subject of 14:20, the one who treads the winepress.[106] This argument makes sense because Revelation often presents an event in veiled form at first and in more detailed or direct form later on.[107] Thus the angel who carries out the vintage prefigures, and 14:20 more explicitly alludes to, the battle of 19:11-21.[108] The portrayal of the risen Jesus in that passage will be discussed in the next subsection. This link between the two passages, however, does not eliminate the impression made upon the audience by 14:14-20 that the risen Jesus is a kind of angel.

### The Risen Jesus as the Word of God

Rev 19:11-16 is the book of Revelation's equivalent of the parousia.[109] The statement, "I saw heaven opened," in v. 11 usually signifies the beginning of

---

105. Carrell concludes that Rev 14:14 involves the risen Jesus temporarily taking on angelic form and function (*Jesus and the Angels*, 175-95, especially 194). Similarly, Gieschen interprets the scene as an "appearance of the angelomorphic Christ" (*Angelomorphic Christology*, 252). Hannah concludes that "it seems unlikely in the extreme that Christ here [14:15-16] is being depicted as dependent upon an angel for communication with God. The purpose of the angel issuing from the temple and relaying the command to Christ is probably only intended to emphasize the divine origin of the edict" (*Michael and Christ*, 155).

106. Hannah, *Michael and Christ*, 155.

107. Yarbro Collins, *Combat Myth*, 8-9, 11-13, 32-44.

108. Yarbro Collins, "The 'Son of Man' Tradition," 565; *Cosmology and Eschatology*, 193.

109. Most commentators reach this conclusion; Aune finds the view of Farrer and Mealy "suggestive" that the unit presents Jesus as the royal bridegroom of Psalm 45 (*Revelation*, 3:1,046-47). There is no clear allusion to Psalm 45, however, in the unit.

a vision or revelation.[110] In this case it may also indicate the manner in which the risen Jesus will return at the time of his parousia, namely in a dramatic manner that recalls the self-revelation and the mighty deeds of God (cf. Isa 64:1-4).[111] The description of the rider as "faithful and true" (πιστὸς καὶ ἀληθινός) identifies him as Jesus Christ.[112] The statement that "he judges and makes war with justice" both describes him and indicates for what purposes he has appeared.

In 19:12, it is said that the one who rides on the white horse has eyes like a flame of fire (οἱ δὲ ὀφθαλμοὶ αὐτοῦ ὡς φλὸξ πυρός). The same element appears in the description of the "one like a son of man" in 1:14 and "the son of God" in 2:18. This motif is similar to the description of the angel in Dan 10:6. Both the Old Greek and Theodotion say that "his eyes were like torches of fire" (οἱ ὀφθαλμοὶ αὐτοῦ ὡσεὶ λαμπάδες πυρός). This characteristic is attributed to the principal angel in *Joseph and Aseneth* 14:8-9.[113] The many diadems or crowns that the rider wears (19:12) signify his kingship, that is, his messiahship.

In 19:13, the rider is described as "dressed in a garment dyed with blood" (περιβεβλημένος ἱμάτιον βεβαμμένον αἵματι). This image is best taken as an allusion to Isa 63:1-6, a theophany of the divine warrior,[114] whose garments are red (ἐρύθημα ἱματίων) (63:1 LXX) as if he had come from treading the wine vat (ὡς ἀπὸ πατητοῦ ληνοῦ) (v. 2). In verse 3 the imagery shifts from treading grapes to treading upon the nations "in wrath" (ἐν θυμῷ), crushing them as earth, and bringing down their blood to the earth. In verse 4 the speaker explains this activity in terms of the day of recompense coming upon them (ἡμέρα γὰρ ἀνταποδόσεως ἐπῆλθεν αὐτοῖς) and the year of redemption, presumably of God's people, being at hand (καὶ ἐνιαυτὸς λυτρώσεως πάρεστιν).

That the purpose of the one who rides a white horse is similar is clear from the heavenly armies that follow him, also on white horses (Rev 19:14), and from the sharp sword that issues from his mouth in v. 15.[115] It is ex-

---

110. Cf. Acts 10:11; Ezek 1:1; Aune, *Revelation*, 3:1,047, 1,052.

111. For passages in which the open heaven is associated with judgment, see Aune, ibid., 3:1,052.

112. Jesus is called "the faithful witness" (ὁ μάρτυς ὁ πιστός) in 1:5 and "the faithful and true witness" (ὁ μάρτυς ὁ πιστὸς καὶ ἀληθινός) in 3:14; "the true one" (ὁ ἀληθινός) in 3:7.

113. Carrell, *Jesus and the Angels*, 57, 203.

114. Yarbro Collins, *Combat Myth*, 224-25.

115. Cf. 1:16; 2:12, 16.

plicitly said that the purpose of this sword is "to trample the nations with it" (ἵνα ἐν αὐτῇ πατάξῃ τὰ ἔθνη). In 19:21 it is said that the kings of the earth and their armies (cf. v. 19) were killed by the sword of the one seated on the horse, the sword that came from his mouth.

That the figure on the white horse is the messiah is made clear by the allusion to Ps 2:9 in Rev 19:15b, "and he will rule them with an iron rod" (ποιμανεῖ αὐτοὺς ἐν ῥάβδῳ σιδηρᾷ).[116] The renewed allusion to Isa 63:2-3 in Rev 19:15c indicates that the risen Jesus, as messiah, is God's agent in judging the nations in battle: "and he will trample the vat of the wine of the wrath and the anger of God the almighty" (πατεῖ τὴν ληνὸν τοῦ οἴνου τοῦ θυμοῦ τῆς ὀργῆς τοῦ θεοῦ τοῦ παντοκράτορος).[117]

It is in this context that the name of the rider on the white horse is said to be "the word of God" (ὁ λόγος τοῦ θεοῦ) in 19:13b. The context makes clear that it is not the philosophical notion of the logos and the similarity between the logos and the wisdom of God that are at issue here, as was the case in the prologue of the Gospel of John. Rather, it is God's effective word that is evoked. In Isa 45:20-25, salvation is offered to the Gentiles, and the hope is that they will accept the offer willingly. If not, God will force them to submit: "I have sworn an oath by my life; the word that overcomes has gone forth from my mouth, a word that will not be made void: 'To me every knee will bend, by me every tongue will swear an oath'" (Isa 45:23).[118]

The most striking analogy to Jesus Christ as the word of God here is in the Wisdom of Solomon in the section "Divine Wisdom or Justice in the Exodus" (chapters 11–19).[119] The argument of this section is structured by seven antitheses.[120] The sixth antithesis is that the Egyptian firstborn are destroyed, but Israel is protected and glorified (18:5-25).[121] The taking away of a multitude of Egyptian children was punishment for the Egyptian

116. Cf. 12:5.

117. The judgment of the nations is just punishment for their persecution and murder of the faithful people of God (6:9-11; 13:7, 15; 17:6).

118. Translation from Joseph Blenkinsopp, *Isaiah 40–55* (AB 19A; New York: Doubleday, 2002), 260; see also the discussion on 262-63.

119. Following Winston's division of the work and title for this section (*Wisdom of Solomon*, xv). His argument, however, that "The description of the Logos [in Wis 18:15] is strikingly similar to that of Sophia earlier in the book" (ibid., 317), is not convincing.

120. Ibid., xv-xvi.

121. Ibid., xvi.

resolve to kill the infants of the Israelites (18:5). The deed is described as follows:

> While restful silence encompassed all things and night was halfway through its rapid course, your all-powerful word leaped from heaven, from the royal throne, into the middle of the doomed land as a relentless warrior bearing as a sharp sword your genuine command; standing, it filled all things with death. It touched heaven yet stood upon earth. (Wis 18:14-16)

Jesus as the word of God comes down from heaven to do battle with the two beasts, the kings of the earth, and their armies (19:11, 19).

Since he is described earlier as having a throne, shared with or given to him by God (3:21), he can be said to have descended from his royal throne (as messiah) to engage in battle.[122] His kingship or messiahship is explicitly reaffirmed at the end of the description, "and he has a name written on his garment and on his thigh: king of kings and lord of lords" (19:16). The indirect account of the battle and the direct statement of its results fit the text of the prototype: "and filled all things with death" (cf. Rev 19:17-21 with Wis 18:16).

The all-powerful word of God is described in Wis 18:16 as standing on the earth and touching heaven. Personified concepts in the *Iliad* and the *Aeneid* were described in a similar way. The angel of the Lord is likewise described as "standing between earth and heaven" in 1 Chr 21:16.[123] Thus the Wisdom of Solomon seems to imply that the word of God was, or could take the form of, an angel. This motif would fit the hypothesis that the risen Jesus is portrayed in Revelation as the principal angel, as well as the (heavenly) messiah.

---

122. Darrell D. Hannah argues, primarily on the basis of Rev 3:21 and 22:1, 3, that the risen Jesus is enthroned on God's own throne ("The Throne of His Glory: The Divine Throne and Heavenly Mediators in Revelation and the Similitudes of Enoch," *ZNW* 94 [2003] 68-96). In 3:21, however, the risen Christ, as speaker, appears to distinguish between his throne (ὁ θρόνος μου) and his father's throne (ὁ θρόνος αὐτοῦ). Egyptian representational art, however, depicts the pharaoh seated at the right hand of a god on the same throne; Othmar Keel, *The Symbolism of the Biblical World* (Winona Lake, IN: Eisenbrauns, 1997) 263, and fig. 353; 368, n. 52.

123. Winston, *Wisdom of Solomon*, 319.

## Conclusion

Although the Gospel of John and the book of Revelation use many of the same terms in their portrayal of Jesus and his work, they differ on several important points. In the Gospel it is clear that Jesus, as the word or logos philosophically understood, is preexistent and divine in the sense of being an emanation of God or being "a god." In contrast, there is no sign in the book of Revelation that "the word" of God is philosophically understood. The starting point is rather the idea of God's effective word (cf. Isa 45:22-23). This idea is then personified, like the word of God in Wis 18:14-16, and described as huge in size, as great as the distance between heaven and earth.

The two works, however, agree that Jesus is the messiah of the heavenly type. They both link the traditional royal epithet "son of God" with the term "messiah." Yet the Gospel elaborates that title in such a way as to interpret Jesus as son of God in a unique sense: he is the only-begotten god. In Revelation the only time that Jesus is explicitly called "the son of God" (ὁ υἱὸς τοῦ θεοῦ) is in the message to Thyatira (2:18). The context, drawing upon the vision of 1:12-16, alludes to Dan 10:6. This allusion suggests that the angel of Daniel 10 is identified here with Jesus as an angelic heavenly messiah. In 5:5 and 22:16, Jesus is portrayed as son of David. In chapter 12, he is depicted as the son of the woman clothed with the sun. If she is the heavenly Israel, it could be inferred that God is the father of the child. The language, however, is symbolic and ought not to be pressed.

The two authors agree that the death of Jesus was motivated by love and is effective for his followers. The book of Revelation emphasizes the power of his blood (1:5b) and the sacrificial character of his death through the image of the slaughtered lamb (ἀρνίον) (5:6). The Gospel interprets the death of Jesus in terms of the binding of Isaac (3:16, 35). It also connects Jesus' death with the time at which the passover lambs were sacrificed (19:14). Unlike the traditional significance of the sacrifice of the passover lamb, the death of Jesus is portrayed as taking away sin (1:29).

For both the Gospel and the book of Revelation, Jesus' identity as messiah is closely linked to his identity as Son of Man or as the manlike figure in Daniel 7. Like Mark, the Gospel links the Son of Man title with the death of Jesus. Like Matthew and Luke, it also connects the Son of Man with judgment. A distinctive interpretation of Jesus as the Son of Man in John is that he is the mediator between heaven and earth (1:51). This new development is linked to the death of Jesus because it is through his being "lifted up" that he is able to draw people to himself, including leading them to the presence of the father in the heavenly world. Revelation, in contrast, suggests that the risen Jesus as the one like a son of man is the principal angel.

Both authors associate Jesus with the wisdom tradition. The Gospel identifies personified wisdom with the word of God as the philosophical logos. Revelation does not go in this direction. It depicts Jesus as "the beginning of the creation of God" in 3:14, which recalls the Greek version of Prov 8:22, "The LORD created me as the beginning of his ways for his works." Although they do not allude specifically to texts about wisdom, certain ambiguous sayings of the risen Jesus in Revelation are best interpreted in relation to personified wisdom. He affirms that he is the first and the last, the alpha and the omega, and the beginning and the end (1:17; 22:13). In light of the evidence that the author of Revelation portrays Jesus as the heavenly messiah who is also the principal angel of God, these sayings are best interpreted as associating Jesus with personified wisdom as God's first creature. Although some elements of these sayings are also attributed to God,[124] it is unlikely that the author intends to identify Christ with God. Rather, the common affirmations signify that Christ participated in the creation and will participate in the full manifestation of the rule of God as God's agent.

The Gospel and Revelation both present Jesus as preexistent and as divine in some sense. In the Gospel, he is either an emanation of God or God's first creature, namely, the only-begotten god. In Revelation, the evidence suggests that he is God's first creature, namely, the principal angel.

---

124. God is presented as the *alpha* and *omega* in Rev 1:8 and as the *alpha* and the *omega* and the beginning and the end in 21:6.

# Conclusion

The idea that the king was in some sense divine had ancient roots in the Near Eastern world. That it was embraced by the Davidic dynasty in Jerusalem is apparent from the royal psalms, which reflect a court protocol inherited from the Canaanites, who were in turn influenced by Egyptian royal ideology in the New Kingdom period. There is no evidence for a cult of the king in ancient Judah, but the rhetoric of the psalms should not be disregarded for that reason. It was primarily a way of marking the king off as superior to other human beings, although not on a par with the Most High. The psalms speak of the king as son of God, and say he is begotten, not adopted. This language is mythical and metaphorical rather than philosophical. It does not employ ontological categories. But it should not be dismissed as "mere" metaphor. It was a powerful way of shaping perceptions about the special relationship between the king and his god.

This high view of the status of the monarchy was severely shaken by the disasters of the Assyrian and especially the Babylonian eras. In the prophetic writings, the divine status of the king is mentioned only once, in Isaiah 9. The Deuteronomistic historian formulated the relationship between God and the Davidic dynasty in covenantal terms and emphasized that the king would be punished for infidelity. Yet it also preserved the promise that "I will be a father to him, and he will be a son to me," even if the language of begetting was dropped and the emphasis was rather on parental discipline.

After the demise of the monarchy, it was easier to speak of a future messianic king in purely ideal terms. Messianic expectation, in the sense of hope for the restoration of the Davidic dynasty, has left some traces in the prophetic literature of the Persian era, but these oracles do not impute divinity in any degree to the future king. There is more extensive evidence for messianic expectation in the Hellenistic period, especially after the usurpation of the monarchy by the Hasmonean line. Many of the references to a future "messiah" in the Dead Sea Scrolls are minimal and refer to him only as the "shoot of David" who will arise in the last days. But a significant number of texts in this period impute to the messianic king a superhuman status.

The Greek translation of the Psalms shows no inhibitions about referring to the king as son of God (Psalms 2, 89), begotten by God (Psalm 110) or addressed as God (Psalm 45). Moreover, the idea that the king is preexistent is introduced into Psalm 110 and possibly implied in Psalm 72. The Greek translation of Isaiah 9 does not call the king "mighty god," but instead describes him as an angel, a possible interpretation of the Hebrew word אל, "god," in the Hellenistic period.

The Dead Sea Scrolls, while normally reticent about imputing superhuman status to the messiah, explicitly interpret the statement in 2 Samuel 7, "I will be a father to him, and he will be a son to me," as a reference to the shoot of David, in 4Q174, the *Florilegium*. Moreover, this text continues with citations from Psalms 1–2, which were often regarded as one psalm in antiquity.[1] The word משיחו, "his messiah," in Ps 2:2 appears to be interpreted as referring to "the elect ones of Israel" in the *Florilegium*. No interpretation of Ps 2:7, "You are my son; today I have begotten you," is preserved. Nonetheless it is difficult to avoid the impression that this psalm was juxtaposed to 2 Samuel 7 here because of the common reference to the king as son of God.[2] It should be noted that Psalm 2 is used extensively in

---

1. *Berakot* 9b. So also the Western Text of Acts. Paul Maiberger, "Das Verständnis von Psalm 2 in der Septuaginta, im Targum, in Qumran, im frühen Judentum und im Neuen Testament," in Josef Schreiner, ed., *Beiträge zur Psalmenforschung. Psalm 2 und 22* (Forschung zur Bibel; Würzburg: Echter, 1988), 85-151, especially 85-89; H. L. Strack and P. Billerbeck, *Kommentar zum Neuen Testament aus Talmud und Midrasch* (München: Beck, 1924, 1989), 2:725; Joseph A. Fitzmyer, *The Acts of the Apostles* (AB 31; New York: Doubleday, 1998), 516.

2. George J. Brooke, "Shared Intertextual Interpretations in the Dead Sea Scrolls and the New Testament," in idem, *The Dead Sea Scrolls and the New Testament* (Minneapolis: Fortress, 2005), 70-94, here 75, pace Annette Steudel, "Psalm 2 im antiken Judentum," in Die-

reference to the messianic king in *Psalms of Solomon* 17, even though his divine sonship is not explicitly noted.[3] Ps 2:7 is juxtaposed to 2 Sam 7:14 in Heb 1:5, and the same psalm verse is cited in conjunction with a reference to "the holy promises to David" in Acts 13:33-34.

Ps 2:7 is very likely to provide the referential background in two other controversial texts from Qumran. The *Messianic Rule,* 1QSa, according to the most likely reading, refers to the time "when God will beget the messiah with them," picking up the language of the psalm. In 4Q246, the *Aramaic Apocalypse* or "Son of God" text, the figure who bears the titles "Son of God" and "Son of Most High" should be identified as the Davidic messiah, as also in Luke 1:32, 35. While 4Q246 does not cite Psalm 2 directly, the psalm provides the most obvious basis for designating the messianic king as son of God.

By the time these texts were written, most probably in the first century BCE, the royal psalms and 2 Samuel 7 were established as sacred scriptures. Even if the royal ideology of ancient Judah had died out at the end of the monarchical period, the language was available for meditation, and was often read as relating to the "end of days." It is not surprising, then, that the language of divine sonship should be applied to the messianic king, who was yet to come.

The most important development regarding the divinity of the messiah in ancient Judaism, however, was the reinterpretation of messianic expectation in light of Daniel's vision of "one like a son of man" (Dan 7:13). In the *Similitudes of Enoch,* the Son of Man is a heavenly, preexistent figure, not a descendant of David, who is seated on a throne of glory as eschatological judge. But he is also called "messiah," in a passage that alludes to Psalm 2 (*1 Enoch* 48:10: "for they have denied the Lord of Spirits and his Anointed One").[4] It is also said of this figure that "all who dwell on earth will fall down and worship before him" (*1 Enoch* 48:5). The verse continues to say that they will glorify and sing hymns to the name of the Lord of

---

ter Sänger, ed., *Gottessohn und Menschensohn. Exegetische Paradigmen biblischer Intertextualität* (Neukirchen-Vluyn: Neukirchener Verlag, 2004), 189-97.

3. See Kenneth Atkinson, *An Intertextual Study of the Psalms of Solomon Pseudepigrapha* (Lewiston, NY: Mellen, 2001), 336-41.

4. Johannes Theisohn, *Der auserwählte Richter* (SUNT 12; Göttingen: Vandenhoeck & Ruprecht, 1975), 56; Stefan Schreiber, *Gesalbter und König. Titel und Konzeptionen der königlichen Gesalbtenerwartung in frühjudischen und urchristlichen Schriften* (BZNW 105; Berlin: de Gruyter, 2000), 331.

Spirits. It is not implied that the Son of Man is worshipped as the supreme God, but rather that people perform *proskynesis* before him in recognition of his authority.

The messiah is also depicted as a "son of man" figure, who comes on the clouds, in *4 Ezra* 13. He is also called "my son," and much of the imagery of the chapter is derived from Psalm 2. *4 Ezra*, however, persists in identifying this figure as "from the posterity of David" (*4 Ezra* 12:32), even though it is not apparent why a descendant of David should come on the clouds.

The reinterpretation of the messiah as heavenly "son of man," in accordance with Daniel's figure, places the traditional language about the king/messiah as "son of God" in a new light. It must be seen in the context of affirmations of the preexistence of the messianic king in the Greek psalter and also in the context of the expectation of heavenly, angelic, savior figures, such as we find in 11QMelchizedek.

### Jesus as Son of God

The early Christian proclamation of Jesus as son of God must be seen in this context of Jewish messianic expectation. Contrary to the thesis of Bousset, who saw this proclamation as a later development in the Gentile church, under Hellenistic influence, the belief that Jesus was "son of God" was entailed in the first instance by the conviction that he was the messiah.

Unlike the "Son of Man" in the *Similitudes of Enoch*, or even the messianic "man" of *4 Ezra*, Jesus was an historical human being, who died ingloriously on a cross. In his lifetime, he did not conform at all to the typical Jewish expectation of a warrior messiah who would drive out the Romans and restore the kingdom of Israel, as his followers had hoped.[5] The affirmation that he was the messiah could be maintained after his death only by the belief that he was raised from the dead and exalted to heaven, and that he would come again as the Son of Man on the clouds of heaven. The identification of Jesus as the Son of Man would have been easier if he himself had spoken, however, mysteriously, of the Son of Man as an eschato-

---

5. Luke 24:21. See further John J. Collins, "Jesus and the Messiahs of Israel," in H. Lichtenberger, ed., *Geschichte–Tradition–Reflexion. Festschrift für Martin Hengel* (Tübingen: Mohr Siebeck, 1996), 3:287-302.

logical judge who was to come. Although it has often been argued that all the Son of Man sayings in the Gospels derive ultimately from Jesus' use of the Semitic idiom "son of man," it is more likely that the oldest sayings are allusions to and interpretations of Dan 7:13-14. Some have argued that the apocalyptic Son of Man sayings are the oldest and that they originated in the experience of Easter. As noted above, it is more credible that the identification of the risen Jesus with the heavenly Son of Man occurred on the basis of Jesus' teaching about that figure.

The letters of Paul provide the oldest evidence for Christology. After "God revealed his son" to Paul (Gal 1:16), he became convinced that Jesus was the messiah and taught the members of the communities he founded that this was the case. He presumably also explained to them what being the messiah entailed. These conclusions are supported by the fact that, in his letters, Paul simply assumes that Jesus is the messiah and that his addressees know what this means. Although Paul does not apply the title "Son of Man" to Jesus, his knowledge of traditions about Jesus as Son of Man is evident in the apocalyptic contexts in which he at times uses the terms "son of God" and "lord" (κύριος). The contexts of Paul's letters and his allusions to scripture make clear that "son of God" and "messiah" are equivalent.

Paul sometimes speaks of Jesus as preexistent. At times he does so by identifying Christ with preexistent, personified wisdom (1 Cor 8:5-6).[6] The same identification may be implied by 2 Cor 4:3-4.[7] The clearest example of the portrayal of Christ as preexistent in the letters of Paul is the prose hymn in Phil 2:6-11. The political rhetoric of the hymn suggests that the description of Christ as "in the form of God" (ἐν μορφῇ θεοῦ) signifies that he is the preexistent messiah.[8] The depiction of Christ as the preexistent heavenly messiah in Philippians is not incompatible with his portrayal in the Corinthian correspondence as personified, preexistent wis-

---

6. It is possible, however, that Paul is speaking about the new creation in 1 Cor 8:5-6; cf. 2 Cor 5:16-17.

7. In 2 Cor 4:4 Christ is called the image of God. The same is said of wisdom in Wis 7:25-26. 2 Cor 4:4, however, can also be interpreted as signifying that Christ became the image of God by means of his death and resurrection (cf. 2 Cor 4:6) or that he is the image of God as the second Adam (cf. Gen 1:26 LXX).

8. That being "in the form of God" signifies that Jesus is the second Adam is unlikely, e.g., because a different Greek word is used to express the idea that humanity was created in God's "image" in Gen 1:26-27 LXX.

dom. The same combination is attested by the *Similitudes of Enoch* (*1 Enoch* 48:2-3, 6).

Whether the salutation of Romans portrays Jesus as preexistent or not is unclear because the language is ambiguous. The reference to Jesus Christ as God's son in 1:1-3, "the gospel of God . . . concerning his son" (εὐαγγέλιον θεοῦ . . . περὶ τοῦ υἱοῦ αὐτοῦ), could mean that he existed already before he was born "according to the flesh." In that case, the portrayal here would be similar to the description of him as "in the form of God" before he was "born in human likeness" (ἐν ὁμοιώματι ἀνθρώπων γενόμενος) in Phil 2:6-7. The alternative is that "son of God" here is an application of the biblical language about the king to Jesus as messiah. In this case "son of God" would be equivalent to being a descendant of David (ἐκ σπέρματος Δαυίδ). In this case being descended from David "according to the flesh" (κατὰ σάρκα) in v. 3 would be a contrasting parallel to the appointment of Jesus as son of God "according to a spirit of holiness" (κατὰ πνεῦμα ἁγιωσύνης) in v. 4. According to this reading, Jesus was son of God as messiah designate during his life on earth and became son of God as a heavenly being through his resurrection. It is not surprising that Paul may have spoken of Christ clearly as preexistent in Philippians and avoided such language in Romans, even though Romans is a later letter. The reason could well be that he thus accommodated his teaching to two different audiences.

The Synoptic Gospels do not portray Jesus as preexistent. In Mark "son of God" signifies first and foremost that Jesus is the messiah (1:11 in its allusion to Ps 2:7 and explicitly in 8:29). During his lifetime Jesus has authority and will suffer as the hidden Son of Man (2:10, 28; 8:31; 9:31; 10:33-34). He will exercise his messiahship as the exalted Son of Man (8:38; 13:26-27; 14:62). Matthew emphasizes Jesus' messiahship in the opening sentence: "the account of the descent of Jesus Christ = messiah, son of David, son of Abraham" (βίβλος γενέσεως Ἰησοῦ Χριστοῦ υἱοῦ Δαυὶδ υἱοῦ Ἀβραάμ). Both Matthew (1:20) and Luke (1:35) portray Jesus as begotten by God in the sense that he was conceived by the power of God and had no human father. In neither case, however, is this idea combined with the notions of preexistence and incarnation. As in Mark, "son of God" and "Son of Man" are equivalent in Matthew. Matthew goes beyond Mark in emphasizing that Jesus as Son of Man has a kingdom (13:41; 16:28) and will act as judge (19:28; 25:31-46).

In Luke, as in Mark and Matthew, it is clear that "son of God" (or "son of the Most High") is equivalent to "messiah." This is clear in the speech of Gabriel to Mary, where Jesus' divine sonship is closely linked to his reception of the throne of his father, David (1:32). In Luke, Jesus as the exalted Son of Man will act as advocate (12:8-9) and as judge (21:36).

The narrative of the Gospel of John begins with the question of who the messiah is. In the first scene priests and Levites ask John the Baptist whether he is the messiah, and he replies negatively and refers to one who is coming after him (1:19-28). In the next scene, the one coming after John is identified as Jesus, and John testifies that he is "lamb of God" and "the son of God" (1:29-34). In the following scene, Jesus as lamb of God is identified as "the messiah" (1:35-42). This narrative sequence and the role of epithets in it suggest that the terms "son of God" and "messiah" are equivalent in John, just as they are in the Synoptics. This equivalence is emphasized in two key passages in John: the confession of Martha (11:27) and the original ending of the Gospel (20:31).

In the healing of the blind man and the episodes that follow it, Jesus is identified both as messiah (9:22) and as Son of Man (9:35-38). This narrative use of epithets implies that "messiah" and "Son of Man" are equivalent in John as well as in the Synoptics (cf. also 1:49 with 1:51).[9] Like the Synoptics, John portrays the Son of Man as judge (5:27). Unlike the case in Mark, Matthew, and Luke, this role in John is at least partially realized (5:24; 9:39). John also has a kind of "suffering Son of Man" type of saying. This type is found in chapter 6, where it is said that the Son of Man will give food that does not perish (6:27). Later this food is identified as the flesh and blood of the Son of Man (6:53). This identification presupposes his death. His death is then interpreted as "ascending where he was before" (6:62). In typical paradoxical irony, the death of Jesus is equated with the glorification of the Son of Man (12:23-25, 32-33).

John differs from the Synoptic Gospels in its elaboration of the divine sonship of Jesus by identifying him with the "word" (λόγος) in the sense of the Middle Platonic "logos." This "logos" is akin to preexistent, personified wisdom. Wisdom was portrayed both as the first creature of God (Prov 8:22-23; Sir 24:9) and as begotten by God (Wis 8:3; Philo, *On Flight and Finding* 9 §§48-50). She is also portrayed as an eternal emanation or effulgence of God and as God's image (Wis 7:26). It is not clear whether Jesus as logos is portrayed as God's first creature or as eternal. The existence of the

9. "Son of Man" and "son of God" are portrayed as equivalent in John 5:25-27.

logos "in the beginning" in John 1:1 could mean at the beginning of creation; the notion of the logos as the first creature is compatible with such an interpretation of the statement. The same is said of wisdom in the Greek version of Prov 8:22. In any case, John portrays Jesus as son of God in a unique way (1:18; 3:16).

John also elaborates the notion of Jesus as Son of Man in distinctive ways. In the dialogue with Nicodemus, the Son of Man is portrayed as a preexistent, heavenly being (3:13). Similarly, the Johannine Jesus as Son of Man speaks about having come into the world (9:35, 39). The most innovative Son of Man saying in John is 1:51, which identifies Jesus as Son of Man with Jacob's ladder (Gen 28:12). This portrayal of the Son of Man as the mediator between heaven and earth is based on a number of other ideas: that crucifixion is exaltation, that crucifixion is ascent to heaven, and that when Jesus is lifted up he will draw all people to himself. The crucifixion of the Son of Man is also a revelatory event (8:28).

In the book of Revelation, as in the letters of Paul and Mark, "messiah" (χριστός) sometimes appears to be used as a proper name for Jesus, but certain passages make clear that the term still had the connotation "messiah" (Rev 11:15; 12:10; 20:4, 6). The epithet "son of God" is used only once in Revelation (2:18). It is associated there with angelic attributes. This association supports the conclusion that the opening vision portrays the risen Jesus as an angelic heavenly messiah.

As the Gospel of John does, Revelation associates Christ with wisdom (3:14) and with the word of God (19:13). These terms are used quite differently, however, in Revelation. The risen Jesus is associated with wisdom in 3:14 as "the beginning of the creation of God." This epithet clearly implies preexistence, but nothing in the work requires the inference that he is eternal. Rather, the implication seems to be that he is God's first creature. The portrayal of Christ as the word of God does not seem to have any philosophical connotations. He is portrayed rather as the effective word of the Lord, probably in angelic form (cf. Wis 18:14-16).

### Worship and Divinity of Jesus

Finally, two issues regarding early Christology should be addressed briefly. One concerns worship of him, the other, his divinity. With regard to the first, Larry Hurtado has argued that the earliest Jewish Christians were already thinking and worshipping Christ in binitarian terms and that this development was a unique "mutation" of Jewish monotheism. One of his key criteria is that these early followers worshipped him or expressed devotion to him in public, corporate, cultic, or liturgical contexts. No "principal agent" of God was so worshipped by their Jewish contemporaries.[10] A significant problem with his argument concerns what "worship" and "devotion" signify.[11] An important instance of "worship" or "devotion" for Hurtado is *proskynesis,* bowing down or self-prostration. The Greek term is used in a variety of ways: traditionally, Greeks performed the gesture before cult images of their gods. This usage does indeed imply worship in a full sense. The Greeks were also aware, however, that Persians performed it before their king of kings. They did not interpret this performance as implying that the Persians thought their kings were gods; rather, they condemned it as self-degradation unworthy of free men. It is not at all clear that the term necessarily implies worship in a full sense in the book of Revelation. In 5:14, the twenty-four elders are portrayed as performing the gesture. Hurtado infers that the elders are worshipping the lamb along with God.[12] In the message to Philadelphia, however, the risen Christ says, "I will cause some from the synagogue of Satan . . . to come and worship before your feet and know that I have loved you" (3:9). This use of the verb "to bow down, to prostrate oneself" (προσκυνέω) makes clear that it does not necessarily mean "worship" in the full sense. It also makes clear that an important, if not primary, connotation is submission to embodied power and authority.[13] In the *Similitudes of Enoch,* it is predicted that all who dwell on earth will fall down and worship before the Son of Man (*1 Enoch* 48:5).[14]

10. Larry W. Hurtado, *How on Earth Did Jesus Become a God?* (Grand Rapids: Eerdmans, 2005), 47-48; idem, *One God, One Lord* (Philadelphia: Fortress, 1988), 11-15; idem, *Lord Jesus Christ* (Grand Rapids: Eerdmans, 2003), 3-11, 29-53.

11. For discussion see Adela Yarbro Collins, "'How on Earth Did Jesus Become a God?' A Reply," in David B. Capes, Helen K. Bond, April Deconick, and Troy A. Miller, eds., *Israel's God and Rebecca's Children: Christology and Community in Early Judaism and Christianity* (Waco, TX: Baylor University Press, 2007), 55-66.

12. Hurtado, *Lord Jesus Christ,* 47, 50, 72-73; more emphatically, 592.

13. The same logic applies to the prose hymn in Phil 2:6-11. Given the political connotations of the hymn, the expectation "that at the name of Jesus every knee would bend" (2:10) signifies primarily recognition of the risen Christ's authority and power. This conclusion is supported by the affirmation that he is "lord" (κύριος) in verse 11; the epithet has strong royal connotations. See Philo, *On Dreams* 1.163 and Chapter 5 above.

14. Crispin H. T. Fletcher-Louis ("The Worship of Divine Humanity as God's Image

The other issue to be addressed in this context is the divinity of Jesus. Richard Bauckham rejects the commonly made distinction between "functional" divinity and "ontic" (or ontological) divinity because it is based on the premise that "first-century Jewish monotheists could attribute divine 'functions' to Jesus without difficulty," but not "divine 'nature.'"[15] Instead he constructs a concept of the unique identity of the God of Israel by way of analogy with human personal identity.[16] He then tries to show that the "exalted Jesus participates in God's unique sovereignty over all things" and that the "preexistent Christ participates in God's unique activity of creation."[17] The question of course is precisely *how* and *to what degree* Christ participates in that sovereignty and activity of creation. This theological language obscures the historical specificity that we have attempted to bring to light in this book. In addition, it should be noted that personified wisdom participates *as a creature* in God's activity of creation according to Prov 8:22 LXX and that the Son of Man in the *Similitudes of Enoch* participates in God's sovereignty by sitting on the throne of God and by acting as judge in the last judgment.

---

and the Worship of Jesus," in Carey C. Newman, James R. Davila, and Gladys S. Lewis, eds., *The Jewish Roots of Christological Monotheism* [JSJSup 63; Leiden: Brill, 1999], 112-28) has argued that this passage is evidence that ancient Jews were willing to worship other figures besides God. Although Hurtado (*Lord Jesus Christ*, 37-39) makes some valid criticisms of Fletcher-Louis's arguments, it is unclear why he interprets the gesture as worship in Revelation 5, yet rejects the idea that it signifies worship in *1 Enoch* 48:5.

15. Richard Bauckham, *God Crucified: Monotheism and Christology in the New Testament* (Grand Rapids: Eerdmans, 1998), 41-42.

16. Ibid., 7-8.

17. Ibid., 28-29, 35-40.

# Bibliography

Abegg, Martin G. "The Messiah at Qumran: Are We Still Seeing Double?" *DSD* 2 (1995) 125-44.

Adam, Klaus-Peter. *Der königliche Held. Die Entsprechung von kämpfendem Gott und kämpfendem König in Psalm 18* (WMANT 91; Neukirchen-Vluyn: Neukirchener Verlag, 2001).

Albl, Martin C. *"And Scripture Cannot Be Broken": The Form and Function of the Early Christian Testimonia Collections* (NovTSup 96; Leiden: Brill, 1999).

Alexander, Philip. *The Mystical Texts* (Companion to the Dead Sea Scrolls; London/New York: T&T Clark, 2006).

———. "3 (Hebrew Apocalypse of) Enoch," *OTP*, 1:223-315.

Allen, Leslie C., *Psalms 101–150* (WBC 21; Waco: Word, 1983).

Alt, Albrecht. "Jesaja 8,23–9,6. Befreiungsmacht und Krönungstag," in Walter Baumgartner, ed., *Festschrift Alfred Bertholet zum 80. Geburtstag gewidmet* (Tübingen: Mohr Siebeck, 1950), 29-49, reprinted in Alt, *Kleine Schriften zur Geschichte des Volkes Israel* (3 vols.; Munich: Beck, 1953), 2:206-25.

Andersen, F. I. "2 Enoch," *OTP*, 1:204-9.

Aschim, Anders. "Melchizedek and Jesus: 11QMelchizedek and the Epistle to the Hebrews," in C. C. Newman, J. R. Davila, and G. S. Lewis, *The Jewish Roots of Christological Monotheism* (JSJSup 63; Leiden: Brill, 1999), 129-47.

Assmann, Jan. "Die Zeugung des Sohnes. Bild, Spiel, Erzählung und das Problem des ägyptischen Mythos," in Jan Assmann, Walter Burkert, and Fritz Stolz, eds., *Funktionen und Leistungen des Mythos. Drei altorientalische Beispiele* (OBO 48; Freiburg: Universitätsverlag/Göttingen: Vandenhoeck & Ruprecht, 1982), 13-61.

Atkinson, Kenneth. *I Cried to the Lord: A Study of the Psalms of Solomon's Historical Background and Social Setting* (JSJSup 84; Leiden: Brill, 2004).

———. *An Intertextual Study of the Psalms of Solomon Pseudepigrapha* (Lewiston, NY: Mellen, 2001).

Attridge, Harold W. *Hebrews* (Hermeneia; Philadelphia: Fortress, 1989).

Attridge, H. W., and R. A. Oden. *Philo of Byblos: The Phoenician History* (CBQMS 9; Washington, DC: CBA, 1981).

Aune, David E. *Revelation* (3 vols.; WBC 52; Dallas: Word; Nashville: Thomas Nelson, 1997-1998).

Auwers, Jean-Marie. "Le psaume 132 parmi les graduals," *RB* 103-4 (1996) 546-60.

Avioz, Michael. *Nathan's Oracle (2 Samuel 7) and Its Interpreters* (Bern: Lang, 2005).

Badian, Ernst. "Alexander the Great between Two Thrones and Heaven: Variations on an Old Theme," in Alastair Small, ed., *Subject and Ruler: The Cult of the Ruling Power in Classical Antiquity* (Journal of Roman Archaeology Supplementary Series 17; Ann Arbor, MI: Journal of Roman Archaeology, 1996), 11-26.

———. "The Deification of Alexander the Great," in *Ancient Macedonian Studies in Honor of Charles F. Edson* (Thessaloniki: Institute for Balkan Studies, 1981), 27-71.

Baines, John. "Ancient Egyptian Kingship: Official Forms, Rhetoric, Context," in John Day, ed., *King and Messiah in Israel and the Ancient Near East* (JSOTSup 270; Sheffield: Sheffield Academic Press, 1998), 16-53.

Barth, H. *Die Jesaja-Worte in der Josia-Zeit. Israel und Assur als Thema einer produktiven Neuinterpretation der Jesajaüberlieferung* (WMANT 48; Neukirchen-Vluyn: Neukirchener Verlag, 1977).

Barthel, Jörg. *Prophetenwort und Geschichte. Die Jesajaüberlieferung in Jes 6–8 und 28–31* (FAT 19; Tübingen: Mohr Siebeck, 1997).

Bauckham, Richard. *God Crucified: Monotheism and Christology in the New Testament* (Grand Rapids: Eerdmans, 1998).

Bauer, Walter. *A Greek-English Lexicon of the New Testament and Other Early Christian Literature* (ed. William F. Arndt, F. Wilbur Gingrich; 3rd ed. rev. by Frederick W. Danker; Chicago: University of Chicago Press, 2000).

Becking, Bob. "'Wie Töpfe Sollst Du Sie Zerschmeissen.' Mesopotamische parallelen zu Psalm 2,9b," *ZAW* 102 (1990) 59-79.

Begg, Christopher. "Josephus' Portrayal of the Disappearances of Enoch, Elijah and Moses: Some Observations," *JBL* 109 (1990) 691-93.

Bell, Lannie. "Luxor Temple and the Cult of the Royal Ka," *JNES* 44 (1985) 251-94.

Berger, Klaus. *Jesus and the Dead Sea Scrolls* (Louisville: Westminster, 1995).

Best, Ernest. *A Commentary on the First and Second Epistles to the Thessalonians*

(Black's New Testament Commentaries; London: Adam & Charles Black, 1972).

Betz, Hans Dieter. *Galatians* (Hermeneia; Philadelphia: Fortress, 1979).

―――. "Plutarch's Life of Numa: Some Observations on Graeco-Roman 'Messianism,'" in Markus Bockmuehl and James Carleton Paget, eds., *Redemption and Resistance: The Messianic Hopes of Jews and Christians in Antiquity* (London/New York: T&T Clark, 2007), 44-61.

Bevan, Edwin R. *A History of Egypt under the Ptolemaic Dynasty* (London: Methuen, 1927).

Beyerle, Stefan. "'Der mit den Wolken des Himmels kommt,' Untersuchungen zu Traditionsgefüge 'Menschensohn,'" in Dieter Sänger, ed., *Gottessohn und Menschensohn. Exegetische Studien zu zwei Paradigmen biblischer Intertextualität* (Biblisch-Theologische Studien 67; Neukirchen-Vluyn: Neukirchener Verlag, 2004).

―――. "'A Star Shall Come out of Jacob': A Critical Evaluation of the Balaam Oracle in the Context of Jewish Revolts in Roman Times," in G. H. van Kooten and J. T. A. G. M. van Ruiten, eds., *Balaam: The Prestige of a Pagan Prophet in Judaism, Early Christianity and Islam* (Themes in Biblical Narrative; Leiden: Brill, 2008).

Black, M. *The Book of Enoch or 1 Enoch* (SVTP 7; Leiden: Brill, 1985).

―――. "Unsolved New Testament Problems: The 'Son of Man' in the Teaching of Jesus," *Expository Times* 60 (1948-1949) 32-36.

Blass, Friedrich, and Albert Debrunner. *A Greek Grammar of the New Testament and Other Early Christian Literature* (trans. from 9th-10th Germ. ed.; ed. Robert W. Funk; Chicago: University of Chicago Press, 1961).

Blenkinsopp, Joseph. *A History of Prophecy in Israel* (rev. ed.; Louisville: Westminster John Knox, 1996).

―――. *Isaiah 1–39* (AB 19; New York: Doubleday, 2000).

―――. *Isaiah 40–55* (AB 19A; New York: Doubleday, 2002).

Bligh, John. *Galatians in Greek: A Structural Analysis of St. Paul's Epistle to the Galatians with Notes on the Greek* (Detroit: University of Detroit, 1966).

Bikerman, E. *Institutions des Seleucides* (Paris: Geuthner, 1938).

Bird, Phyllis A. "'Male and Female He Created Them': Gen 1:27b in the Context of the Priestly Account of Creation," *HTR* 74 (1981) 129-59.

Boccaccini, Gabriele, ed. *Enoch and the Messiah Son of Man: Revisiting the Book of Parables* (Grand Rapids: Eerdmans, 2007).

Bockmuehl, Markus, and James Carleton Paget, eds. *Redemption and Resistance: The Messianic Hopes of Jews and Christians in Antiquity* (London and New York: T&T Clark: 2007).

Boring, M. Eugene. *Sayings of the Risen Jesus: Christian Prophecy in the Synoptic Tradition* (SNTSMS 46; Cambridge: Cambridge University Press, 1982).

Borsch, F. H. *The Son of Man in Myth and History* (London: SCM, 1967).

Böttrich, Christfried. "Konturen des 'Menschensohnes' in äthHen 37–71," in Dieter Sänger, ed., *Gottessohn und Menschensohn. Exegetische Studien zu zwei Paradigmen biblischer Intertextualität* (Biblisch-Theologische Studien 67; Neukirchen-Vluyn: Neukirchener Verlag, 2004), 53-90.

Bousset, Wilhelm. *Kyrios Christos: A History of the Belief in Christ from the Beginnings of Christianity to Irenaeus* (Nashville: Abingdon, 1970; German original, 1913).

Bousset, Wilhelm, and Hugo Gressmann. *Die Religion des Judentums im späthellenistischen Zeitalter* (3rd ed.; Tübingen: Mohr Siebeck, 1966).

Bovon, François. *Luke 1* (Hermeneia; Minneapolis: Fortress, 2002).

Boyarin, Daniel. *Borderlines: The Partition of Judaeo-Christianity* (Philadelphia: University of Pennsylvania Press, 2004).

Breasted, James H. *Ancient Records of Egypt* (Chicago: University of Chicago Press, 1906).

Brettler, Marc Zvi. *God Is King: Understanding an Israelite Metaphor* (JSOTSup 76; Sheffield: JSOT, 1989).

Breytenbach, Ciliers. "Hypsistos," *DDD*, 439-43.

Brooke, George J. "Kingship and Messianism in the Dead Sea Scrolls," in John Day, ed., *King and Messiah in Israel and the Ancient Near East* (JSOTSup 270; Sheffield: Sheffield Academic Press, 1998), 434-55.

———. "Shared Intertextual Interpretations in the Dead Sea Scrolls and the New Testament," in idem, *The Dead Sea Scrolls and the New Testament* (Minneapolis: Fortress, 2005), 70-94.

Brown, Raymond E. *The Birth of the Messiah: A Commentary on the Infancy Narratives in the Gospels of Matthew and Luke* (new updated ed.; ABRL; New York: Doubleday, 1993; 1st ed. 1977).

———. *The Gospel according to John* (2 vols.; AB 29; Garden City, NY: Doubleday, 1966-1970).

Brown, William P. "A Royal Performance: Critical Notes on Psalm 110:3aγ-b," *JBL* 117 (1998).

Brunner, Helmut. *Die Geburt des Gottkönigs. Studien zur Überlieferung eines altägyptischen Mythos* (Ägyptologische Abhandlungen 10; Wiesbaden: Harrassowitz, 1964).

Budde, K. *Jesaja's Erleben. Eine gemeinverständliche Auslegung der Denkschrift des Propheten (Kap. 6,1–9,6)* (Gotha: Klotz, 1928).

Bultmann, Rudolf. *The History of the Synoptic Tradition* (rev. ed.; New York: Harper & Row, 1968).

———. *Theology of the New Testament* (2 vols.; New York: Scribner, 1951).

Burkert, Walter. *Greek Religion* (Oxford: Blackwell, 1985).

Burkett, Delbert. *The Son of Man Debate: A History and Evaluation* (SNTSMS 107; Cambridge, UK: Cambridge University Press, 1999).

Carmignac, J. "Le document de Qumran sur Melkisédeq," *RevQ* 7 (1970) 343-78.

Carrell, Peter R. *Jesus and the Angels: Angelology and the Christology of the Apocalypse of John* (SNTSMS 95; Cambridge: Cambridge University Press, 1997).

Cartlidge, David R., and David L. Dungan. *Documents for the Study of the Gospels* (Philadelphia: Fortress, 1980).

Casey, Maurice. *From Jewish Prophet to Gentile God: The Origins and Development of New Testament Christology* (Louisville: Westminster John Knox, 1991).

————. *Son of Man: The Interpretation and Influence of Daniel 7* (London: SPCK, 1979).

Casey, P. M. "The Use of the Term 'Son of Man' in the Similitudes of Enoch," *JSJ* 7 (1976) 11-29.

Cerfaux, L., and J. Tondriau. *Le culte des souverains dans la civilisation gréco-romaine* (Tournai: Desclée, 1957).

Chadwick, Henry. *The Early Church* (Pelican History of the Church 1; Harmondsworth, UK/Baltimore: Penguin Books, 1967; reprinted 1969).

Charlesworth, J. H. "The Son of David: Solomon and Jesus (Mark 10.47)," in Peder Borgen and Søren Giversen, eds., *The New Testament and Hellenistic Judaism* (Peabody, MA: Hendrickson, 1995), 72-87.

Charlesworth, J. H., H. Lichtenberger, and G. S. Oegema, eds. *Qumran-Messianism: Studies on the Messianic Expectations in the Dead Sea Scrolls* (Tübingen: Mohr Siebeck, 1998).

Chester, Andrew. *Messiah and Exaltation* (WUNT 207; Tübingen: Mohr Siebeck, 2007).

————. "The Christ of Paul," in Markus Bockmuehl and James Carleton Paget, eds., *Redemption and Resistance: The Messianic Hopes of Jews and Christians in Antiquity* (London/New York: T&T Clark, 2007), 109-21.

Chialà, Sabino. *Libro delle parabole di Enoc* (Studi Biblici 117; Brescia: Paideia, 1997), 39-51.

Childs, B. S. *Isaiah* (OTL; Louisville: Westminster, 2001).

Chilton, Bruce. "Jesus *ben David*: Reflections on the *Davidssohnfrage*," *JSNT* 14 (1982) 88-112.

Clements, R. E. "The Immanuel Prophecy and Its Messianic Interpretation," in idem, *Old Testament Prophecy: From Oracles to Canon* (Louisville: Westminster John Knox, 1996).

Collins, John J. *The Apocalyptic Imagination* (2nd ed.; Grand Rapids: Eerdmans, 1998).

————. *The Apocalyptic Vision of the Book of Daniel* (HSM 16; Missoula, MT: Scholars Press, 1977), 123-52.

————. "The Background of the 'Son of God' Text," *BBR* 7 (1997) 51-62.

————. *Daniel: A Commentary on the Book of Daniel* (Hermeneia; Minneapolis: Fortress, 1993).

————. "Enoch and the Son of Man: A Response to Sabino Chialà and Helge Kvanvig," in Gabriele Boccaccini, ed., *Enoch and the Messiah Son of Man: Revisiting the Book of Parables* (Grand Rapids: Eerdmans, 2007), 216-27.

————. "Genre, Ideology and Social Movements in Jewish Apocalypticism," in J. J. Collins and J. H. Charlesworth, eds., *Mysteries and Revelations: Apocalyptic Studies since the Uppsala Colloquium* (JSPSup 9; Sheffield: Sheffield Academic Press, 1991), 25-32.

————. "A Herald of Good Tidings: Isaiah 61:1-3 and Its Actualization in the Dead Sea Scrolls," in Craig A. Evans and Shemaryahu Talmon, eds., *The Quest for Context and Meaning: Studies in Biblical Intertextuality in Honor of James A. Sanders* (Leiden: Brill, 1997), 225-40.

————. "Isaiah 8:23–9:6 and Its Greek Translation," in Anssi Voitila and Jutta Jokiranta, eds., *Scripture in Transition: Essays on Septuagint, Hebrew Bible, and Dead Sea Scrolls in Honour of Raija Sollamo* (JSJSup; Leiden: Brill, 2008).

————. "Jesus and the Messiahs of Israel," in H. Lichtenberger, ed., *Geschichte–Tradition–Reflexion. Festschrift für Martin Hengel* (Tübingen: Mohr Siebeck, 1996), 3:286-302.

————. "Messianism and Exegetical Tradition: The Evidence of the LXX Pentateuch," in idem, *Jewish Cult and Hellenistic Culture* (JSJSup 100; Leiden: Brill, 2005), 58-81.

————. "Mowinckel's *He That Cometh* Revisited," *Studia Theologica* 61 (2007): 3-20.

————. *The Scepter and the Star: The Messiahs of the Dead Sea Scrolls and Other Ancient Literature* (ABRL; New York: Doubleday, 1995).

————. "Sibylline Oracles," *OTP*, 1:390-405.

————. "The Sign of Immanuel." Forthcoming in *The Proceedings of the Oxford Seminar on Prophecy*, edited by John Day.

————. "The 'Son of God' Text from Qumran," in M. de Boer, ed., *From Jesus to John: Essays on Jesus and New Testament Christology in Honour of Marinus de Jonge* (Sheffield: JSOT, 1993), 65-82.

————. "The Son of Man in First-Century Judaism," *NTS* 38 (1992) 448-66.

————. "Stirring Up the Great Sea: The Religio-Historical Background of Daniel 7," in idem, *Seers, Sibyls and Sages in Hellenistic-Roman Judaism* (JSJSup 54; Leiden: Brill, 1997), 139-55.

————. "A Throne in the Heavens: Apotheosis in pre-Christian Judaism," in J. J. Collins and M. Fishbane, eds., *Death, Ecstasy, and Otherworldly Journeys* (Albany: State University of New York, 1995), 41-58.

————. "What Was Distinctive about Messianic Expectation at Qumran?" in J. H.

Charlesworth, ed., *The Bible and the Dead Sea Scrolls* (Waco, TX: Baylor University, 2006).

————, and P. W. Flint. "243-245. 4Qpseudo-Daniel$^{a-c}$ ar," in G. Brooke et al., *Qumran Cave 4. XVII. Parabiblical Texts, Part 3* (DJD 22; Oxford: Clarendon, 1996), 96-164.

Colpe, C. *Die religionsgeschichtliche Schule. Darstellung und Kritik ihres Bildes vom gnostischen Erlösermythus* (Göttingen: Vandenhoeck & Ruprecht, 1961).

————. "ὁ υἱὸς τοῦ ἀνθρώπου," *TDNT*, 8 (1972), 400-477.

Condra, Ed. *Salvation for the Righteous Revealed: Jesus amid Covenantal and Messianic Expectations in Second Temple Judaism* (AGJU 51; Leiden: Brill, 2002).

Conzelmann, Hans. *1 Corinthians* (Hermeneia; Philadelphia: Fortress, 1975; 1st German ed. 1969).

————. *An Outline of the Theology of the New Testament* (New York: Harper & Row, 1969).

Cook, Edward M. "Aramaic Language and Literature," in Eric Meyers, ed., *The Oxford Encyclopedia of Archaeology in the Ancient Near East* (New York: Oxford, 1997), 1:178-84.

————. "4Q246," *BBR* 5 (1995) 43-66.

Cooke, Gerald. "The Israelite King as Son of God," *ZAW* 32 (1961) 202-25.

Coppens, Joseph. "Le Psaume CX et l'Idéologie Royale Israélite," in *The Sacral Kingship: Contributions to the Central Theme of the VIIIth International Congress for the History of Religions* (Rome, April 1955) (Leiden: Brill, 1959), 333-49.

Cross, Frank Moore. *The Ancient Library of Qumran* (3rd ed.; Sheffield: Sheffield Academic Press, 1995).

————. *Canaanite Myth and Hebrew Epic* (Cambridge, MA: Harvard University Press, 1973), 248-57.

Crossan, John Dominic. *The Historical Jesus: The Life of a Mediterranean Jewish Peasant* (San Francisco: HarperSanFrancisco, 1991).

Dahl, Nils Alstrup. *The Crucified Messiah and Other Essays* (Minneapolis: Augsburg, 1974).

Dalman, Gustaf. *Die Worte Jesu mit Berücksichtigung des nachkanonischen jüdischen Schrifttums*, vol. 1: *Einleitung und wichtige Begriffe, nebst Anhang. messianische Texte* (Leipzig: Hinrichs, 1898); ET *The Words of Jesus Considered in the Light of Post-Biblical Jewish Writings and the Aramaic Language* (Edinburgh: T&T Clark, 1909).

Darnell, John C. "Hathor Returns to Medamûd," *Studien zur Altägyptischen Kultur* 22 (1995) 47-94.

Daumas, F. *Les Mammisis des temples égyptiens* (Paris: Les Belles Lettres, 1958).

David, Martin. *Die Adoption im altbabylonischen Recht* (Leipzig: Weicher, 1927).

Davila, James R. "Melchizedek, the 'Youth,' and Jesus," in idem, ed., *The Dead Sea*

*Scrolls as Background to Postbiblical Judaism and Early Christianity: Papers from an International Conference at St. Andrews in 2001* (STDJ 46; Leiden: Brill, 2003), 248-74.

————. *The Provenance of the Pseudepigrapha* (JSJSup 105; Leiden: Brill, 2005).

Davies, W. D., and Dale C. Allison. *The Gospel according to St. Matthew* (3 vols.; ICC; Edinburgh: T&T Clark, 1988-1997).

Davis, Norman, and Colin M. Kraay. *The Hellenistic Kingdoms: Portrait Coins and History* (London: Thames and Hudson, 1973).

Day, John. "The Canaanite Inheritance of the Israelite Monarchy," in John Day, ed., *King and Messiah in Israel and the Ancient Near East* (JSOTSup 270; Sheffield: Sheffield Academic Press, 1998).

————. *God's Conflict with the Dragon and the Sea* (Cambridge: Cambridge University Press, 1985).

Delling, G. "παρθένος," *TDNT*, 5 (1967).

Dietrich, Manfried, Oswald Loretz, and Joaquín Sanmartín. *The Cuneiform Alphabetic Texts from Ugarit, Ras Ibn Hani and Other Places* (Münster: Ugarit-Verlag, 1995).

Dietrich, Manfried, and O. Loretz, and J. Sanmartin, eds. *Die keilalphabetischen Texte aus Ugarit* (Neukirchen-Vluyn: Neukirchener Verlag, 1976).

Dietrich, W. *Prophetie und Geschichte* (FRLANT 108; Göttingen: Vandenhoeck & Ruprecht, 1972).

Donahue, John R. "Recent Studies on the Origin of 'Son of Man' in the Gospels," in Raymond E. Brown, S.S., and Alexander A. DiLella, O.F.M., eds., *A Wise and Discerning Heart: Studies Presented to Joseph A. Fitzmyer in Celebration of His Sixty-Fifth Birthday, CBQ* 48 (1986) 484-98.

Donner, H. "Adoption oder Legitimation? Erwägungen zur Adoption im Alten Testament auf dem Hintergrund der altorientalischen Rechte," *OrAnt* 8 (1969) 87-119.

Dowden, Ken. "Io," in Simon Hornblower and Anthony Spawforth, eds., *Oxford Classical Dictionary* (3rd ed.; Oxford: Oxford University Press, 1996), 762-63.

Duhm, Bernhard. *Das Buch Jesaja* (Göttingen: Vandenhoeck & Ruprecht, 1892, 4th ed. 1922).

Duling, Dennis C. "Solomon, Exorcism, and the Son of David," *HTR* 68 (1975) 235-52.

Dunn, J. D. G. *Christology in the Making* (London: SCM, 1980).

————. "'Son of God' as 'Son of Man' in the Dead Sea Scrolls? A Response to John Collins on 4Q246," in S. E. Porter and C. A. Evans, eds., *The Scrolls and the Scriptures: Qumran Fifty Years After* (JSPSup 26; Sheffield: Sheffield Academic Press, 1997), 198-210.

Dürr, Lorenz. *Psalm 110 im Lichte der neueren alt-orientalischen Forschung* (Münster: Aschendorff, 1929).

Elnes, E. E., and P. D. Miller. "Elyon," in K. van der Toorn et al., *Dictionary of Deities and Demons in the Bible* (2nd ed.; Leiden: Brill, 1999), 293-99.

Emerton, John A. "The Site of Salem," in J. A. Emerton, ed., *Studies in the Pentateuch* (VTSup 41; Leiden: Brill, 1990), 45-71.

————. "Some Linguistic and Historical Problems in Isaiah VIII.23," *JSS* 14 (1969) 151-75.

Engnell, Ivan. *Studies in Divine Kingship in the Ancient Near East* (Uppsala: Almqvist and Wiksell, 1943).

Eshel, Esti. "The Identification of the 'Speaker' of the Self-Glorification Hymn," in D. W. Parry and E. Ulrich, eds., *The Provo International Conference on the Dead Sea Scrolls* (STDJ 30; Leiden: Brill, 1999), 619-35.

Eslinger, Lyle. *House of God or House of David: The Rhetoric of 2 Samuel 7* (JSOTSup 164; Sheffield: Sheffield Academic Press, 1994).

Fiebig, Paul. *Der Menschensohn: Jesu Selbstbezeichnung mit besonderer Berücksichtigung des aramäischen Sprachgebrauches für "Mensch"* (Tübingen/Leipzig: Mohr Siebeck, 1901).

Finkelstein, Israel, and Neil Asher Silberman. *The Bible Unearthed: Archaeology's New Vision of Ancient Israel and the Origin of Its Sacred Texts* (New York: The Free Press, 2001)

Fishbane, Michael. *Biblical Interpretation in Ancient Israel* (Oxford: Clarendon, 1985).

Fitzmyer, Joseph. *The Acts of the Apostles* (AB 31; New York: Doubleday, 1998).

————. "The Aramaic 'Son of God' Text from Qumran Cave 4 (4Q246)," in idem, *The Dead Sea Scrolls and Christian Origins* (Grand Rapids: Eerdmans, 2000), 41-61.

————. "4Q246: The 'Son of God' Document from Qumran," *Bib* 74 (1994) 153-74.

————. "Further Light on Melchizedek from Qumran Cave 11," in idem, *Essays on the Semitic Background of the New Testament* (Missoula, MT: Scholars Press, 1974), 245-67, reprinted in *The Semitic Background of the New Testament* (Grand Rapids: Eerdmans, 1997), 245-67.

————. *The Gospel according to Luke I–IX* (AB 28; New York: Doubleday, 1981).

————. "The New Testament Title 'Son of Man' Philologically Considered," in idem, *A Wandering Aramean: Collected Aramaic Essays* (SBLMS 25; Missoula, MT: Scholars Press, 1979), 143-60; reprinted in idem, *The Semitic Background of the New Testament* (Grand Rapids: Eerdmans, 1997), 143-60.

————. *The One Who Is to Come* (Grand Rapids: Eerdmans, 2007).

————. *Romans* (AB 33; New York: Doubleday, 1993).

————. "The Semitic Background of the New Testament *Kyrios*-Title," in idem, *A Wandering Aramean: Collected Aramaic Essays* (SBLMS 25; Missoula, MT: Scholars Press, 1979), 115-42; reprinted in idem, *The Semitic Background of the New Testament* (Grand Rapids: Eerdmans, 1997), 115-42.

————. "The Study of the Aramaic Background of the New Testament," in idem, *A Wandering Aramean: Collected Aramaic Essays* (SBLMS 25; Missoula, MT: Scholars Press, 1979), 1-27; reprinted in idem, *The Semitic Background of the New Testament* (Grand Rapids: Eerdmans, 1997), 1-27.

Fletcher-Louis, Crispin. *All the Glory of Adam: Liturgical Anthropology in the Dead Sea Scrolls* (STDJ 42; Leiden: Brill, 2002).

————. "The Worship of Divine Humanity as God's Image and the Worship of Jesus," in Carey C. Newman, James R. Davila, and Gladys S. Lewis, eds., *The Jewish Roots of Christological Monotheism* (JSJSup 63; Leiden: Brill, 1999), 112-28.

Fossum, J. E. "The New religionsgeschichtliche Schule: The Quest for Jewish Christology," in E. Lovering, ed., SBLSP 1991, 638-46.

Foster, B. R. *Before the Muses: An Anthology of Akkadian Literature* (3rd ed.; Bethesda, MD: CDL, 2005).

————. *From Distant Days: Myths, Tales and Poetry from Ancient Mesopotamia* (Bethesda, MD: CDL, 1995).

Frankfort, Henri. *Kingship and the Gods: A Study of Ancient Near Eastern Religion as the Integration of Society and Nature* (Chicago: University of Chicago Press, 1948).

Fraser, P. M. *Ptolemaic Alexandria* (Oxford: Clarendon, 1972).

Furnish, Victor Paul. *II Corinthians* (AB 32A; Garden City, NY: Doubleday, 1984).

Gardiner, Alan H. "The Coronation of King Haremhab." *JEA* 39 (1953) 14-15.

Gathercole, Simon J. *The Preexistent Son: Recovering the Christologies of Matthew, Mark, and Luke* (Grand Rapids: Eerdmans, 2006).

Geissen, Angelo. *Der Septuaginta-Text des Buches Daniel Kap. 5-12, zusammen mit Susanna, Bel et Draco sowie Esther Kap. 1,1a-2, 15* (Papyrologische Texte und Abhandlungen 5; Bonn: Habelt, 1968).

Germond, Philippe. *Sekhmet et la Protection du Monde = Aegyptiaca Helvetica* 9 (1981).

Gerstenberger, Erhard S. *Psalms: Part One, with an Introduction to Cultic Poetry* (FOTL XIV; Grand Rapids: Eerdmans, 1988).

————. *Psalms: Part Two, and Lamentations* (FOTL XV; Grand Rapids: Eerdmans, 2001)

Gese, H. "Natus ex virgine," in idem, *Vom Sinai zum Zion. Alttestamentliche Beiträge zur biblischen Theologie* (München: Kaiser, 1974).

————. *Zur biblischen Theologie* (3rd ed.; Tübingen: Mohr Siebeck, 1989).

Gianotto, Claudio. *Melchisedek e la sua Tipologia* (Brescia: Paideia, 1984).

Gibson, J. C. L. *Canaanite Myths and Legends* (Edinburgh: Clark, 1977).

Gibson, Jeffrey B. "Jesus' Wilderness Temptation according to Mark," *JSNT* 53 (1994) 3-34.

Gieschen, Charles A. *Angelomorphic Christology* (AGJU 42; Leiden: Brill, 1998).

Görg, Manfred. *Gott–König–Reden in Israel und Ägypten* (Stuttgart: Kohlhammer, 1975).

Grainger, John D. *Seleukos Nikator: Constructing a Hellenistic Kingdom* (London: Routledge, 1990)

Grayson, A. K. *Babylonian Historical-Literary Texts* (Toronto: University of Toronto, 1975).

Green, Peter. *Alexander the Great* (New York: Praeger, 1970).

Gressmann, Hugo. *Der Messias* (Göttingen: Vandenhoeck & Ruprecht, 1929).

Grundmann, Walter. "χρίω κτλ., A. General Usage," *TDNT,* 9 (1974).

Gunkel, Hermann, and Joachim Begrich. *Introduction to the Psalms* (Macon, GA: Mercer University Press, 1998). Translated from the fourth ed. of *Einleitung in die Psalmen* (Göttingen: Vandenhoeck & Ruprecht, 1933).

Gutbrod, W. "νόμος κτλ., D. The Law in the New Testament," *TDNT,* 4 (1967).

Habicht, Christian. *Gottmenschentum und griechische Städte* (Zetemata 14; München: Beck, 1956).

Hamilton, Mark W. *The Body Royal: The Social Implications of Kingship in Ancient Israel* (Leiden: Brill, 2005).

Hannah, D. D. *Michael and Christ: Michael Traditions and Angel Christology in Early Christianity* (WUNT 2.109; Tübingen: Mohr Siebeck, 1999).

———. "The Throne of His Glory: The Divine Throne and Heavenly Mediators in Revelation and the Similitudes of Enoch," *ZNW* 94 (2003) 68-96.

Hanson, Paul D. "Zechariah 9 and an Ancient Ritual Pattern," *JBL* 92 (1973) 37-59.

Hare, Douglas R. A. *The Son of Man Tradition* (Minneapolis: Fortress, 1990).

Hartenstein, Friedhelm. "'Der im Himmel thront, lacht' (Ps 2,4)," in Dieter Sänger, ed., *Gottessohn und Menschensohn. Exegetische Studien zu zwei Paradigmen biblischer Intertextualität* (Biblisch-Theologische Studien 67; Neukirchen-Vluyn: Neukirchener Verlag, 2004), 158-88.

Hatch, Edwin, and Henry A. Redpath, eds. *A Concordance to the Septuagint and Other Greek Versions of the Old Testament* (Oxford: Clarendon, 1897).

Hay, David. *Glory at the Right Hand: Psalm 110 in Early Christianity* (SBLMS 18; Nashville: Abingdon, 1973).

Hays, Richard B. *The Faith of Jesus Christ: The Narrative Substructure of Galatians 3:1–4:11* (2nd ed.; Grand Rapids: Eerdmans; Dearborn, MI: Dove Booksellers, 2002; 1st ed. 1983).

Healey, John F. "Dew," *DDD,* 251.

———. "The Immortality of the King: Ugarit and the Psalms," *Or* 53 (1984) 245-54.

Hengel, Martin. *Judaism and Hellenism: Studies in Their Encounter in Palestine during the Early Hellenistic Period* (2 vols.; Philadelphia: Fortress, 1974).

———. "Setze dich zu meiner Rechten! Die Inthronisation Christi zur Rechten

Gottes und Psalm 110,1," in Marc Philonenko, ed., *Le Trône de Dieu* (Tübingen: Mohr Siebeck, 1993), 108-94.

———. *The Son of God: The Origin of Christology and the History of Jewish-Hellenistic Religion* (Philadelphia: Fortress, 1976; German ed. 1975).

Higgins, A. J. B. *The Son of Man in the Teaching of Jesus* (SNTSMS 39; Cambridge: Cambridge University Press, 1980).

Hillers, D. R. *Micah* (Hermeneia; Philadelphia: Fortress, 1984).

Hinnells, John R. "The Zoroastrian Doctrine of Salvation in the Roman World," in E. J. Sharpe and J. R. Hinnells, eds., *Man and His Salvation: Studies in Memory of S. G. F. Brandon* (Manchester: Manchester University Press, 1973), 125-48.

Hofius, Otfried. *Der Christushymnus Philipper 2,6-11* (2nd ed.; WUNT 17; Tübingen: Mohr Siebeck, 1976).

Høgenhaven, Jesper. *Gott und Volk bei Jesaja. Eine Untersuchung zur biblischen Theologie* (Leiden: Brill, 1988).

Hölbl, Günther. *A History of the Ptolemaic Empire* (London: Routledge, 2001).

Holladay, William M. *Jeremiah 1* (Hermencia; Minneapolis: Fortress, 1986).

Hooke, S. H., ed. *Myth, Ritual, and Kingship: Essays on the Theory and Practice of Kingship in the Ancient Near East and in Israel* (Oxford: Oxford University Press, 1958).

Horbury, William. *Jewish Messianism and the Cult of Christ* (London: SCM, 1998).

———. "The Messianic Associations of 'The Son of Man,'" in idem, *Messianism among the Jews and Christians* (London and New York: T&T Clark, 2003), 144-51.

———. *Messianism among Jews and Christians: Biblical and Historical Studies* (New York and London: T&T Clark, 2003).

Horton, Fred L. *The Melchizedek Tradition* (SNTSMS 30; Cambridge: Cambridge University Press, 1976).

Hossfeld, Frank-Lothar, and Erich Zenger. *Psalms 2: A Commentary on Psalms 51–100* (Hermeneia; Minneapolis: Fortress, 2005).

Hultgård, Anders. *L'eschatologie des Testaments des Douze Patriarches* (Uppsala: Almqvist & Wiksell, 1977).

Hurtado, Larry W. *How on Earth Did Jesus Become a God? Historical Questions about Earliest Devotion to Jesus* (Grand Rapids: Eerdmans, 2005).

———. *Lord Jesus Christ: Devotion to Jesus in Earliest Christianity* (Grand Rapids: Eerdmans, 2003).

———. *One God, One Lord: Early Christian Devotion and Ancient Jewish Monotheism* (Grand Rapids: Eerdmans, 2003).

Jeremias, Joachim. *New Testament Theology: The Proclamation of Jesus* (New York: Charles Scribner's Sons, 1971).

Johnson, Aubrey R. *Sacral Kingship in Ancient Israel* (2nd ed.; Cardiff: University of Wales Press, 1955).

Joyce, Paul M. "King and Messiah in Ezekiel," in John Day, ed., *King and Messiah in Israel and the Ancient Near East* (JSOTSup 270; Sheffield: Sheffield Academic Press, 1998), 323-37.

Juel, Donald. *Messianic Exegesis: Christological Interpretation of the Old Testament in Early Christianity* (Philadelphia: Fortress, 1988).

Kaiser, O. *Isaiah 1–12: A Commentary* (2nd ed.; OTL; Philadelphia: Westminster, 1983).

Keel, Othmar. *The Symbolism of the Biblical World* (Winona Lake, IN: Eisenbrauns, 1997).

Kitchen, K. A. *Ramesside Inscriptions: Historical and Biographical* (Oxford: Oxford University Press, 1971).

Kittel, Rudolf. *Die hellenistische Mysterien und das Alte Testament* (Stuttgart: Kohlhammer, 1924).

Klein, Jacob. "Sumerian Kingship and the Gods," in Gary Beckman and Theodore J. Lewis, *Text, Artifact, and Image in the Ancient Near East* (BJS 346; Providence, RI: Brown University, 2006), 115-31.

Knibb, M. A. "The Date of the Parables of Enoch: A Critical Review," *NTS* 25 (1979) 345-59.

———. "The Martyrdom and Ascension of Isaiah," *OTP*, 2:143-76.

———. "The Structure and Composition of the Book of Parables," in Gabriele Boccaccini, ed., *Enoch and the Messiah Son of Man: Revisiting the Book of Parables* (Grand Rapids: Eerdmans, 2007), 48-64.

———, and R. J. Coggins. *The First and Second Books of Esdras* (Cambridge Bible Commentary; Cambridge: Cambridge University Press, 1979).

Knohl, Israel. *The Messiah before Jesus: The Suffering Servant of the Dead Sea Scrolls* (Berkeley: University of California, 2000).

Knoppers, Gary. "Ancient Near Eastern Royal Grants and the Davidic Covenant: A Parallel?" *JAOS* 116 (1996) 670-97.

Kobelski, Paul J. *Melchizedek and Melchiresha'* (CBQMS 10; Washington: Catholic Biblical Association, 1981).

Koch, Klaus. "Der König als Sohn Gottes in Ägypten und Israel," in Eckart Otto and Erich Zenger, eds., *"Mein Sohn bist du" (Ps 2,7). Studien zu den Königspsalmen* (Stuttgarter Bibelstudien 192; Stuttgart: Verlag Katholisches Bibelwerk, 2002), 1-32.

———. "Messias und Menschensohn," in idem, *Vor der Wende der Zeiten. Beiträge zur apokalyptischen Literatur* (Neukirchen-Vluyn: Neukirchener Verlag, 1996), 235-66.

Koenen, Ludwig. "Die Adaptation ägyptischer Königsideologie am Ptolemäerhof," in W. Peremans, ed., *Egypt and the Hellenistic World* (Studia Hellenistica 27; Leuven: Leuven University Press, 1983), 142-90.

Kovacs, Judith, and Christopher Rowland. *Revelation* (Blackwell Bible Commentaries; Oxford: Blackwell, 2004).

Kraus, Hans-Joachim. *Psalms 1–59* (CC; Minneapolis: Fortress, 1993; translated from the 5th ed. of *Psalmen 1. Teilband, Psalmen 1–59* [BK; Neukirchen-Vluyn: Neukirchener Verlag, 1978]).

Kugel, James L. *The Traditions of the Bible: A Guide to the Bible as It Was at the Start of the Common Era* (Cambridge, MA: Harvard University Press, 1998).

Kuhn, H.-W. "Rom 1,3f und der davidische Messias als Gottessohn in den Qumrantexten," in C. Burchard and G. Theissen, eds., *Lesezeichen für Annelies Findeiss* (Heidelberg: Wissenschaftlich-theologisches Seminar, 1984), 103-13.

Kvanvig, H. S. *Roots of Apocalyptic* (Neukirchen-Vluyn: Neukirchener Verlag, 1988).

—————. "The Son of Man in the Parables," in Gabriele Boccaccini, ed., *Enoch and the Messiah Son of Man: Revisiting the Book of Parables* (Grand Rapids: Eerdmans, 2007), 179-215.

Laato, Antti. "Psalm 132 and the Development of the Jerusalemite/Israelite Royal Ideology," *CBQ* 54 (1992) 49-66.

—————. "Psalm 132: A Case Study in Methodology," *CBQ* 61 (1999) 24-33.

—————. "Second Samuel 7 and Ancient Near Eastern Royal Ideology," *CBQ* 59 (1997) 144-69.

—————. *A Star Is Rising: The Historical Development of the Old Testament Royal Ideology and the Rise of the Jewish Messianic Expectations* (Atlanta: Scholars Press, 1997).

—————. *Who Is Immanuel?* (Åbo: Åbo Akademie, 1988).

Lambert, W. G. "Kingship in Ancient Mesopotamia," in John Day, ed., *King and Messiah in Israel and the Ancient Near East* (JSOTSup 270; Sheffield: Sheffield Academic Press, 1998), 54-70.

—————. "Three Unpublished Fragments of the Tukulti-Ninurta Epic," *AfO* 18 (1957-58) 48-51.

Lampe, Geoffrey W. H. *A Patristic Greek Lexicon* (Oxford: Clarendon, 1961).

Leprohon, Ronald J. "Royal Ideology and State Administration in Pharaonic Egypt," in Jack Sasson, ed., *Civilizations of the Ancient Near East* (4 vols.; New York: Scribner's, 1995).

Leivestadt, R. "Der apokalyptische Menschensohn ein theologisches Phantom," *Annual of the Swedish Theological Institute* 6 (1967-1968) 49-109.

—————. "Exit the Apocalyptic Son of Man," *NTS* 18 (1971-1972) 243-67.

Levenson, Jon D. *The Death and Resurrection of the Beloved Son: The Transformation of Child Sacrifice in Judaism and Christianity* (New Haven: Yale University Press, 1993).

—————. *Sinai and Zion* (San Francisco: Harper, 1987).

Levine, B. A., and J. M. Tarragon. "Dead Kings and Rephaim: The Patrons of the Ugaritic Dynasty," *JAOS* 104 (1984) 649-59.

Lewis, Theodore J. *Cults of the Dead in Ancient Israel and Ugarit* (HSM 39; Atlanta: Scholars Press, 1989).

L'Heureux, C. E. "The Ugaritic and Biblical Rephaim," *HTR* 67 (1974) 265-74.

Lichtheim, Miriam. *Ancient Egyptian Literature,* vol. 1: *The Old and Middle Kingdom* (Berkeley: University of California Press, 1975).

Liddell, Henry George, and Robert Scott, eds. *A Greek-English Lexicon* (9th ed.; Henry Stuart Jones; Oxford: Clarendon, 1940).

Liebers, Reinhold. *"Wie geschrieben steht"; Studien zu einer besonderen Art frühchristlichen Schriftbezuges* (Berlin/New York: de Gruyter, 1993).

Lietzmann, Hans. *Der Menschensohn: Ein Beitrag zur neutestamentlichen Theologie* (Freiburg im Breisgau/Leipzig: Mohr Siebeck, 1896).

Lindars, B. *Jesus, Son of Man* (Grand Rapids: Eerdmans, 1983).

―――. *New Testament Apologetic: The Doctrinal Significance of the Old Testament Quotations* (London: SCM, 1961).

Longman III, Tremper. "The Messiah: Explorations in the Law and Writings," in Stanley Porter, ed., *The Messiah in the Old and New Testaments* (Grand Rapids: Eerdmans, 2007).

Lüdemann, Gerd. *Paul, Apostle to the Gentiles: Studies in Chronology* (Philadelphia: Fortress, 1984; German 1980).

Lust, Johan. *Messianism and the Septuagint: Collected Essays,* ed. K. Hauspie (Leuven: Leuven University Press, 2004).

Luz, Ulrich. *Matthew 1–7: A Commentary* (Hermeneia; Minneapolis: Fortress, 2007).

Machinist, Peter. "The Epic of Tukulti-Ninurta I: A Study in Middle Assyrian Literature" (Ph.D. dissertation, Yale, 1978).

―――. "Kingship and Divinity in Imperial Assyria," in Gary Beckman and Theodore J. Lewis, eds., *Text, Artifact, and Image: Revealing Ancient Israelite Religion* (Providence, RI: Brown University Press, 2006), 152-88.

Mack, Burton L. *A Myth of Innocence: Mark and Christian Origins* (Philadelphia: Fortress, 1988).

Maiberger, Paul. "Das Verständnis von Psalm 2 in der Septuaginta, im Targum, in Qumran, im frühen Judentum und im Neuen Testament," in Josef Schreiner, ed., *Beiträge zur Psalmenforschung. Psalm 2 und 22* (Forschung zur Bibel; Würzburg: Echter, 1988), 85-151.

Malherbe, Abraham J. *The Letters to the Thessalonians* (AB 32B; New York: Doubleday, 2000).

Manson, T. W. "The Son of Man in Daniel, Enoch and the Gospels," *BJRL* 32 (1949-50) 183-85.

Manzi, F. *Melchisedek e l'angelologia nell' Epistola agli Ebrei e a Qumran* (AnBib 136; Rome: Pontifical Biblical Institute, 1997), 96-101.

Marcus, Joel. *The Way of the Lord: Christological Exegesis of the Old Testament in the Gospel of Mark* (Louisville: Westminster/John Knox, 1992).

Martínez, F. García. "The Eschatological Figure of 4Q246," in idem, *Qumran and Apocalyptic: Studies on the Aramaic Texts from Qumran* (Leiden: Brill, 1992), 162-79.

———. "Old Texts and Modern Mirages: The 'I' of Two Qumran Hymns," in idem, *Qumranica Minora I: Qumran Origins and Apocalypticism* (STDJ 63; Leiden: Brill, 2007), 105-25.

———. "Two Messianic Figures in the Qumran Texts," in idem, *Qumranica Minora II* (STDJ 64; Leiden: Brill, 2007), 20-24.

——— and J. C. Tigchelaar. *The Dead Sea Scrolls Study Edition* (Leiden: Brill, 1997).

———, E. J. C. Tigchelaar, and A. S. van der Woude: *Qumran Cave 11, II* (DJD 23; Oxford: Clarendon, 1998).

Martyn, James Louis. *History and Theology in the Fourth Gospel* (rev. ed.; Nashville: Abingdon, 1979; 1st ed. 1968).

Mastin, B. A. "A Neglected Feature of the Christology of the Fourth Gospel," *NTS* 22 (1976) 32-51.

McCarter, P. K. *2 Samuel* (AB 9; New York: Anchor, 1984).

McCarthy, Dennis J. *Treaty and Covenant* (AnBib 21A; Rome: Pontifical Biblical Institute, 1981).

———. "II Samuel 7 and the Structure of the Deuteronomic History," *JBL* 84 (1965), 131-38.

Mehl, Andreas. *Seleukos Nikator und sein Reich* (Studia Hellenistica 28; Leuven: Leuven University Press, 1986).

Meier, Samuel A. "Shahar (Deity)," *ABD*, 5:1,150-51.

Mettinger, Tryggve N. D. "Cui Bono? The Prophecy of Nathan (2 Sam. 7) as a Piece of Political Rhetoric," *Svensk Exegetisk Årsbok* 70 (2005) 193-214.

———. *King and Messiah: The Civil and Sacral Legitimation of the Israelite Kings* (ConBib OT 8; Lund: Gleerup, 1976).

Metzger, Bruce M. *A Textual Commentary on the Greek New Testament* (2nd ed.; Stuttgart: German Bible Society/United Bible Societies, 1994).

Meyer, Arnold. *Jesu Muttersprache: Das galiläische Aramäisch in seiner Bedeutung für die Erklärung der Reden Jesu und der Evangelien überhaupt* (Freiburg im Breisgau/Leipzig: Mohr Siebeck, 1896).

Meyers, Carol L., and Erich M. Meyers. *Zechariah 9–13* (AB 25C; New York: Doubleday, 1993).

Milik, J. T. "4QVisions d'Amram et une citation d'Origène," *RB* 79 (1972) 77-92.

————. "Les modèles araméens du livre d'Esther dans la Grotte 4 de Qumrân," *RevQ* 59 (1992).

Montgomery, James A. "Anent Dr. Rendel Harris's 'Testimonies,'" *Expositor* 22 (1921) 214-17.

————. *A Critical and Exegetical Commentary on the Book of Daniel* (ICC; Edinburgh: T&T Clark, 1927; reprinted 1979).

Moore, Ernest. "ΒΙΑΖΩ, ΑΡΠΑΖΩ and Cognates in Josephus," *NTS* 21 (1975) 519-43.

Moran, W. L. *The Amarna Letters* (Baltimore: Johns Hopkins, 1992).

Mørkholm, Otto. *Antiochus IV of Syria* (Copenhagen: Gyldendal, 1966).

Mosca, Paul. "Daniel 7 and Ugarit: A Missing Link," *Bib* 67 (1986) 496-517.

Moss, Candida R. "The Transfiguration: An Exercise in Markan Accommodation," *Biblical Interpretation* 12 (2004) 69-89.

Mowinckel, Sigmund. *He That Cometh: The Messiah Concept in Israel and Later Judaism* (Nashville: Abingdon, 1956; reprint, Grand Rapids: Eerdmans, 2005).

————. *The Psalms in Israel's Worship* (Grand Rapids: Eerdmans, 2004; first English ed., Oxford: Blackwell, 1962).

Müller, Ulrich B. *Messias und Menschensohn in jüdischen Apokalypsen und in der Offenbarung des Johannes* (Gütersloh: Mohn, 1972).

Newman, C. C., J. R. Davila, and G. S. Lewis, eds. *The Jewish Roots of Christological Monotheism: Papers from the St. Andrews Conference on the Historical Origins of the Worship of Jesus* (JSJSup 63; Leiden: Brill, 1999).

Newsom, Carol A. "4Q419," in Esther Eshel et al., *Qumran Cave 4, VI: Political and Liturgical Texts, Part 1* (DJD 11; Oxford: Clarendon, 1998).

————. *Songs of the Sabbath Sacrifice: A Critical Edition* (HSS 27; Atlanta: Scholars Press, 1985).

Nickelsburg, G. W. E. "Discerning the Structure (s) of the Enochic Book of Parables," in Gabriele Boccaccini, ed., *Enoch and the Messiah Son of Man: Revisiting the Book of Parables* (Grand Rapids: Eerdmans, 2007), 23-47.

————. *1 Enoch 1* (Hermeneia; Minneapolis: Fortress, 2001)

Nickelsburg, G. W. E., and J. C. VanderKam. *1 Enoch: A New Translation Based on the Hermeneia Commentary* (Minneapolis: Fortress, 2004).

Nilsson, Martin. *Geschichte der griechischen Religion* (3rd ed.; München: Beck, 1974).

Noth, Martin. *The Laws in the Pentateuch and Other Studies* (Philadelphia: Fortress, 1966).

O'Connor, David, and David P. Silverman, eds. *Ancient Egyptian Kingship* (Probleme der Ägyptologie 9; Leiden: Brill, 1994).

Olson, Daniel C. "Enoch and the Son of Man in the Epilogue of the Parables," *JSP* 18 (1998) 27-38.

Orlov, A. A. *The Enoch-Metatron Tradition* (TSAJ 107; Tübingen: Mohr Siebeck, 2005).

Otto, Eckart. "Das Deuteronomium als Archimedischer Punkt der Pentateuchkritik auf dem Wege zu einer Neubegründung der de Wette'schen Hypothese," in M. Vervenne and J. Lust, eds., *Deuteronomy and Deuteronomic Literature: Festschrift C. H. W. Brekelmans* (BETL 133; Leuven: Peeters, 1997), 321-29.

―――. "Politische Theologie in den Königspsalmen zwischen Ägypten und Assyrien. Die Herrscherlegitimation in den Psalmen 2 und 18 in ihrem altorientalischen Kontexten," in Otto and Zenger, eds., *"'Mein Sohn bist du,'"* 33-65.

―――. "Psalm 2 in neuassyrischer Zeit. Assyrische Motive in der judäischen Königsideologie," in Klaus Kiesow and Thomas Meurer, eds., *Textarbeit. Studien zu Texten und ihrer Rezeption aus dem Alten Testament und der Umwelt Israels. Festschrift für Peter Weimar* (AOAT 294; Münster: Ugarit-Verlag, 2003), 335-49.

―――, and Erich Zenger, eds. *"Mein Sohn bist du" (Ps 2,7): Studien zu den Königspsalmen* (Stuttgart: Katholisches Bibelwerk, 2002).

Owen, Paul, and David Shepherd. "Speaking Up for Qumran, Dalman and the Son of Man: Was *Bar Enasha* a Common Term for 'Man' in the Time of Jesus?" *JSNT* 81 (2001) 81-122.

Parker, Simon. "The Birth Announcement," in Lyle Eslinger and Glenn Taylor, eds., *Ascribe to the Lord: Biblical and Other Studies in Memory of Peter C. Craigie* (JSOTSup 67; Sheffield: JSOT, 1988).

Parker, S. B. "Shahar," *DDD*, 754-75.

Patton, Corrine L. "Psalm 132: A Methodological Inquiry," *CBQ* 57 (1995) 643-54.

Paul, Shalom M. "Adoption Formulae: A Study of Cuneiform and Biblical Legal Clauses," *Maarav* 2/2 (1979-1980) 173-85.

―――. *Amos* (Hermeneia; Minneapolis: Fortress, 1991).

Perlitt, L. *Bundestheologie im Alten Testament* (WMANT 36; Neukirchen-Vluyn: Neukirchener Verlag, 1969).

Perrin, N. "The Creative Use of the Son of Man Traditions by Mark," *Union Seminary Quarterly Review* 23 (1967) 357-65.

―――. *Rediscovering the Teaching of Jesus* (New York: Harper & Row, 1967).

―――. "Mark XIV. 62: The End Product of a Christian Pesher Tradition?" *NTS* 12 (1965-1966) 150-55.

―――. *A Modern Pilgrimage in New Testament Christology* (Philadelphia: Fortress, 1974).

―――. "The Son of Man in Ancient Judaism and Primitive Christianity: A Suggestion," *BR* 11 (1966) 17-28.

―――. "The Son of Man in the Synoptic Tradition," *BR* 13 (1968) 3-25.

————, and Dennis Duling. *The New Testament: An Introduction* (2nd ed.; New York: Harcourt Brace Jovanovich, 1982).

Peters, Melvin K. H. "Septuagint," *ABD*, 5:1,093-1,104.

Pettazzoni, R. "Aion-(Kronos) Chronos in Egypt," in idem, *Essays on the History of Religions* (Leiden: Brill, 1954).

Pietersma, Albert. "Messianism and the Greek Psalter," in M. A. Knibb, ed., *The Septuagint and Messianism* (BETL CXCV; Leuven: Peeters, 2006), 49-75.

Pietsch, M. *"Dieser ist der Spross Davids . . . ." Studien zur Rezeptionsgeschichte der Nathanverheissung* (WMANT 100; Neukirchen-Vluyn: Neukirchener Verlag, 2003).

Pomykala, K. E. *The Davidic Dynasty Tradition in Early Judaism: Its History and Significance for Messianism* (SBLEJ 7; Atlanta: Scholars Press, 1995).

Porter, Stanley, ed. *The Messiah in the Old and New Testaments* (Grand Rapids: Eerdmans, 2007).

Préaux, Claire. *Le monde hellénistique. La Grèce et l'Orient de la mort d'Alexandre à la conquête romain de la Grèce* (323-146 av. J.-C.) (Paris: Presses universitaires de France, 1978).

Price, S. R. F. *Rituals and Power: The Roman Imperial Cult in Asia Minor* (Cambridge: Cambridge University Press, 1984).

Puech, Émile. *La croyance des Esséniens en la vie future. Immortalité, résurrection, vie éternelle?* (Paris: Gabalda, 1993).

————. "Fragment d'une Apocalypse en Araméen (4Q246 = pseudo-Dan[d]) et le 'Royaume de Dieu,'" *RB* 99 (1992) 98-131.

————. "Notes sur le Fragment d'Apocalypse 4Q246 — 'Le Fils de Dieu,'" *RB* 101-4 (1994) 533-57.

————. "Préséance sacerdotale et messie-roi dans la Règle de la Congrégation (1QSa ii 11-22)," *RevQ* 16 (1993-1995).

————. "246. 4Qapocryphe de Daniel ar," in G. Brooke et al., *Qumran Cave 4, XVII: Parabiblical Texts, Part 3* (DJD XXII; Oxford: Clarendon, 1996), 165-84.

Rad, Gerhard von. *Old Testament Theology* (New York: Harper & Row, 1965).

————. "The Royal Ritual in Judah," in idem, *The Problem of the Hexateuch and Other Essays* (New York: McGraw-Hill, 1966), 222-31, originally published as "Das judäische Königsritual," *ThLZ* 73 (1947) 211-16.

Rahlfs, Alfred. *Septuaginta* (2 vols.; Stuttgart: Württembergische Bibelanstalt, 1935).

Rainbow, P. "Melchizedek as a Messiah at Qumran," *BBR* 7 (1997) 179-94.

Reitzenstein, R. *Poimandres. Studien zur griechisch-ägyptischen und frühchristlichen Literatur* (Leipzig: Hinrichs, 1904).

Reitzenstein, R., and H. H. Schaeder. *Studien zum antiken Synkretismus, aus Iran und Griechenland* (Berlin and Leipzig: Teubner, 1926).

Rendsburg, Gary A. "Psalm CX 3B," *VT* 49 (1999) 548-53.

Roberts, J. J. M. "Isaiah and His Children," in Ann Kort and Scott Morschauser, eds., *Biblical and Related Studies Presented to Samuel Iwry* (Winona Lake, IN: Eisenbrauns, 1985), 193-203.

———. "The Old Testament's Contribution to Messianic Expectations," in J. H. Charlesworth, ed., *The Messiah* (Minneapolis: Fortress, 1992), 39-51.

———. Review of Markus Saur, *Die Königspsalmen,* in *CBQ* 67 (2005) 700.

———. "Whose Child Is This? Reflections on the Speaking Voice in Isaiah 9:5," *HTR* 90 (1997).

Robinson, James M., Paul Hoffmann, and John S. Kloppenborg, eds. *The Critical Edition of Q* (Hermeneia; Minneapolis: Fortress; Leuven: Peeters, 2000).

Roehrig, Catharine H., ed. *Hatshepsut: From Queen to Pharaoh* (New Haven: Yale University Press, 2006).

Römer, Thomas. *The So-Called Deuteronomistic History: A Sociological, Historical, and Literary Introduction* (London/New York: T&T Clark, 2007)

Romm, James. *Alexander the Great: Selections from Arrian, Diodorus, Plutarch, and Quintus Curtius* (Indianapolis/Cambridge: Hackett, 2005).

Rooke, Deborah W. "Kingship as Priesthood: The Relationship between the High Priesthood and the Monarchy," in John Day, ed., *King and Messiah in Israel and the Ancient Near East* (JSOTSup 270; Sheffield: Sheffield Academic Press, 1998), 187-208.

———. *Zadok's Heirs* (Oxford: Oxford University Press, 2000).

Rösel, Christoph. *Die messianische Redaktion des Psalters. Studien zu Entstehung und Theologie der Sammlung Psalm 2–89* (Stuttgart: Calwer, 1999).

Rösel, Martin. "Die Interpretation von Genesis 49 in der Septuaginta," *BN* 79 (1995) 54-70.

———. "Die Jungfrauengeburt des endzeitlichen Immanuel," *Jahrbuch für Biblische Theologie* 6 (1991) 134-51.

Rost, Leonard. *Die Überlieferung von der Thronnachfolge Davids* (BWANT 3/6; Stuttgart: Kohlhammer, 1926).

Rouillard, H. "Rephaim," *DDD,* 692-700.

Rowland, Christopher. "A Man Clothed in Linen: Daniel 10.6ff and Jewish Angelology," *JSNT* 24 (1985) 99-110.

———. *The Open Heaven* (London: SPCK; New York: Crossroad, 1982).

———. "The Vision of the Risen Christ in Rev. I.13ff.: The Debt of an Early Christology to an Aspect of Jewish Angelology," *JTS* 31 (1980) 1-11.

Sanders, E. P. *Jesus and Judaism* (Philadelphia: Fortress, 1985).

Sarna, Nahum M. "Psalm 89: A Study in Inner-Biblical Exegesis," in Alexander Altman, ed., *Biblical and Other Studies* (Cambridge, MA: Harvard University Press, 1963).

Saur, Markus. *Die Königspsalmen* (BZAW 340; Berlin: de Gruyter, 2004).

Savignac, J. De. "Essai d'interprétation du Psaume CX à l'aide de la littérature égyptienne," *OTS* 9 (1951) 105-35.

Schaper, Joachim. *Eschatology in the Greek Psalter* (WUNT 2/76; Tübingen: Mohr Siebeck, 1995).

―――. "The Persian Period," in Markus Bockmuehl and James Carleton Paget, eds., *Redemption and Resistance: The Messianic Hopes of Jews and Christians in Antiquity* (London/New York: T&T Clark, 2007), 38-61.

―――. "Der Septuaginta-Psalter als Dokument jüdischer Eschatologie," in Martin Hengel and Anna Maria Schwemer, eds., *Die Septuaginta zwischen Judentum und Christentum* (Tübingen: Mohr Siebeck, 1994), 38-61.

Schibler, Daniel. "Messianism and Messianic Prophecy in Isaiah 1–12 and 28–33," in Philip E. Satterthwaite, Richard S. Hess, and Gordon J. Wenham, *The Lord's Anointed: Interpretation of Old Testament Messianic Texts* (Grand Rapids: Baker, 1995), 87-104.

Schiffman, L. H. *The Eschatological Community of the Dead Sea Scrolls* (SBLMS 38; Atlanta: Scholars Press, 1989).

Schimanowski, Gottfried. *Weisheit und Messias. Die jüdischen Voraussetzungen der urchristlichen Präexistenzchristologie* (Tübingen: Mohr/Siebeck, 1985).

Schnackenburg, Rudolf. *The Gospel according to St. John* (3 vols.; London: Burns & Oates, 1968-1982; 1st German ed. 1965-1975).

Schniedewind, W. M. *Society and the Promise to David: The Reception History of 2 Samuel 7:1-17* (New York: Oxford, 1999).

Schreiber, Stefan. *Gesalbter und König. Titel und Konzeptionen der königlichen Gesalbtenerwartung in frühjüdischen und urchristlichen Schriften* (BZNW 105; Berlin: de Gruyter, 2000).

―――. "Henoch als Menschensohn. Zur problematischen Schlussidentifikation in den Bilderreden des äthiopischen Henochbuches (äthHen 71,14)," *ZNW* 91 (2000) 1-17.

Schweitzer, Albert. *Von Reimarus zu Wrede. Eine Geschichte der Leben–Jesus–Forschung* (Tübingen: Mohr Siebeck, 1906); ET *The Quest of the Historical Jesus* (New York: Macmillan, 1968; first complete ed., London: SCM, 2000).

Seeligmann, Isaac Leo. *The Septuagint Version of Isaiah and Cognate Studies* (Tübingen: Mohr Siebeck, 2004).

Segal, Robert A., ed. *The Myth and Ritual Theory: An Anthology* (Oxford: Blackwell, 1998).

Seux, M.-J. *Épithètes Royales Akkadiennes et Sumériennes* (Paris: Letouzey et Ané, 1967).

Sherwin-White, Susan, and Amélie Kuhrt. *From Samarkand to Sardis: A New Approach to the Seleucid Empire* (Berkeley: University of California Press, 1993).

Shiner, Whitney T. "The Ambiguous Pronouncement of the Centurion and the Shrouding of Meaning in Mark," *JSNT* 78 (2000) 3-22.

Shipp, R. Mark. *Of Dead Kings and Dirges: Myth and Meaning in Isaiah 14:4b-21* (Academia Biblica 11; Atlanta: Society of Biblical Literature, 2002).

Silverman, David P. "The Nature of Egyptian Kingship," in David O'Connor and David P. Silverman, ed., *Ancient Egyptian Kingship* (Probleme der Ägyptologie 9; Leiden: Brill, 1994), 157-84.

Sjöberg, Erik, and Gustav Stählin. "בן אדם und בר אנש im Hebräischen und Aramäischen," *Acta Orientalia* 21 (1953) 57-65, 91-107.

————. "ὀργή κτλ., D: The Wrath of God in Later Judaism," *TDNT*, 5 (1967).

Skehan, P. W. "Two Books on Qumran Studies," *CBQ* 21 (1959) 71-78.

Slater, T. B. "One like a Son of Man in First-Century-CE Judaism," *NTS* (1995) 193-98.

Smith, Mark S., *The Early History of God: Yahweh and Other Deities in Ancient Israel* (Grand Rapids: Eerdmans, 2002).

Smith, Morton. "Ascent to the Heavens and Deification in 4QMᵃ," in Lawrence H. Schiffman, ed., *Archaeology and History in the Dead Sea Scrolls* (JSPSup 8; Sheffield: JSOT, 1990), 181-88.

Smith, Stephen H. "The Function of the Son of David Tradition in Mark's Gospel," *NTS* 42 (1996) 523-39.

Spronk, Klaas. *Beatific Afterlife in Ancient Israel and in the Ancient Near East* (AOAT 219; Kevelaer: Butzon & Bercker/Neukirchen-Vluyn: Neukirchener Verlag, 1986), 161-96.

Stamm, J. J. "Die Immanuel-Weissagung und die Eschatologie des Jesaja," *ThZ* 16 (1960) 439-55.

————. "La prophétie d'Emmanuel," *RHPR* 23 (1943) 1-25.

Stanton, Graham. "Messianism and Christology: Mark, Matthew, Luke and Acts," in Bockmuehl and Paget, eds., *Redemption and Resistance,* 78-96.

Starbuck, Scott R. A. *Court Oracles in the Psalms: The So-Called Royal Psalms in Their Ancient Near Eastern Context* (SBLDS 172; Atlanta: Society of Biblical Literature, 1996).

Steudel, Annette. "The Eternal Reign of the People of God — Collective Expectations in Qumran Texts (4Q246 and 1QM)," *RevQ* 65-68 (1996) 507-25.

————."Psalm 2 im antiken Judentum," in Dieter Sänger, ed., *Gottessohn und Menschensohn. Exegetische Paradigmen biblischer Intertextualität* (Neukirchen-Vluyn: Neukirchener Verlag, 2004), 189-97.

Steymans, Hans Ulrich. *Psalm 89 und der Davidbund* (Österreichische Studien 27; Berlin: Lang, 2005).

Stone, M. E. *Features of the Eschatology of Fourth Ezra* (Atlanta: Scholars Press, 1989).

————. *Fourth Ezra: A Commentary on the Book of Fourth Ezra* (Hermeneia; Minneapolis: Fortress, 1990).

————. "The Question of the Messiah in 4 Ezra," in J. Neusner, W. S. Green, and

E. Frerichs, eds., *Judaisms and Their Messiahs* (Cambridge: Cambridge University Press, 1987), 209-24.

Stonemann, Richard. *The Greek Alexander Romance* (London: Penguin, 1991).

Strack, H. L., and P. Billerbeck: *Kommentar zum Neuen Testament aus Talmud und Midrasch* (München: Beck, 1924, 1989).

Suter, D. W. *Tradition and Composition in the Parables of Enoch* (SBLDS 47; Missoula, MT: Scholars Press, 1979).

———. "Weighed in the Balance: The Similitudes of Enoch in Recent Discussion," *Religious Studies Review* 7 (1981) 217-21.

Sweeney, M. A. *Isaiah 1–39, with an Introduction to Prophetic Literature* (FOTL XVI; Grand Rapids: Eerdmans, 1996).

———. *King Josiah of Judah: The Lost Messiah of Israel* (Oxford: Oxford University Press, 2001).

Taylor, J. Glenn. *Yahweh and the Sun: Biblical and Archaeological Evidence for Sun Worship in Ancient Israel* (JSOTSup 111; Sheffield: JSOT, 1993).

Theisohn, Johannes. *Der auserwählte Richter* (Göttingen: Vandenhoeck & Ruprecht, 1975).

Thompson, Leonard L. *The Book of Revelation: Apocalypse and Empire* (New York: Oxford University Press, 1990).

Tigay, J. H. "Adoption," *EncJud* (1971) 300-301.

Tobin, Thomas H. "Logos," *ABD*, 4:348-56.

Tödt, Heinz Eduard. *The Son of Man in the Synoptic Tradition* (Philadelphia: Westminster, 1965).

Tournay, R. J. *Voir et entendre Dieu avec les Psaumes* (Cahiers de la Revue Biblique 24; Paris: Gabalda, 1988).

Tuckett, Christopher M. *Christology and the New Testament: Jesus and His Earliest Followers* (Louisville: Westminster John Knox, 2001).

VanderKam, J. C. "Righteous One, Messiah, Chosen One, and Son of Man in 1 Enoch 37–71," in J. H. Charlesworth, ed., *The Messiah* (Minneapolis: Fortress, 1992), 169-91.

Van der Kooij, Arie. "Die Septuaginta Jesajas als Dokument jüdischer Exegese. Einige Notizen zu LXX — Jes. 7," in *Übersetzung und Deutung. Studien zu dem Alten Testament und seiner Umwelt Alexander Reinard Hulst gewidmet von Freunden und Kollegen* (Nijkerk: Callenbach, 1977).

Van der Woude, A. S., ed. "Melchisedek als himmlische Erlösergestalt in den neugefundenen eschatologischen Midraschim aus Qumran Höhle XI," *OTS* 14 (1965) 354-73.

Van Driel, G. *The Cult of Assur* (Assen: van Gorcum, 1969).

Van Henten, J. W. "The Hasmonean Period," in Markus Bockmuehl and James Carleton Paget, eds., *Redemption and Resistance: The Messianic Hopes of Jews and Christians in Antiquity* (London/New York: T&T Clark, 2007), 15-28.

Van Kooten, G. H., and J. T. A. G. M. van Ruiten, eds. *Balaam: The Prestige of a Pagan Prophet in Judaism, Early Christianity and Islam* (Themes in Biblical Narrative; Leiden: Brill, 2008).

Vaux, Roland De. "The King of Israel, Vassal of Yahweh," in idem, *The Bible and the Ancient Near East* (New York: Doubleday, 1971), 152-80.

Veijola, T. *Die Ewige Dynastie: David und die Entstehung seiner Dynastie nach der deuteronomistischen Darstellung* (Helsinki: Suomalainen Akatemia, 1975).

―――. *Verheissung in der Krise. Studien zur Literatur und Theologie der Exilszeit anhand des 89. Psalms* (Helsinki: Suomalainen Tiedeakatemia, 1982).

Vermes, G. *The Authentic Gospel of Jesus* (London: Allen Lane/Penguin Books, 2003).

―――. *The Complete Dead Sea Scrolls in English* (rev. ed.; London: Penguin, 2004).

―――. *Jesus and the World of Judaism* (Philadelphia: Fortress, 1984).

―――. *Jesus the Jew: A Historian's Reading of the Gospels* (Philadelphia: Fortress, 1973).

―――. "The Use of בר נש/בר נשא in Jewish Aramaic," Appendix E in Matthew Black, *An Aramaic Approach to the Gospels and Acts* (3rd ed.; Oxford: Clarendon, 1967), 310-30.

Vermeylen, J. *Du Prophète Isaïe à l'apocalyptique: Isaïe, I-XXXV, miroir d'un demi-millénaire d'expérience religieuse en Israël* (Paris: Gabalda, 1977).

Vielhauer, Philipp. *Aufsätze zum Neuen Testament* (Theologische Bücherei 31; München: Kaiser Verlag, 1965).

―――. "Gottesreich und Menschensohn in der Verkündigung Jesu," in Wilhelm Schneemelcher, ed., *Festschrift für Günther Dehn* (Neukirchen: Buchhandlung des Erziehungsvereins, 1957), 51-79.

―――. "Jesus und der Menschensohn: Zur Diskussion mit Heinz Eduard Tödt und Eduard Schweizer," *Zeitschrift für Theologie und Kirche* 60 (1963) 133-77.

Vollenweider, Samuel. "Der 'Raub' der Gottgleichheit: Ein religionsgeschichtlicher Vorschlag zu Phil 2.6(-11)," *NTS* 45 (1999) 413-33.

Volz, Paul. *Jüdische Eschatologie von Daniel bis Akiba* (Tübingen: Mohr Siebeck, 1903).

Vos, Louis A. *The Synoptic Traditions in the Apocalypse* (Kampen, the Netherlands: Kok, 1965).

Wagner, Thomas. *Gottes Herrschaft. Eine Analyse der Denkschrift (Jes 6,1–9,6)* (VTSup 108; Leiden: Brill, 2006).

Walck, Leslie W. "The Son of Man in the *Similitudes of Enoch* and the Gospels," in Gabriele Boccaccini, ed., *Enoch and the Messiah Son of Man: Revisiting the Book of Parables* (Grand Rapids: Eerdmans, 2007), 299-337.

Walker, Donald Dale. *Paul's Offer of Leniency (2 Cor 10:1): Populist Ideology and*

*Rhetoric in a Pauline Letter Fragment* (WUNT 2.152; Tübingen: Mohr Siebeck, 2002).

Wasserman, Emma. "The Death of the Soul in Romans 7: Sin, Death, and the Law in the Light of Hellenistic Moral Psychology" (Ph.D. diss., Yale University, 2005).

Wegner, Paul D. *An Examination of Kingship and Messianic Expectation in Isaiah 1–35* (Lewiston, NY: Mellen, 1992).

Weinfeld, Moshe. "The Covenant of Grant in the Old Testament and in the Ancient Near East," *JAOS* 90 (1970) 184-203.

———. *Deuteronomy and the Deuteronomic School* (Oxford: Oxford University Press, 1972).

Weiss, Johannes. *Die Predigt Jesu vom Reiche Gottes* (Göttingen: Vandenhoeck & Ruprecht, 1892); ET *Jesus' Proclamation of the Kingdom of God* (Lives of Jesus; Philadelphia: Fortress, 1971).

Wellhausen, J. *Die Kleinen Propheten übersetzt und erklärt* (Berlin: Reiner, 1898).

Wildberger, Hans. *Isaiah 1–12* (CC; Minneapolis: Fortress, 1991; trans. from *Jesaja, Kapitel 1–12* [BK; Neukirchen-Vluyn: Neukirchener Verlag, 1980])

Williamson, H. G. M. "The Messianic Texts in Isaiah 1–39," in John Day, ed., *King and Messiah in Israel and the Ancient Near East* (Sheffield: Sheffield University Press, 1998), 238-70.

———. *Variations of a Theme: King, Messiah and Servant in the Book of Isaiah* (The Didsbury Lectures, 1997; Carlisle, Cumbria: Paternoster, 1998).

Winston, David. *Logos and Mystical Theology in Philo of Alexandria* (Cincinnati, OH: Hebrew Union College Press, 1985).

———. *The Wisdom of Solomon: A New Translation with Introduction and Commentary* (AB 43; Garden City, NY: Doubleday, 1979).

Wise, Michael O. *The First Messiah: Investigating the Savior before Christ* (San Francisco: HarperSanFrancisco, 1999).

———. "מי כמוני באלים": A Study of 4Q491c, 4Q471b, 4Q427 and 1QH$^a$ 25:35-26:10," *DSD*, 7 (2000) 173-219.

Wolff, H. W. *Joel and Amos* (Hermeneia; Philadelphia: Fortress, 1977).

———. *Micah* (CC; Minneapolis: Augsburg, 1990).

Wrede, William. *The Messianic Secret* (Cambridge, UK: J. Clarke, 1971; reprinted Greenwood, SC: Attic Press; 1st German ed. 1901).

Würthwein, E. "Jesaja 7,1-9. Ein Beitrag zu dem Thema: Prophetie und Politik," in idem, *Wort und Existenz. Studien zum Alten Testament* (Göttingen: Vandenhoeck & Ruprecht, 1970), 127-43.

Wyatt, Nicolas. *Myths of Power: A Study of Royal Myth and Ideology in Ugaritic and Biblical Tradition* (Ugaritisch-Biblische Literatur 13; Münster: Ugarit-Verlag, 1996).

———. *"There's such Divinity doth Hedge a King"* (Aldershot: Ashgate, 2005).

Xeravits, Géza G. *King, Priest, Prophet: Positive Eschatological Protagonists of the Qumran Library* (Leiden: Brill, 2001).

Yarbro Collins, A. "The Apocalypse of John and Its Millennial Themes," in Martin McNamara, ed., *Apocalyptic and Eschatological Heritage: The Middle East and Celtic Realms* (Dublin: Four Courts Press, 2003), 50-60.

―――. "The Apocalyptic Son of Man Sayings," in Birger A. Pearson, ed., *The Future of Early Christianity: Essays in Honor of Helmut Koester* (Minneapolis: Fortress, 1991), 220-28.

―――. *The Beginning of the Gospel: Probings of Mark in Context* (Minneapolis: Fortress, 1992).

―――. "The Charge of Blasphemy in Mark 14:64," *JSNT* 26 (2004) 379-401; reprinted in Geert van Oyen and Tom Shepherd, eds., *The Trial and Death of Jesus: Essays on the Passion Narrative in Mark* (Leuven: Peeters, 2006), 149-70.

―――. *The Combat Myth in the Book of Revelation* (Harvard Dissertations in Religion 9; Missoula, MT: Scholars Press for the Harvard Theological Review; reprinted Eugene, OR: Wipf & Stock, 2001).

―――. "Composition and Performance in Mark 13," in the Festschrift for Seán Freyne, ed. Anne Fitzpatrick McKinley, Margaret Daly-Denton, Brian McGing, and Zuleika Rodgers (Leiden: Brill, forthcoming).

―――. *Cosmology and Eschatology in Jewish and Christian Apocalypticism* (JSJSSup 50; Leiden: Brill, 1996).

―――. *Crisis and Catharsis: The Power of the Apocalypse* (Philadelphia: Westminster, 1984).

―――. "Establishing the Text: Mark 1:1," in Tord Fornberg and David Hellholm, eds., *Texts and Contexts: Biblical Texts in Their Textual and Situational Contexts: Essays in Honor of Lars Hartman* (Oslo: Scandinavian University Press, 1995), 111-27.

―――. "'How on Earth Did Jesus Become a God?' A Reply," in David B. Capes, Helen K. Bond, April Deconick, and Troy A. Miller, eds., *Israel's God and Rebecca's Children: Christology and Community in Early Judaism and Christianity* (Waco, TX: Baylor University Press, 2007), 55-66.

―――. "The Influence of Daniel on the New Testament," in John J. Collins, *Daniel* (Hermeneia; Minneapolis: Fortress, 1993), 90-105.

―――. "Jesus' Action in Herod's Temple," in eadem and Margaret M. Mitchell, eds., *Antiquity and Humanity: Essays on Ancient Religion and Philosophy Presented to Hans Dieter Betz* (Tübingen: Mohr Siebeck, 2001), 45-61.

―――. *Mark: A Commentary* (Hermeneia; Minneapolis: Fortress, 2007).

―――. "Mark and His Readers: The Son of God among Greeks and Romans," *HTR* 93 (2000) 85-100.

―――. "The Origin of the Designation of Jesus as 'Son of Man,'" *HTR* 80 (1987)

391-408 (396), reprinted in eadem, *Cosmology and Eschatology in Jewish and Christian Apocalypticism* (JSJSup 50; Leiden: Brill, 1996), 139-58.

—. "Psalms, Phil. 2:6-11, and the Origins of Christology," *Biblical Interpretation* 11 (2003) 361-72.

—. "The 'Son of Man' Tradition and the Book of Revelation," in James H. Charlesworth, ed., *The Messiah: Developments in Earliest Judaism and Christianity* (Minneapolis: Fortress, 1992), 536-68.

—. "The Worship of Jesus and the Imperial Cult," in Carey C. Newman, James R. Davila, and Gladys S. Lewis, eds., *The Jewish Roots of Christological Monotheism: Papers from the St. Andrews Conference on the Historical Origins of the Worship of Jesus* (JSJSup 63; Leiden: Brill, 1999), 234-57.

Zenger, Erich. "'Es sollen sich niederwerfen vor ihm alle Könige' (Ps 72,11). Redaktionsgeschichtliche Beobachtungen zu Psalm 72 und zum Programm des messianischen Psalters Ps 2-89," in Otto and Zenger, "'Mein Sohn bist du,'" 66-93.

Zetterholm, Magnus, ed. *The Messiah in Early Judaism and Christianity* (Minneapolis: Fortress, 2007).

Zevit, Ziony. "Israel's Royal Cult in the Ancient Near Eastern *Kulturkreis*," in Beckman and Lewis, eds., *Text, Artifact, and Image,* 189-200.

Ziegler, Joseph. *Susanna, Daniel, Bel et Draco* (Septuaginta: Vetus Testamentum Graecum 16.2; Göttingen: Vandenhoeck & Ruprecht, 1954).

Zimmermann, Johannes. *Messianische Texte aus Qumran* (WUNT 2.104; Tübingen: Mohr Siebeck, 1998).

Zuntz, Günther. "Ein Heide Las das Markusevangelium" in Hubert Cancik, ed., *Markus-Philologie: Historische, literargeschichtliche und stilistische Untersuchungen zum zweiten Evangelium* (WUNT 33; Tübingen: Mohr Siebeck, 1984), 205-22.

Zvi, Ehud Ben, *Micah* (FOTL XXI B; Grand Rapids: Eerdmans, 2000).

# Index of Modern Authors

# Index of Scripture and Other Ancient Literature